Sophie Halaby in Jerusalem

An Artist's Life

Laura S. Schor

With a Foreword by Kamal Boullata

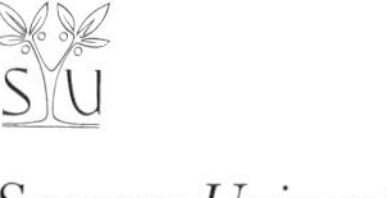

Syracuse University Press

The generous assistance of the George N. Shuster Faculty Research Fund at Hunter College is gratefully acknowledged.

First Edition 2019

19 20 21 22 23 24 6 5 4 3 2 1

∞ The paper used in this publication meets the minimum requirements of the American National Standard for Information Sciences—Permanence of Paper for Printed Library Materials, ANSI Z39.48-1992.

For a listing of books published and distributed by Syracuse University Press, visit https://press.syr.edu.

ISBN: 978-0-8156-3653-3 (hardcover)
978-0-8156-1112-7 (paperback)
978-0-8156-5484-1 (e-book)

Library of Congress Cataloging-in-Publication Data

Available from publisher upon request.

Manufactured in the United States of America

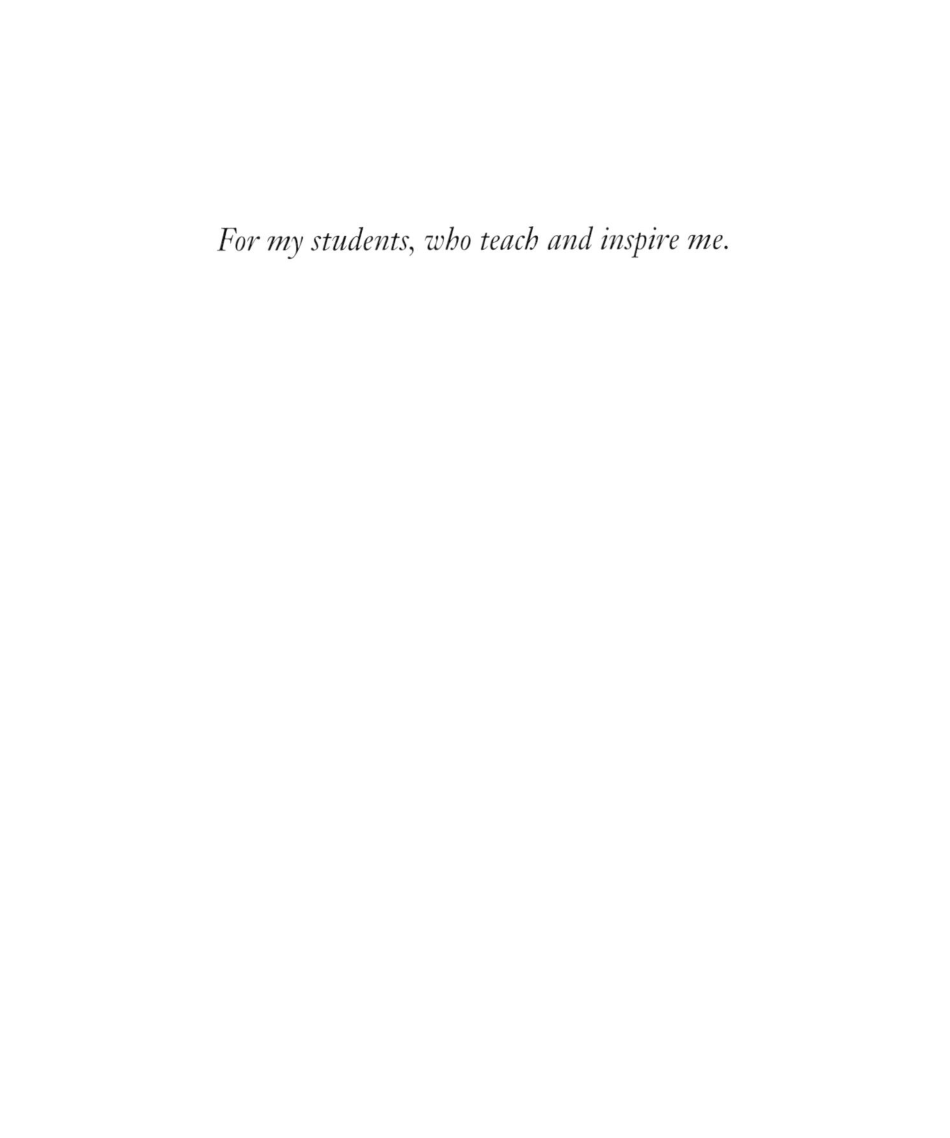

For my students, who teach and inspire me.

Contents

Illustrations

Maps

A gallery of prints by Sophie Halaby follows page 132

Foreword

KAMAL BOULLATA

The cosmopolitan world of Jerusalem in which Sophie Halaby (1906–97) thrived as an artist was demolished in May 1948, following Ben Gurion's declaration of a Jewish state in the coastal heart of Palestine. After decades of what the city's Arab natives had simply referred to as *al-ittirabat*, or "the troubles," the declaration fatally divided the city between Jew and Arab. The fugitive artist's family home, visible from a safe distance beyond barbed wires, now laid among the ruins in no-man's-land. In the meantime, the artist resumed her life with her mother and younger sister, in the Arab part of her hometown, which survived under the jurisdiction of Jordan. By June 1967, however, in a six-day blitzkrieg, the Israeli military forces annexed the remaining part of the city in addition to taking over the rest of historic Palestine. Consequently, all of Jerusalem's Arab natives, be they Muslim or Christian, like the Halaby women, were reduced, according to Israeli law, to mere "residents" in the city of their ancestors, a status that could be arbitrarily revoked at any time. Cut off from the Arab world overnight, the Old City of Jerusalem, its environs, and all the territories that fell under Israeli military occupation were in time turned into separate ghettos, monitored by around-the-clock surveillance cameras, and barricaded behind towering walls.

The book in your hands traces the life story of a pioneering artist whose sole desire throughout her painting career was to explore the vision of Jerusalem. Before the historian Laura Schor set foot in the ghetto where Halaby lived and died, leaving hardly any trace save what survived of her paintings, she had authored numerous studies on other pioneering women. They include a book on women workers in nineteenth-century France, followed by biographies of women such as the French feminist-socialist Flora Tristan (1988), who was the grandmother of the painter Paul Gauguin. Schor has also written two other biographies on pioneering Jewish women who left their mark on their times. The first concerns the Parisian philanthropist Baroness

Betty Rothschild (2006), who is the subject of a sumptuous portrait by Jean-Auguste-Dominique Ingres, and her subsequent book turns attention to Annie Landau (2013), the British headmistress who presided over the Evelina de Rothschild School in the Jerusalem that inspired Sophie Halaby's earliest paintings.

Having myself been born in Jerusalem and raised in the divided city, I knew Halaby as a member of our Christian Orthodox community. Throughout that time, however, I never thought that her art would in any way bear upon my own career as an artist. And yet, perhaps a personal anecdote that sheds light on my earliest connection to the subject of this book is worth recounting.

I was a schoolboy in my early to mid-teens dabbling with painting when I first saw one of Halaby's watercolors. It was displayed in the window of the shop her sister, Anastasia (better known as Asia), opened on Zahra Street. To aid refugees bereaved of their livelihood following the national catastrophe, Asia dedicated her time to selling traditional embroideries executed by peasant women who had lost their lands.

In her shop window, in which a variety of embroidered textiles were displayed, Asia featured a different still-life painting by her sister every week. In retrospect, I cannot help but think of how the aesthetic sensibility of the Halaby sisters echoed that of the seventeenth-century Dutch painter Margaretha van Godewijk, who was the first artist in Europe to paint flower arrangements and is equally remembered for her exquisite floral embroideries. At the time, however, I simply reveled in the joy of seeing how the freshness of the flower arrangements in the paintings of my hometown's professional artist disclosed a poignant contrast to the geometric floral patterns adorning the clothing of women villagers.

Thus, I made it a weekly pilgrimage to walk all the way from my Jaffa Gate neighborhood, within the Old City, to Zahra Street, outside the city walls, in the hope of seeing a new painting. Before returning home, I often stopped next door to the Halaby's shop, where Michel Sahhar, a member of our church community, had a bookstore. Michel often lent me books I could not afford to buy. One day, after seeing an exhibition of my paintings held at the Arab Orthodox Club, on the Musrara alley bordering on no-man's-land, Michel asked me to select one of my Old City streetscapes for display among the books in his bookstore's window. Thanks to the Halaby sisters, the upper den in Sahhar's Bookstore eventually turned into an intimate art gallery, the first of its kind in town. On a couple of occasions, paintings by my friends, Sari Khoury and Samia Taktak, were displayed along with my own works. From the sale of my paintings, I was finally able to pay Michel for the books of my choice. In time, the sales of my works enabled me to afford to go to Rome to start my art education.

The few Palestinian talents who preceded Halaby in seeking an art education in Europe were men, like Mubarak Sa'ed (1876–1961) from Jerusalem and Hanna al-Mismar (1898–1988) from Nazareth. Each of them was sponsored by his own denominational church in the hope that upon his return he would contribute to his church's adornments. In contrast, Halaby was not only the first woman but also the first independent talent in Palestine who was determined to go on her own to further her art studies abroad. Paris, the world capital of art during the late 1920s and early 1930s, was where the twenty-three-year-old talent from Jerusalem opted to pursue her art studies.

As soon as Laura Schor got scent of Halaby's art, she flew to Jerusalem and Amman to see with her own eyes what remains of the artist's work following her death in 1997. Schor met with people, mostly women, who had known the artist at different periods of her life. Through their personal voices, Schor started lucidly threading the pieces of Halaby's life story together. For further research, she traveled to Paris and Oxford to authenticate or double-check this or that detail from French and British sources. Simultaneously, the historian never ceased to seek recourse in what Virginia Woolf once called "the humane art" of letter writing; Schor additionally followed up with her contacts by email and by phone. In the process, she left no stone unturned.

Schor's biographical study of Halaby is the first book on an Arab woman painter of the latter's generation. Her vigilant and painstaking research conducted over the years brings the pioneering artist from Jerusalem back to life. As the historian leads her reader through a minefield of explosive depths crammed with culprits and victims, she forges a way beyond religious or nationalist blinders to reveal the sheer humanity of the artist. In the process, the reader learns what a creative woman experienced during a tragic period in her country's history and how she never ceased striving to capture in her painting what has been eternally beautiful in the city of her forefathers. By restricting her writing to the unfolding of history during the artist's lifetime, Schor grants her readers the space to find their own ways to appreciate how Jerusalem occupied a special place in the heart and mind of the artist.

While the surviving collection of Halaby's paintings includes representations of the human figure, most of which go back to her student days in Paris, the bulk of her lifelong artistic output focused on still-life paintings of wild flowers—which we learn that the artist used to gather on the hills around Jerusalem—along with a wide range of Jerusalem landscapes. With such a devout concentration on two subjects year after year, one cannot help but wonder what the artist was seeking to express besides the mere pleasure of painting.

The one and only common denominator between Halaby's two favorite subjects seems invisible to the viewer. For the artist, it is the intuitive experience of savoring time at home after being elsewhere. Having always been one of the few cities in the world in which time has continued to be inseparable from space, Jerusalem called its pioneering artist to invent a language of visual expression beyond that of time—something perfected by the French Impressionists, who Halaby must have assiduously studied during her years in Paris. The archaeological artifacts that, as we learn, were permanently displayed along with her paintings in Halaby's living quarters, may only imply a hint of the artist's sensitized awareness of how time lives on in her hometown.

Reading through this book, we discover that Halaby's landscape paintings of Jerusalem represent not what her eyes were seeing but what they remembered. Her still-life paintings, by contrast, preserved for her the fleeting freshness of the wild flowers she had brought indoors. In their depiction, the artist memorialized the passing of time through another season she had lived. Thus, Halaby's oscillation between landscape and still-life painting may be viewed as not only two limbs of one body but as two parts completing one another, whereby space and time are wed together as they are in the Jerusalem in which the artist lived. By restricting her writing to the history of Jerusalem during Halaby's lifetime, Schor, in the footsteps of the artist, summons our attention to reflect on how rooted the artist's sense of belonging was to the place itself.

From the roof of the house the Halaby sisters had built on a highland right outside the city walls, they could glory in a boundless vista of the Old City and the surrounding hills, which provided the artist with the subject for her still-life paintings. But for the landscape artist, that vista was never enough of a view to embody the Jerusalem of her heart. Over different times of the year, just as often as the artist left her garden to pick the seasonal flowers from nature, Halaby would go out to capture the sight of her Jerusalem from different distant sites.

Like Halaby, any Jerusalemite knows that when driving from Jaffa or from Jericho up to Jerusalem, the first sign looming in the distance indicating the approach to the city is the tip of the belfry of the Russian Church of the Ascension crowning the Mount of Olives. It was in such tantalizing distances, in the middle of nowhere, that the artist often chose to set up her easel. By painting the bare landscapes before her, from the gradual approach to Jerusalem topped by some brushstrokes suggesting the Russian belfry, Halaby gave

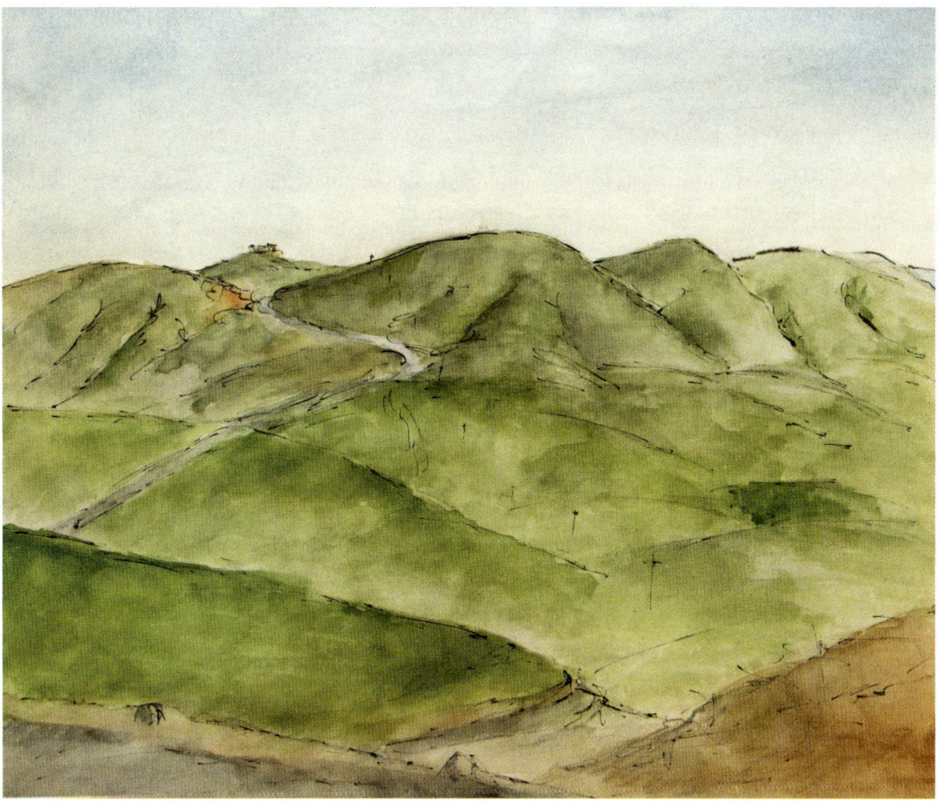

1. *A Road to Jerusalem*. Painting by Sophie Halaby, originally untitled. Yvette and Mazen Qupty Collection.

body to the bubbling joy the Jerusalem native feels upon catching sight of the first sign of coming home. That specific church, furthermore, represented a personal history for the artist since it was her great-uncle who was instrumental in having it built where it stands. By detailing the family's ties to the Russian churches gracing the Mount of Olives, Schor paves the way for us to appreciate a recurring theme in Halaby's Jerusalem paintings.

Soon after the fall of the West Bank of the Jordan River and the Gaza Strip under Israel's military occupation, a young generation of visual artists and dilettantes emerged in the cultural ghetto as its leaders graduated from regional art schools in Jerusalem, Baghdad, and Alexandria. Inspired by the pictorial language popularized in the posters and publications of the Palestine Liberation Organization, their imagery assembled emblematic fragments borrowed from folkloric traditions, national symbols, and verbal referents. With the clandestine support of the PLO, the mass reception of their pictorial expression was unprecedented. Marching to the beat of the same drummer, collective art exhibitions mushroomed at every national occasion, representing a new form of expressing resistance to Israel's military occupation.

Halaby's form of resistance continued to be rooted in the quality of an artistic creativity that was free from the tired and ready-made rhetoric. For her, seeing how Jerusalem, in the work of the leading talents, was reduced to a cliché in the symbolic form of the golden Dome of the Rock must have simply looked like a coarse vulgarization of Jerusalem's prime significance.

While all indications imply that Sophie Halaby, like her more politically active sister, shared the national aspirations of all those resisting the Israeli military occupation and the injustice suffered by the people of Palestine, it is important to note that she never participated in any of the nationalistic art exhibitions. In contrast, knowing what women go through in an infective patriarchal society, in 1986 the eighty-year-old artist lent her works to be included in the first art exhibition by Palestinian women who could have been the age of her grandchildren.

During the last years of Halaby's life, after her father and mother were long buried on the Mount of Olives, next to older members of her family, the lone artist of Jerusalem who never sought the limelight continued to cherish the time she spent in total solitude amid her lifetime collection of paintings and archaeological findings. Halaby must have bathed in the serenity and certitude with which Georgia O'Keeffe, another artist who lived her last years in seclusion, once articulated in a letter to her friend Sherwood Anderson: "Whether you succeed or not is irrelevant, there is no such thing. Making your unknown known is the important thing." We owe thanks to Laura Schor, who, as soon as she learned of Halaby's art, made it known with all the fidelity in her capacity as a historian. Her testimony in this book opens up for readers the first panoramic window revealing not only how the cosmopolitan life of a pioneering Palestinian painter was lived but also—in a cruel twist—what Halaby's closest confidant in the ghetto committed directly before and after her scarcely noticed death.

Sophie Halaby in Jerusalem

Introduction

Sophie Halaby was a Jerusalemite and an artist of great talent. She lived in Musrara, a vibrant neighborhood outside the walls of the Old City, from her birth in 1906 until 1948, when she found temporary refuge in a Russian Orthodox convent in the Old City. She lived the rest of her creative and productive life on Nur al-Din Street in Wadi Joz, a section of Jerusalem governed by Jordan and later occupied by Israel. The political vicissitudes of her times—war, threat of war, and occupation—shaped her life. However, her art focused on the enduring beauty of the landscape and flowers of Jerusalem, not on the traumatic experiences of her life. Sophie's thoughts and sentiments are expressed in her work; they were sketched in pen and ink or red and black chalk and painted with egg tempera, oils, and watercolors. As her personal and professional papers disappeared after her death in 1997, her drawings and paintings constitute the only direct testimony of her ideas and feelings about Jerusalem.

Sadly, these works are not included in the collections of international museums of renown; nor are they on permanent public view in any Palestinian museum. Most of her paintings are held in two private collections; Yvette and Mazen Qupty in Jerusalem and George al-Ama in Bethlehem collectively own hundreds of Sophie Halaby's sketches, watercolors, and oil paintings. Some of these paintings have appeared in temporary exhibits in Jerusalem and Bethlehem in recent years. Catalogs of some of these exhibits feature reproductions of her work. Unfortunately, the vast majority of these works, as well as additional paintings owned by individuals living in the United States, the United Kingdom, and Jordan, have never been shown to the public. None of the works has been properly digitized and made available to scholars.

Writing a biography of Sophie Halaby thus posed difficult challenges. There were few traditional historical sources to consult. The lack of these sources is a familiar problem for scholars writing women's history, a field that has developed significantly during the past fifty years. Scholars in this field have turned to a variety of techniques borrowed from cultural anthropology, literature, and art history. I used all of these methodologies to broaden and deepen my research, interviewing scores of Sophie's family and friends, parsing the memoirs of her contemporaries, and studying her artistic works.

The study of Palestinian women poses special challenges, as the contemporary political situation injects political overtones into all aspects of life, including the act of conducting interviews for scholarly purposes. My research on Sophie Halaby began with interviews with those who remembered the artist and who were willing to answer my questions. Some of the people I approached wondered why I, an American historian with no connection to Palestine, was interested in Sophie Halaby. Others said that their memories of Palestine were too unhappy and thus refused to talk about the Jerusalem artist. Fortunately, there were many who responded positively to my desire to learn more about the woman they remembered.

Using oral testimony as a source poses both challenges and opportunities different from those encountered when using archival evidence. Speaking with multiple interview subjects sometimes resulted in conflicting information. To resolve the dilemma of different versions of stories I often returned to the people interviewed to ask the question again, explaining that I had heard a different version of the story from someone else. For those subjects comfortable with using email, following up a face-to-face interview with email summaries of what had been learned and posing additional questions was a useful technique. For others, follow-up phone calls were the best method. One distinct advantage of oral testimony is that the interviewee sometimes raises issues of which the historian was unaware.

I kept in touch with my first informants, mostly living in the United States and in Jerusalem, for many years and often found their additional information of great value. More recently, family and friends of the late artist living in England and Jordan joined my roster of interviewees. Collectively, these interviews resulted in many hours of shared understanding and trust between Sophie's family, friends, and me. Our discussions often elicited long-forgotten memories that enabled me to fill lacunae in the written records.

More than two decades ago, Ellen Fleischmann sketched the challenges she faced as a doctoral student doing dissertation research on Palestinian women during the British Mandate. She assumed that she would find written sources—letters, organizational records, memoirs, newspapers, and legal papers. She discovered that some of these sources—particularly personal papers and organizational archival materials—were long lost, destroyed, or dispersed. If they were still in existence, they were largely irretrievable or inaccessible. As a consequence, Fleischmann realized that she would be forced to depend on oral history as a major alternative source.[1]

Fleischmann had been trained in graduate school to find and use written sources. She recognized that privileging document-based history led to the exclusion of work about women. Fleischmann continued her research by learning ways to engage Palestinian women as narrators of their own history. She jettisoned tape-recorders and lists of interview questions, finding them an obstacle to candor. As she continued the process, she recognized that informality of approach and serendipity were her best chances for success. She routinely asked everyone who expressed interest in her work if they had a mother, grandmother, or neighbor who might remember the Mandate period. She also dropped all academic jargon and sought to bridge the gap between herself, an American university student, and the women and men she interviewed.

Like Fleischmann, I became a historian several decades ago. I focused on the contributions of women to history, since I found the past described by academic historians was often incomplete and hence distorted. In my earlier work on nineteenth-century women workers, I searched to find their words in letters to the editor of the worker press, in memoirs addressed to daughters and nieces, and in early feminist newspapers. More recently, working on the twentieth century has allowed me to use oral testimony as a source. Using living voices, as opposed to those written down and preserved, has been an enlightening experience. The women and men I interviewed educated me. Some were particularly kind in sharing precious letters and photographs. Others shared stories—memories of Sophie Halaby and her world. I always appreciated their efforts to tell their stories and recognized the collective process we were engaged in to create a more complete and hence more accurate story of the past.

Sophie lived through difficult times. At the end of the British Mandate, Palestine as a country disappeared from maps. According to writer and historian Elias Sanbar, the Palestinian people "were erased along with the lines on the map."[2] Rosemary Sayigh, an anthropologist who has been interviewing Palestinian women for decades, agreed with Sanbar that the Nakba left all Palestinians stateless and invisible, but she noted that the voices of Palestinian women were particularly missing from history books.[3] Jean Said Makdisi, a memoirist and astute observer, echoed this sentiment, issuing a clarion call for a different kind of history that would feature those long-silenced voices: "It has seemed to me that the account of the past as told by academic historians and social scientists was somehow incomplete, and therefore distorted, or at least diminished from the full-blown felt reality to which women's lives and perceptions contribute a great deal. Sounds and smells, pictures, clothes, interiors, gardens, songs and dances, were most often left out of the academic accounts, sacrificed to the telling of a more abstract story."[4]

The integrated history called for by Makdisi awaits its historian. Happily, there has been continuous growth in publishing women's stories, primarily memoirs in recent years. The words of Sophie's contemporaries, women like Serene Husseini Shahid, Fadwa Tuqan, Ghada Karmi, Anbara Salam Khalidi, Hanan Ashrawi, Hala Sakakini, Samia Nasir Khoury, Betty Dagher Majaj, and Jean Said Makdisi help to fill the void left by the unfortunate loss of Sophie's papers. Some of these women, like Sophie, remained in Jerusalem, others lived in neighboring Arab countries, and still others moved to Europe or the United States. All of them remained culturally and psychologically attached to Jerusalem. Hence their observations about the Nakba, the Six-Day War, and Israel's occupation of the West Bank and Gaza provide a reasonable facsimile of what Sophie may have felt and thought. These memoirs complemented the oral histories, enabling me to create a picture of Sophie's life.

Sophie's biography is marked by violence, war, and loss of home and property. Nevertheless, she constructed a life of beauty in her new home and of meaning in her work. Sophie filled her studio with roses and tulips from her garden as well as with wild irises and cyclamens that she picked on the nearby hills. She worked every day in her studio, painting and repainting the hills she contemplated through her windows and the flowers she carefully arranged before giving them eternal life on canvas. She hosted friends and participated in social groups, often with her lifelong companion, her sister, Asia. Sophie was a modern woman who respected traditions. She yearned for a society based on freedom and dignity for the Palestinian people. Her art is a window into the life she envisaged. Sophie's art inspired me. Studying her slow development from a purely representational artist to one whose work, especially her landscapes, became increasingly abstract demonstrated her personal commitment to her art and her abiding love for Jerusalem.

While researching the life of Sophie Halaby, I was led to reflect on many issues central to Palestinian history: the conflicts between traditional and Western ideas of women's roles at home and in society, the development of Palestinian nationalism, and the definition of Palestinian identity. As the daughter of an affluent and educated Jerusalem family, Sophie attended school, studied foreign languages, worked for the British administration, and participated in social welfare activities. As she and her classmates became women, they were faced with complicated decisions: Should they continue their studies, which often entailed going abroad? Should they marry or remain single? Should they maintain traditions or modernize dress and lifestyle? Should they become involved in women's groups and in national politics? In addition to the lively ideological battles occasioned by these questions, Sophie and her friends faced periods of alternating peace and violence caused by tensions among the competing ideologies of British colonialism, Jewish Zionism, and Arab nationalism.

Sophie Halaby's life traversed the years when Palestinian identity evolved. At the end of the Ottoman Empire, Muslim and Christian Jerusalemites saw themselves as part of a pan-Arab community and identified as Arabs or Palestinians interchangeably. Following the conquest of the area by the British, the borders of Palestine were defined; local residents of all faiths began to identify as Palestinians. They also referred to themselves by religious denomination or simply as Arabs and Jews. After 1948 and the founding of the State of Israel, Muslims and Christians displaced from their homes referred to themselves primarily as Palestinians, though they sometimes identified as Arabs. In response to the 1967 Israeli occupation of East Jerusalem and the West Bank, Palestinian identity strengthened.

Sophie's life was deeply affected by Arab and Zionist nationalism, which challenged the aspiration of intercommunal tolerance promulgated at her school, the Jerusalem Girls' College. She was twenty-three years old in 1929 when violence shattered the calm of Jerusalem. She was thirty years old at the beginning of the Arab Revolt in 1936. At the time of the Nakba, when she found refuge in the Old City, she was forty-two. In 1967, when Israeli soldiers ordered her out of her home in East Jerusalem, she was sixty-one. She was forced to lie outside on the ground in front of her house while Israeli officers ransacked it, looking for snipers and weapons; shrapnel from a stray missile destroyed her studio. Like most Palestinians, Sophie lost family members and friends to the recurrent violence. These traumatic events had a lasting impact.

Sophie's life was also influenced by continuous physical changes to her city. Each of the colonial powers that controlled Jerusalem—the Ottomans, the British, the Jordanians, and the Israelis—asserted love for the city and vowed to protect its cultural heritage. However, the balance between preservation and renovation, between maintaining cultural heritages and providing opportunities for development, were often cause for confrontation, even violence. Sophie was aware of the changes in the boundaries, topography, and cityscape of Jerusalem, but she loved the bare hills of the city. Though living as an independent, modern woman, she was affronted by the continuous architectural changes to the city. In her paintings, she quietly protested the presence of European architecture by eliminating the new buildings and the new roads that connected them from her landscapes of untouched hills.

Aside from political and nationalist concerns, there were other profound influences on Sophie's life and art. She was the first Arab woman from Jerusalem to study art in Paris, arriving there in 1929 and returning home in 1933. Her sojourn was an opportunity for her to experience life as a modern woman in the artistic capital of the world. She lived among other young women who came from a variety of European and American cities to study in Paris. Like Sophie, many of these women were iconoclasts in their home countries, women who were determined to perfect their skills and to build careers. They held ideas that were not widely shared by their contemporaries. Sophie returned to Jerusalem an artist and an independent thinker.

She identified herself in a directory of Jerusalem Arab businesses as a professional woman, specifically as a painter of watercolor greeting cards with Palestinian subjects. At the beginning of the Arab Revolt, Sophie put down her watercolors and drew a series of political cartoons criticizing British rule and Zionist goals. She soon returned to her studio and to her watercolors and oil paint. In 1948, Sophie Halaby was the only Palestinian artist who succeeded in saving her work amid the dislocation and destruction of war. She resumed painting, working alone in her new studio in East Jerusalem for decades. Looking back at those years, Mary Joury, a younger contemporary lamented, "We didn't pay enough attention to Sophie Halaby. We didn't know her work was important."[5]

In late life, Sophie became aware of work by a younger group of artists who supported the Palestine liberation movement with their paintings. She was curious about their work, attended their exhibits, but did not modify her style or her subject matter in response to theirs. Sophie Halaby's Jerusalem remained the vision she saw from her studio windows in East Jerusalem. The familiar beauty of the Mount of Olives without its buildings was what she chose to paint, not the wars, uprooting, or evidence of the rapid change to Jerusalem. Her persistent painting of Jerusalem as she willed it to be was her private form of resistance.

Sophie Halaby experienced repeated sorrows, yet she was resilient and worked hard to create a record of her feelings about Palestine in her paintings. Her persistent devotion to painting the hills and flowers of Jerusalem reflected an obsession with the culture and traditions of her people like that described by Suad Amiry in her poem, "An Obsession." Amiry speaks directly to Palestine as to an absent friend, musing on her obsessive longing for and devotion to her lost home. She asks:

Would you *ever* let go of me
For a lifetime
For a year
A month
An hour
A minute
Even a second?

She answers her rhetorical question: "No."

Amiry lists the losses experienced by the Palestinian people: villages, pianos, Persian carpets, baby photo albums, libraries, horses, donkeys, cats, and her own pet monkey, Shasa. She adds the blooming almond trees and the pomegranates that were not picked in the spring of 1948, the firing on farmers who returned to try to harvest their fields, the bride's wardrobe and wedding presents left behind.

Amiry's poem addresses the trauma of loss that is so often a central concern of the Palestinian artist. In a stanza titled: "Yes, an Obsession," she writes:

My dreams are all about you
And my nightmares are all because of you
My happiness is related to you
My expectations are all concerning you
And my disappointments pile up beside you.

Her conclusion, a stanza titled, "How very *exhausting* it is," echoes the sentiments expressed in Sophie's paintings:

Above all I have to keep my sanity with all the brutality around you
Every hour, every minute and every second
If ever I do come to terms with what had happened to you
I must banish that part of my brain
That cherishes reason, logic, justice.[6]

Sophie was buried on the Mount of Olives with few people in attendance. Her community of friends and family was no longer robust. Her sister, Asia, was in the last stages of dementia in a nursing home. Olga Wahbe, ninety-three years old, her cousin and close friend, was at the funeral, along with Dr. John Tleel, also a steadfast friend. A temporary marker was placed on her grave, which still awaits a permanent headstone. Happily, Sophie's work continues to live. In 2003, her sketches were included in an exhibit of *Pioneers of Palestine Art* sponsored by the al-Wasiti Foundation. In 2007, her paintings were included in an exhibit of *Palestinian Women Artists* at al-Hoash. Most recently,

Samia Halaby contributed an article about her cousin Sophie to a special issue of the *Jerusalem Quarterly* devoted to visual culture.[7]

Aided by the many women and men I have interviewed, by the memoirs of Sophie's contemporaries, by Sophie's art, and by the books by scholars dedicated to understanding the history of Palestine, I have tried to write a truthful history of Sophie Halaby and the place she loved. My book begins with a chapter about Sophie's complex identity as a multilingual child born to a Russian Orthodox mother and an Arab Orthodox father, and the British education she received at the Jerusalem Girl's College. It continues with a chapter about Sophie's experiences following her graduation from high school and during her studies as an art student in Paris. The third chapter describes her return to Jerusalem and the political cartoons she contributed to a weekly newspaper during the Arab Revolt. The fourth chapter begins with Sophie's leaving West Jerusalem, finding refuge in the Old City, taking a second brief trip to Paris for further study, and the construction of her new home including a private studio in East Jerusalem, where she resumed her life as a working artist. The fifth chapter describes the destruction of this studio in 1967 and its reconstruction, as well as her reaction to life under the Israeli occupation of Jerusalem. The sixth chapter is devoted to Sophie's work as it was integrated into the Palestinian art canon.

I hope that her life will inspire others, as she has inspired me, to work for a better present and future for Jerusalem and for the Palestinian people. The discovery of sufficient evidence to construct Sophie's biography took place over many years, in many locations. As a traditional bibliography is insufficient explanation of how this work was written, I have described the process of searching for Sophie Halaby in an afterword to this book.

1

Forming Sophie's Identity

1906–1924

> My short time at the all-British preparatory school had a lasting impact. It gave me a dual character. I really belonged to two worlds, the European and that of the Middle East. I was not quite sure which culture to identify with, but it made my life much more interesting.
>
> —John Melkon Rose, *Armenians of Jerusalem*

Russian-Palestinian Heritage

Sophie Halaby, like John Melkon Rose, author of the above excerpt, belonged to more than one world. Her mother, Olga Akimovna Khudobasheva, was Russian; her father, George Halaby, was the scion of an established Christian Arab Jerusalem family. In the early twentieth century, there were more than ten thousand foreign residents in Jerusalem; many children, like Sophie, were of mixed parentage.[1] Like Melkon Rose, Sophie attended a British school. Unlike Rose, her thoughts about culture and identity have not become part of the historical record. Fortunately, records of her classes, letters and observations of her teachers, and notes of her accomplishments in the Jerusalem Girls' College exist and can be used to glean a sense of her early education and of the complex identity—European and Palestinian—that nourished her childhood years.

Sophie's mother was born in Stavropol, then part of the Russian Empire, the youngest of ten children. Her father had served in the army and later became chief of police in the small town of Eisk. Olga left her home in the Caucasus to study education in Kiev. Following graduation, she was hired to teach in a Russian school in Palestine. In 1902, she was named headmistress of a girls' school of 350 pupils and 15 teachers in El-Mina, near Tripoli, Lebanon. Her career as an educator ended with her marriage to George Halaby in the iconic Russian Orthodox Cathedral of the Holy Trinity in the Russian Compound of Jerusalem.[2]

George Halaby was the eldest son in a family of eleven children, all born in Jerusalem. Like many Christian Arabs living in Palestine, George was educated in Russian schools. He excelled in his studies. Encouraged by his uncle Ya'qub Egorovich Halaby, the dragoman, or translator and facilitator, of the Russian Mission, George continued his education in Moscow, graduating from the Moscow Ecclesiastical Seminary in 1888. Following graduation, he received a scholarship from the Imperial Orthodox Palestine Society (IOPS) to study at the Kiev Theological Academy, from which he graduated in 1892.[3] He may have remained in Kiev for a few years after graduation, working in some capacity for his uncle and the IOPS, or returned to Palestine immediately, where he may have taught in a Russian school. George was appointed dragoman of the mission in 1901 after his uncle's death.[4]

Birth and death records of the Halaby family are kept in the Church of Mary Magdalene on the Mount of Olives in Jerusalem. They reveal that George Halaby was born in Jerusalem on March 3, 1864, and died there on April 4, 1945. He is buried in the church graveyard just above the Garden of Gethsemane. The records state that Olga was born on February 5, 1864, and died on December 31, 1952. These dates are carved into the headstone that adorns the plot where she was buried, next to her husband. Despite being engraved in stone, Olga's birthdate is puzzling. If she was born in 1864, as the record states, she gave birth to her first child, Nicola, at the age of forty, an unusual occurrence in the early part of the twentieth century. The fact that her husband was born in 1864 suggests that someone recording the dates may have copied the year of George's birth into Olga's records.[5]

Regrettably, the church records are silent about the birthplace of Sophie, formally known as Sonia. Friends and family have different recollections of her birthplace—some believe she was born in Kiev, while others are certain she was born in Jerusalem. Scholars are also divided on this issue.[6] Sophie was identified as Russian by her teachers in Jerusalem and as Palestinian by her British employers. She carried a Palestinian passport when she traveled to Paris. Throughout her life, she maintained a deep commitment to the heritage of both cultures.

The birthplace of Sophie's siblings, Anastasia, known as Asia, and Nicola, are likewise uncertain. Asia was born in 1909 and died in Jerusalem in 1998. She is buried next to her sister. Nicola was born in 1904 and died in in 1991 in Philadelphia. The Halaby family, with the exception of Nicola, is buried in adjacent plots in the iconic graveyard beneath the golden cupolas of the Russian Church. Ya'qub Halaby is buried nearby, as are several members of the Wahbe family, who were close relatives. The Wahbe and Halaby families intermarried several times in different generations, attesting to their continuing closeness.[7]

Sophie and her siblings, Nicola and Asia, enjoyed a comfortable childhood as the result of inherited wealth that originated with two Halaby brothers who fled persecution in Aleppo around 1500; one settled in Jerusalem and the other in Jaffa.[8] The family wealth was enhanced by Sophie's great-uncle Ya'qub, who was among the first Arabs educated in Russian schools. His fluency in Russian, Turkish, and Arabic were prerequisites for attaining the coveted position of dragoman in Jerusalem. Ya'qub was the first to be appointed to this position, holding it from 1865 until his death in 1900, years of significant land acquisition and development by Russia in Jerusalem. Ya'qub Halaby was an Ottoman subject, an important factor in facilitating land purchase for the Russian Orthodox Church, since only Ottomans could buy land in Palestine without special dispensation. He mastered the complex rules of the Ottoman legal system, becoming a skillful negotiator. These attributes made him the ideal partner for Father Antonin Kapustin, a strategic planner of great skill who arrived in Jerusalem in 1865 and was soon appointed head of the Russian Mission, a position he held until his death in 1894.[9] During this period, Ya'qub acquired land that increased the Halaby family wealth.

Kapustin was eager to create a strong presence for the Russian Orthodox Church in Jerusalem, where the Catholic Church and the Greek Orthodox Church already owned land, churches, monasteries, schools, and hospices. He was aware of the growing interest in land acquisition by protestant churches—Lutheran, Presbyterian, Anglican, Quaker, and other Evangelicals. Supported by an ample budget and by the skills of Ya'qub Halaby, Father Kapustin set to work purchasing land for the Russian Ecclesiastical Mission.[10]

The first large Russian property purchased in Jerusalem was the Maidan, the traditional Ottoman parade ground that occupied roughly seventeen acres outside the sixteenth-century walls of the Old City. This purchase provided accommodations for the ten-thousand Russian pilgrims who arrived each spring, most of whom walked from Jaffa to Jerusalem. The first buildings to be erected in the Russian Compound, or Moskobiyah, as this area became known, were a women's hospice and the Russian consulate in the southeast, a hospital and a building for the Russian Ecclesiastical Mission in the southwest, and a large men's hospice in the northwest. In 1872, the Cathedral of the Holy Trinity, where Sophie's parents would later be wed, was consecrated in the center of the compound. In 1890, the Imperial Hospice, designed for affluent travelers, was built. The buildings were named for members of the tsar's family.[11]

Father Kapustin and Ya'qub also worked on the small plot adjacent to the Church of the Holy Sepulchre inside the Old City, which had been purchased by Russia in the 1850s. When construction began, archaeological ruins were found, halting further development for decades. Excavation under the leadership of Father Kapustin and Conrad Schick, a German architect and archaeologist, identified a majestic staircase believed to be the eastern steps to the original fourth-century Church of the Holy Sepulchre. Other findings included a gate threshold believed to belong to the Judgment Gate, now in the Church of the Holy Sepulchre, through which Jesus is believed to have left Jerusalem to ascend the Hill of Calvary, where he is believed to have been crucified. The Alexander Nevsky Church, named for a thirteenth-century warrior prince, was erected above the excavation site.[12] A large stone, presumably from Calvary, was placed in this church. In 1948, when Sophie Halaby and her family fled their home in the Musrara section of Jerusalem, they found refuge in a small convent connected to this church.

Ya'qub also facilitated the purchase of a large plot on the Mount of Olives, where he and Father Kapustin built churches and convents. Their work was supported by the IOPS, whose members collected hundreds of thousands of rubles annually on Palm Sunday to support the work in Palestine. In addition to churches and convents, the society built and staffed schools for the youth of Palestine. These schools, which taught Russian as well as Arabic, continued to grow, becoming the largest system of elementary schools in the Holy Land until the fall of the Russian Empire.

Father Kapustin built the Church of the Ascension on the Mount of Olives, modeled on the Hagia Sofia. The church, surrounded by a beautiful garden, had a spectacular view of the Dead Sea. The adjacent two-hundred-foot-tall bell tower became part of the Jerusalem skyline in 1870. Sophie and Asia prayed regularly in the decades after 1948 in this church; its tower is visible in several of Sophie's paintings. The nuns in the Convent of the Mount of Olives, added later, became Sophie's friends. On the other side of the Mount of Olives, facing the Dome of the Rock, the Church of Mary Magdalene was built in 1886, in honor of Empress Marya Alexandrova. Its seven golden onion domes added a Russian architectural note to the Jerusalem skyline, but though Sophie was familiar with the church and close to nuns who lived in its adjacent convent, its iconic image is not present in any of her works.[13]

Ya'qub Halaby served as dragoman for thirty-five years. In addition to facilitating the purchase of land for the Russian Church, it is likely that he also acquired substantial holdings for himself. At the time of his death in 1900, his position and presumably some of his land passed to his nephew, George,

Sophie's father. The Halaby family owned considerable landed property in Jerusalem. Though they spent some time in Kiev before and during World War I, there is evidence that the Halaby family were living comfortably in Jerusalem in 1911 when a group of Russian theological students from Kiev arrived on pilgrimage. A history of their trip notes that George Halaby hosted students from the Kiev Academy, led by Father Alexander Glagolev, in his home in Musrara. The author commented: "How pleasant it is to see that this Arab by origin is filled with the best sentiments towards our great country—Russia. He is married to a Russian."[14]

World War I

Three years later, when the Ottoman Empire declared war on the British, French, and Russian Empires, foreign nationals of enemy countries were exiled from Palestine. The priests and the entire staff of the Russian Mission left for Alexandria. All Russian schools and churches were closed. George Halaby, the dragoman who held Ottoman nationality, was appointed administrator of the mission in their absence. The Ottoman military command seized the entire Russian Compound. The Russian hospital, designed to care for pilgrims, was turned into a hospital for wounded Ottoman soldiers; the hospices built to house pilgrims became soldiers' barracks. Officers were billeted in the Imperial Hospice. George was left in charge of the spaces deemed unimportant to the war effort.

Ordinary soldiers like Ihsan Hasan Turjman, who served as a clerk in the Ottoman military headquarters in Jerusalem and later in Nablus and Hebron, wondered: "What will be the fate of Palestine?" The assumption of his friends and family was that the Ottoman Empire would be dismembered and that Palestine would become part of Egypt under the tutelage of the British. Others thought that Palestine would be annexed to Syria in an autonomous Arab East. There was also another faction—the Young Turks—who wanted Palestine to remain part of the Ottoman Empire. Jemal Pasha, the Ottoman commander in Jerusalem, used the support of this group to justify his repression of Arab nationalists.[15]

Though George Halaby was not ordered to leave Palestine, the safety of his family was in jeopardy. In Jerusalem, old men, Jews and Christians, were pressed into forced labor, cleaning streets and hauling lumber to serve the Ottoman war effort. George, fifty years old, was vulnerable. His son, Nicola, twelve years old, was not yet of draft age, but youngsters only a few years older were being conscripted. Most worrisome, Olga Halaby risked arrest as a Russian national. According to family oral history, the entire Halaby family fled Jerusalem, returning to Kiev to wait out the war.

Edward Said, who was born in Jerusalem and experienced exile, mused later in life: "While it perhaps seems peculiar to speak of the pleasures of exile, there are some positive things to be said for a few of its conditions. Seeing 'the entire world as a foreign land' makes possible originality of vision. Most people are principally aware of one culture, one setting, one home; exiles are aware of at least two, and this plurality of vision gives rise to an awareness of simultaneous dimensions, an awareness that—to borrow a phrase from music—is contrapuntal."[16]

It was during this tumultuous period that the young Sophie developed the plurality of vision that would inform her art. There are no written records of the family's exile from Jerusalem, but family oral history recounts that the Halaby family spent the war years in Kiev and subsequently fled the fighting pursuant to the Bolshevik Revolution for Jerusalem in late 1917.[17] The story of their flight from Jerusalem to Russia and back to Jerusalem was retold repeatedly, emphasizing the duality of the family—part Russian and part Palestinian. In 1948, the family would be uprooted again, leaving their home in Musrara to take refuge in the Old City of Jerusalem. From that point, Sophie would live the rest of her life in East Jerusalem, painting the hills and flowers of her city repeatedly. Sophie's art was a product of her complex identity, forged in wartime exile, but also influenced by her British education in Jerusalem and by her travels in Paris to study art. Sophie told some people that she was born in Kiev and others that she was born in Jerusalem. This playful inconsistency was an element of her originality; secrecy and confounding others about her origins was a feature of her personality.

Sophie told Sisters Tamara and Veronica of the Convent of the Mount of Olives that she was born in Kiev and that the Halaby family lived there during her childhood, returning to Jerusalem after the Bolshevik Revolution. She illustrated her stories with a family photo album of pictures of the children in Kiev. This album was among the treasured possessions brought from Kiev to Jerusalem. It was saved again when the family left their home in Musrara for the Old City in 1948. It made a final voyage to the new Halaby home in East Jerusalem. In 1957, the photo album, documenting the family's life in Kiev, was shown by Sophie to the girl who would become Sister Veronica. The eight-year-old, who came from a neighboring Arab village to study at the convent, was curious about Sophie's life in Russia.[18]

The photos of bright floral pinafores and floppy white hats worn by Sophie and Asia enchanted the young Veronica. She remembered the girls' braids, tied in ribbons for the long Kiev summer days, and photographs of a small boy, possibly Nicola, in his sailor suit with short pants and straw boater. There may have been a picture of a governess who taught them English or French. The daily dose of cod liver oil, eaten with a piece of black bread to remove the taste, may have appeared in another photo.[19] The album clearly facilitated a connection between the middle-aged artist and her young friend. Unfortunately, the childhood photos that had traveled so far and that contained so many clues to the lives of the Halaby children were destroyed along with all of Sophie's other papers at the end of her life.[20]

The Kiev that Sophie knew, and later heard about in stories told by her parents, was far larger and more modern than Jerusalem. Its population of about 250,000 was more than six times that of Jerusalem. In 1892, Kiev opened the first tramline in the Russian empire. The city prospered, shipping sugar and grain exports along the Dnieper River. Kiev was the scene of conflict among Russian, Polish, and Ukrainian nationalist groups, as well as periodic outbursts of anti-Semitic pogroms during the years of the war.[21] Nevertheless, the Halaby family found refuge there, enjoying a comfortable life. Nannies and governesses were likely employed, and schools were available for all three children, as Kiev opened schools for girls at the turn of the twentieth century that offered opportunities to study music and art as well as history and mathematics. Nicola would have attended a school that encouraged science as well as math, history, and geography.[22] The Bolshevik Revolution brought great instability to Kiev as imperial forces withdrew and competition for control between Cossacks and Red troops led to violence.

George Halaby recognized the danger to his family posed by the revolution and received news of the British advance in Jerusalem with relief. The Halaby family probably arrived in Jerusalem shortly after the victorious British forces. They found a city that had suffered greatly during the war. The food supply of Jerusalem, which was brought in from the surrounding villages, had been confiscated to feed Ottoman soldiers, causing the price of basic foodstuffs to escalate by 50 percent; a locust epidemic in 1915 caused destitute villagers to seek refuge in Jerusalem, resulting in even greater stress on the food supply. Jemal Pasha, commander of the Ottoman Fourth Army in Jerusalem, had ordered the collection of agricultural tithes in kind, not in money. Producers hid their harvests, fearing confiscation of their grain by the government. The price of coal and kerosene soared. The trees of the city were cut down and used to power the narrow-gauge railway that stretched from Constantinople to Beersheba.[23]

Bertha Spafford Vester, one of a very small number of foreigners permitted to remain in the city during the war, managed the American Colony, established as a Christian cooperative community decades before the war. Under her guidance, the colony operated a clinic; two hospitals, supported by the Red Crescent Society, whose Jerusalem branch was established in 1915; and soup kitchens that fed twenty-five hundred hungry Jerusalemites each day. Vester recorded the misery of women who offered to sell their babies for a pittance just to be sure of a few more meals. She described one mother who left her skeletal twin babies at midnight hanging from the colony's front gate. Worst of all, in her estimation, were the many destitute young girls who sold themselves to German and Turkish troops.[24]

Though there had been no battles in the Holy City, Ottoman authorities had used Jerusalem as a military headquarters from the beginning of the war. Suspected traitors, including the Mufti of Gaza and his son, were hanged at the Jaffa Gate of the Old City. Scores were imprisoned and tortured. Their cries continued to echo in the collective consciousness of the fearful city. In the summer and fall of 1917, as the British army advanced from the south, Turkish soldiers fled Jerusalem carrying money, records, drugs, surgical instruments, furniture, and food. In deference to the religious status of the city, there was no bombardment.[25] Khalil Sakakini, the leading Arab educator of Jerusalem at the time, observed the devastation of Jerusalemites: "Our men are hanged, our children become orphans, we are overloaded with taxes, donations, and responsibilities dealing with the war. Our important families are exiled, and we are dying from hunger and patience."[26]

The entry of General Allenby on foot through the same Jaffa Gate into the Old City on December 11, 1917, was staged to demonstrate that the British were liberating the city from the Turks, not occupying it as conquerors. Bertha Spafford Vester saw the event differently. She recalled: "We thought then we were witnessing the triumph of the last crusade." Jerusalemites celebrated—church bells rang, and flowers were showered on British officers. Vester quoted the book of Psalms, "Truly we should sing with the tongue smiling . . . the Lord hath done great things for us, therefore we are glad."[27]

Historian Laura Robson, writing nearly one hundred years after the arrival of the British, analyzed the British presence in Palestine without emotion. She recognized that despite the triumphant feelings recorded by Vester, Palestinian Christians saw their political fortunes erode. The British, she asserted, created a myth of historic enmity among the three Abrahamic religions in order to demonstrate the continuing need for their presence. This ultimately led to strife. Muslim and Christian became oppositional categories for the first time.[28]

Unaware as they were of British colonial plans, Jerusalemites greeted the arrival of British troops with great expectation of relief from the deprivation and hostilities of the war years.[29] Vester recorded that she saw Jews and Muslims joining their Christian neighbors in spontaneous merrymaking, happy that the privations of wartime were ending. She saw a Jewish man embrace a Greek Orthodox priest, whose tall, clerical hat went askew in the exuberance of fraternal feelings. Allenby's proclamation on the steps of the citadel was designed to reassure all religious groups that the British would govern with fairness: "Every sacred building, monument, holy spot, shrine, traditional site, endowment, pious bequest, or customary place of prayer, of whatever form of the three religions, will be maintained and protected according to the existing customs and beliefs of those to whose faiths they are sacred."[30]

Foreign nationals, who had been exiled and whose property was confiscated, began to trickle back to Jerusalem. Strangers greeted each other in the street, congratulating one another on surviving. People, including thousands of deserters from the Turkish army, emerged from hiding. General Allenby responded to the needs of Jerusalemites by issuing practical orders to bring daily supplies of wheat and other food essentials from Cairo to address the severe privations of the civilian population. The Syria and Palestine Relief Fund, founded by Bishop Rennie MacInnes, added to the food supplies and also donated wool to make blankets and warm clothing. The American Zionist Organization and the American Red Cross contributed personnel, equipment, and funds.

Allenby, recognizing the need for long-term relief aid, invited Mabel Warburton, former headmistress of the British Syrian School in Beirut, and Anne Irvine, formerly of the Scottish mission in Tiberias, to come to Jerusalem to create a system to care for the thousands of orphans roaming the Old City. Warburton and Irvine, who had both been exiled in Cairo during the war, were experienced teachers and relief workers; both spoke some Arabic. They arrived in January and began rounding up destitute children, bringing them in from the streets, feeding them, smearing them from head to foot with sulfur ointment to treat their scabies, and combing paraffin through their hair to rid them of head lice. Gradually, they found families who could continue to care for some of the children.[31]

As the crisis in the Old City waned, British officials identified a new problem: German Kaiserwerth Deaconess nuns were spreading "hateful lies" about the British to orphans in their care outside the walls. Their orphanage, Talitha Kumi, a large stone house surrounded by a garden built by Conrad Schick in the mid-nineteenth century, served hundreds of orphans.[32] British authorities exiled the Deaconess nuns to Cairo and asked Warburton to take charge of these orphans. Warburton agreed to the task with the understanding that she would be allowed to create a secondary school for girls on the premises. Allenby approved the plan; Warburton and Irvine moved to an old stone house on the Jaffa Road adjacent to the orphanage; it would be their home for the next five years. They began the process of transforming the orphanage building into the school that Sophie and Asia would attend, the English Girls' High School.[33]

Home in Musrara

The Halaby family was welcomed back to the city, where they had friends and family. Mother Catherine of the Russian Convent at Mary Magdalene, a long-time friend of the family, reported that George and Olga settled with their children in a home in Musrara belonging to the family. This may have been the same house they lived in before leaving Jerusalem or a neighboring house. (The Halaby family owned several houses in Musrara.) Diana Safieh, a friend of the family, remembered visiting them there.[34] Evidence of the Halaby family's presence in Musrara is also found in the diary of Khalil Sakakini, who reported a dream in which he walked on the new road between the houses of the Halaby family and that of Fraidy al-Alami.[35] It is likely that Uncle Ya'qub bought the property in Musrara decades earlier at the time he worked on completing the purchase of the Russian Compound.

In Jerusalem, George discovered that the British were using the Russian Compound as an administrative center. Throughout the years of the British Mandate, the new Soviet government claimed ownership of the Russian Compound and of all Russian church property in Palestine. The British did not respond to Soviet demands for restitution. Meanwhile the Russian Orthodox Mission, no longer supported by either the government or the people of Russia, was in dire financial trouble. In 1922, the Russian Orthodox Church Outside of Russia was established in opposition to the new Soviet government, but it was only in February 1933 that Father Antony Sinkevich arrived in Jerusalem as archimandrite, the highest ranked church official in Palestine. He would serve there for seventeen years, responsible for managing all mission property and its occupants. The British continued using the Russian Compound throughout the Mandate but allocated Father Antony space in the compound for mission headquarters. There, Father Antony received foreign dignitaries as well as the British high commissioner.[36]

Father Antony and George Halaby developed a close relationship, reprising the one enjoyed previously by Father Kapustin and Ya'qub Halaby. Though there was no longer a need for a traditional dragoman, as Ottoman nationality was no longer a requirement for buying land, George was able to help Father Antony marshal evidence regarding the ownership of land and buildings claimed by the Soviet government and counter-claimed by the Russian Orthodox Church Outside of Russia. George retained the title and the connections associated with his rank. Sophie kept his official documents long after his death.[37] A young friend of Sophie described George as a "theologist" and a "gentleman" who spent hours writing at his desk.[38]

The Halaby home in Musrara was located in one of the few mixed neighborhoods of Jerusalem. Wasif Jawhariyyeh, born in 1897, a popular oud player and musician, described this storied neighborhood, among the earliest communities built outside the city walls, followed by the development of the neighborhoods of Sheikh Jarrah, Yemin Moshe, Baq`a', and later, Katamon and Talbieh. Jawhariyyeh saw the move out of the Old City as an opportunity for hundreds of families to replace their fetid, ancient housing with modern tiled buildings secured with mortar and fortified by iron railings. He noted that Musrara was the first Jerusalem neighborhood whose homes had electricity; the first cars in the city were driven on nearby Jaffa Road. Arabic as well as classical Western music playing on new phonographs could be heard from open windows. Cinemas opened, featuring motion pictures from faraway Hollywood.[39] Jawhariyyeh thought that the cafés located at the periphery of the new neighborhoods around Musrara and the Russian Compound or near the Jaffa Gate "were nodes where Christian, Muslim, Jewish, and Armenian populations could interact."[40] This interaction characterized the urban, educated population of the city.

Sophie, though still a young girl, was doubtless aware of the liveliness and modernity of the Musrara neighborhood described by Jawhariyyeh. She would certainly also have been conscious of the traditional Jerusalem sights and sounds that were captured in the memoirs of the young Felicity Ashbee, who arrived with her family from England in 1918. Ashbee wrote about peasant women who wore brightly embroidered black dresses and Muslim women who covered their faces with veils. The melon market near the Jaffa Gate, with its piles of stacked green melons, and the thronging, shouting Arabs buying and selling, were also memorable, as was the Armenian, Mr. Ohan, whose shop was laden with carpets and embroideries hung from the ceiling, brass and copper bowls and candlesticks, and old silver plates and dishes. Ohan, she recalled, always offered guests coffee in tiny blue and white china cups without handles. Ashbee liked walking along the rampart walls from which she could see the Church of Mary Magdalene, which she called "the fairytale Russian church, its golden onion-shaped domes glowing as if they were on fire, emerging out of the cypresses and olive trees of Gethsemane." She remembered the pottery workshop of Mr. Ohanessian, whose workers were making replacement tiles for the renovation of the Dome of the Rock, and she recalled watching an old Arab who resurfaced copper saucepans with tin, noting that "he did it so quickly—like magic." She also remembered the oily sesame cakes and the halva that were sold in the market.[41]

While these or similar sights would have been unavoidably familiar to young Sophie, her neighbors in nearby Musrara were different from those described by Ashbee. They were educated men and women. Dr. Tawfiq Canaan, the first Arab physician to graduate from the Syrian Protestant College (later the American University of Beirut), who was an authority on leprosy and became an important ethnographer of Palestine, lived there with his family. His wife and sister-in-law were active in women's and nationalist causes. His daughter, Leila (later Leila Mantura), was a good friend of another neighbor, Ruth Schwartz (later Ruth Dayan) and of Ruth's sister, Reuma (later Reuma Weizmann). Other neighbors, including Musa Alami, Arif al-Arif, and Awni Abd al-Hadi, became leaders of the Palestinian National Movement. Professor Zvi Banet, a scholar of Islam, and Ya'akov Shapira, who became Israel's minister of justice, also lived nearby.[42] Dr. Helena Kagan, recently arrived from Russia, lived close by with her mother. Dr. Kagan was the first pediatrician in Jerusalem; she cared for Jawhariyyeh's children. Dr. Albert Ticho, the famous ophthalmologist, who treated Jordanian royalty as well as poor Arab peasants, lived above his clinic with his artist wife.[43]

Anna Ticho had arrived from Vienna, where she had studied art, in 1912. She was eighteen years old and engaged to marry her first cousin, Albert Ticho. Anna described her first impressions of the city: "I came from Vienna, from the land of forests, water, and wild beauty. We entered Jerusalem in the evening hours. The delicate colours and contours of the bare hills dissolved into the evening light and there was a breathtaking silence over the hills. I felt overwhelmed and was in love with this land at first sight. This love grew on me. And the expression of the spirit of Jerusalem became my life's work. I befriended its stones, thistles, the primitive architecture of the little Arab houses which nestle in the hills and its giant olive trees."[44]

Sophie was younger and had not yet studied painting, yet she must have experienced similar attraction to the beautiful hills that became the focus of her mature work. The sights, sounds, and smells of the city that greeted her—the bright sunlight and clear air, the Bedouins in their ornate garb, the call of the muezzin, the smell of camels, were different from life in Kiev. The narrow streets of the Old City, the beautiful stone walls, the minarets and mosques where vendors of cool drinks, licorice, and raisin juice called their wares and clapped brass castanets to attract the attention of possible customers intrigued her. Serene Husseini Shahid described the sheikhs, priests, and rabbis dressed in black, their heads covered with the different headgear demanded by their respective religions. She also wrote about the peasant women from neighboring villages who walked to the Old City to sell their wares, carrying fruit and vegetables in hand-woven baskets on their heads, holding one hand on a hip and the other on the basket for balance. She described their long black dresses, intricately embroidered in characteristic patterns of red, green, and pink, and their flowing embroidered white shawls swinging gracefully as they walked.[45] These striking sights were part of Sophie's world.

The Halaby family adjusted to their new environs. During the years in Kiev they spoke Russian in public, while Arabic was a private family language. In Jerusalem, Arabic was ubiquitous; Russian became the private family language. They attended the nearby Holy Trinity Cathedral; at home they drank tea with lemon from a Russian samovar, not the Turkish coffee popular in Jerusalem. Shortly after their arrival in the city, all three children were registered in English-language schools, where they absorbed English culture, a new layer to be integrated into their Russian-Palestinian identities. The children adapted quickly to their new environs. Soon, all three siblings were able to read English books and magazines. They spoke and corresponded with friends in English, though they spoke Arabic with shopkeepers and servants. In 1961, Nicola wrote in English to Aunt Vera in Birzeit, apologizing for not being able to write Arabic properly, but noting that he would be able to understand a reply in Arabic.[46]

For Sophie, the ability to adapt to Russian, Palestinian, and English culture was an essential ingredient of her life, and it became a part of her artistic world. Said's conceptualization of a "contrapuntal" identity was true for Sophie, who refused to select one culture as dominant. All three reverberated in her life and work.

Antiquity and Modernity in Jerusalem

While Jerusalem had been an important city under the Ottomans, Damascus remained a more important center of government and commerce. By making Jerusalem the capital of Mandate Palestine, the British gave the landmarks of the city new importance: the Ottoman Citadel (later, David's Citadel) and the Dome of the Rock became symbols of Palestine; they were featured on new postage stamps. Under the direction of the Pro-Jerusalem Society planners, the cubic, domed structures characteristic of the domestic architecture of the Old City became icons of the Palestinian landscape.[47]

As soon as the immediate needs for food and water for Jerusalem's population were met, British authorities turned to other pressing issues—housing, hygiene, and education were high on their agenda. Ronald Storrs, the new governor of the city, opposed all physical manifestations of modernity in the architecture of the city. Storrs saw the emergence of Jaffa Road as a major commercial artery and the new modern neighborhoods championed by Jawhariyyeh in the north and west as incompatible with the essence of Jerusalem, the Holy City. He was determined to preserve his vision of the ancient city through plans for new buildings and urban design that were in keeping with the architectural style of the Old City, which would be shielded from commerce and modernization by a new park. To this end, he founded the Pro-Jerusalem Society. Sophie's feelings about Jerusalem would be profoundly affected by the debate between those who celebrated modernizing efforts and others who wished to maintain Jerusalem as a Holy City.

Storrs and the planners and architects he hired to staff his department saw the monumental European buildings constructed in previous decades—like the Italian Hospital and the Germanic Augusta Victoria—as blemishes on the landscape of the city. One of the first British architects to assist Storrs was Charles Robert Ashbee (Felicity's father), a leading figure of the Arts and Crafts movement of England, who lamented the intrusion of these "antiregionalistic" structures: "Coming into the City from the old pilgrim route . . . we notice how the ancient Jerusalem is all but obliterated: we see the once golden dome no longer, we see a bastard Florence, a bastard Nuremburg, a bastard Moscow, an imitation Lourdes, a Bavarian suburb and an imitation Oxford. . . . Round and about the City circuit within or without the walls we note an arrogant assertion of the various national codes. All modern buildings seem to have been strangely prophetic of the War."[48]

Ashbee couldn't tear down these iconic buildings, so he directed his attention to less permanent structures. He took aim at the corrugated iron shacks that stood near the Jaffa Gate serving a variety of commercial purposes and replaced them with structures built according to authentic, indigenous design reminiscent of the khans used by peasants who came to Jerusalem to sell their produce. Ashbee, like Storrs, was deeply offended by the Ottoman clock tower erected over the Jaffa Gate in 1906. Clock towers became symbols of the spirit of change and civic pride under the Ottomans; they also represented a new sense of measuring time, replacing the sundial. Thus, it is not surprising that when Storrs raised the five hundred pounds necessary for its dismantling, city notables petitioned the governor to spare the tower that had cost the community a considerable sum to erect. Storrs, ever eager to show the spirit of compromise, promised to reerect the clock elsewhere.[49]

Unlike British officials, who sought to safeguard traditional building structures, "marrying modern progress with treasured antiquity" in the words of Alan Cunningham, the last high commissioner, Zionist officials championed modernity and aggressive development. Nevertheless, they hired Patrick Geddes, a British planner, to build an important symbol—the Hebrew University. Though he worked for ten years, from 1918 to 1928, he succeeded only in completing the National Library (today, housing the law faculty of the Hebrew University). In this dome-shaped building, Geddes sought not only to restore harmony between ancient Hebrew culture and its "authentic habitat," but also to incorporate an element of architectural unity among Jewish, Christian, and Muslim cultures—the dome. Indigenous Palestinian culture—as exemplified by the dome roofs in the sunshine—expressed the historical life of the land to Geddes and was perfectly compatible, in his view, with its new modern spirit.[50]

Sophie Halaby grew up in this milieu of competing visions for her new city. Her Jerusalem was becoming more Christian as the peal of church bells was added to the familiar muezzin calls. It was also becoming more Jewish as European immigrants opened shops and cafés in the growing city center. The extraordinary quality of the bright sunlight that pervaded the city was mentioned by many new arrivals to the city. Anna Ticho, the Viennese artist, noted that she was blinded by the brightness and stopped painting for several years until she adjusted to the strong light.[51] Sophie, who had family photo albums of her childhood in Kiev, was aware of the difference between the colors of Kiev and the light of Jerusalem. She was also already aware of the dome-shaped buildings, which were featured in some of her mature work.

Susan P. Emery, a young art teacher who arrived in Jerusalem from England at about the same time as the Halaby family, conveyed vivid impressions of the city in letters home to her mother. She described getting up at 3:30 a.m. with another teacher to see the sun rise from the top of the Mount of Olives:

> I think I have never seen anything more marvelous than the view from the top. Beneath a dark blue cloud stretched a great belt of golden sky, against which the Mountains of Moab stood out in vivid purple. At the foot of the mountains the Dead Sea lay, just catching the golden light; and all between was the Wilderness of Judea, bare, and rocky and brown, with never a leaf upon it. We waited a little, and suddenly the sun came up behind the mountains, and the whole of the Jordan Valley was flooded with glowing pink and

> gold light, spreading along the mountains as far as we could see. The Dead Sea is 20 miles away, and nearly 4,000 feet below, and the tops of the mountains must be 50 miles or more away, but the air is like crystal, and the Sea looks like a big pond, and the hills of Moab quite close.[52]

British landscape painter Thomas Seddon, writing from Jerusalem in the first half of the nineteenth century, captured the colors on the hills surrounding the city:

> At present, the color varies singularly. Whenever the light shines directly on them, the hills look white, with lines of yellow running over them from the dry parched herbage; but when the sun is low, so that the sides of the rocky ledges are in shadow, the hill is of a glorious purple, mixed with the golden and brown tints of the herbage. The white rock is also very susceptible of color, from the rays of the morning or evening sun, and the little early that is visible being reddish. The Mount of Olives every evening is of a wonderfully beautiful, rather red purple.[53]

This natural beauty, the richness of color and light, would have been evident to Sophie, and it would be captured in her later artwork.

The Jerusalem Girls' College

Beginning in the mid-nineteenth century, a plethora of missionary schools—French, Italian, German, Russian, and Anglican—were established in Jerusalem, teaching European languages. Jewish schools taught in Yiddish, Ladino, and Hebrew, as well as in a variety of European languages. Islamic schools, which were state schools under the Ottomans, taught in Arabic. These schools became the center of controversy in the years before World War I when the Turks required that Turkish replace Arabic as the language of instruction. Missionary and Jewish schools, which received no government subsidy, were permitted to continue to teach in the language of their countries as long as they added a class in Turkish. In the past, poor Arab families often sent their children, especially their daughters, to missionary schools, which provided food and clothing as well as education. As a result of the change in legislation, affluent Muslim and Christian families, believing that Western languages would be of greater utility to their children than Turkish, began to send their children to missionary schools in greater numbers.[54]

Following decades of unsuccessful missionizing, it became increasingly clear to Anglican clergy in Jerusalem that Muslim and Jewish children would not convert. A secondary effort to encourage Orthodox Christian children to become Anglican had also failed. Thus, Anglican Bishop Blyth renounced missionizing as an objective and adopted a new goal for his church in Jerusalem: to influence Christian, Muslim, and Jewish boys and girls to cooperate with each other. Just before the turn of the century, Blyth established St. Mary's School to teach tolerance and cooperation to Jerusalem's daughters and St. George's School (later St. George's College) to instill "godliness and morality" in the boys of the city.[55]

The new focus on the church's role as a catalyst for peaceful coexistence rather than a means to proselytize can be seen in an article published in 1905 about St. George's School in the journal *Bible Lands*. The author presented a new definition of the role of a Christian gentleman as one who studied and worked with others of different religious backgrounds without rancor: "[A] prominent feature of our school is that it contains boys of all religions. Christians, Greeks, Latins, Anglicans, Mohammedans and converted Jews . . . we have not had one single fight for religion's sake. So nobly do the boys answer to the summons of this liberal public school appeal to a higher life, and strenuously and pluckily they do strive after the Christian gentleman ideal."[56]

No Anglican leader was more eloquent than Mabel Warburton, recently brought to Jerusalem by General Allenby, in supporting Bishop Blyth's call for fostering tolerance among the different communities in Jerusalem. Warburton believed that communities living together in tolerance would lead to peace. Her students, including Sophie Halaby, at the English Girls' High School (later the Jerusalem Girls' College or JGC) prayed regularly for the peace of Jerusalem, but Warburton believed in action as well as prayer. She shared Bishop Blyth's belief that the girls and women of Jerusalem had a vital role to play in cultivating an atmosphere of tolerance. In her opening day remarks in 1922, a session attended by all the pupils, Warburton spoke of the unique position of the city—the difficulties, the advantages, the opportunities of being its residents: "We have no common national name or national tradition to appeal to, to rouse our enthusiasm and to encourage our service; yet no other city in the world has such memories and such monuments of noble endeavor or offers such inspiration and such opportunity to those who seek its good. If the peoples who meet in Jerusalem can be taught to live in peace, united in common desire for its welfare, what an object lesson on universal brotherhood would be offered to the world!"[57]

Sophie's headmistress, Mabel Warburton, was a powerful mentor. Warburton had attended Cheltenham Ladies' College from 1895 to 1897, and she was greatly inspired by its famous principal and pioneer of women's education, Dorothea Beale. She came to Jerusalem an experienced teacher, having spent over a decade at the British Syrian Training College in Beirut. Her enthusiasm was fueled by a combination of religious conviction, sense of service, and devotion to girls' education. Three missionary societies supported her work: the Christian Missionary Society, the Jerusalem and the East Mission, and the Church Mission to Jews.[58]

The Mandatory government, in adherence to Allenby's promise to respect the sensibilities of each community in Palestine, planned to open schools that taught children of Muslim and Christian heritage in Arabic in one school system while teaching Jewish children in Hebrew in a separate system. Warburton was concerned that this approach made it less likely that the different communities would be able to understand each other and work together. She was determined to have pupils from each of the communities enrolled in her school and to teach them in a common language, English. To attain her goal, she had to find suitable teachers to staff the large old stone building that had housed the Talitha Kumi orphanage.

Anne Irvine agreed to stay on to help her friend launch the school. Mabel Warburton traveled to Beirut, where she located five of her former pupils whose teacher training had been interrupted by the war. These young women had substantial ability in English and knowledge of British school organization. She invited them to join the staff as prefects, senior students with a leadership role in organizing younger students and assisting the teachers. They soon made their way to Jerusalem on a British destroyer. She also hired two young English women who had attended Cheltenham Ladies' College—Mabel Mellor and Susan P. Emery. Years later, Emery described Warburton as a very cheerful, extroverted woman, who believed in the potential of her entire staff.[59]

Warburton's school opened in September 1918, at first accepting girls between the ages of six and fifteen. The majority of the pupils were Muslim; there were a small number of Jews and a variety of Christians—Armenian, Greek Orthodox, and Russian Orthodox. Sophie and Asia were in attendance from the beginning. At first, Emery had grave doubts, founded in Western prejudices, about Warburton's plan to create a culture of tolerance. She wrote to her mother: "It is queer, one hears people at home talk of the return of the Jews to Palestine, but it wouldn't be any good, one sees, for they are hated by both Christians and Moslems . . . the Moslems hate the Christians, but they still join forces against the Jews. Nothing but a thorough-going despotism for one hundred years will pull this country together . . . it will take ages to instill into the people any idea of public service, or truthfulness, or cleanliness."[60]

Emery's colonialist views did not last. Warburton's power of persuasion was so powerful that Emery became her partner in the Anglican educational initiative to build a culture of tolerance in Palestine.

Unlike earlier missionary schools that served the very poor, often providing food and clothing as well as education, the English Girls' High School attracted students from wealthier and more established homes; fees were introduced, as were distinctive school uniforms. Warburton was successful from the first year in creating a culture of learning and of fairness that remained the hallmark of the school. The youngest children were taught in Arabic but had an English lesson every day. From the age of eleven all teaching was in English. Since the first class included girls of varying degrees of competence in English, all were expected to help each other learn. Working together, they learned a good deal from each other. Many of the pupils were the first in their families to study English. The language became an important part of the bond uniting all pupils.

Among the first to enroll were Sophie's cousins, the Wahbe sisters—Nadia, Olga, Sonia, and Louba—who were homeschooled until Warburton's school opened in 1918. Olga recalled, "I had my early education almost all the Elementary one at home as both father and mother were teachers and both graduates of the teachers seminarics under Imperial Russian Orthodox patronage." Olga, like her cousin Sophie, began her formal schooling knowing three languages: "In Arabic I had a very thorough background, Arabic grammar, syntax, rhetoric, literature, taught by my father and kept on by private tutorial teaching until my entry into University. I knew Russian and French and had before the age of twelve read most of the classics—many of which were translated into Russian. I had read Charles Dickens, the Christmas Carol, and Little Dorrit, and David Copperfield, and many others, and Chekov's stories, Turgenev's, and many of Tolstoy's, Henrik Ibsen's plays, Kalilah and Dimna, and the historical novels of Zeidan."[61]

Olga's parents subscribed to publications and magazines in three languages, including some illustrated ones that made lasting impressions on the young girl. Their friends were an educated circle who also influenced Olga and her siblings. The family background of the Wahbe sisters and their Halaby cousins was typical of their educated classmates: their parents had begun the transition from traditional to modern life by learning European languages. Sophie's mother, Olga, spoke Russian, French, and a little Arabic. Her father, George, spoke Arabic, some French, and was fluent in Russian. Aunt Vera was multilingual in Arabic, Russian, English, and probably French. When she returned to Jerusalem, Vera married Assaf Wahbe, also an educated Jerusalemite. In Jerusalem, Olga and Vera, sisters-in-law and close friends, were comfortable walking around the city without male escort and without traditional veils. These educated women believed that their daughters would have a bright future in British Jerusalem. Despite periodic concern about political unrest caused by growing nationalist movements, they had no plans to return to Russia (now under Soviet rule), to emigrate elsewhere, or to send their children abroad, except for short periods of advanced studies.[62]

The Halaby and Wahbe cousins followed the curriculum developed for them by Miss Warburton and were deeply impressed by the example of their headmistress. Olga remembered: "Miss Warburton had a great personality and when she approached we felt her presence which always inspired us and gave us courage and love for work." These two qualities—courage and love for work—were part of the ethos developed at the English Girls' High School. Here, young Jerusalemites read about English girls who solved problems on their own by thinking logically and acting swiftly. They read books like the popular Chisholm's *The Jolly Book for Girls*, whose girls took action to save others from catastrophe. Unlike Chisholm's heroines, who were a homogeneous group—all Protestant—the girls of the English Girls' School were keenly aware that they were a diverse group. Olga noted the warm feeling of inclusion created in the school for "all of us, Arabs, Greeks, Armenians, Russians, English, Americans, Germans, Jews, Bahais. . . . We were all made to feel as though we were one—there were no differences except in customs, heritage, language, but all joined in school activities as one great family."[63]

This extraordinary opportunity to learn together as girls and young women was a rare opportunity in Jerusalem and was remembered fondly by graduates. Even when the development of nationalistic rhetoric, sometimes accompanied by violence, caused fear in the city, within the walls of the English Girls' School harmony prevailed. This ethos of tolerance carried over to alumnae meetings. Graduates of diverse backgrounds continued to share news of continuing education, travel, marriages, and children. They met regularly in each other's homes and at the school for alumnae gatherings.[64]

Susan P. Emery, hired to teach art, believed that the lessons learned in school soon became part of the home lives of pupils too. In a letter to her mother in England, she observed, "This unity of work and games, of Christian teaching and School Assembly, made a very great contribution to the well-being of Jerusalem, since the hundreds of homes from which the pupils came were drawn, at least in some degree, into fellowship."[65] She repeatedly credited Miss Warburton for ending the discriminatory system that had existed in missionary schools whereby Arab teachers were called by their first names while British teachers were addressed with the title Miss and their surnames. Arab teachers had not been included in staff meetings, and they were the only teachers required to supervise students during recess. Warburton changed those policies, challenging traditional behavior and showing by example the benefits of collaboration and of mutual respect.[66]

Emery was an important influence on the young Sophie, who attended the English Girls' High School from 1918 until she graduated in 1924.[67] At first, Emery's thoughts about the students' artistic skills demonstrate the same Orientalism that led her to doubt Warburton's mission, and that tainted many Europeans in Jerusalem: "If they learnt drawing until they were fifty they would not be any good at it. They are not at all original. The Jews, especially, are awfully clumsy with their hands." Emery, however, after working in Jerusalem for many months shed her preconceptions and recognized her pupils as individuals.[68] Her presence provided the young Sophie Halaby with an important role model. The intrepid art teacher commanded an unusual presence in Jerusalem, carrying a sketchpad with her whenever she walked through the streets of the city. Her letters home were full of descriptions of sketching in the early morning light, at midday, and at dusk.

Miss Warburton, anticipating a growing need for teachers in Palestine, began almost at once to develop a teacher-training course that was added to the secondary-school curriculum. For those interested in office work, she developed another set of courses, the commercial curriculum. This program included typing, shorthand, and bookkeeping. Within two years there were two hundred pupils who remained in school beyond their secondary exams. The young women who took advantage of these additional classes filled the offices and schools established by the British Mandate.

The Talitha Kumi building was barely satisfactory in the first years of the school; Warburton projected the need for more room to accommodate the growing number of students and to provide specialized classrooms such as laboratories and studios to meet the needs of an expanding curriculum. She began to plan a campus that would feature a modern school building with airy classrooms, a separate facility with hygienic water closets, a dormitory for housing girls who lived too far away to commute to school, a building that included a large assembly hall and dining facility, and a garden for play as well as for lessons in botany and gardening. She found a suitable plot of land on which to build a school that matched her aspirations adjacent to the Ratisbonne monastery in Rehavia and arranged a loan for its purchase.[69] The new school buildings were certainly of great interest to Sophie and her classmates.

While these new buildings were being built, an ancient building, the old Ottoman Citadel, was renamed the Tower of David and used to host the first art exhibit in the city. The exhibit was the major cultural event of 1921 in Jerusalem. Organized by the British town planner, Ashbee, it featured hundreds of works and was the most ambitious and prestigious event of its kind in Palestine, attracting two thousand visitors. The display was divided into sections: Islamic art, architectural plans, international art, and the Hebrew Union of Artists. This latter category included paintings by several women who were amateur artists and not members of the union: Mrs. Albina, wife of the deputy police commissioner of Jerusalem; Mrs. Gordon, an Englishwoman; and Mrs. Drucker, who exhibited pictures she had painted in India. In another measure of inclusiveness, Ashbee arranged for a small selection of Bedouin textiles to be shown.[70]

Reduced admission fees for students were announced, and many students attended with their teachers. Sophie was likely one of them. She may have gone a second time with her mother, who collected embroidered fabric that she bought from village women who brought fresh fruit and vegetables to Musrara.[71] Sophie and her sister would later collect such textiles themselves. Sophie was fifteen years old when she looked at the works on display. What did she think of them? Was she inspired by the paintings or by the embroidery? Regrettably, she left no clues to her thoughts in 1921. Three years later, Sophie passed a matriculation test in drawing, which she studied throughout her school years.[72]

The English Girls' High School was renamed the Jerusalem Girls' College in 1922 at the opening of the first of the new school buildings, a hostel built to accommodate fifty students and six staff. Warburton announced at the inauguration that she had changed the name of the school to indicate her ambition to provide the girls of Jerusalem with increasing opportunities for higher education in order to fulfill her vision of creating a cohort of educated and dedicated women to work for intercommunal harmony in the city. The architect, George Shiber, a Christian Arab who worked with Ashbee and the Pro-Jerusalem Society, was praised in *Palestine Weekly*: "The Hostel was entirely of Palestine workmanship, and built entirely of Palestine material. It was a great tribute to the tradition of building in Palestine, and reflected credit on the architect, who had carried out the smallest details so thoroughly."[73]

Governor Storrs presided at the opening ceremony. He noted that the masons, carpenters, painters, plasterers, and quarrymen—Christian, Muslim, and Jew—had worked together in absolute harmony of spirit. He added: "If it is true that the spirit of those who work on a building stays with that building and never leaves it, I venture to hope that the spirit of those excellent hardworking men, each respecting his own religion and that of his fellow workers, may remain with it and all connected with it as long as it exists. If the girls who are sent here have the spirit of mutual toleration grafted onto their lives, and use it when they go out into the world, there can be no doubt whatever but that their influence over the future of this country can be for nothing but good."[74]

Once established in the new buildings, Warburton worked to enhance the curricular program, creating teacher-training classes and other college-level courses for students.[75] A keen sportswoman, she believed strongly in extracurricular activities as a means of building character. The new campus facilitated the growth of school clubs that provided another opportunity for girls of different religious and cultural backgrounds to form friendships. The glee club was very popular, as were the drama, pen pal, and sports clubs. Perhaps the most beloved of the clubs was the Girl Guides, a program for scouting activities that began with Brownies, continued with Guides, and culminated with Rangers. Each level of achievement was rewarded with special badges worn on the distinctive Guide uniform. Sports competitions with Guides from different schools provided opportunities for leadership as well as for achievement in sports and for singing and dance performances. It is likely that Sophie joined most of her classmates in the Girl Guides.

Warburton cited the achievements of her mentor, Miss Dorothea Beale, principal of Cheltenham College, who had expanded the student body of her school, enhanced the curriculum, and developed a program in teacher training. Warburton adopted Beale's motto: "There is work for women to do in this world, prepare yourself that *you* may nobly and worthily perform your part."[76] To this end, she created a liberal arts program—Scripture, history, geography, nature study, mathematics, Arabic, English, French, handwork (sewing and drawing), singing, and physical exercises—at the Jerusalem Girls' College. Sophie followed this rich curriculum.

At the conclusion of each year, pupils received a detailed report card attesting to their achievements and to their behavior. They were graded in both conversational and literary English, as well as Bible, history, geography, mathematics, literary Arabic, conversational French, and physiology—including the structure of the body, skeleton, joints, muscles, circulation, digestion, respiration, and nervous system. Sophie's study of physiology prepared her for the classes in anatomy she would take later in Paris. Formal drill, games, and class walks completed the program. For many, the report card became a treasured object, a manifestation of belonging to an elite group of educated girls.[77] Collectively, these pupils were called the "college girls," easily identified as they walked through the streets of the city by their distinctive green uniforms.

Diploma Day ceremonies were a celebratory event attended by important dignitaries as well as by the families of the graduates. A platform was erected in the garden surrounding the new school buildings for the occasion. Miss Warburton was joined on the platform by High Commissioner Sir Herbert Samuel, Sir Gilbert and Lady Clayton, and Archdeacon Waddy. The first row of seats was reserved for the patriarchs of the Greek and Armenian churches and the French consul; the second row was for heads of government departments. The event included sports competition, singing, and a display of handicrafts.[78] After graduation, the alumnae joined the Old Girls Guild, which had started in 1920, at a series of informal gatherings—lectures, volunteer work, and social events. Sophie Halaby and Olga Wahbe graduated in 1924 and joined the guild.[79]

The school, its teachers and headmistress, and the extracurricular activities all had a lasting impact on Sophie Halaby and her classmates. Izzat Tannous, a student at St. George's School who became a physician and Palestinian national leader, explained the extraordinary influence this type of school had on young people in Jerusalem:

> If I have said so much about that period of my life spent at St. George's School, it is because this institution played such a big role in my life. My character and my personality were shaped within its walls, in its classrooms, on its playground and, not least, in the bishop's drawing room where we were entertained by the bishop's family. We were treated like gentlemen and we were expected to act as such. . . . The moral standard of the school and the sportsmanship that prevailed within its premises had a great influence on the lives of all the students. . . . It was the honesty and devotion of these great people which stimulated our love of the Western World.[80]

During her years at the Jerusalem Girls' College, Sophie's identity as a Russian-Palestinian developed and matured. The school stimulated in Sophie a love of the Western world like that described above by Izzat Tannous, but Sophie soon understood that the ideals she learned in school were often betrayed by the realities of life in British-controlled Jerusalem. Unlike Tannous, she also had to overcome the peculiar limitations set on her aspirations due to beliefs about proper gender roles.

Palestinian Identity

Warburton's vision of a peaceful Jerusalem where her pupils (and their families) practiced tolerance was based on her mistaken assessment that there was no national feeling among her students. Testimony of the students suggests that they, on the contrary, did in fact have nationalist feelings. Olga Belkind, a graduate of the college, observed that the positive relations among the students did not extend to their families: "They did not visit our homes and we did not visit theirs." Widad Rizik, who attended the English Girls' School in Haifa, which was led by Susan P. Emery, Warburton's protégée, went further to describe the influence of life outside the classroom on the relations among students: "We were two separate entities (Arabs and Jews), and I must say we didn't like each other very much, because in our consciousness, the Balfour promise was being discussed and rejected and we heard about these things, and politics is so much part of life here."[81]

British officials continued to believe that national beliefs were nonexistent among Jerusalem's students. Stewart Perowne, who worked for the Education Department of the Mandate and taught at St. George's College, agreed with Warburton's assessment. In a letter to his father he wrote: "By giving them an English education, therefore, one is not really de-nationalizing them, because for the most part they have not the remotest idea of what their nationality implies; they have no traditions, and they are likely to find, on the whole, more akin to their own aspirations in Nelson and Cromwell than in Salah ed Din and Suleiman the Magnificent."[82] Perowne and Warburton failed to recognize the nationalist spirit growing among their students.

John Melkon Rose, the Armenian who attended St. George's College, cited above, understood that he belonged to two worlds, the European and the Middle Eastern. This feeling of multiple identities was true for many children of "mixed marriages," as they were called, like Sophie and her siblings. Thus, rather than having no national feelings, these children had complex national feelings. For some, like Widad Rizik, these multiple identities were experienced as a problem. Rizik described the confusing results of her British education: "You're not one of your own people. Although I don't begrudge anybody, I don't envy those people who are more Arab than I. But I'm different. Everyone who went to the English High School is different. We're not part of the community and we never will be. . . . 'Who am I? I am not British and I'm not Arab,' and this is a problem."[83]

Izzat Tannous, looking back at his time at St. George's, explained further the contradictory feelings students had about their English schools. Tannous appreciated the moral standard of the school and its spirit of sportsmanship. He lauded the honesty and devotion of the teachers, which stimulated love of the Western world. Nevertheless, Tannous felt deceived by the "despotism with which the Arab people were treated, and in particular the people of Palestine, at the hands of the Western powers after the First World War."[84] He concluded that this behavior compelled the Arabs to lose faith in the sincerity of the West.

Rashid Khalidi, in his acclaimed book *Palestinian Identity*, sought to untangle the different strands of thought that went into the creation of Palestinian identity. He explained: "it would be normal for a Palestinian today to identify *primarily* as an Arab in one context, as a Muslim or Christian in another, as a Nabulsi or Jaffan in yet another, and as a Palestinian in a fourth."[85] Beginning in the early Mandate period, Khalidi affirmed a growing sense of political and national identification among politically conscious, literate, and urban Palestinians, like George and Olga Halaby.[86] Though Sophie's parents identified as Palestinians, they encouraged their children to master the English language and to learn the culture of the British, recognizing its growing importance in Jerusalem. For Sophie, the influence of the English Girls' School had lasting importance, but her identity as a Palestinian and as a member of the Russian Orthodox community remained firmly in place. Khalidi's understanding of the complexity of Palestinian identity adds another dimension to Sophie's contradictory stories about her birthplace and childhood cited above. These discrepancies may reflect the whims of an eccentric artist or they may have been intentionally designed to hide deeply held personal feelings of identity.

2

Becoming a Modern Woman

1924–1933

> They [Jerusalem women] have nearly forgotten all the Eastern ways of doing things and are equal to the Western women in education and freedom. They are educated from childhood in primary schools, then in higher schools, colleges, and universities. So by the time they are 20 they are able to do any sort of business, either as a teacher or in government offices . . . in public they can speak and set their opinions, they go to lectures and live in societies. They read and find out what they don't know and what is happening in other places. If she thinks she can be of any use, she is willing to help. If she marries, it is by her will, and they live to help one another always asking one another's opinions about things, so they form a happy family and they give the best education to their children.
>
> —Annig Khalihigian, Armenian student, Jerusalem Girls' College, cited in Ruth Woodsmall, Survey on Status of Middle Eastern Women

Old Girls' Guild

The families who sent their daughters to the Jerusalem Girls' College wanted them to study English—the language of the new government and increasingly the language that would guarantee their daughters access to higher education abroad and to teaching and office jobs in Jerusalem. They recognized that learning English culture was also important in establishing them as modern girls. Thus, parents of girls who saw a professional future for their daughters and those who wanted their daughters to marry educated men enrolled them in the school. Some of them were notable Muslim families like the Nashashibis and Husseinis, whose daughters were likely to marry Muslim community leaders. Others, like the Valeros, were prominent Sephardic Jewish families whose daughters were likely to study abroad and to marry successful business leaders. Soon, the majority of the parents, like Sophie's, were Christian. Many were Greek Orthodox or Armenian and had attended missionary schools where they studied Russian or French. They sent their sons to St. George's College and their daughters to the Jerusalem Girls' College. They were pleased to see their daughters attending classes in their classic English schoolgirl uniforms on the new modern campus in Rehavia. They were happy that their daughters spoke English and made friends among the social elite of Jerusalem, who hailed from different communities, and who, like them, participated in the modernizing social and cultural life of Jerusalem.

Miss Warburton elaborated on her vision for the school in a pamphlet designed to raise funds for the additional buildings she planned. She noted that among the many changes taking place in Palestine under British rule, a most remarkable one was in the position of girls and women. Before the war, only a very few girls received anything in the way of a liberal arts education, and she observed that it was those few—teachers, nurses, social workers—who were hired immediately as Palestine developed. During the war, she believed, financial difficulties and the conscription of men had made it necessary for girls and women to support the family. Those trained in mission schools as teachers and nurses in many cases became the sole earners, helping their families survive. This, she contended, led to a better understanding of the value of educating girls after the war.[1]

Miss Warburton, a member of the Old Girls' Guild of Cheltenham Ladies' College, thought that the graduates of the Jerusalem Girls' College should continue to affiliate with their alma mater and to support its work in the way that the Cheltenham graduates supported their college. In 1923, she formally established the Old Girls' Guild of the Jerusalem Girls' College, with herself as president. The Old Girls in Jerusalem were a distinctive group in the city, recognizable to each other and to all Jerusalemites by their English chatter. Some married; others became professionals. All served their communities in a variety of ways. Those who moved away returned to Jerusalem for reunions, meetings of the Old Girls, lectures, and social events.

Sophie Halaby became a member of the guild in 1924 and remained attached to her school friends for the rest of her life. The *Old Girls' Annual Report* of 1924 recorded Sophie's success in the Oxford and Cambridge school certificate exams with credit in English, History, Geography, French, Russian, and Drawing. Olga Wahbe took and passed the exams at the same time. Both cousins were serious students who were interested in additional study. Their exam scores entitled them to pursue higher education, but there was as yet no university for them to attend in Jerusalem.[2] In 1923, a Board of Higher Studies had been established to promote university level education, an issue raised by both Governor Storrs and Mabel Warburton in prior years, but the board proceeded very slowly, limiting their work to conducting the Palestine matriculation exam, which eventually did away with the need for the Oxford and Cambridge exams, and creating a curriculum for the Palestine Diploma.[3]

Following graduation, Olga began teaching in Bethlehem and was soon awarded the first scholarship given to a woman student to attend the American University of Beirut (AUB). She continued her education in Beirut, earning a BA degree. Sophie, like most of her classmates, remained in Jerusalem and went to work for the British administration. It is likely that her interest in drawing led her to seek out opportunities to visit artists in Jerusalem in order to observe their work. She went with Olga to visit the studio of Khalil Halaby, a relative and a successful icon painter.[4] Sophie also met George Aleef, a Russian immigrant who had sought refuge in Jerusalem following the revolution. Aleef painted cityscapes of Jerusalem, using oils and watercolors; he displayed mosques, churches, and synagogues peacefully juxtaposed. Since he couldn't make a living selling his work, he soon began teaching art at an elementary school in the nearby village of Bethany.[5] Visiting studios was the only way for Sophie to continue studying art, as there were no permanent collections of art in museums or galleries in Jerusalem for her to visit in the 1920s.[6]

Sophie's brother, Nicola, a graduate of St. George's College, was in Leicestershire, England, studying engineering in Loughborough Technical College.[7] Sophie was already hoping to continue her education abroad. In the interim, she remained close to her former classmates, attending their summer conference and chairing a committee that investigated a topic of great interest to her: the challenge of continuing education following graduation. Sophie's committee discussed several avenues to achieve the goal of continuing education: First, independent reading was advocated. The committee encouraged guild members to borrow books from the school library and from the YMCA. Second, correspondence courses were available. Third, there were many lectures open to the public in Jerusalem, especially in the field of archaeology. During the general discussion that followed Sophie's report, a suggestion was made to create reading circles in which each member would buy a book, read it, and share it with everyone else in the circle.[8]

The Old Girls' summer conference also included reports on how to form and run a Girl Guide group, what goes into making an ideal Sunday School, how to improve life in villages, and how to teach children the value and practice of prayer. Sophie's interests were more aligned with continuing education than with social service. She agreed to investigate opportunities for correspondence courses. From the activities described in the *Old Girls' Annual Report*, it would appear that graduates who remained in Jerusalem met frequently both at the school and elsewhere in the city. In the absence of other social networks and recreational activities in the early years of the Mandate, the Old Girls' Guild continued to attract members and to influence their activities in the years following graduation.

Membership in the guild provided alumnae with a sense that they were involved in the modernization of their country. Like their parents, Sophie and her siblings considered themselves leaders in Palestine's emergence as a modern Arab nation. As Laura Robson observed, Christians had become an important part of an emerging middle class, a class defined by their educational attainments and their commitment to modernity.[9] In the coming years, Sophie and her former classmates would struggle to fulfill the roles they created for themselves.

Working for the British

Sophie Halaby was eighteen years old when she began to work for the British administration in 1924. Years later, she told American historian Tom Ricks that she had worked in the British motor pool. She showed him a photo of herself, a petite woman in the work uniform of her group, posing behind the wheel of a large truck.[10] She continued to work for the Mandatory government while living at home in Musrara for five years. Her brother, Nicola, was in England, studying engineering; her sister, Asia, continued to study at the Jerusalem Girls' College; her cousin Olga was in Beirut at the AUB. Sophie discovered what it was like to work, to earn money, and to be relatively independent. As a youngster, she had learned to take pride in performing well at schoolwork. Now, she put her knowledge of English and of British culture into practice on the job.

Like her fellow students at the Jerusalem Girls' College Sophie knew the importance of being properly attired. The stylish green uniform of her school days, with its pleated skirt, fashionable jacket, and becoming hat was easily recognizable in Jerusalem. It was at once a statement of modernity and of propriety. Sophie learned to value outward appearances both from her teachers, who rewarded perfect compliance with school uniform regulations, and from her mother, who is remembered as an elegant woman.[11] As a young adult, Sophie paid attention to the way she dressed, developing a personal style. New fabric shops for elite customers opened on Mamilla Road. Here, Sophie could purchase a *cupon*, a piece of fabric three meters long that was one of a kind and just enough for a dress. Family and friends remembered her being attired in clothing of the finest fabric, which she often made herself.[12] Sophie could also peruse the new stores opened in Baq`a', where she could browse among a selection of ready-made dresses at a shop established by Mayo and Khoury. She could buy shoes at the elegant shop owned by Handal and Qurunful or at Garabedian's fashionable shoe shop on Jaffa Street.[13]

There were many additional signs of changing times for women in Jerusalem. Trendy short haircuts were styled at a salon established by Sarkis. Helen Bentwich wrote home enthusiastically in 1925 about her own modern haircut, calling it "shingles."[14] Young women enrolled in exercise classes at the YWCA led by Katy Abdo, a Jerusalem Girls' College graduate. Undergarments were made to order by Madame Bauer, who had a shop near the Russian Compound. All of these elements were challenges to Arab traditions about proper deportment for women that featured long hair covered by a head covering and loose-fitting dresses.[15] Sophie gradually created a style that suited her: clothing, shoes, hairstyle, all announced that she was a modern young woman.

Working for the British administration left Sophie time to read books, attend lectures and concerts, and maintain friendships with the Old Girls. Though Sophie is sometimes depicted as a reclusive woman, it is more accurate to describe her as a serious young woman who was eager to learn more about the world, especially about the arts. Attending lectures was the most common form of continuing education in Jerusalem in this period. Bertha Spafford Vester noted hundreds of lectures in her diary. Among them, Humphrey Bowman, director of the Department of Education, read from a series of short plays illustrative of modern British drama in the library at St. George's Close; Hilda Ridler, inspector of girls' schools, lectured at the YWCA on "Literature as Recreation"; Norman Bentwich, the attorney general, lectured at the American Colony on social work programs at Toynbee Hall in London; Dame Millicent Fawcett, a British suffragist, spoke about the vote for women at the Association for Social Services; and Mrs. Bartlett, visiting from India, spoke on "Experiences as Inspectress of Schools in India."[16] It is likely that Sophie attended many of these lectures as part of her effort to continue her education.

The YWCA opened in Wyndham House on the Street of the Prophets, near Musrara, in 1921. Also called the House of World Friendship, the Y included a hostel and an employment bureau. Girls were welcomed as junior members from the age of eleven to sixteen, after which they were eligible to be full members. In 1927, 391 women—journalists, hospital sisters, missionaries, and students—from ten nations resided in the hostel. Some of the residents attended the Jerusalem Girls' College. The employment bureau motto was: "By love serve one another." Of the 446 girls who applied for jobs that year, 183 were placed. Membership in the YWCA in Jerusalem was cosmopolitan: Arabs, Greeks, Armenians, Russians, British, Americans, and Germans joined; some Jews and Muslims were also members. They all attended classes, lectures, discussion circles, and used the library.[17] Sophie's association with the YWCA probably began with a junior membership. Membership in the Y was one way Sophie could continue to be involved with the educated women of the city. She remained affiliated with the Y for the rest of her life.

Like all government employees, Sophie was awarded several official holidays. Government employees did not work on June 3, the anniversary of King George V's birthday. On November 11, Armistice Day, work was suspended for two hours starting at 11:00 a.m., when all were expected to maintain two minutes of silence in honor of those who perished during World War I. Finally, December 9 was another government holiday, marking the annual observance commemorating the surrender of the Ottoman forces to General Allenby. On that day, leading Christian, Muslim, and Jewish Jerusalemites gathered in St. George's Cathedral. Susan P. Emery, Sophie's art teacher, observed in a letter to her mother: "We had the usual solemn service at the Cathedral this morning, officially attended by all heads of Government and Churches. It is a most impressive service. I love to see Jews, Moslems and Christians all taking part in the same thing for once."[18] Religious holidays were also observed according to a schedule published by the Mandatory authorities.[19]

In 1924, the cathedral service was followed by a major celebration marking the opening of King George V Street. High Commissioner Herbert Samuel, Governor Ronald Storrs, and Mayor Regheb Nashashibi all participated in the festive event. Modern young women like Sophie were among the hundreds of celebrants marking the creation of a new thoroughfare running perpendicular to Jaffa Road and new possibilities for offices and shops.[20] These young women also attended events sponsored by the Jerusalem Music Society, a group supported by Ronald Storrs that was keen to bring classical music performed by European artists to Jerusalem. Thelma Yellin, a cellist who hailed from England and taught periodically at the Jerusalem Girls' College, was a frequent performer. Traute Grunfelder, from Germany, sometimes accompanied her on the piano. They often played works by Boccherini, Beethoven, and César Franck. As there was no permanent music hall in the city, they performed in various venues, including the Opera Cardinal Ferrari (today the Terra Sancta) and the Evelina de Rothschild School (today the Israel Minister of Education offices). These European women modeled modern roles for Sophie and her friends.

In the mid-1920s, Sophie had achieved a position of high status for a young Russian Arab woman. She had passed the Oxford and Cambridge matriculation exams, a feat accomplished annually by only a handful of Jerusalem students.

Her job working for the British administration also conferred prestige in Jerusalem. Nonetheless, while enjoying her newfound independence, she was certainly aware of subtle and overt discrimination in her work. At the Jerusalem Girls' College, Sophie learned to value "British fairness," but this doctrine was routinely tested in the realities of the work world. Government offices had two pay scales, one for Europeans and another for Palestinians. While Miss Warburton classified Sophie as "Russian," her British employer hired her on the Palestinian pay scale. Jews and Muslims suffered additional discrimination from firm refusals by British bosses of requests to take off for holiday observances. Orthodox Christians, like Sophie, fared somewhat better, but they too had to negotiate special privileges. All Arabs chafed at the glass ceilings placed on their opportunities for promotion. They were not promoted to supervisory roles managing Europeans, regardless of experience and talent.[21]

Hala Sakakini recalled an incident described by her Aunt Melia that illustrated the discriminatory behavior of some British officials:

> When Aunt Melia was a teacher in a Government school, a certain Miss Ridler, an English woman, was Inspector of Girls' Schools. She was an arch-colonialist, a conservative of the old style. She expected all the "native" teachers to pay homage to her, and any person who stood up to her she could not tolerate. . . . Aunt Melia told us about some of her colleagues who were nauseatingly servile. . . .
>
> One day the teachers in my aunt's school were lining up the girls in the playground in order to enter classes after break. Miss Ridler was present. . . . She demanded that each teacher salute her in military fashion as she passed before her, and the girls were to do the same. . . . One class after another passed in front of Miss Ridler. The teachers lifted their hands in salute and the girls followed suit. When Aunt Melia's turn came, she passed by without saluting, in clear and unmistakable defiance of the order. . . . Miss Ridler called out sharply that they should return to the starting point, line up again and go in saluting. But Aunt Melia refused to comply and Miss Ridler had to give up.[22]

Another example of ethnic discrimination occurred in the government hospital, located in the Russian Compound near Sophie's home in Musrara. Originally constructed in 1859 for Russian pilgrims, it was converted to a British hospital in 1918. It was the largest government hospital in Palestine, with 105 beds, an x-ray ward, a surgical ward, and a maternity ward. This hospital served the British and the Arab populations; however, following colonial practice, a separate wing was created to serve British bureaucrats, officers, and policemen.[23]

Working for the British Mandate was complicated. Sophie and her peers confronted a predicament whose source was the tension between their duty as civil servants and their deeper loyalties to family, religion, and nation. There were additional problems caused by unease between Arab Christians and Muslims, as a disproportionate number of Christians were employed in government work. Arab teachers were obliged to disseminate what they regarded as a distorted version of history; Arab policemen were called upon to suppress anti-Zionist disturbances; Arab judicial officers were asked to prosecute Arabs accused of racial violence. On April 30, 1927, *Filastin* carried an editorial, "The Duties of the Arab Official," which stated, "The Arab official is the point of contact between the local government and the people. . . . The official must be frank in his opinions and not be the echo of those of the British."[24]

Ten years later, a government report included the following testimony by an Arab employee: "We have made every effort to remember our obligations as civil servants. . . . But alongside [these] are the dictates of our consciences. . . . In addition to our general duties as civil servants, a particular duty lies on us as Arab officers, which is that of serving as a link between the Government and the Arab population . . . of interpreting to the public the acts of the Government in their true light, and of explaining to the Government the feelings and needs of the Arab population."[25]

As she developed seniority in her position, Sophie was surely subject to increasing discrimination. Her brother, Nicola, had graduated from St. George's College and had continued the family tradition begun by their father and his sister, Aunt Vera, of studying abroad. Perhaps influenced by the work of the Pro-Jerusalem Society and the building projects planned for the city, Nicola studied civil engineering, expecting to return to Jerusalem to work on major construction projects.[26] His letters home would have raised for Sophie the possibility of continuing her studies in Europe.

Asia graduated from the Jerusalem Girls' College in 1926 and continued to take classes to obtain a Secondary School Certificate. Though she could have become a teacher, Asia followed Sophie in working for the administration, a position she maintained until the British left Palestine. Cousin Olga Wahbe completed her BA degree at the AUB, graduating in 1928. She soon began working in Ramallah as an instructor in the Government Teachers' Training College.[27]

While Sophie remained particularly close to Asia and Olga, her membership in the alumnae association kept her up to date with all those who graduated. As a member, she received an annual issue of the *Jerusalem Girls' College Magazine* (*JGC Magazine*), which often featured articles contributed by graduates who were studying in Beirut. These articles provided Old Girls who remained in Jerusalem an opportunity to learn about life for young women who pursued advanced education. One student wrote that she felt very lucky to be studying at the AUB, where the teaching was quite different from the Jerusalem Girls' College, as there was much outside reading to do. Another asserted that there was no need for women to fear attending college. Faculty and students at AUB, she asserted, were gradually adjusting to the presence of women. She advised women students to seek out friendships in the library and in social gatherings like skating, billiards, and bowling. She concluded: "The world is changing rapidly and we expect a woman's life, whether in business, at home, or in college, to change."[28]

Modern Ideas vs. Eastern Traditions

Regrettably, any diary in which Sophie may have recorded her musings about these matters has been lost. If she wrote letters to friends or family in this period, they have disappeared. Based on her actions in the coming years, she behaved as a modern woman, traveling to Paris to get the art education she wanted and participating in exhibits in Paris, where she won a prize for one of her paintings. Not long after she returned home to Jerusalem, she listed herself in a professional directory as a painter of post cards. Some time later she sold paintings to two of her cousins, explaining that she was a professional and couldn't just give them away.[29]

Modernization was a topic under serious discussion by Jerusalem girls and women in all of the religious communities of Jerusalem, some of it recorded by Ruth Woodsmall, an American social scientist who conducted a study on the changing status of women in the Middle East. Woodsmall asked Jerusalem Girls' College students to reflect on the differences between the life of a woman now and before World War I. She explained that they were experiencing a period of rapid change and asked: "What values in Eastern life should be carefully safeguarded?"[30]

Annig Khalihigian, the Armenian student cited above, expressed a progressive and optimistic view of change. She asserted that women before the war were no more than servants in the house, taught from earliest childhood to do housework; learning to read and write was not thought important. They were forbidden to speak in public and were told whom they would marry and when; some covered their faces with veils when they went out. Annig contrasted this grim picture with what she viewed as a much better contemporary life for Jerusalem's girls and women. Despite the crisis faced by the

Armenian community in 1915, with many thousands of refugees fleeing to the Armenian section of the Old City of Jerusalem, Annig saw life constantly improving.[31]

Other respondents, like Meliha Yamulki, a Muslim student, were explicit in connecting perceived social progress to westernization. Meliha claimed that European women had won many freedoms still denied to Eastern women, and she believed that in Palestine, Muslim women had less freedom than Christian women. She lamented that women were not permitted to enter clubs to discuss national social issues with men, and she feared that women would not be permitted to attend university with men until "the fanaticism" of Muslims was abolished. She raised two additional issues that she believed were detrimental to Muslim women: first, inheritance laws that awarded men double that which was awarded to women; second, divorce laws that enabled men to leave their wives but didn't permit women to leave their husbands. Meliha distinguished between Muslim religious observance and Muslim cultural values, pointing out that the Muslim religion did not forbid women from showing their faces, nor did it forbid advanced education for women.

Aviva Lerner, a Jewish student, encouraged those seeking higher education to continue despite the sneers of male students, and she urged women to demand the right to vote, to sit in Parliament, and to form societies to aid the needy. She also thought that women must be free to select their husbands. Lerner expected women to make some mistakes along the route to freedom, since their only models were men. She concluded: "Try to acquire his skill, his industriousness, his professional cleverness, which he has had time to learn while you were in bondage. But do not try to imitate his manliness by dress, by action or by hiding your womanhood."[32]

Not all the students were unequivocal in their enthusiasm for modernization and westernization. Mary Deeb, a Greek Orthodox student, observed that Eastern women were trying to follow their European sisters in their intellectual achievements, in their lifestyle, and even in their dress. She believed that European women, her teachers, had encouraged these changes and "are our best friends." On the other hand, Mary noted, there were some Eastern values worth preserving and teaching to European women. For example, the hospitality of Eastern women, their kindness to strangers, their honesty, and their loyalty were attributes that should be preserved. Mary also noted the importance of family bonds and respect for parents as Eastern virtues to be cherished. Finally, she asserted that Eastern languages, possibly Greek and Arabic, were both beautiful and ancient and that their literature should be held in higher esteem than the literature of modern European languages.

Carmel Halabi (unrelated to Sophie Halaby), another Greek Orthodox student, felt that Western, that is, European or American, inventions like motorcars, airplanes, telephones, telegrams, and the radio were all wonderful additions to Eastern life. However, she recognized that adoption of Western ways had unanticipated consequences. For example, the use of electrical tools in carpentry led to a loss of jobs for traditional workers. The use of foreign languages in place of local languages led to a loss of local culture. The adoption of European fashion by peasant women led to the disappearance of traditional embroidered dresses. She feared that Eastern families would be broken by divorce, a Western custom less practiced in the East. Halabi saw benefits to life in Jerusalem but was concerned about the deleterious implications.

Fadwa Abdelwahab, a Muslim student, presented a nuanced view of the class implications of changing women's traditional status. She noted that there were three classes of women in Palestine: The first class were peasants, who left their homes early in the morning, worked like beasts in the fields, did not wear veils, mixed freely with men while working, yet at home were servants to their husbands. The second class were the fashionable, who imitated Western styles, wearing sleeveless, low-cut dresses, applying make-up, and speaking French. These city-dwelling women were, nevertheless, also dependent on their husbands and had not achieved freedom. Thc third class included women who were moving toward freedom through education. They recognized the defects in their society and strove to improve. At home, they were nearly equal to their husbands. Fadwa closed her astute observations about the intersection of gender and social status with this advice: "The Eastern woman ought to choose wisely before rising to demand her rights. Her freedom depends on the education of the majority. Let the Moslem woman be unveiled but not too suddenly, slowly yet surely she shall gain her end."[33]

Woodsmall's survey documents the sentiments of students at the Jerusalem Girls' College, who strived for autonomy while simultaneously expressing the wish to preserve Eastern traditions. While we cannot know which of these ideas Sophie espoused, it is certain that she would have been exposed to them, and that negotiating these different views had a significant influence on her identity, her life choices, and her art. Sophie was attracted to aspects of modern life—the freedom to make her own decisions about marriage, advanced studies, and travel abroad. She was, however, aware of the discrimination against Arabs in British employ and troubled by the contrast between the ideals of modernization and their reality in Jerusalem. In later years, she would become aware of how these conflicts were reflected in the architectural changes made in the name of modernization in Jerusalem.

Both Sophie and Asia valued traditional Palestinian culture. Their mother, Olga, amassed a collection of embroidered cloth bought from village women who came to Musrara to sell fruits and vegetables. Olga collected their work for decades, teaching her daughters how to recognize patterns associated with each village. Widad Kawar, the celebrated authority on Palestinian embroidery, recalled that she had learned to appreciate the intricate patterns of embroidery representative of different villages in the Halaby home. After the expulsion of thousands of Palestinian villagers from their homes in 1948, Asia created an embroidery workshop to support displaced and impoverished women by fostering the production of traditional embroidery. She helped them to provide for their families by selling their embroidered tablecloths, bookmarks, and pincushions to tourists, eventually marketing their work as products of the "Arab Refugee Handicrafts Centre." Sophie supported her in this work for decades. Kawar credited the sisters with having saved Palestinian embroidery traditions after 1948. Sophie and Asia chose to lead independent lives while supporting traditional Palestinian culture.[34]

To continue the process of modernization, especially for young women, some called for the creation of a university in Jerusalem for those who were unable to leave Palestine for further education. In the summer of 1922, Ronald Storrs had proposed a British university for both Arabs and Jews, to be established in the city. Zionist opposition was strong, viewing the plan as competition for the fledgling Hebrew University, whose foundation stones had been set in 1918. Nevertheless, Britain was eager to provide British higher education, which they saw as greatly superior to the American program offered in Beirut, to Palestinians and residents of other British territories in the Middle East. Mabel Warburton supported this plan as did Terese Nasnas, a graduate of the Jerusalem Girls' College enrolled at the AUB, who wrote: "The thing we miss most is a university. I hope our present College will grow into a big university."[35] Despite lengthy discussions and reports issued by committees, the creation of a British university in Jerusalem ultimately foundered due to budgetary reasons.[36]

Becoming an Artist

In the years following her graduation, Sophie made decisions that had a lasting impact on her adult life. She watched many of her former schoolmates marry and have children, attending numerous weddings and christenings. Sophie did not marry. This was not unusual in a city where educated women outnumbered the supply of similarly educated men. In a world of changing familial roles and uncertain future, the independence of remaining at home as a single woman was an attractive option. She watched as friends became teachers, nurses, social workers, and office workers, but these occupations did not appeal to Sophie. She was an independent woman; some even called her eccentric.[37] Her goal to become a professional artist was unique for her time and her city.

There was only one art school in Jerusalem in the 1920s. Founded by Boris Schatz in 1906, the Bezalel Academy, located near Sophie's home, on Ethiopia Street, was dedicated to creating Jewish and Zionist art. It had very few women students and no Arab ones. The first Arab to study at Bezalel was Nihal Bishara, who took classes there from 1942 through 1944. Therefore, though it had painting teachers, it was not possible for Sophie to study there.[38]

For Sophie, the AUB was also not an option for further study, as it did not open an art department until 1954. She had no formal teacher or mentor in the years following her graduation in Jerusalem. She remained at her office job. At this time, there were very few professional artists in Palestine, men or women. There were a few accomplished craftsmen—icon painters, embroiderers, and ceramicists—who made their living from their work. There were also a few European artists who had visited Jerusalem; David Roberts, the Scotsman, who achieved fame and fortune for his lithographs, was probably the best known. Postcards featuring his drawings were sold to tourists in the Old City. There were a small number of European women who spent months or years in Jerusalem painting. Miss Moore, the sister of one of the teachers at the Jerusalem Girls' College, spent many months sketching the city. Mrs. Hannah Gray Hill, who lived on Mount Scopus, painted panoramic views. These artists, however, were amateurs. While she waited for an opportunity to continue her studies abroad, Sophie may also have followed a correspondence course like the one undertaken by Margo Dabbas Tamari, who followed a program established by École ABC in France.[39]

In search of artistic inspiration, Sophie may have visited the studio of Anna Ticho, the Viennese painter who lived nearby. She would have seen Ticho's early work, sketches of Arab patients who came to her husband's clinic for treatment. She probably attended the first exhibit of Ticho's work at her home in 1926.[40] She also likely visited the studio of Mubarak Sa'ad, who studied painting with Catholic priests, often working from photographs.[41] Sophie was also able to study illustrations of French and Italian paintings in magazines, books, and postcards, all of which were increasingly available in Jerusalem bookstores. She would have known about the work of Jamal Badran, who had returned to Jerusalem from several years' study in Cairo at the School of

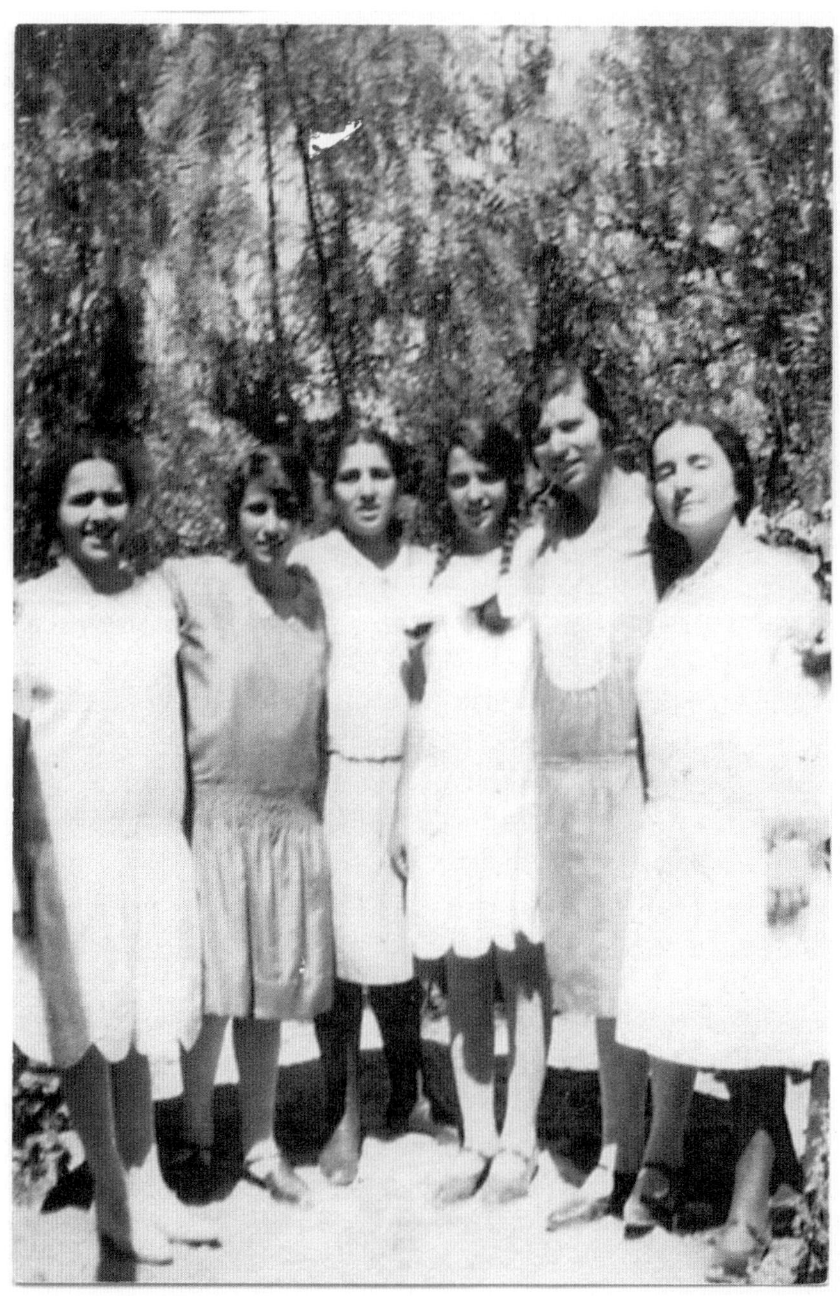

2. Sophie Halaby with her sisters and cousins, ca. 1929. *Left to right*: Nadia Wahbe, Sonia Wahbe, Asia Halaby, Louba Wahbe, Olga Wahbe, Sophie Halaby. Courtesy of Lily W. Porter and Nelly W. Barrett.

Applied Arts and Crafts, specializing in leatherwork and decorative arts. His work on the restoration of the Dome of the Rock and of the Al-Aqsa Mosque was of interest, but it was only in the late 1930s, after Sophie returned from Paris, that Badran, having received a second degree from London's Central School of Arts and Crafts, established a school to teach a variety of artistic skills in Jerusalem.[42] In addition to the inspiration she received from artists around her, Sophie was visually stimulated by the natural beauty of Jerusalem, by the depictions of the city she saw in magazines and books, and by frescoes and paintings in Russian ecclesiastical art.

Sophie was also influenced by her regular attendance at the Cathedral of the Holy Trinity in the Russian Compound and by periodic visits to other Russian religious sites in the city—the Alexander Nevsky Church in the Old City, the Church of Mary Magdalene and the Church of the Ascension, both on the Mount of Olives, and the Russian Orthodox Gorny Convent in Ein Karem. All of these buildings were decorated with elaborate murals and ornate icons depicting biblical scenes. These works presented the young artist with biblical subject matter and a variety of artistic techniques.

The artists who had the strongest impact on Sophie as she made decisions about where to study were Susan P. Emery, her drawing teacher at the Jerusalem Girls' College, who was a graduate of the London Central School of Arts and Crafts, and Anna Ticho, who was educated in Vienna. Though Emery had studied in London and Ticho in Vienna, Sophie knew that the best place to study art, especially for women, was Paris. The fact that no young woman had gone from Jerusalem to study art in Paris was an obstacle; however, at the age of twenty-three, Sophie was apparently prepared to overcome all objections. A photograph of Sophie and her sister, Asia, with their cousins Olga, Nadia, Louba, and Sonia, taken around this time, perhaps in anticipation of Sophie's departure, shows all of them stylishly attired with drop-waist dresses; they appear ready to stride forward toward modern life. The photo is the only piece of evidence that allows the historian a glimpse of Sophie at the time she left for Paris.

French Influence in Jerusalem

Jacques d'Aumale, the French consul general in Palestine, appointed in 1928, was the man who facilitated the fulfillment of Sophie's plan to study art in Paris. D'Aumale traveled to Jerusalem via Cairo, taking the train across the Kantara Bridge, which had been built by the British during the war. He reported the "rocky" crossing of the Sinai and his amazement at seeing the

Imperial Airfield at Kalandria and the big military cemetery. Upon arrival in Jerusalem, d'Aumale was immediately aware of the strong influence of Britain on the cultural and economic life of Palestine; he sought to find ways to restore French influence in the country. He was responsible for oversight of the construction of a major new neo-Renaissance-style building to house the consulate general in Jerusalem. Here, in a beautiful spot overlooking the Old City, d'Aumale would host lectures in French and concerts by French artists throughout the remainder of his tenure. These lectures and concerts were an opportunity to showcase French culture. They were widely covered in the press and attracted large audiences. It is highly likely that Sophie and her sister attended some of these events, as they both had studied French and passed matriculation exams in the subject.[43]

More importantly for Sophie's future, d'Aumale soon implemented a new program designed to win Palestinian friends for France. Responding to the lack of opportunities for higher education in Palestine, d'Aumale created a scholarship program for high school graduates who wished to pursue their education in France. Students from a variety of disciplines applied.[44]

It is unclear how many applications were submitted for this program and how many were funded. Surviving documentation of this effort is slim. All five of the applications that survive in the French diplomatic archives were for young Jewish men whose interests in mining, architecture, veterinary medicine, and physical education were consonant with the Zionist agenda. Jacques Kahanoff submitted his birth certificate and his academic credentials as part of his application to the École nationale supérieure des mines. Mr. Rechter, an architect, was admitted to the third year of study at the École nationale des ponts and chaussées. Israel Spektor applied to study veterinary medicine in Toulouse. His application was denied, at first, as documentation from his secondary school was deemed inadequate. The British embassy in Paris assisted with forwarding necessary certificates and notarization, and Spektor's application was later approved. Maurice Levy's application to attend veterinary school in Alfort was also approved. Finally, Moise Garti was accepted to study at the École supérieure d'éducation physique at Joinville.[45] Sophie's application and those of all the other applicants were not retained. The existing files make clear the kind of documents Sophie needed: school and employment certificates, a passport, and letters of recommendation.

Sophie's application would have included a copy of her school diploma as well as a certificate attesting to her successful completion of the Oxford and Cambridge matriculation. It would have included a letter of support for her good conduct from the headmistress and one attesting to good work habits from her employer. Similar letters exist for Fortunée Sitton, a fellow Jerusalem Girls' College graduate, whose family kept copies for more than eighty years.[46] It is likely that Sophie also retained her papers. The well-known artist, Samia Halaby, a cousin who visited Sophie in 1966, referred to a thick file that Sophie showed her about Asia's accomplishments as an example of her record-keeping skills. Regrettably, all of Sophie's papers were destroyed after her death.[47] Sophie's application to continue her artistic studies was a bold initiative. Few young Palestinian women went to Europe to study in her era. Most of those who did were graduates of the Jerusalem Girls' College.

Sophie was awarded a four-year scholarship to study art in Paris.[48] This was an unusual achievement for a woman. During the interwar years, a small group of international women artists were gaining recognition in Paris, but, as Paula Birnbaum noted, they were marginalized on the basis of gender and ethnicity in the art press. Critics trivialized their work, neglected to mention their names, and often spoke of their liaisons with famous male artists.[49] As Sophie prepared to join the small group of women studying art in Paris in the few academies offering places to women students, there were still moral qualms about nude models sitting for women students. Nevertheless, Sophie was determined. She was awarded the grant and prepared to leave for Paris.

Jerusalem Riots: 1929

While Sophie was organizing for her trip, assembling her dossier to satisfy the French government that she was worthy of a scholarship to study abroad, and obtaining documents from her employers attesting to her good conduct, violence erupted in Jerusalem and in nearby Hebron. The area had begun to return to normal following a massive earthquake in 1927 that had left 450 people dead in Palestine. Musical performances featuring Thelma Yellin on cello and Margery Bentwich on violin restored interest in classical music following a period of emergency caretaking for quake victims. On March 12, 1929, violin virtuoso Bronisław Huberman gave his first performance in Jerusalem. Six weeks later, High Commissioner John Chancellor opened the new, nonsectarian Nathan and Lina Strauss Health Center dedicated to preventive medicine.[50]

Despite outward signs of cultural and civic development, nationalists—both Jewish and Arab—were regrouping to gain advantage. In 1929, Tisha B'Av, a Jewish fast day commemorating the destruction of both holy temples in Jerusalem, fell on August 15. Approaching the Western Wall, young men raised the Zionist flag and sang the Zionist anthem, "Hatikvah," provoking

Arab resistance by introducing Zionist symbols to the site of previous riots. The following day, the birthday of the Prophet Mohammad, Arabs went down from al-Aqsa to the Western Wall and desecrated Jewish holy books. An attempt by the British to reconcile both sides failed, and lynchings of Arabs and Jews ensued. The riots spread to Hebron and then north to Haifa and Safed. Trials of the accused resulted in the death penalty for twenty-six Arabs and two Jews. Most appealed and had their sentences commuted. In Jerusalem, thirty-one Jews and fifty Arabs were killed, with many more wounded.[51] Following the riots, all recreational events in Jerusalem were canceled. There were no plays, no concerts, and no soccer matches.

Violence continued to challenge the control of British authorities. On November 12, Dr. Albert Ticho, the revered ophthalmologist who treated Arabs and Jews and the husband of artist Anna, was attacked with a knife at the entrance to his clinic in Musrara. The knife punctured his lung. For days the attempted assassination was the main topic of conversation in the city. The Jaffa-based Arab newspaper, *Filastin*, offered a twenty-five-pound reward for information leading to the arrest of the would-be assassin. Twelve days later, on November 24, Attorney General Norman Bentwich, husband of Helen Bentwich, was shot and wounded while walking through government offices.[52]

The harsh response of the British administration to the violence of 1929 was a catalyst for the development of Arab nationalism. A group of lawyers educated in the government law school founded by Norman Bentwich issued "The Protest of the Arab Advocates." Using their legal training, they challenged the high commissioner to answer the following questions:

1. Did Your Excellency, in describing the acts of murder committed against the Jews as being barbarous, rely on official reports of the Health Department and hear the evidence of the Arabs? And did these reports state that Arab victims were murdered in an extraordinary Western civilized manner?
2. Was Your Excellency informed that the Arab martyrs were unarmed, save with the conviction that they were defending their Holy Places, their political and religious rights, and their national dignity?
3. We challenge Your Excellency to state one atrocious act committed by Arabs whether in Hebron or any other place!
4. Was Your Excellency informed that many Arab houses were burnt, destroyed, and looted?
5. Was Your Excellency informed that the disciplined and civilized British soldiers have killed offenceless Arab women, children, and old men?[53]

The Arab response to the events of 1929 also gave rise to politically conscious women's groups. *Filastin* published a thank-you note to the Ladies Committee for Aiding the Distressed in Jerusalem for raising 340 Palestine pounds. The ladies replied with modesty: "In this we have participated in the minimal way in our duty toward our nation and our homeland. We don't deserve to be thanked for it."[54] A decade earlier, Mabel Warburton had described the girls in her school as having no common national name or tradition to bind them. This was clearly no longer true. National feelings were growing among all the communities of Palestine. Although Warburton had hoped for an ethos tolerant of all faiths, what emerged was a sharp divide between Jews, who were labeled Zionists, and Arab Nationalists, including Christians and Muslims.

The First Arab Women's Congress convened in Jerusalem on October 26, 1929. This group had a clear nationalist purpose. Unlike the Social Service Association, established in 1918 as an intercommunal women's group of Jews, Christians, and Muslims that was chaired by the wives of British officials, the Arab Women's Congress was open only to Christian and Muslim women who supported the nationalist effort. Anbara Salam Khalidi recalled attending the First Congress, which was chaired by Zakiyya al-Husseini, wife of Musa Kazim Pasha al-Husseini. Khalidi described her: "She was at the forefront of women activists, known for her frank talk; she was intelligent, tall and attractive. She had the ear of all the men in the Mandate, from the High Commissioner down to the lowliest of officials."[55]

The women at the Arab Women's Congress took to the streets in a protest demonstration, ending at Government House. Bertha Spafford Vester noted that they paraded through the streets in many automobiles on the way to see Sir John Chancellor, the high commissioner. They protested against the Balfour Declaration, against Norman Bentwich, the attorney general who was Jewish and hence, they believed, incapable of being impartial, and against corporal punishment in government schools. In reference to this last request, they asked for the dismissal of Jerome Farrell, assistant director of education, who had ordered the beating of boys in a school in Nablus. The high commissioner invited the women protestors to come into Government House for coffee. They refused to drink the coffee until Chancellor agreed to do all in his power to address the issues they raised.[56] It was estimated that over two hundred women from all over Palestine attended. It is unlikely that Sophie or Asia Halaby was among them, as Sophie was keen on being issued a Palestinian passport that would allow her to travel abroad and Asia continued to work for the British administration. Nevertheless, they were aware of the activities of the protesting women, whom they knew as neighbors and friends.

By the spring of 1930 the violence had subsided, but the feelings of insecurity had not disappeared. Helen Bentwich captured the spirit of the times in a letter home: "You ask if we think we shall ever settle down to pleasant conditions again. Quite frankly . . . the answer is no. I don't know what will happen or how long we shall be able to stick it, or they us. It's an experience, and the danger and the hostility we've been through gives one the feeling one had during the war. The danger seems over now—I think there are too many soldiers and police for further outbreaks—but the hostility on all sides still exists. . . . Mostly we go on day to day, not talking of it except to each other."[57]

Art Student in Paris

Nicola, Sophie's brother, returned home from his studies in England about this time. He had been abroad since completing his high school education at St. George's College in Jerusalem. Nicola, a civil engineer, began to work with Austen St. Barbe Harrison, the chief architect of the Mandatory Department of Public Works. He worked on three of the major projects supervised by Harrison: the General Post Office (now the Central Post Office), the Palestine Archaeological Museum (now the Rockefeller Museum), and Government House (now housing the United Nations Special Coordinator for the Middle East Peace Process), all completed in the 1930s.[58] Perhaps Nicola's return home was a catalyst for Sophie's obtaining family approval to leave. Another precipitating factor might have been the violence that had erupted that summer, ending a relatively harmonious period that began with the arrival of the British.

The British Mandatory government issued seventy thousand Palestine passports between 1924 and 1948.[59] There was no list of passports granted or files of applications for passports in Kew, the British National Archive devoted to diplomacy, in the Israel State Archive, or the Central Zionist Archive. Thus, the exact date of Sophie's embarking for Paris remains unknown. Likewise, her arrival date in Paris and the route she took are also unknown. It is likely that she traveled by ship from Jaffa, sailed to Marseilles, and continued from there by train to Paris.

Sophie arrived in Paris in late 1929 or early 1930, settled somewhere in the city, and began to study at one of the art studios open to women. The Académie Julian and the Académie Colarossi were the best known, but there were others that accommodated women students from the late 1920s. These academies taught hundreds of women, many arriving from abroad. Work in the studio was almost entirely technical, with long sessions of life classes, including dissections of corpses and lectures on anatomy. In addition to classes on drawing and painting, there were sessions for sculpture, watercolor, and miniature painting. Instructors reviewed and critiqued the work of each student. One of the portraits saved by Sophie, that of an old man, has an additional arm and hand, likely drawn by her teacher to correct her original depiction. The studios created a system of competitions designed to improve the skills of their students and to prepare them to submit their work to the salons.[60]

Like Mary Cassatt, who arrived in Paris a few decades before her, Sophie spent a lot of time in museums and galleries. Cassatt wrote to a friend explaining the effect of seeing for the first time Degas's pastels in the window of a gallery on Boulevard Haussmann: "I used to go and flatten my nose against that window and absorb all I could of his art. It changed my life. I saw art then as I wanted to see it."[61] While there are no letters recording Sophie's reaction to the art she saw in Paris, there is a visual record. Sophie's paintings of nude women, seen from the back, were clearly influenced by Ingres, whose work she would have studied in the Louvre. Sophie's nudes, dated 1930, were created for studio competition. Several of them are included in the collections of Mazen Qupty and George al-Ama. Kamal Boullata wrote with great appreciation of these works, which feature the bare back of a seated woman. Boullata noted the influence of Ingres, but pointed out that in contrast to the French neoclassical painter, who encouraged the spectator to become a voyeur, Sophie seemed to be recovering the woman's body from within. He added that she identified with the model's back the way a male painter identified with his own features in a mirror.[62]

Visiting galleries was part of the art education of all Parisian art students. Sophie may have attended an exhibit of paintings by Anna Ticho, her neighbor in Jerusalem, at a popular bookstore and exhibit gallery located near the Paris Opera. The Quatre Chemins Gallery advertised Ticho's works in November 1930 with an announcement that read: "Ticho—Peintures, Aquarelles, Dessins (Palestine)."[63] The word "Palestine" in the announcement would have attracted Sophie's attention. She may have already thought of exhibiting her own works with the caption "Palestine."

Sophie lived at 93 Boulevard Saint-Michel at the Foyer International des Etudiantes (International Women Students' Hostel) from January 7 through July 4, 1931. Her registration form includes her nationality, "Palestinian," and her place of birth, "Jerusalem." Sophie occupied room 217. She was in the heart of the Latin Quarter, a center for students and artists.[64] As a resident in the Foyer, Sophie was sheltered from the two stereotypes of womanhood that were celebrated in French popular culture: the "garçonne," or modern, sexually liberated workingwoman, and the "mère de famille nombreuse," or mother of many children.[65] Neither image was attractive to Sophie. The culture of the Foyer, designed as an oasis of study for women from all over the world, was a safe home where she continued to develop her artistic skills and her understanding of her place in the world.

The most impressive room in the Foyer was the library, located on the sixth floor, reached by an elevator. A Francis I fireplace of majestic proportions dominated the room; crests of all the nations were placed between the recessed windows. The collection included six thousand volumes in French, English, German, and Russian. Nearby, there was a small meditation room, a solarium, and an airy rest room. A model infirmary was also set up in the Foyer. One floor above the library was an enclosed terrace that opened onto a parapet, enabling students to walk the perimeter of the building. From these vantage points, students could see the graceful Sacré-Cœur, the iconic Eiffel Tower, the noble Saint-Sulpice, and the lush Luxembourg Gardens. Residents were surrounded by the major architectural elements that made Paris a city beloved by millions.[66]

The main floor had a cafeteria that could serve one thousand students and a beautiful auditorium that served as a tearoom during the day. On the next floor were salons, clubrooms, and soundproof music practice rooms. An informal reading room supplied the girls with French newspapers and the leading foreign periodicals.

Sophie's room, which was on the second floor, was a combination living room and bedroom, painted in a pastel hue, housing a wide divan covered with fabric, with matched pillow and drapery. It was modern and quite different from the Damascene furniture featuring mother-of-pearl accents favored by her family in Jerusalem. Ample closets provided space for all of her belongings. A desk, designed by the American heiress Grace Whitney Hoff, included glass-covered shelves above and spacious drawers below. All the furniture was made of solid oak. Adjacent to this room was a tiled dressing room featuring hot and cold running water. Utility rooms on each floor housed electric irons, sewing machines, and washtubs.

Residence in the Foyer was limited to one hundred young women who planned to earn their own living and who were registered as students in Paris. Sophie was selected for residency by a committee, guided by letters of recommendation and, in many cases, by personal knowledge of a student's circumstances.[67] Acceptance into this selective international group of ambitious young women was an important step in Sophie's developing identity as a modern woman and an artist.

Everything at the Foyer was designed to support the students in their endeavors to learn. Their needs for daily life were taken care of by the staff.

Opportunities for socializing with other educated women were abundant. When Sophie returned to Jerusalem, she maintained a similar approach to the necessities of life, living comfortably at home with her parents in Musrara. In later life, Sophie would live with Asia in East Jerusalem. There she called in for dinners and hired help to care for her home so that she could concentrate on art. She socialized with Jerusalem Girls' College alumnae and, at the American Colony Hotel, with English-speaking visitors to Jerusalem, continuing the pattern of lively interaction with educated women that she had experienced in Paris.[68]

A project of Grace Whitney Hoff, the Foyer opened in 1906 as a hostel for American and British women students. Used during World War I as a relief center, the building reopened in 1919 as the Foyer International des Etudiantes, reflecting its enhanced mission. Whitney Hoff reasoned that peace was the greatest need in the postwar world and saw in young women students of all nations the hope for its achievement. In the months before Sophie's arrival, she guided a significant renovation of the building, fitting it with a modern heating system, an incinerator, electric motors, dumbwaiters, and ventilating machines, all below ground. The kitchen housed supply rooms, gas stoves, electric refrigerators, huge soup kettles, and a vegetable-washing basin made of blue mosaic tiles. Whitney Hoff was determined that the students would receive the most comfortable, modern accommodations possible.

She explained her vision in an address to the students at the dedication:

> To you, students, I address a decisive appeal. It is to stand secure as an example of pure womanhood, which rises above the feverish agitation, the tumult and dissonance of modern life. . . . It is woman finally who forces herself to create a union between the real and the ideal. . . .
>
> As I transfer to the Foyer International des Etudiantes the key to this building, I ask the administration of the movement to open the door wide for students to use their trained minds, not only in the circumscribed area of personal needs, but to unfold to them the vision of the future, which means preparation for universal peace. . . .
>
> Let there be a beacon light of hope issuing from this Foyer out to this great City which leads the world in art and educational privileges. Let there be impartiality, magnanimity, and largeness of purpose, constructiveness, tolerance, cooperation, and above all unity of spirit.[69]

Sophie must have understood and appreciated the words of Whitney Hoff. She had learned similar ideas from Mabel Warburton, but she had also experienced the reality of discrimination working for the British Mandate and during the violence of 1929 in Jerusalem. In the Foyer she was able to test her thoughts and feelings about the realities and limits of peaceful coexistence and cooperation in the community of a wide variety of young women who had flocked to Paris from all over Europe and the United States, convinced that they would find greater freedom and opportunity for personal and professional development than in any other city in the world.[70] In the protected environment of the Foyer, students of different backgrounds, including Sophie, gained strength to face the challenges awaiting them at home. A young woman from Beirut wrote that in the Foyer, women from all over the world could learn to understand each other. A Polish student noted, "There is surely love here—how does it happen?" A Russian girl added, "I cannot believe that I am not dreaming, to have such happiness living here after the nightmare of the past." A British girl agreed, "How is this place so filled with happy people? If you feel down on your luck, you are sure to meet a smiling face and it makes you smile too."[71] Surely Sophie shared some of the feelings of the women who shared her home.

Sophie settled into the routine of the Foyer. The language spoken by the residents was French. On alternate Sundays, tea was served with a musical program. Art exhibits, lectures, and discussion groups were regular features aimed at widening the interests of the students. Sophie learned to exhibit her work, adding her paintings to the long wall designated for student exhibits. There were also courses in physical culture and dancing, opportunities for spiritual refreshment, excursions, and parties featuring national costumes, as well as coupons for theater and concert performances in the city. One of the volunteer workers at the Foyer, Annette Tritton, an Englishwoman and daughter of a member of the World Committee of the YWCA, probably became a friend and mentor to Sophie. Tritton, an art student herself, was deeply engaged in the life of the Latin Quarter and was able to help Sophie select a studio where she could learn the most and a salon that would exhibit her works.[72]

Tritton organized two annual exhibits at the Foyer: The first featured sketches made in the open air during the summer and were shown in the garden studio; the second was an exhibit of finished products of the winter's work in Paris. Both exhibits resulted in prizes for the winning artists. The winning sketch became the property of the Foyer; the winning painting was sent to the United States. One of the winning works was *A Mother with Two Children* by Elizabeth Nourse, an American who arrived in Paris with her sister, Louise, to study painting in 1887. Nourse studied at the Académie Julian and exhibited her works, gradually gaining a following. She remained close to the students at the Foyer, living nearby on rue d'Assas with her sister and taking active interest in the students until her death in 1938. The French government bought one of her paintings to hang in the Luxembourg Museum beside those of James Abbott McNeill Whistler, Winslow Homer, and John Singer Sargent.[73] The model of the Nourse sisters' living arrangements may have influenced Sophie when she and her sister Asia decided to live together in Jerusalem.

In addition to the friends and mentors Sophie found at the Foyer, it is likely that she also sought out the Russian community in Paris. The large and ornate Alexander Nevsky Cathedral on rue Daru had an impressive list of aristocratic members, who might have been interested in her work and who were able to buy paintings or to support a gallery exhibit. Regrettably, there is no evidence that she attended this church, whose service would have been familiar to her from the Church of the Holy Trinity that she attended with her family in Jerusalem. Recent work on the archive of the church has produced lists of famous members. Sophie Halaby's name is not among them.[74] She may have taken some classes at the Académie Vassilieff or the Académie Russe, both schools founded for Russian art students in Paris, which attracted many women students. Chaim Soutine and Ossip Zadkine taught at these academies.[75]

Sophie left the Foyer for several months beginning in July 1931. The young art student spent most of her time working hard to learn everything she could while she lived in Paris. Perhaps she moved to share a room with Pauline Paul, a graduate of the Jerusalem Girls' College recently arrived from Jerusalem. Paul recorded her impressions of being an art student in Paris for the *JGC Magazine*:

> The days here pass very quickly. One gets involved almost unconsciously in this Paris life of unceasing turmoil. . . . I am following art courses in Paris, especially drawing, painting, and music, and only here did I find out what work can be. Every morning I go to the Art Studio where I paint and draw either from live models or still life. I love portrait drawing and painting. We have two professors who correct in our studio . . . though personality and individuality are maintained of course. Almost every day I meet Sophie Halaby, who works at the same place. We often talk of the Girls' College together.[76]

Sophie may have spent a few months copying famous works in the Louvre and the Luxembourg. The artistic richness of the museums and galleries must have led to an expansion of her thinking about art. Carrying her sketchpad as her teacher Susan P. Emery had in Jerusalem and stopping to draw whatever caught her eye became a lifelong habit.[77] As her artistic sensibility matured, she became aware of the continuing controversy among art critics regarding work that was nonrepresentational. Artists who were called Impressionists, Post-Impressionists, Dadaists, Cubists, and Surrealists were the subjects of lively debate. Sophie lived in Paris during the years when Cezanne, Matisse, Gauguin, Van Gogh, Modigliani, Seurat, Signac, Picasso, Braque, Cassatt, Degas, and so many others achieved notoriety. She would have gone to see their works and read about them in artistic journals.

Art Exhibits and Criticism

Lesser-known artists like the "Palestinian group" were reviewed in the art journal *L'art vivant*. Exhibiting in the Zak Gallery, this group included Jacques Zuker, whose "charming blues" were noted by the reviewer; Moussia Toulman, whose sculpture of a torso was applauded; Bernstein, whose drawings were held up for praise; Moshe Castel, whose work of the countryside with its greens and reds found favor; Aron Dejez, who captured city life; and, finally, Moshe Mokady, who etched expressive figures on a red base.[78] All of these artists were Jews who held Palestinian passports.

As this review makes clear, in the early 1930s "Palestinian" was a term used for all the people who lived within the borders of the British Mandate. It is not known if Sophie attended this exhibit or what she thought about these paintings that purported to capture the feeling of Palestine. It is likely that she was increasingly aware of the work of some Jewish artists from Palestine, who painted landscapes of Jerusalem, a subject that was of great interest to her. A few months after this review, Sophie titled two of the paintings that she exhibited at the Salon des Tuileries *Palestine* and *Jerusalem*.

Sophie's artistic identity was influenced by gender as well as by nationality. Despite continued bias, the art journals of the period reviewed the well-known women artists. One reviewer of an exhibit at the Galerie Charpentier commented on the work of Marie Bashkirtseff, Louise Breslau, and Magdeleine Real del Sarte. Mme Olga Mordvinoff was singled out for her pastels as well as for an oil painting.[79] Another reviewer focused on the Galerie Pigalle, which hosted an annual exhibit organized by Mme Camax-Zoegger, the president of the recently founded Society of Modern Women Artists: "The male elite of Paris is forced at least once a year to admit that women may be imbued with talent, intelligence, and creativity." He concluded that there is nothing "feminine," meaning weak, in the style of Chana Orloff or Jane Poupelet.[80]

There is no evidence of Sophie's thoughts about these articles, but we do know that she was extremely productive during these months, as she succeeded in placing four of her works at the Salon des Tuileries in their 1932 show, which opened in May and was up for two months. This salon was created in 1924 in response to the critique of artists who found the selection process used by the Académie des Beaux Arts to be biased in favor of traditional work. In his inaugural speech, Albert Besnard, director of the salon, stressed the role of liberty in the artistic community as a precursor to artistic innovation. Those works of Sophie's selected for the exhibit reflected her love of her homeland as well as her new interests in Paris. They also indicate that she could paint from memory as well as from reality. In addition to her two works *Palestine* and *Jerusalem*, she exhibited two more, *Un Coin de Montparnasse* and *Nature Morte*. Regrettably, these works have not been located.

There was no consensus about the Salon des Tuileries of 1932 in the art journals of that year. *Les Beaux-Arts* enthused that of all the salons that had just opened, the Tuileries seemed to be the most interesting and lively. The author noted that the exhibit included numerous nude paintings, many of which were stylistically excellent. Another review, more critical in nature, appeared in the *Revue de l'art*. This reviewer derided the artists as lazy and mindless, "a generation that is concerned with capturing a rare mood rather than creating a new style."[81]

Sophie's work was not mentioned in any reviews. She returned to the Foyer in late summer 1932 for nearly a year, living in room 616. She was no longer a newcomer either in the Foyer or in the city's art scene. Presumably, she continued to study while she planned submissions for the 1933 season. Two of her paintings were accepted by the Salon des Tuileries that spring: *Nature Morte* and *Fleurs*. Sophie won a prize for her *Portrait d'une femme* that year. The article reporting the prize, for a competition at the Académie des Beaux Arts in December, listed the artist's name as "Sophie G. Halaby."[82]

The review of the 1933 Salon des Tuileries in the *Revue de l'art* was once again negative. The reviewer believed that there were few good works displayed and that, regrettably, impressionist works seemed to be everywhere.[83] Sophie left the Foyer, and possibly Paris, before the review came out. Nevertheless, she had to be aware of the continuing critical controversy about various forms of nonrealistic painting, a source of friction in the art world for the previous half-century. Even so, Sophie's fiercely independent spirit, described by Kamal Boullata, impelled her to paint as she experienced her subjects. Her realistic renderings of fruit and flowers gradually transformed into more abstract work.[84]

In addition to the general controversy over realism, the art world also debated the issue of whether there was an appropriate genre for women artists.

They pondered: Should women continue to focus on representational flower painting, landscape, and portraiture, long considered their strengths, or should they join the impressionist salons, following Mary Cassatt and Berthe Morisot? Another question that emerged was whether women artists should focus on motherhood as a subject. Chana Orloff wrote: "For me, a woman is especially and above all, a mother, and she does not live completely unless she experiences motherhood; also, I am convinced that for a woman artist, maternity is necessary, because life is the most profound source of art."[85]

German artist Paula Modersohn-Becker, who spent years studying in Paris, disagreed. She feared marriage and family life, explaining: "I very much want to be in control and . . . I have gotten used to directing my own life." She enthused about the freedom of expression she saw in works of Degas, Daumier, and Millet, observing, "They don't seem to care whether what they are making is a 'picture' or not, or whether the public always understands them. The important thing to them is that it be art."[86] Explaining her choice to live on her own, she wrote, "Some people give their lives to others, and some give their lives to an idea." She questioned, "Does it mean that the former are to be praised and the latter blamed?" She concluded, "People must do what nature demands of them."[87]

Like Modersohn-Becker, Sophie remained fiercely protective of her approach to art. She sketched and painted for years while living at home in Jerusalem; she didn't exhibit her work, which continued to evolve, until the 1950s. In the 1970s, when Palestinian artists were encouraged to focus their work on nationalist images, she refused to change her subject matter or her style. Fearful that some might confuse her work with that of her cousin Samia Halaby, who was part of the nationalist art movement, she told Samia to be certain to sign her full name to her paintings (rather than just a first initial) so that no one would confuse their works.[88]

Sophie probably left Paris at the end of September 1933 and traveled through Italy, stopping for a few weeks to paint while en route home. Several of her paintings include Italian scenes. She took with her the memory of conversations with fellow artists, the education in the studios, and the experience of exhibiting in Paris. For four years, Sophie had had access to museums, art studios, galleries, exhibition space, and, perhaps most importantly of all, she had lived in an atmosphere that privileged art and artists. She didn't leave us thoughts about her time in Paris, so we have to imagine them from the words of others, from the life she led, and from her paintings. Modersohn-Becker, who came from a small town in Germany, wrote about her stay in Paris, "I am becoming somebody. I'm living the most intensely happy period of my life."[89]

Abel Pann, a Jewish artist from Belarus, who lived among artists in the famous La Ruche for many years, felt differently. In his autobiography, he explained why an artist who came from abroad might leave the city: "All that has been done here has been created by others. My people and I have no part in it. Here I am a stranger."[90] Sophie Halaby apparently shared this sentiment. As is the case for many who study abroad, Sophie's experience of life in a foreign environment served to deepen her identity.

Sophie and several other Jerusalem Girls' College graduates had the self-confidence to seek advanced education in the cultural capitals of the world. They attended concerts and theaters; they appreciated the beauty of Paris and London, the gardens, old churches, museums and galleries.[91] Their mastery of foreign languages and understanding of European history and culture allowed them to participate effectively in their new environments. Their stories were shared with students and alumnae, inspiring others to follow in their footsteps, to be bold in their aspirations to continue their education and to contribute to society. Most, like Sophie, returned to Jerusalem, where their Western spirit would meet up with Eastern realities.

Some had studied medicine, nursing, education, and library science. They were soon working in important positions in Jerusalem and elsewhere in Palestine in jobs previously not open to women. In becoming a professional artist, Sophie pioneered a new avenue for creativity for Arabs in Palestine whose work had previously been restricted to church and mosque ornamentation. Sophie did not need patronage; she had sufficient family support to open a studio at home, to experiment with different media, and to paint subjects she selected. The independence she enjoyed in pursuing her artistic studies and in developing a unique style was thoroughly modern. Sophie's Parisian art study gave her skills to express her passion for painting that was born in Jerusalem. The natural beauty of Jerusalem remained her muse as she continued to develop these skills.

Sophie maintained strong ties with the alumnae of the Jerusalem Girls' College. They were her closest friends. During the years she spent in Paris, she maintained her membership in the Old Girls' Guild, which grew to one hundred dues-paying members, many of whom met every ten days. Four of the Old Girls were studying at AUB, two taking liberal arts courses, two others preparing for medical school. When the medical students qualified, they would be the first Arab women to become physicians. They were both Christians who had entered the course of study with a view to caring for Muslim women, who often refused care from male doctors. Health care was a strong interest for many graduates. One nurse described the five hundred babies registered at the Mother and Child center she served. Another nurse spent a month in England caring for patients in a hop-pickers' hospital.[92]

Miss Warburton also continued to be a presence in Sophie's life through her columns in the *JGC Magazine*, which Sophie received in Paris. Warburton continued to express her strong conviction about the importance of women's contributions to the world. She wrote in the *Magazine*, "Our generation has seen immense changes and the world of today is very different from the world of fifty years ago. What the world will become in the next half century will depend very largely upon the women."[93]

In spite of growing Arab and Jewish nationalism and the violence that marred the peace of Jerusalem, Warburton remained steadfast in her conviction that peace was possible and that women had a role to play in creating solutions to the conflicts in the world. She encouraged her students and her alumnae to believe in themselves. She urged them to value the importance of their contributions to their families, to their communities, and to the larger world. She reminded them that they had had an opportunity to begin to learn the meaning of life in school, "not only for learning new knowledge and gaining new ideas, but for living together in the relationships of a community." She observed that scientific knowledge is not enough. "We live in a world of persons. Still more than knowledge of things do we need knowledge of people."[94] Sophie's experiences of life in the Foyer as well as of working with diverse students in the studios of Paris deepened her understanding of Warburton's thinking. She returned to Jerusalem a modern woman who believed in the importance of her work as an artist. There she would be faced with unanticipated challenges posed by competing national stories.

3

The Art and Politics of Jerusalem

1933–1948

> SITUATION PALESTINE GRAVER, HUNDRED FAMILIES REFUGEES ON STREETS, RESULT OF ILLEGAL DEMOLISHING IN JAFFA INSPITE OF ORDER HIGH COURT. TYRANNY FORCED WOMEN TO JOIN REVOLUTIONISTS ON HILLS, ONE KILLED, OTHERS WOUNDED. PEASANTS' HOMES DESTROYED AND RANSACKED, PROVISIONS SCATTERED, PRODUCE CONFISCATED, WOMEN MOLESTED, UNBEARABLE CONDITIONS. GENERAL SUFFERING. TRADITIONAL BRITISH JUSTICE NOWHERE, CONFIDENCE LOST, HOPES FRUSTRATED. ENTREAT YOU IN NAME OF HUMANITY PUT END CHAOS AND TYRANNY, PROTECT BRITISH HONOUR. DON'T BREAK BRITISH ARAB MOSLEM FRIENDSHIP FOREVER.
>
> —Arab Women's Committee, cable to secretary of state for the colonies, printed in *Palestine and Transjordan Weekly*, July 11, 1936

New Construction in Jerusalem

Sophie returned home to Musrara in 1933. The architecture of the New City had changed in her absence. Several new buildings had been built, reflecting the growing presence of the British Mandate in Jerusalem. The most prominent were Government House, the Scottish Memorial Church, the King David Hotel, the International YMCA, the Edison Theatre, and the Sansur office building. Though Sophie left no written description of these buildings, she was certainly aware of them. Several contemporaries described the changes to the city in letters and diaries. Significantly, Sophie did not paint any of these new buildings.

Helen Bentwich, part of the English elite of Jerusalem, had lived in the city from 1918 until 1930. When she returned in 1932, she described the controversy relating to new construction in Jerusalem, where new buildings were supposed to fit into the style of older, traditional buildings.

> There is a new Government House, a theatre, a hotel de luxe, two new banks, a huge YMCA building, a Scottish Church and hostel, some new Zionist offices, and innumerable private houses in every area. There is a powerful Town Planning Commission in Jerusalem which does its best to regulate the positions of the new buildings; but the rest is left to the individual architect, frequently with deplorable results as to the suitability of the style to the surroundings. Many architects act on the theory that a few domes and some extraneous arches added to a building of any form or shape will inevitably supply the required Oriental atmosphere.[1]

Augusta Victoria, the palatial structure on the Mount of Olives built by Kaiser Wilhelm, had served as Government House from the beginning of the Mandate, but the building had been badly damaged during the 1927 earthquake, and a new Government House had been planned before Sophie left for Paris. By the time Sophie returned to Jerusalem, it was completed. Situated on a hill nearly two miles to the south of the Old City, the new building was octagonal and featured locally quarried stone. Designed by the architects Austen Harrison and Clifford Holliday, the building contained domes and interior arches, crossed vaults, and a monumental fourteen-foot-high ceramic fireplace of Armenian tiles created by David Ohanessian.[2] Nicola Halaby was an engineer for the building project, which had already become the center of British high society in Palestine.[3] Sophie surely visited Government House upon her return to Jerusalem.

Helen Bentwich thought that Government House lacked grandeur, though it was suitable for its purpose. She preferred the architecture of St. Andrews Church, also known as the Scottish Memorial Church, which was built on a small hill just above the railway station and fit into the general plan of the city.

Eunice Holliday, whose husband, Clifford, was the architect of the church, was appreciative of the new King David Hotel that had opened in 1931 on Julian's Way (today King David Street). She noted that this hotel brought a new level of opulence and sophistication to the city. She described a supper dance at the hotel on New Year's Eve: "It was a lovely place, much more luxurious and better run than anything Jerusalem has had before. The management was very lavish with et ceteras, and we were provided, in the course of the evening, with crackers (in abundance), squeakers, whistles, paper hats, balloons, rattles, streamers, little balls et cetera."[4]

Helen Bentwich, on the other hand, regarded the new hotel as a gigantic box, awaiting tourists. The two-story, two-hundred-room, sixty-bathroom edifice was built of locally quarried pink sandstone. The exterior, Helen thought, was too solid to be vulgar and too plain to be majestic. The interior, on the other hand, was a not unpleasing mixture of Hittite and Futurism, in her view. Swiss interior decorator J. P. Hoffschmid had been asked to draw on the "ancient Semitic style" evocative of the time of King David. He designed a high-ceilinged, marble-floored lobby in muted beige and green colors, accented by Egyptian, Assyrian, Hittite, Phoenician, and Greek motifs in public areas. Food was served by waiters dressed in long white robes with broad red sashes, fezzes, and white gloves. Helen concluded: "The fleshpots of Egypt have at last been brought to Jerusalem, and it is no longer necessary to visit Cairo for an atmosphere of luxury and good food."[5]

In 1931, the Arab entrepreneur Michael Sansur opened a modern office building, rococo in style. The building displayed its ownership in proud signs announcing the name, "the Sansur Building," on front and back. British authorities tried to rename the square where Jaffa Road, Ben Yehuda Street, and Luntz Street meet "Sansur Square," but its earlier designation, Zion Square, remained the only one used. Arab and Jewish lawyers rented office space and met together at Café Europa on the ground floor of the Sansur Building. The Europa was the most exclusive café in Jerusalem, offering French champagne and cups of coffee at twice the price of other shops. In addition to lawyers, the building housed offices for Batta Shoes, Elite Chocolate, several banks, and several groups of accountants. British, Jewish, and Arab intellectuals met at the less expensive Piccadilly, Kapulsky, Alaska, and Vienna cafés, each at a different corner of the square. The popular Café Atara was nearby. These British and Jewish cafés served men and women, while nearby Arab cafés—Umayah, Jawhariyyeh, and al-Ma'aref—served men only. New cinemas brought entertainment from Europe and the United States. The Zion, Rex, Eden, Tel-Or, al-Sharq, and aforementioned Edison were popular with Jerusalemites. The YMCA offered concerts by the Palestine Symphony Orchestra, whose members were Jews and Arabs.[6]

The Edison Theatre was completed in 1932. This fifteen-hundred-seat auditorium, named for Thomas Edison, was the only air-conditioned public hall in the city. The elegant cultural center of Jerusalem for several decades, the Edison featured performances by popular world-renowned artists: singers such as Yves Montand and Juliette Greco, classical musicians such as Arturo Toscanini and Jascha Heifetz, and the famous British actress Sybil Thorndike. It also showed films, of which the Russian and German were best, according to Helen Bentwich.[7]

The YMCA, built directly opposite the King David Hotel, had a 164-foot-tall tower, making it one of the tallest structures in Jerusalem. Designed by Arthur Louis Harmon, architect of the Empire State Building in New York

City, it was dedicated on April 18, 1933, by Lord Allenby, several months before Sophie returned from Paris. This building would become a significant fixture in her social life in later years. The words inscribed at the entrance to the building were taken from Allenby's address: "Here is a place whose atmosphere is peace, where political and religious jealousies can be forgotten and international unity fostered and developed."[8] The inscription was translated into Arabic and Hebrew so that all the communities in Jerusalem could read it and be influenced by its message.

Helen Bentwich looked favorably on the indoor swimming pool and outdoor soccer stadium, the first of these sports facilities for the city.[9] The building also housed a fifty-thousand-volume library and a six-hundred-seat auditorium with a 2,519-pipe organ, a gift of the Julliard Music Foundation. Sophie had the opportunity to attend classical music performances featuring renowned artists that took place monthly at the Foyer.[10] In Jerusalem, she had further occasion to enjoy classical music in this new auditorium.[11] The well-stocked library was surely also important to Sophie, who had previously sought a solution to the lack of access to libraries in Jerusalem.[12]

In addition to the new buildings and cultural attractions, Sophie would have also noticed great improvement in the roads of Jerusalem. All were "tarred," which was a great relief to those who had to navigate them in wet weather. King George Street, opened in 1924 to supply the new Western residential suburbs of the city, had been dubbed "King George's quagmire," but it was now, in Bentwich's view, "as good as any road need be." There were one-way streets, like the newly opened Princess Mary Way; there were parking places and no-parking places. Moreover, British constables, on horseback and wearing white-sleeved uniforms, saw to it that the traffic laws were obeyed.[13]

When Sophie returned to Jerusalem, she was no longer the aspiring student artist who had left home in 1929. She was twenty-seven years old and a skilled professional who had exhibited her work and won a prize in Paris, the cultural capital of Europe. She returned home with dozens of paintings and sketches and installed them in her home studio along with the brushes, paints, special art paper, and canvases that she brought with her. She continued to use that special art paper, imported from Paris, for the rest of her life.[14] Within the Arab community, she was identified as the first local woman who had studied in Paris; she enjoyed a measure of celebrity. One indication of the significance accorded her pioneering sojourn in the French capital is that eight decades later she was still known for it in Jerusalem.[15]

While she lived abroad, taking classes with women of many different nationalities and living among them at the Foyer, Sophie matured. Studying in art studios with women artists who hailed from many European countries and the United States, she saw herself as part of the small community of modern women who devoted their lives to art. It was during these important years that Sophie developed skills that she employed to paint the hills and flowers of Jerusalem. These Western skills would continue to inform her style, even as that style evolved and became highly personalized.

No written record of Sophie's thoughts from this period was preserved in diaries or letters. Nevertheless, her return home in the autumn of 1933 is a clear indication of her Palestinian loyalties. Khalil Sakakini, the inspired memoirist, who, like Sophie, spent time in the West, expressed his complicated love of country in his writing: "Every human and every nation must have its own existence. I love the English *ummah* (nation) and I admire its morals, principles, power, and greatness . . . but I am not English. . . . I love America, that free, energetic, and noble country, but I am not American. . . . I may get sick of my life as an Easterner; I may grow sad for my condition and feel humiliated by my shame and despair over not accomplishing my dreams and goals; I may even want to be freed of my Easterness, but I cannot but be an Easterner."[16]

Sophie's vision of Jerusalem and of her place in the city is captured not in prose but in her many paintings of the hills surrounding the city and of the flowers that grew in and around it. Though she visited the sites described above and participated in the cultural activities hosted there, Sophie was not inspired artistically by modern additions to her city. She painted Jerusalem as she saw and loved it, erasing all of the new buildings that brought European influence into its borders.

Dissonance: Nationalism and Colonialism in Jerusalem

The simultaneous growth of nationalism alongside the continuous pressure of colonial ideology led to dissonance for those, like Sophie Halaby, who valued Palestinian tradition while simultaneously admiring her European teachers and their modern ways. The building boom in Jerusalem described above was a product of the new ideas brought to Palestine by the British. It provided jobs and a sense of development in the city, but it didn't stop the growth of nationalism. As Salim Tamari noted, the attraction to modern life and the growth of national spirit operated on different planes simultaneously.[17] While Sophie was in Paris, two ceremonial funerals were held on the Haram al-Sharif, in the Old City. The Indian Muslim religious leader and scholar Muhammad Ali Jauhar, who had died in London, was interred in January 1931 within the perimeter of the compound through the efforts of Hajj Amin al-Husseini, the grand mufti and the head of the Muslim Supreme Council. Accompanied by hundreds of Arab Boy Scouts in uniform, this event had both religious and political significance. Five months later, the funeral of Sharif Hussein bin Ali, the leader of the Arab Revolt during World War I, was also held on the Haram al-Sharif. The burial of Hussein, who had spent the last years of his life in Amman, the capital of his son Abdullah's kingdom of Transjordan, in this sacred place was designed to reinforce the Hashemite family connection to Jerusalem.[18] These expressions of Muslim nationalism took place in the Old City, on a spot holy to Muslims and Jews, and close to the Church of the Holy Sepulchre.

Years earlier, Khalil Sakakini, the educational supervisor for Arab schools in Palestine and founder of the progressive Dusturiyyah School, had rejected political and religious communities, declaring in his diary: "I am not Christian and not Buddhist, not Muslim and not Jewish, just as I am not Arab or British, not German and not Turkish."[19] Sakakini's opposition to religious nationalist fervor did not stop its development and its continued association with the Haram al-Sharif. Wasif Jawhariyyeh described another funeral, that of Musa Kazem Pasha al-Husseini, who died in March 1934: "All major Palestinian cities declared mourning, and delegations from all over the country came to Jerusalem to be at the funeral. . . . People came in their thousands and walked in a grand procession from Sheikh Jarrah (Husseini's home) to Temple Mount in one uninterrupted flow. There, after the funeral and the eulogies given by the country's greatest men of letters, scholars, and leaders, he was buried in the court of the Temple Mount as a sign of appreciation of his efforts, his struggle, and the loyalty he had shown in his lifetime."[20]

As Nadim Bawalsa has pointed out, Sakakini's definition of nationalism, which he taught in his school, was the pursuit of knowledge and humanity.[21] This was quite different from the nationalist religious spirit described by Wassif Jawhariyyeh. Religious nationalism was felt throughout the year in Jerusalem, but was intensified in spring when the holidays of Nebi Musa for Muslims, Easter for Christians, and Passover for Jews all occurred within days of each other. Nebi Musa celebrations brought large numbers of Muslims from Nablus and Hebron carrying banners, beating drums, and clanging cymbals while singing folk songs, walking to the Haram al-Sharif en route to the tomb of the Prophet Moses.[22] Christian pilgrims also flocked to the city to celebrate Easter, while Jews came to pray at the Western Wall. The king and queen of Belgium were in Jerusalem to see the rituals in 1933.

Despite tensions in the city, the spring holiday season passed without incident that year.[23]

While religious national rituals gained adherents, Jerusalemites also celebrated British rituals. The British War Cemetery on Mount Scopus attracted a large group of Anglophiles on Armistice Day for the annual commemoration of soldiers who died fighting with the British during World War I. The Anglican archbishop presided, lauding the heroism of men who came from distant lands and gave their lives to restore peace to the Holy City. Poppies were distributed, and bagpipes were played. Some, like Bertha Spafford Vester, pasted their poppies into a diary. (Vester's poppies are now in the Library of Congress.) Many of those, like Sophie and Asia, who attended British schools or worked for the British administration, were among the hundreds who attended the ceremony.[24]

British culture remained pervasive in Jerusalem. The new YMCA was the venue for an annual grand concert featuring a military band, including pipers, as well as for soloists like cellist Thelma Yellin and vocalist Ellen Garbedian. The celebration of the birthday of King George V was held on the outskirts of Jerusalem at the Talavera Barracks, a celebration in which both the Transjordan Frontier Force and the Palestine police participated. The elite of all communities participated in these events. Another regular event was a summer "garden fête" hosted by the Jerusalem Girls' College. Tea and refreshments were served to the leaders of Jerusalem, who came to watch English country dancing and to listen to a concert performed by students. Watercolors and sketches, along with fresh cut flowers and homemade cakes, were for sale.[25]

British rituals did not obscure the emerging political struggle between the two national groups—Jews and Arabs. In Jerusalem, Jewish immigration was a constant irritant to the Arab community; the related issue of Jewish land acquisition was another source of friction. The use of Hebrew and Arabic in public signage became a flashpoint for those concerned with national symbols in public space. Allocation of government resources was yet another arena of conflict. Elections to the city government and the conduct of its affairs all reflected the underlying tension.[26]

In the 1930s, ignoring the growing opposition of Arab leaders, Zionists focused their efforts on increasing Jewish immigration. The deteriorating situation for Jews in Germany led to more applications for immigration to Palestine. In 1931, 4,075 Jews had reached Palestine. The following year, the number of immigrants doubled, reaching 9,553. In 1933, the year of Sophie's return home, immigration tripled from the previous year, reaching 30,327. Within two years, Jewish immigration had more than doubled again, reaching 61,854 in 1935. The 1930s were years of economic depression in Europe and the United States, but this was a period of prosperity in Palestine. Polish and German immigrants brought capital, invested their money, and created jobs for Jews and Arabs. For a time, prosperity created the illusion of possible peace, but Arab nationalists decried the sale of Arab-owned land to Jews, denouncing both buyers and sellers.[27]

Not long after Sophie returned home, the First National Arab Fair, featuring a Palestinian Pavilion, opened in the Palace Hotel (now the Waldorf Astoria). The month-long exhibit had a distinctly political intent; it was designed to increase trade and to inspire pan-Arab solidarity. Brocades and silks from Damascus, Cairo, and Baghdad were displayed, along with a large selection of copper and brass artifacts. Pastry cooks came from Beirut and Damascus and produced delicious sweets: *baklaweh*, *knafeh*, *atayif*, and *bourma*. Flavored ices were on sale as well as ice cream, pistachios, and a variety of fruits. From Syria came *qamr el din*, sheets of dried apricot paste, from which is made a dessert flavored with rose water. Glazed fruit was sold in hand-painted wooden boxes: apricots, pears, plums, sugar apples, and whole walnuts. In the center of each box was a crown of sugared pistachios. Also on sale were inlaid mother-of-pearl boxes, silk-lined, filled with chocolates and containing a silver-plated spoon. A whole room was filled with a selection of soaps made in Nablus and Jaffa. Furniture made in Jaffa was also on display. Arabic music played, and a troop of acrobats performed. Turkish coffee was served.[28]

In later life, Sophie decorated her home with pillows made of richly brocaded textiles, mother-of-pearl boxes, and copper and brass household goods like the ones on display at the Arab Fair. She favored local crafts, often purchasing items in the villages she visited near Jerusalem.[29] Selling housewares was not the only purpose of the fair. Hajj Amin al-Husseini used the festive occasion to announce his plan to create an Arab university in Jerusalem. Husseini showed drawings by a Cairo architect for several schools: the school of religious knowledge to be housed in the Haram compound, medical and law schools to be located in the Palace Hotel, and an agricultural college to be built on the Mount of Olives. None of these plans were realized due to lack of funds.[30]

The paintings of Zulfa al-Sa'di featured at the exhibit would have been of particular interest to Sophie. Al-Sa'di was the scion of a venerable Sufi family who lived in the Old City, as did her teacher, Nicola Saig, a well-known icon painter. At twenty-three years old, al-Sa'di was a few years younger than

Sophie. She was the first woman to study with Saig and one of the first Muslims. Like her mentor, al-Sa'di was influenced by traditional icon painting. Kamal Boullata noted that al-Sa'di did not simply capture facial features, but, like Byzantine icon painters, she wrote within her oil paintings the names of the persons she depicted. Among others, she painted Saladin, who fought against the Crusaders, and contemporary political leaders like Sharif Hussein, who fought the Ottomans in 1916. Kamal Boullata explained: "The Arabic lettering within her oil paintings served to assert the Arab character of her portraits, heralding in the process the adoption of portraiture as a new type of Palestinian national icon."[31]

Faten Nastas Mitwasi observed that al-Sa'di's portraits were clearly political. "Her imagery delivered a straight forward political, anti-colonial message, well understood by her public."[32] Sophie had studied portraiture in Paris. In contrast to al-Sa'di, her portraits, including her nude paintings, were deeply personal; they had no overt political content.

Al-Sa'di also exhibited still-life paintings that were foreign to the European tradition. One was a collection of local produce—tomatoes, green peppers, eggplant, garlic, and radishes. Another still life featured wild cactus fruit. Sophie had painted still-life paintings in Paris; the work she did there reflected her European training, often including a classical bust adjacent to a glazed fruit bowl. Once back in Jerusalem, she painted local scenes and objects, including garlic and olive oil in a cruet. Al-Sa'di frequently painted from photographs, a technique eschewed by Sophie's teachers.[33]

Shortly after the exhibit of Arab culture closed, Sophie had another opportunity to see art in Jerusalem. Anna Ticho, who, like Sophie, painted outdoors from nature, exhibited drawings and watercolors on Sunday, January 14, 1934, at Steimatsky's Gallery, entered through the popular bookstore on Jaffa Road. Consul J. M. Kadleki of Czechoslovakia introduced the artist and her work. He invited viewers to examine the paintings of Jerusalem and other sites in Palestine, and of Palestinian people. Ticho's exhibit remained on view for two weeks.[34]

A few months later, a second Arab exhibit, promoted by the Arab Fair Company, opened in Jerusalem. Hala Sakakini recalled the fireworks that were set off every night of the exhibit in the summer of 1934 and the food and handicrafts from Palestine and other parts of the Arab world. A café served Arabic ice cream; there was music, acrobats, and a circus. The exhibit included leather goods from Egypt, woolen blankets from Iraq, a multitude of sweets and fruit preserves from Damascus, brocades and silks from Syria, perfumes and confectionary from Lebanon, brass and copper objects from the Levant, soap from Nablus, mother-of-pearl from Bethlehem, wool rugs from Beersheba and Gaza, handwoven towels from Majdal, furniture made in Jaffa, and carved olive wood products from Jerusalem.[35]

As a result of these exhibits, Sophie became increasingly aware of the rivalry, carried out through competition in the arts, between Zionists and Palestinians for control of the narrative of local history in the years following her return home. She continued to draw and paint, but she didn't show her work in Jerusalem in the years following her return from Paris. From the existing evidence, it appears that Sophie did not exhibit her paintings again until the mid-1950s, twenty years after her return home.

Faced with competing nationalist agendas—Arab and Jewish—British authorities tried with some success to keep the peace by improving living conditions and by maintaining administrative structures to govern the city. Salim Tamari listed the achievements of the British in Palestine:

> The creation of modern institutions of government, including a new civil service and police force, and the centralization of the national bureaucracy in Jerusalem; the modernization of the land code and the taxation system; the creation of a legal corpus to replace (and supplement) the Ottoman code; the conduct of a national census (1922 and 1931), and the creation of a population registry; the creation of rudimentary features of citizenship and icons of unfulfilled sovereignty (currency, stamps, passports); a modern secular educational system; and finally an infrastructure of roads and communication system, including a broadcasting authority—the Palestine Radio in 1931.[36]

Nevertheless, the British, once welcomed by residents hopeful that their rule would be less intrusive in Palestinian life than that of the Ottomans, were now identified as a colonial power. Tamari accurately observed that all of the above achievements happened while "laying the ground for Partition and for the creation of the State of Israel."[37]

Nowhere was dissonance more visible than in the controversy over language. Lack of a common language was a problem in Palestine throughout the years of the Mandate. British schools for Arab children taught in Arabic; Zionists schools taught Jewish children in Hebrew. As Mabel Warburton had predicted, this led to little intergroup communication. English, taught in Anglican schools, became the language of better educated Arabs and Jews who wished to work for the British Mandatory government.[38] It also became the social language of the educated class who, like Sophie, continued to speak English with their friends long after they graduated. Speaking English was only part of the value system imparted by the British. Nancy Stockdale noted that years after the teachers had passed away, the impact of their efforts to infuse their own values into the lives of Palestinians continued to shape the memories and experiences of their former pupils.[39] In sharp contrast, nationalist Arabs and Jews rejected the English language, denouncing it as the language of the colonial power.

Sophie returned to Jerusalem in the autumn of 1933, where she encountered these and other instances of Arab and Jewish nationalism alongside British colonialism. The Jerusalem Girls' College, where she had been an outstanding student, remained the anchor of continuity for her. As a prominent alumna, Sophie was expected to visit her old school to speak to students about her experiences in Paris and to attend a variety of social events during the year. Her sister, Asia, still working for the British, and her cousin Olga Wahbe, who had recently been appointed vice principal of the Government Women's Teacher Training College, often accompanied her. The ongoing affiliations with their alma mater encouraged them to believe that all the communities of Jerusalem could live in peace.

Miss Warburton, who had been awarded the Silver Jubilee Medal, issued in honor of the twenty-fifth anniversary of the coronation of King George V, returned to Jerusalem in 1935 for two years.[40] She remained close to the members of the Old Girls' Guild of the college, including Sophie and Asia. The membership roster included graduates of all religious backgrounds. Some of the graduates, like Sophie, left Jerusalem for study or work. Yocheved Dar taught in Persia, for example, while Victoria Nasir taught in Jaffa, and Terese Nusnas studied in Beirut.[41]

Other former classmates navigated the dissonance between colonialism and nationalism by creating organizations to help members of their own community using skills learned in their Western school. Mrs. Dimitri Salameh presided over the Society for the Needy and the Sick, which focused its efforts on helping members of the Orthodox Christian community. Another graduate of the Jerusalem Girls' College, Katherine Siksek, secretary of the organization, explained their work: "This society extends its help to the Arab Orthodox in Jerusalem. . . . But we are often called upon to help pilgrims who are taken sick and have lost what they have treasured for their pilgrimage. Also destitute Orthodox villagers residing for their daily work in Jerusalem benefit freely from our society, similarly to the actual residents."[42]

Sophie's cousin, Sultaneh Halaby, another graduate, worked with Katy Antonius in raising funds for the Arab Women's Association of Jerusalem, which established an infant welfare center to aid Muslim and Christian children and women.

The Jerusalem Girls' College found ways to appeal to parents who were increasingly nationalistic, and yet who were also interested in modernization and teaching their children English. A total of 221 pupils were registered: 144 Christians, 47 Muslims, and 30 Jews, representing thirteen different nationalities. Six languages were taught. Among the pupils were representatives of the most influential families in Jerusalem. The Jerusalem Girls' College and St. George's College were among a small number of institutions where Arab and Jewish children lived and worked in harmony.[43]

In the summer of 1935, the indomitable Miss Warburton addressed a public meeting devoted to Christian education in Jerusalem. In contrast to Hajj Amin al-Husseini's plan for an Arab university presented the previous year, Warburton believed that Christian schools should "implant in the pupils, the future leaders of the country, Muslim, Jew, and Christian, that width of outlook, balance of mind, and sensibility to the claims of others, which will help to build up a better understanding between the peoples of the Holy Land."[44] The establishment of a British university in Jerusalem, she thought, would be a catalyst that would raise the standards of secondary school teaching and would be especially useful to the Arab population of the city. Sophie, who remained active in the alumnae community, would likely have supported this initiative. Lack of funds left this project, like that of the Arab university, on the drawing board.

Winifred Coate, the new headmistress of the college, noted changes in the prevailing attitude of the Arab population, which she attributed to growing nationalism. She feared that ethnic antipathies were strengthening in Palestine and that children, reflecting the political and religious prejudices of their parents, would be less inclined to subscribe to the belief in tolerance for all. She therefore believed they needed, more than ever, constructive teaching to respond to the new challenge. Her suggestion was to increase sporting activities among the students as a remedy. Coate noted, "Girls keen on their games readily sink national and other differences in loyalty to their captain or their team." This meager effort to inculcate tolerance withered in the growing nationalist climate.[45]

In August 1935, a group of seventy women representing all three religious groups met at the headquarters of the Women's Christian Temperance Union on Mamilla Road. They were addressed by Ethiopian Empress Menen Asfaw, then visiting Jerusalem, who made an appeal for peace. Many women attested to the suffering of women during war and issued a message to the League of Nations titled "Jerusalem Women Appeal to Peace." One of the speakers was

Sophie's cousin, Melia Halaby. Bertha Spafford Vester, a longtime member of the Social Service Association, which included Christians, Muslims, and Jews, was disappointed with the lack of unity among the women who called for peace. She noted in her diary that when the Jewish women got up to speak, the Arab women walked out of the meeting.[46]

The Arab Revolt

Arab nationalists, angry with British rulers for their unwillingness to staunch the flow of Jewish immigration to Palestine, met in Jerusalem under the leadership of Hajj Amin al-Husseini on May 8, 1936. Their meeting concluded with a resounding challenge: "No taxation without representation." Husseini called for civil disobedience and a general strike to protest British pro-Zionist policies. This was the beginning of the Arab Revolt, which lasted three years.[47]

The newly formed Higher Arab Committee, led by Husseini, directed the first phase of the revolt from May 1936 to July 1937. A general strike was enforced for the first six months, bringing commercial and economic activity in Palestine to a standstill. Jerusalemites like the Halaby family participated in the strike by refraining from buying goods sold in Jewish-owned shops. Nevertheless, Asia continued to work for the British administration and Nicola continued to work with the English architect Austen Harrison on two new buildings: the General Post Office on Jaffa Road and the Palestine Archaeological Museum. Both buildings opened during the revolt in 1938.[48]

Dorothy Norman, teaching at the Jerusalem Girls' College, described the chaotic situation resulting from the strike in a letter to her family on May 19, 1936: "None of our busses ran yesterday so we have rather few girls again though many struggled to get to school in the face of great difficulties in order to do their examinations. This morning I walked down our bus-route to collect such girls as were waiting and bring them to school on foot. I found to my horror an enormous bloodstain on the pavement where a man was shot yesterday; but curiously it is so common here to see messes in the road that I was not perhaps as horrified as I ought to have been!"[49]

Mabel Warburton, who had tried to create an environment of tolerance and intercommunal cooperation, recognized the fragility of the edifice she had constructed. She penned her private thoughts in the summer of 1936:

> It is nice to think of a peaceful countryside in England these days. We are in a desperate condition of things here. . . . Until the spirit of fear is eradicated,

> I see no hope for either Arab or Jew in this country. You cannot have two peoples living in a perpetual spirit of fear and suspicion . . . what is worrying us all is how long this state of things is to continue. . . . There is no doubt that Great Britain has greatly lost in prestige, but I believe that even the most malcontents would in their heart of hearts rather have British rule than that of any other Western power. One can't help wishing sometimes that we were out of it all, and someone else had the Mandate, but I suppose that is cowardly.[50]

Palestinian women, including some educated by Miss Warburton, played a major role during the Arab Revolt, which continued for several years. They advocated the boycott of products brought from England and those produced by Zionist companies. They also organized demonstrations against the British Mandate and Zionist immigration. Some women participated in transferring and smuggling weapons past British Army checkpoints. Others organized fundraising campaigns to assist the families of those who died in the revolt.[51]

During the summer months of 1936, a new English-language publication appeared in Jerusalem, *Palestine and Transjordan: A Weekly Review of Political, Economic, Legal and Social Affairs in Palestine, Transjordan and Other Parts of the Arab World*. Sultaneh Halaby, Sophie's cousin, wrote a letter to the editor that was printed on July 27, 1936, titled "The Jews and Palestine": "There were no Jews in Palestine until Babylonian-Persian times, 6th to 5th century B.C. The Biblical figures, Joshua and David, were Hebrews, not Jews. The Jews are a people of the Law published [*sic*] in the time of Ezra and Nehemia. Israelites occupied the middle and northern part of Palestine; the Hebrews occupied the southern part."[52]

Sultaneh, who had studied the Bible at the Jerusalem Girls' College, used what she had learned to champion a Palestinian nationalist narrative. Engaged as she was in nationalist politics, she may have suggested that her artistic cousin Sophie submit some political cartoons to the new weekly. Ellen Fleischmann noted that many elite urban women took part in demonstrations, collected money to fund the revolt, enforced the strike, and sent petitions to the government.[53]

Sophie, as was her inclination, responded to the revolt by producing art. The eight cartoons that were printed in *Palestine and Transjordan* are a clear expression of her political views. Sophie's cartoons began to appear at the end of August. They captured her changing views of British leaders and her growing opposition to Zionism. Her ideas were similar to those of other elite Arabs, many of whom admired aspects of British culture but had become disenchanted with the British for allowing excessive Jewish immigration to the city. Families like the Halabys, the Dajanis, the Salamehs, the Khaders, the Nashashibis, the Albinas, and the Deebs were all involved with the new Arab Chamber of Commerce that advertised in the weekly. They considered the major issues of the day to include the threat of growing Jewish immigration to the livelihood of Arab businessmen, irreconcilable differences in culture between Jewish immigrants and indigenous Arab populations, and frustration at the inability of the British to resolve the situation.

Sophie's first four cartoons appeared from the end of August to mid-October 1936. The first image featured Chaim Weizmann, president of the World Zionist Organization, dressed like an agricultural pioneer, in short sleeves, short pants, and sandals. Weizmann, who typically was photographed in three-piece suits, is seated in the middle of a map of Palestine, blowing bubbles that are labeled Balfour Declaration, Jewish National Home, Arab-Jewish Friendship, and Jewish Propaganda.[54] Sophie's support for the ideal of tolerance clearly did not extend to acceptance of the Balfour Declaration or the plan for a Jewish National Home. In her drawing, the Arab-Jewish Friendship bubble has burst.

The second image is based on the biblical story of the powerful yet besotted Samson, here pictured as a British lord, and the wily Delilah. Drawn with a stereotypically Jewish nose and wearing immodest garb, this Delilah is a Jewess who, like the original Philistine, is loyal to her people and skillfully cuts Samson's hair, rendering him powerless. In the background is a sketch of Jerusalem with its iconic mosques and bell towers. The implication is that the British are easily tricked by the Jews and are being betrayed by them. The third cartoon features a scrawny Chaim Weizmann leading a wobbly Winston Churchill off a cliff into a field of "Islamic Anger." Weizmann's vision of the future of Palestine, a land of Jewish stars, is featured in a corner of the image.[55] These two cartoons echo the sentiment in the epigraph at the beginning of this chapter. The British, once regarded as friends, were no longer deemed trustworthy.

The fourth cartoon juxtaposes the benign language of the Covenant of the League of Nations with a military scene featuring a British officer with troops marching, airplanes circling, and Arab snipers hidden behind hilltops. A British official holds his head in worry, expressing the failure of the British Mandate to create well-being and to support the peoples who were entrusted to their care.[56] This cartoon reveals Sophie's despair at what has happened to her country.

Hajj Amin al-Husseini called off the general strike for three months, from November 1936 through January 1937, while a British fact-finding

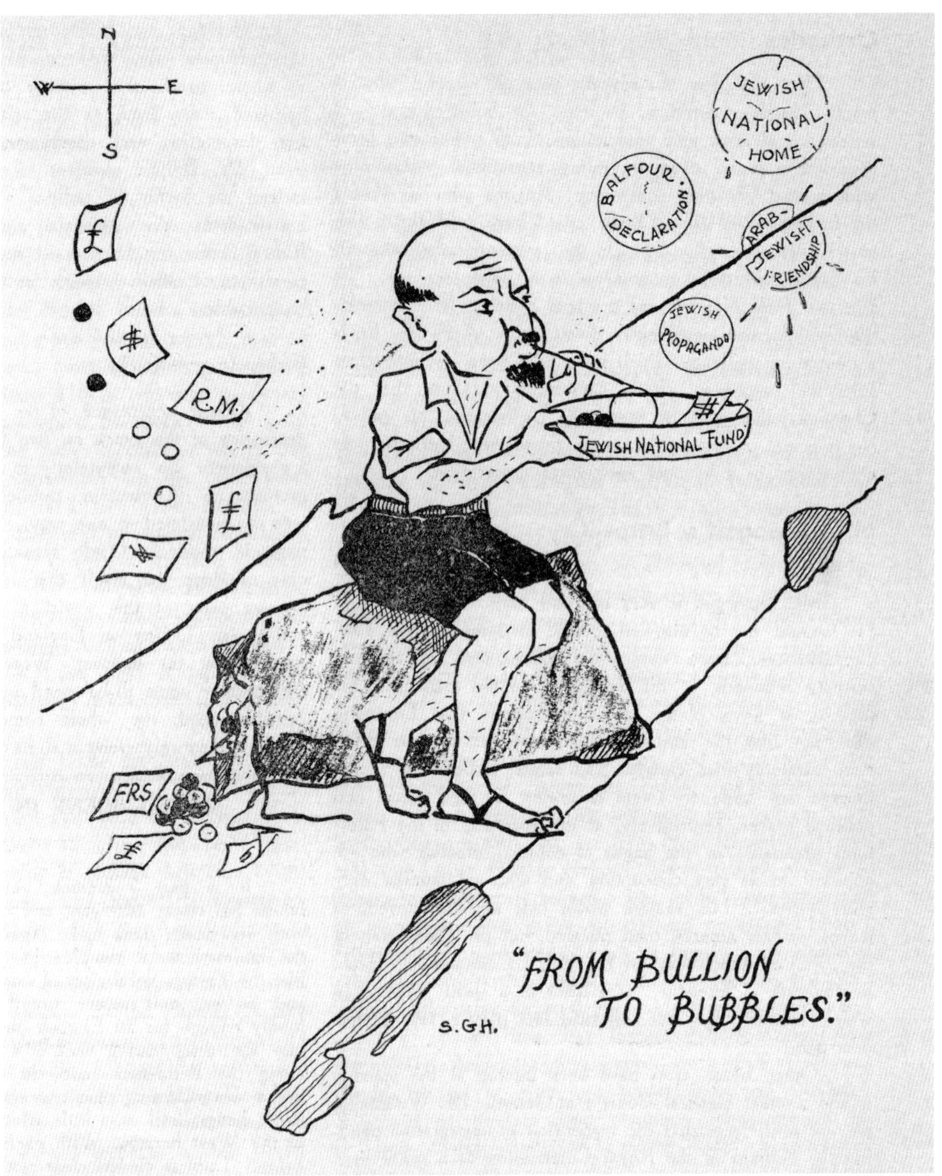

3. From bullion to bubbles. Dorot Jewish Division, New York Public Library.

inquiry, the Peel Commission, toured Palestine. During this period, Sophie contributed three more cartoons; each reflected her growing critique of the failure of the British to offer just treatment to the Arabs. The first of this group of images depicts "Sir Michael," referring to Sir Michael Hogan, chief justice of Palestine, refusing the offer of a new scale of justice to replace the one that came out of a box with a Jewish star. Here, Sophie reveals Arab anger

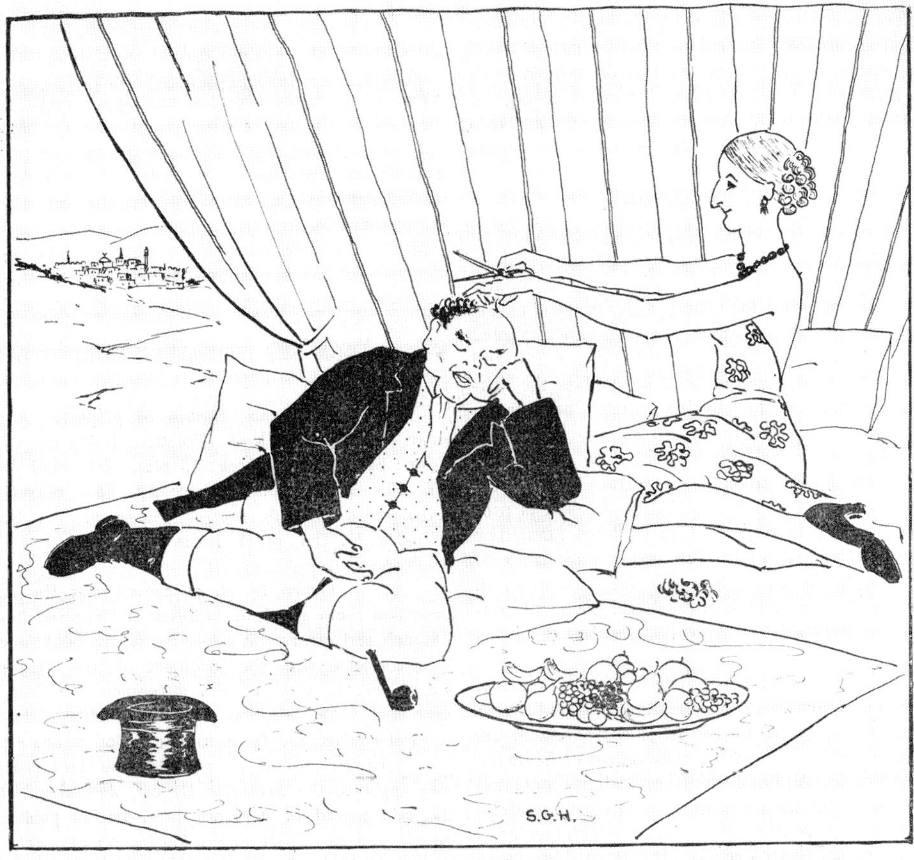

4. Delilah: It's your own fault, Samson . . . you should keep your eyes open. Dorot Jewish Division, New York Public Library.

at the role of Norman Bentwich, a Jew, who had been appointed attorney general at the beginning of the Mandate. Many Arabs were convinced that he was incapable of impartiality. The next image is a scene of crying boys in front of the Hospital of the Order of Saint John (a hospital for the blind). A nurse representing the Royal Commission (perhaps pointing out that there were no women appointed to the Commission) stands at the entrance to the building and asks: "Why are you crying, Abdullah?" The boy explains that Isaac, a Jewish boy, was responsible for his tears. He had started the fight by throwing dust at John, the British boy, who then threw dust in Abdullah's eye. Abdullah concluded, "If you come out, Nurse, they'll do the same with you. They don't know how to play any other game." The drawing expresses Sophie's frustration with the inability of the Peel Commission to learn the

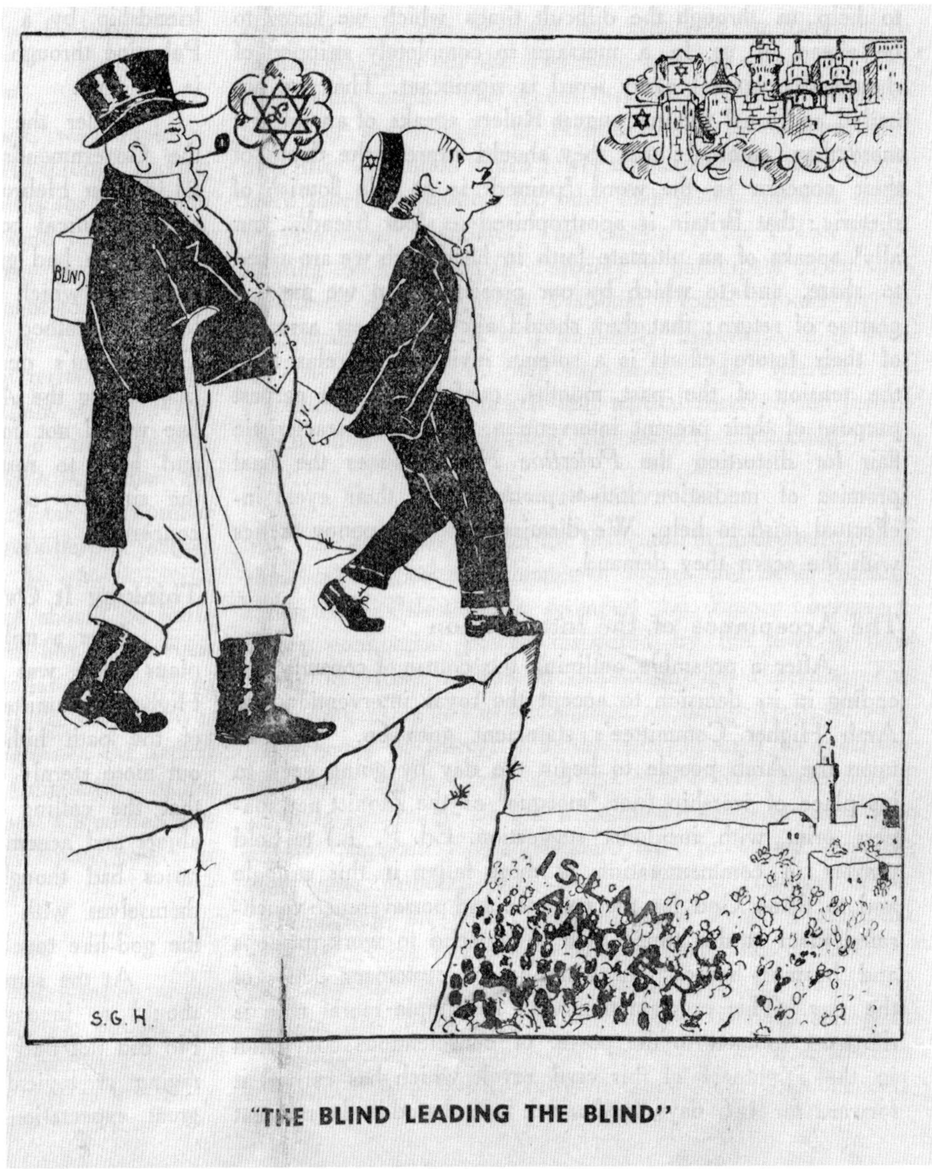

5. The blind leading the blind. Dorot Jewish Division, New York Public Library.

full facts of the country's situation due to what she perceived as the aggressive behavior of the Jews.[57]

A week later, Sophie presented another depiction of Chaim Weizmann, this time as a lecturer explaining, with a rash of misleading numbers, the capacity of Palestine to absorb Jewish immigrants to a British official seated at a school desk. Sophie's cartoons identified growing Jewish immigration as

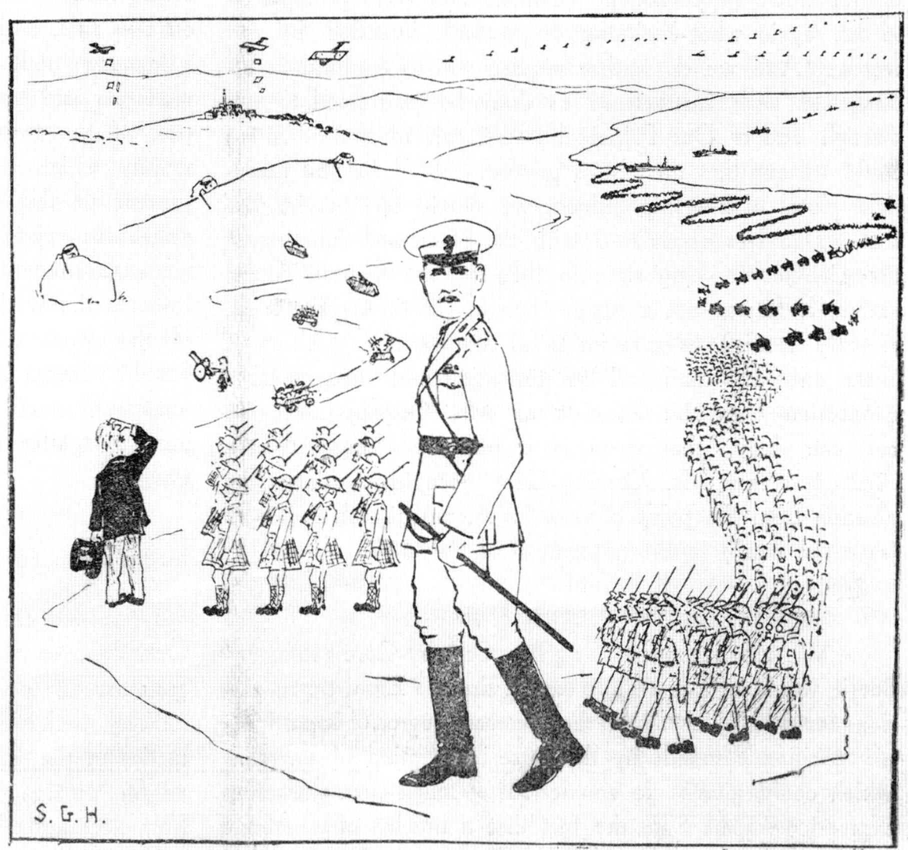

"To those colonies and territories..... there should be applied the principle that the well-being and development of such peoples form a sacred trust of civilisation......"
(Article 22 (1) of the Covenant of the League of Nations.)

6. "To those colonies and territories there should be applied the principle that the well-being and development of such peoples form a sacred trust of civilization." Dorot Jewish Division, New York Public Library.

the major problem. While she again depicted the Jews as duplicitous and the British as naïve, in actuality the major catalyst for Jewish immigration at this time were the Nuremburg Laws of 1935, which took both the Jews and the British by surprise.[58]

For several months, elite residents of Jerusalem enjoyed the cessation of violence while the Peel Commission met. Social life resumed with a musical

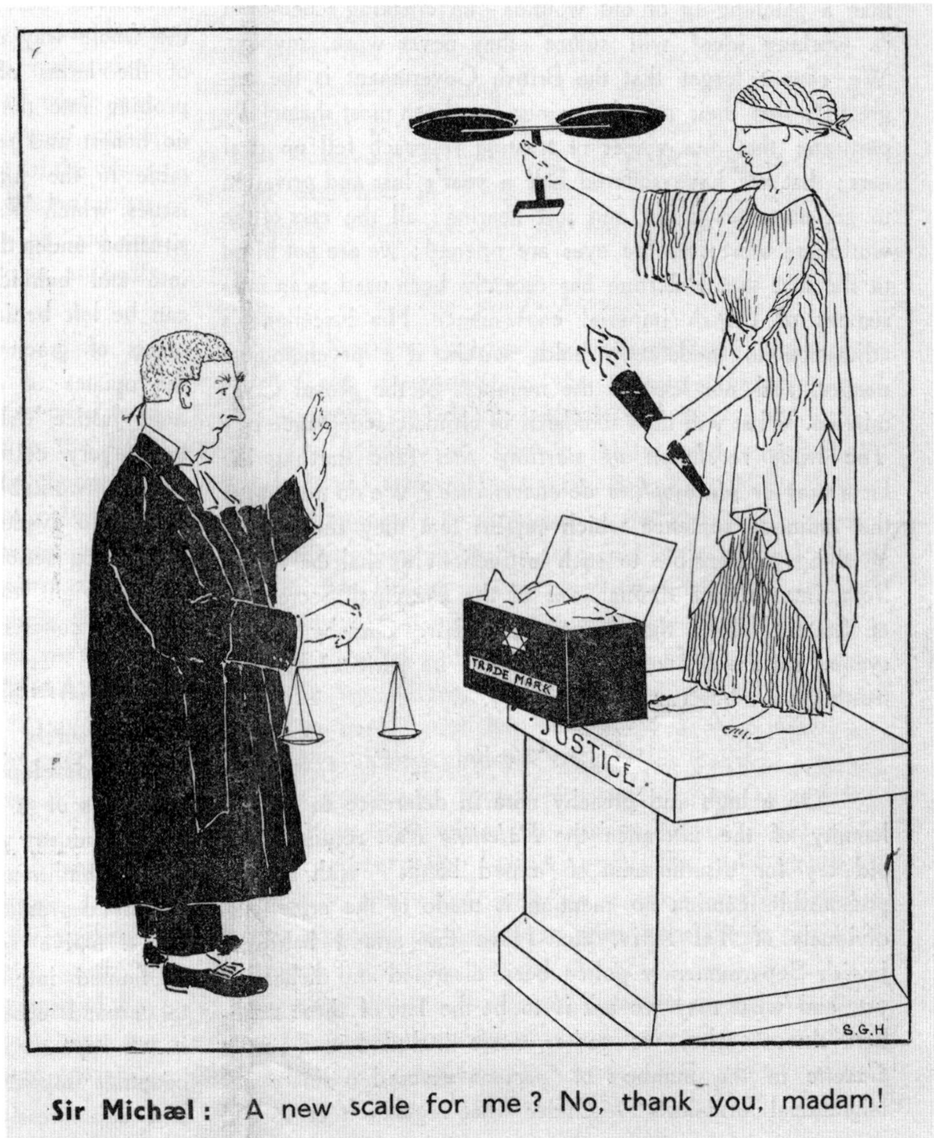

7. Sir Michael: A new scale for me? No, thank you, madam! Dorot Jewish Division, New York Public Library.

interlude on January 3 when Arturo Toscanini, the acclaimed maestro, conducted the Palestine Orchestra in a Beethoven concert at the Edison Theatre. Bertha Spafford Vester noted in her diary, "From an early hour yesterday morning in the lane off Ben Yehuda Rd, where the booking agent's office is located, there was a queue which overflowed into the main road, watched over by two constables who saw to it that people were admitted only five or six at a time."[59]

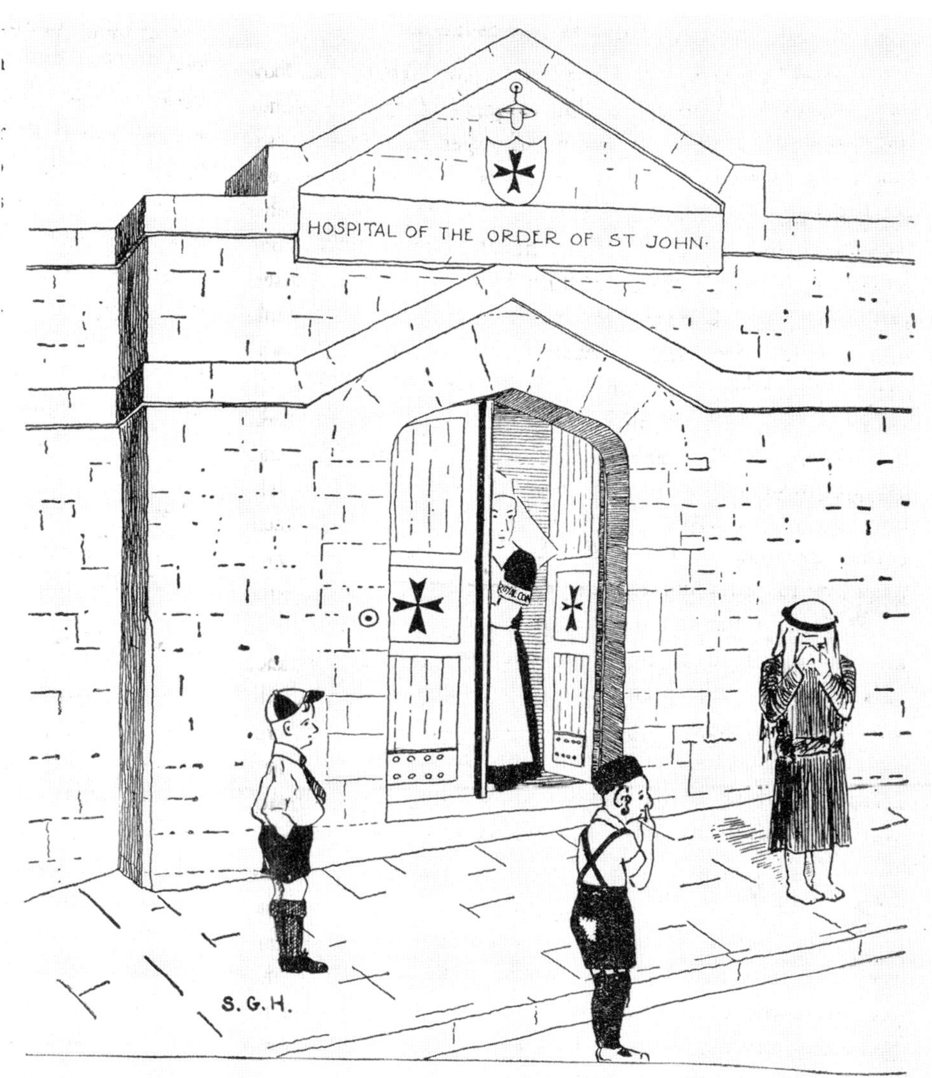

Nurse (Royal Commission): Why are you crying, Abdullah?

Abdullah: Young Isaac threw dust in John's eyes, and John threw dust in mine! If you come out, Nurse, they'll do the same with you. They don't know how to play any other game.

8. Nurse (Royal Commission): Why are you crying, Abdullah? Dorot Jewish Division, New York Public Library.

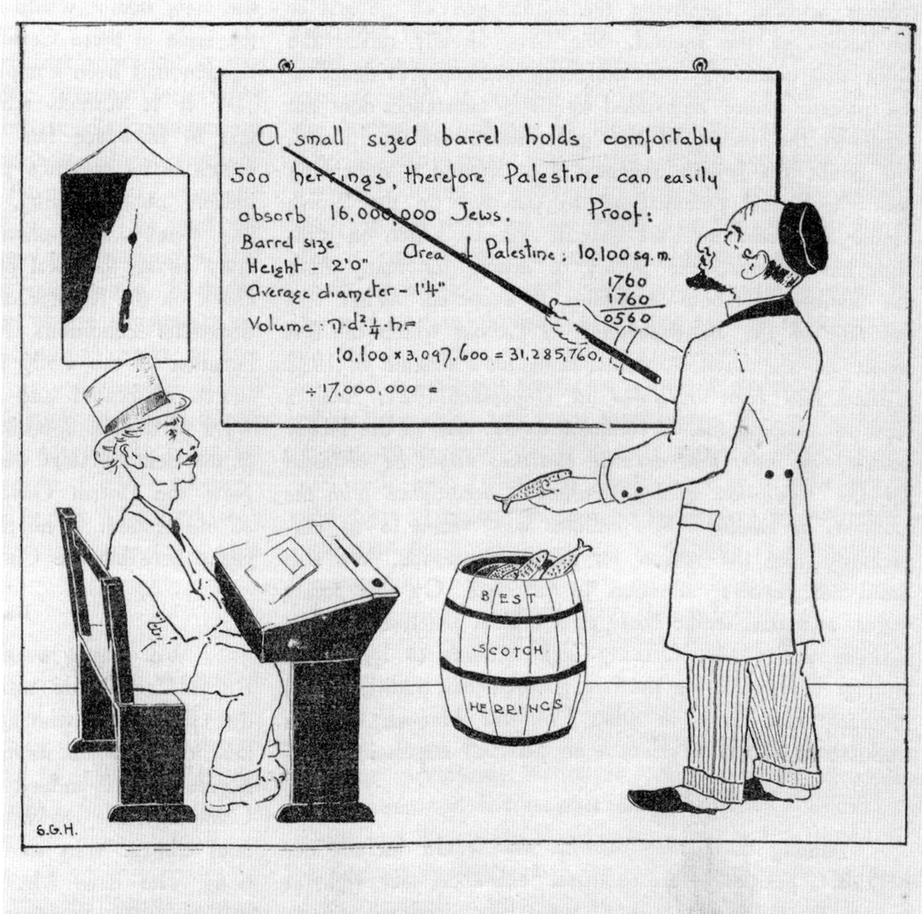

A LESSON IN TAKING A "CONSERVATIVE VIEW OF THE ECONOMIC CAPACITY."

9. A lesson in taking a "conservative view of the economic capacity." Dorot Jewish Division, New York Public Library.

Simultaneously, in a move apparently designed to appease Arabs, a folk museum opened in the Muristan, a complex of streets and shops in the Christian Quarter of the Old City. A committee of volunteers led by Mrs. Neville Barbour, the wife of a British official, gathered a collection of objects ranging from carved wooden coffee pounders from the North to the characteristic black pottery from Gaza, and including jewelry, metalwork, household tools, and an array of women's traditional clothing. This exhibit was intended to testify to the culture and traditions of Arabs in Palestine.[60] Though the

British tried to demonstrate an appreciation for Arab culture, the timing of the exhibit, which appeared while many Arabs were anxiously awaiting the findings of the Peel Commission, was such that it failed to win the good will of the Arab community.

Sophie's last cartoon was a strong denunciation of British policy. This cartoon appeared on March 6, 1937, after the report of the Peel Commission—recommending a partition of Palestine into a Jewish state, a Palestinian state to be incorporated into Transjordan, and enclaves reserved for Mandate control—was published and rejected by the Arab Higher Committee. It features a British official rocking the cradle of twin babies, one Arab and one Jewish, both crying. The cradle is labeled "Palestine Mandate." This poignant cartoon is different in tone from the previous ones. It suggests that the British were unable to sing a song that would be intelligible and comforting to two babies with incompatible languages and needs. The British official wipes his brow in frustration at his failure to pacify the babies.[61] The failure of the Peel Commission to find a solution to the growing dissatisfaction of the Arab population of Palestine was sobering to the artist. Jewish refugees from Hitler's Europe were moving into Musrara and other mixed neighborhoods of Jerusalem. Many were educated people like Sophie. In view of the nationalist sentiments of both Jews and Arabs, she worried that the two cultures would not find a way to live together in peace. It is likely that she continued to participate in political discussions with friends and family, but she hereafter ceased using her artistic talent to comment on the British, the Jews, or the Arabs.

Despite growing Arab nationalism, British officials continued to believe in their mission as a Mandatory government in Palestine. They celebrated the coronation of King George VI and Queen Elizabeth on May 12, 1937, with a service of thanksgiving at St. George's Cathedral. The radio broadcast of the king from Buckingham Palace, assuring all people within the British Empire of the goodwill of the monarchy, was printed in the *Palestine Post*. The manager of the King David Hotel hosted a ball in honor of the occasion. Miss Annie Landau, the headmistress of another English-language girls' school, hosted a coronation moonlight garden party, to which were invited all the elite families of the city.[62]

In the wake of the Arab Higher Committee's rejection of the Peel Report, Arab nationalist violence increased. British officials responded with renewed determination to break the will of the leaders. Following the assassination of a British administrator in Nazareth, scores of Arab leaders were arrested and exiled; the most prominent were sent to the Seychelles Islands in the

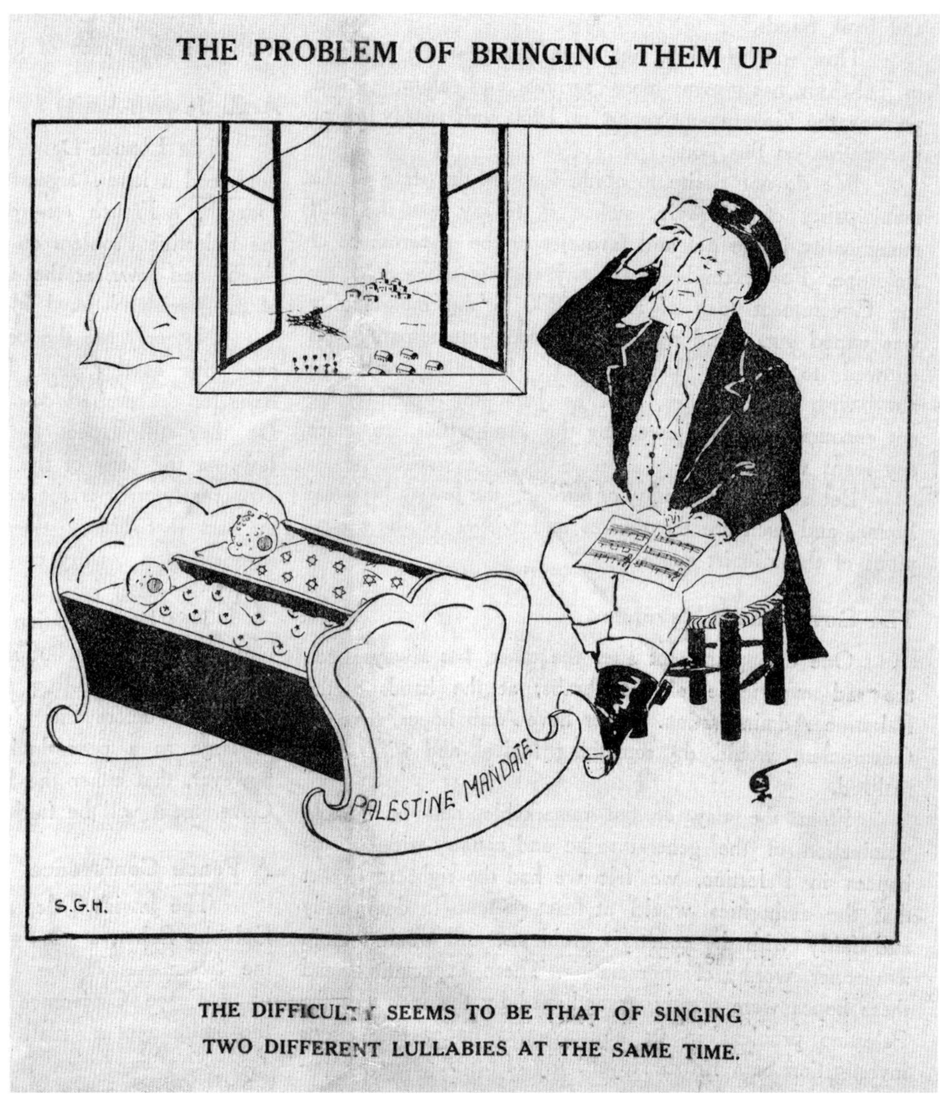

10. The difficulty seems to be that of singing two different lullabies at the same time. Dorot Jewish Division, New York Public Library.

Indian Ocean. Hajj Amin al-Husseini found temporary refuge on the Haram al-Sharif. He later escaped to Lebanon, moved to Iraq, Italy, and finally, Germany. He continued to influence Palestinian nationalist efforts from exile.[63]

In an effort to boost Arab businesses suffering from the strikes and sporadic violence, the Arab Chamber of Commerce published the *Directory of Arab Trade, Industries, Crafts, and Professions in Palestine and Trans-Jordan*. Two members of the Halaby family were included in the directory: Sophie and Nicola. S. G. Halaby was the only entry under the category "Christmas Cards,

Jerusalem." Her work was described as "hand-painted watercolor greeting cards with Palestinian subjects." Her address was given as Musrara Quarter; her post office box was 464. Nicola Halaby was listed as N. G. Halaby under the heading "Mechanical Engineers, Jerusalem." His name was followed by "D.L.C. (Hons.)" His address was more specific, Baldwin Street, which was the main street in Musrara. His post office box was the same as Sophie's. Some of the other entries in the directory included phone numbers. It is likely that the Halaby family did not yet have a phone.[64]

During the final period of the revolt, the Muslim-dominated Arab Strike Committee demanded symbolic support from all Arabs. They issued regulations requiring all men to cease wearing the tarboosh, the fez-like hat that had been customary headwear under Ottoman rule, which was worn by George Halaby, and begin wearing the kaffiyeh, the traditional Bedouin head covering made of a folded scarf or kerchief. Ladies and girls were told to wear a mantle, a light chiffon veil, over their hair. No Arab was to use electric lights, nor play the gramophone or listen to the radio.[65] Rebel leaders insisted that Christians observe Friday as their day of rest and demanded "donations" from Arabs, mostly Christian, working for the British government.[66] For many Arab Christians, these directions were seen as a violation of their freedom. Bertha Spafford Vester reported on a spirited conversation at the home of the Salameh family, Christians and friends of Sophie from the Jerusalem Girls' College, who complained about the change of headdress. Bertha wrote with little sympathy for their distress: "Christian Arabs had glibly joined the Moslem nationalist movement. Now they are getting a taste of what Moslem rule would be like."[67]

In the face of continuing violence, the Old Girls' Guild of the Jerusalem Girls' College held a reunion that captured the feelings of an earlier time. From April 22 to 24, 1937, fifty-two women—Christians, Muslims, Jews, Armenians, Greeks, and an Assyrian—attended. The reunion was organized by a committee elected by the entire membership of the guild. The committee included several Jews, though they were a minority of the members. Friendships among girls of different nationalities—especially between Jews and Arabs—remained strong in the view of Winifred Coate, who reported on the event. Their ties were taken for granted and caused no comment. At a picnic, songs were sung in English, Arabic, Hebrew, French, and Spanish, and everyone sang all the songs.[68]

Despite the success of the reunion, Mabel Warburton was deeply disturbed by both the Peel Commission report and the violence that ensued. She sent her thoughts, "Partitioning Jerusalem: A City Divided against Itself," to the *London Times* on August 2, 1937. The *Times* declined to publish it, claiming it had no space. Warburton focused on the part of the Peel Report that dealt with Jerusalem, fearing that the Jewish sectors of Jerusalem would be added to the newly proposed Jewish state. Presciently, she was concerned about the integrity of the city and the potential loss of its special role in the world. Warburton's views, expressed in this essay, were built on the ideas she had first described at the opening of her school for girls in 1918:

> It is in the realm of the cultural and spiritual that the true hope of the world today lies. The vision of the Holy City, not just the medieval part within the ancient walls, but the modern city with its pulsing cosmopolitan life, becoming as visualized in the Hebrew prophets, a centre from which a word of peace might go forth to the warring nations, is one which thrills the imagination of the world. Not a political capital, not primarily a centre for trade and commerce, but Jerusalem as a city apart, its security guaranteed by all the nations, as a place which all alike, of every creed and race may look on as a spiritual home. A city, on whose gates would be written, "All national, racial, religious prejudices put off, O ye who enter here!"[69]

Sophie had been educated with these ideals, but her feelings had changed during the revolt, as is evident in her cartoons. Warburton, clinging to the ideal of Jerusalem as a vehicle for world peace, longed for a cultural renaissance in the city. She saw positive signs in the Hebrew University, with its "magnificent group of Jewish scholars gathered from all parts of the world." She noted its proximity on the top of Mount Scopus to the British War Cemetery on one side and the Christian churches of the Mount of Olives on the other. She hoped that British and American archaeological experts as well as the erudite scholars of the various Catholic orders would join the university's scholars in their pursuit of learning. She referred to a proposed Muslim university and an Institute of Christian Research; both, she believed, would lead to that cultural renaissance.[70]

Warburton quoted Norman Bentwich, the former attorney general, now serving as Weizmann Professor of International Peace at Hebrew University: "Jerusalem in its essential idea belongs not to one or two peoples but more than any other city of the world is a metropolis of mankind. . . . Since the League [of Nations] has been in operation the need has become increasingly obvious for a spiritual union by the side of and supplementing the political union. . . . If such a union is realized, its proper habitation would be Jerusalem, which the prophets conceived as a capital of the universal kingdom and which has been the principal source of spiritual influence on humanity."[71]

While some continued to speak about justice and understanding, Arab nationalists took control in Beersheba, Bethlehem, Nablus, Ramallah, and, for a time, the Old City of Jerusalem. The Arab Women's Committee, cited above, continued to express strong feelings, now focused on weapons. On July 16, 1938, the text of their memorandum to the high commissioner was printed in the *Palestine and Transjordan Weekly*:

> The Arabs as a whole have on more than one occasion submitted to government that the Jews are in possession of vast amounts of arms and other infernal means which they have brought into the country clandestinely to be used as weapons to exterminate the Arabs, but government did not seem to heed such advice. . . .
>
> The recent outrages in Haifa, Jerusalem, and Jaffa and their occurrence simultaneously . . . show that such attacks were premeditated and organized by responsible persons or bodies. . . .
>
> Your Excellency, we abhor bloodshed no matter of what race it may be, and we sincerely hope that such strong measures will be taken as will prevent further bloodshed.[72]

British authorities, ignoring the pleas of the Arab Women's Committee, responded with growing force to the Arab insurrection. On October 24, 1938, Coate wrote to her board in London to describe the deteriorating situation in Jerusalem: "When I first got back here in September I found everyone full of gloomy rumours; the college was not going to open; if it did, there would be no pupils; the Christians would be too poor, the Moslems too anti-British, and the Jews too frightened to return; the buses would not run, etc. To all enquiries—and after a few days the phone was ringing all day long—I said that everything was going to be as usual—and fortunately this proved to be true. There had been a rumour that I and all the staff were going to stay in England and not return."[73]

Despite the fear, Coate reported that 254 pupils were attending classes: 140 Christians, 75 Muslims, and 39 Jews. In addition, there were 42 in the classes for British children. However, everything was not as usual. In 1938, 1,000 Palestinians were killed in skirmishes with the British, 54 were executed by hanging, and 2,463 were imprisoned. The following year, 55 were executed, 1,200 were killed in action, and more than 5,000 were incarcerated. A new report published by another commission concluded that partition was not practicable. While these reports were being written, Anne Irvine, whose association with the Jerusalem Girls' College went back to its opening days, described the convivial spirit of the alumnae whose meetings continued despite the strife. Irvine went to Tel Aviv to host some alumnae parties and described seeing Simha Mizrahi, a nurse at Bnei Brak, and Alice Mekalhalian, also a nurse, who was working at a hospital overlooking the sea in Jaffa.[74]

In May 1939, Malcolm MacDonald, colonial secretary of state, issued a white paper reversing the Peel Report, announcing conditional independence for a unitary Palestinian state after an interval of ten years, admission of fifteen thousand Jewish immigrants annually into Palestine for five years, and the protection of Palestinian land rights against Zionist acquisition. This new policy represented a sharp reduction in the number of Jewish immigrants who had been arriving in Palestine, most fleeing from Nazi Germany. In a repudiation of the Balfour Declaration, the white paper called for the creation of a Palestinian state with an Arab majority and safeguards for a Jewish minority. The white paper was approved by the British House of Commons but denounced by the Permanent Mandates Commission. A new source of terror, this time from Zionists angered over the limitation on immigration in the face of Jewish vulnerability to Nazi conquest, ensued.[75]

Despite the British repudiation of the Peel Report, Rashid Khalidi explained that the Arab Revolt was a serious failure for the Arabs:

> The Arab economy of Palestine was devastated by years of strikes, boycotts, and British reprisals, and the fighting forces suffered casualties—5,000 killed and 10,000 wounded—that were proportionately huge in an Arab population of about a million, and included the loss of hundreds of the bravest and most enterprising military cadres killed in battle or executed by the British. Finally, the traditional Palestinian leadership, which had been obliged by grassroots pressure to come together to form a joint national leadership, the Arab Higher Committee, at the outset of the general strike in 1936, was shattered by the end of the revolt, divided anew by differences over tactics, which were once again exploited by the British. Many individual leaders were exiled by the British in 1937, and others fled, some never to return to the country.[76]

During the early part of the Arab Revolt, Sophie acted on her growing opposition to British colonialism and Zionism. Her foray into political discourse through the cartoons gave voice to her feelings. Sophie was particularly influenced by one aspect of the national struggle. She responded enthusiastically to nationalist arguments against selling land to Jews. The Halaby family owned many parcels of land. In later life, she struggled to protect the land that she inherited. Her attachment to the land is seen in landscape paintings that are a prominent feature of her mature artwork. As she matured as an artist, her feelings for the land were revealed in increasingly abstract watercolors of the city she loved. These paintings—watercolors and oils—capture the artist's unique vision of Jerusalem.

World War II

Arab and Jewish attacks on the British and on each other ended with the British declaration of war on September 3, 1939. Many Jewish Palestinians joined the British in their fight against Hitler despite British policy restricting Jewish immigration and sale of land to Jews. By the end of the war, thirty thousand Jewish men had enlisted.[77] Arabs in Palestine were divided in their sympathies. Some remained loyal to Hajj Amin al-Husseini, who broadcast Nazi propaganda from Berlin throughout the war. Others remained loyal to their British employers. Asia Halaby was one of the latter. She was one of very few Arab women who volunteered to serve with the Auxiliary Territorial Services (ATS). Sophie remained at home in Musrara, painting. She was removed from direct participation in the war effort, though certainly concerned about her sister's welfare.

The first ATS group in the Middle East included about fifty women, all European, who did intelligence work in Ma'adi, outside Cairo. In November 1941, the remnants of this group were moved to Alexandria, where they joined Jews and Arabs who had been recruited in Palestine. There were strong political feelings among the recruits and some language barriers, as not all spoke English. The ATS eventually recruited five thousand women in the Middle East. Most of them were Jews recently arrived from Europe, joined by Cypriots, Greeks, and Palestinian Jews and Arabs, including Asia Halaby. They trained in Sarafand, on the coast south of Haifa, the largest British base in the Middle East.[78] Asia, who was fluent in English, Arabic, Russian, and French, served as a translator on the base. The women were taught a variety of skills including drafting, driving and mechanics, nursing, switchboard operation, radio operation and repair, and electrical work. Asia, who already had a driver's license, studied mechanics to be able to repair her vehicle during long trips. With her knowledge of English, experience working for the Mandate, skill as a driver, and take-charge personality, Asia was made an officer before leaving the base at Sarafand.[79]

Once they arrived in Egypt, the volunteers were assigned the task of driving ambulances and other vehicles. They often worked in very hot weather and sandstorms. Asia, according to family lore, repeatedly drove through the desert; she was probably assigned to company 503, which was responsible for driving the Cairo to Alexandria road. When she was home on leave in Jerusalem, Asia wore her British uniform and drove her jeep through the city. Vicken Kalbian recalled that this action would typically have generated crowds of chanters and spitters angered by a Palestinian who supported the British. However, because of the prominence of the Halaby family, Asia did not experience anything of the sort.[80] Asia's participation in the war effort meant that Sophie was more aware of war news than most Arab Jerusalemites.

In Jerusalem, despite British policy restricting land purchases by Jews throughout Palestine, the flow of Jewish volunteers to serve the British Army, including women who volunteered to serve in the ATS, continued. In 1941, Crete and Greece fell to the Germans, bringing the battlefield much closer to home. The mayor of Jerusalem, Regheb Nashashibi, hosted a rare intra-communal garden party in August. Jews, Arabs, and British residents were invited. This party was an unusual expression of solidarity in the face of the enemy. Bertha Spafford Vester, the stalwart woman who had organized soup kitchens during World War I, hosted another party in September to celebrate the sixtieth anniversary of the American Colony. She noted that war had again brought the women of Jerusalem together to sew and knit for soldiers. Jews, Christians, and Muslims attended this party as well.[81]

At a time when many Palestinians were suffering from lack of food and goods due to the war, the Palestine Broadcasting Service launched a new series of radio programs designed for educated Arab women. *The New Arab House* showcased the advancements of Arab women and encouraged their contributions, not to the Arab nation, but to general society. Mrs. Salwa Sa'id, a graduate of AUB and the daughter of the former mayor of Beirut, was hired to develop programs based on "scientific knowledge" of subjects. Sa'id saw the European home as a site of "art, order, beauty, and comfort," while the Arab home was, in her view, "chaotic, ostentatious, uncomfortable, impractical, stiff, worn-out, stuffy, and stale."[82] She addressed her "Arab sisters" on the following topics: household management, household planning, the natural position of the house, household furnishings, household organization, cleanliness and tidiness, household economy, the kitchen, the dining room, the maid, and the manservant. Her rather tone-deaf effort to westernize Arab homes during wartime was championed by *Filastin*, which printed transcripts of her broadcasts.[83]

This radio program reinforced colonial ideas about home décor that competed with the local crafts promoted in the Arab Fairs a few years earlier. The call for service to the larger community resonated in the context of the war, but the assumption that the European home was superior to the Arab home surely angered Sophie and her friends, who were struggling with war shortages. To conserve fuel, all private cars were banned from the roads. To feed the troops, two meatless days a week were imposed. Flour, bread, and sugar were rationed. Later, eggs were added to the ration list. The food controller issued a special booklet describing "101 ways to eat potatoes," and encouraged civilians to make the food a dietary staple.[84]

In 1942, the war moved closer to Jerusalem as Rommel's armies advanced with alarming speed, taking Tobruk on the Libyan coast in July. For a time it was feared that the British would be driven out of Egypt; Asia and other ATS recruits were assigned to drive ambulances with wounded Australians from Alexandria to their hospital thirty miles outside of the city. The battle of El Alamein, in Egypt, led by General Montgomery, who had arrived in Palestine in 1939 to lead the British response to the Arab Revolt, brought two hundred thousand British, Australian, New Zealander, Indian, and South African soldiers, plus smaller contingents of French and Greek soldiers, into the field. Ten days of fighting turned the tide of the war in favor of the Allies. Asia and the ATS recruits were assigned to dangerous work ferrying the wounded to field hospitals. Asia's participation in this effort was magnified in family lore. Some believe that she was a driver for General Montgomery.[85] It is more likely that she supported the battle commanded by the general.

Some of the wounded required treatment in hospitals far from the battlefield. Ambulance drivers were charged with taking them hundreds of miles under fire after preparing them for evacuation. At the end of 1943, a conference attended by Churchill, Roosevelt, and other Allied leaders, was held in Cairo. The ATS drivers were asked to supervise the preparation of villas. Other ATS volunteers handled secret telegrams.[86]

At home in Jerusalem, the Jerusalem Girls' College continued to operate throughout the war. Parents of many Jewish refugees sought places for their daughters in this school. Eileen Fenton, vice principal during the war, reported: "We could have filled the school over and over with Jewish children. These were Jewish people who had come to Palestine because there was no where else to go, getting away from Hitler . . . who hoped that their children would be able again to live in Europe somewhere, and therefore wanted them to have a European education."[87]

The *Palestine Post* published details of the European concentration camps on November 25, 1942. In Jerusalem, the Jewish Agency declared three days of official mourning culminating with a fast day on December 2. From noon until midnight all Jewish shops and businesses closed. All musical concerts, dances in cafés and restaurants, and cinema performances were canceled. Sophie was aware of this action, which affected all residents of Jerusalem. She would also have known about the broadcast from Rome on March 19, 1943, of Hajj Amin al-Husseini, who used the occasion of the Prophet's birthday to state: "The Jews have a dangerous aim by which they challenge 400 million Muslims, and that is their express desire to occupy holy Islamic institutions including the al-Aksa Mosque in Jerusalem under the pretext that this Mosque is the Temple of Solomon."[88]

In the spring of 1944 the mayor of Jerusalem, Mustafa al-Khalidi, a Muslim, became ill. His deputy, Daniel Auster, a Jew, was appointed acting mayor. Jews, who made up 61 percent of the city's population, demanded that the next mayor be Jewish. The Arabs rejected this demand, holding a protest strike. Auster remained acting mayor until July, when the high commissioner, in frustration with the impasse, appointed six British officials to govern the city, effectively doing away with the office of mayor.[89]

Despite Hajj Amin al-Husseini's support of Hitler, most Arabs in Jerusalem remained loyal to the British. On June 11, 1944, crowds came out to watch the parade held to celebrate the Allied landing in Normandy. Three hundred khaki-clad ATS women marched through the city, Asia likely among them. Sophie would probably have been present. The *Palestine Post* noted, "There was a general feeling that these girls were part of the forward march of the United Nations on the part of liberation." The crowd of onlookers was so great on Ben Yehuda Street that the girls were almost forced to fight their way down the street.[90]

War continued in Europe as the Halaby family faced personal sorrow in Jerusalem. George Halaby, Sophie's father, died on April 27, 1945. He was buried in a family plot in the graveyard at the Church of Mary Magdalene on the Mount of Olives, near his uncle Ya'qub. The special privilege of being buried on this spot was an indication of the close ties between the Halaby family and the Russian Orthodox Church. Nicola became the head of the Halaby household, replacing his father on the Musrara board.[91] He didn't become the dragoman for the Russian Mission, as the position established under the Ottomans had become superfluous during the British Mandate.

The End of the Mandate

Eleven days later, Jerusalem celebrated VE (Victory in Europe) Day. The festivities reflected the conflicting priorities of the increasingly divided communities. At the Jewish Agency building, the Zionist colors—blue and white—were draped and bordered in black in mourning for the Jews murdered in Europe. The Jewish crowd demanded an end to the immigration quotas of the 1939 white paper. An Arab counterdemonstration formed at the Jaffa Gate; the marchers chanted nationalist slogans and marched through the commercial section of the city. The British refused an American request to allow one hundred thousand survivors of concentration camps into Palestine; they also refused Arab demands for immediate Arab majority rule.[92]

Amid these tensions, social life in Jerusalem returned to prewar rhythms. During the twenty-eight years of British rule, over 2,023 clubs and organizations (charities, cooperatives, sport clubs, and cultural and literary societies) had been registered in Jerusalem. The YMCA boasted 1,950 members in 1947. Garden cafés in the villages around the city resumed entertaining Jerusalemites eager for a taste of country air. The Everest and the Panorama reopened near Beit Jala, while the Hamra, the Aida, and the Harb served customers in Ramallah. In Ein Karem, the Ash-Sharafeh was prized for its beautiful views. In the New City, the Alaska, Atara, Europa, and Vienna cafés enjoyed brisk business, as did the Viennese Tearoom. Dinner dances at the King David Hotel resumed, and eight cinemas—the Edison, al-Sharq, Zion, Eden, Rex, Regents, Studio, and Tel Or—showed Hollywood films like *Ninotchka*, *Alexander's Ragtime Band*, and *Gone with the Wind*.[93]

The Jonas Art Gallery opened on Mamilla Road, near the YMCA. This was Jerusalem's first art gallery.[94] The owners were Luta Jonas, the widow of Ludwig Jonas, a painter, and Eleonora Willinsky, a Russian immigrant. Ya'akov Steinhart, who had opened Steinhart's Art School in Jerusalem, was the first to exhibit there. The gallery rapidly became a cultural landmark in Jerusalem, but the artists who exhibited there were exclusively Jewish. Ya'akov Pines, Moshe Mokady, Miriam Elkan, Ludwig Surin, Marcel Janco, and Ya'akov Nussbaum all showed their work. Marcel Janco merited a one-man show that was reviewed in the *Palestine Post* in November 1945. A few months later, "Fifteen Palestinian Artists" were exhibited at the Jonas Gallery. The reviewer, Thomas Meysels, noted, "The sole newcomer is A. Sternberg with two nudes in watercolour of such exceptional quality that one may look forward with interest to other work of hers."[95] Sophie would have been curious about these works; Moshe Mokady had studied art in Paris and was reviewed in *L'art vivant* in 1932.[96] The Jonas Gallery enjoyed a brief period of success. A British officer and art lover, Paul Anthony, became a regular visitor. He fell in love with Luta; they married, and she returned with him to England.[97] The gallery closed soon thereafter.

The *Palestine Post* published a column, "Jerusalem Art Notes," beginning in the late 1930s. It listed the Palestine Conservatoire of Music as a venue for an art exhibit in 1938, the Art Gallery on Tancred Lane (behind Barclay's

Bank) in 1942, Universitas Book Shop on Princess Mary Avenue in 1944, and Bookbinder's Gallery on Jaffa Road in 1946. The British Council also provided exhibit space for artists: Edvard Matusczak displayed recent works in July 1946; in September, Rosemary Coyle was given an exhibit. The Bezalel Museum also featured exhibits of Jerusalem artists, including Anna Ticho, in 1947. The artists featured in these exhibits were primarily Jewish, and some were foreign visitors. No Arab artists were included.[98]

With the end of World War II, the hostility between Arabs and Jews in Jerusalem, relatively quiescent during the war, resumed. Jerusalem became a center of violence perpetrated by gangs jockeying for position as the intent of the British to leave Palestine became increasingly clear. Every few weeks, the city was shaken by an explosion, followed by the wailing of sirens, indicating the beginning of another curfew. On July 22, 1946, an explosion at the King David Hotel set off by Zionist nationalists killed ninety-one people, including many government employees. The British had taken over the south wing of the hotel in an attempt to create a safe place for its workers. Among the dead was Nadia Wahbe, Sophie and Asia's cousin. Nadia's sisters, Sophie and Louba, were wounded. All three had worked for the British Mandate in offices at the King David.[99] The explosion left a gaping hole in the hotel, a daily reminder of the bombing for all who stopped for coffee at the popular Piccadilly Café on Mamilla Road or visited the YMCA, directly across the street from the hotel. It was a defining moment for Sophie and Asia Halaby, who had been very close to their Wahbe cousins since early childhood.[100]

John Melkon Rose described the growing violence that affected all Jerusalemites: "By 1946, conditions were so bad that Jews and Arabs kept to their respective sides of the city. Buses were ambushed or shot at and explosives placed under cinema seats, in cafes and other places of entertainment, in markets. Armor-plated buses were introduced to protect civilians. We became used to living precariously."[101]

The Jerusalem Girls' College, long a bastion of stability, experienced declining enrollment. Almost continuous curfews made it difficult for pupils to reach school, and Arab parents worried that the Rehavia neighborhood was no longer safe for their daughters. In response, teachers began to patrol the streets before classes started, protecting pupils from street gangs and rock throwing. In February 1947, the Mandatory government took action. They announced "Operation Polly," evacuating all nonessential British subjects. The wives and children of Mandate officials were forced to leave the city within forty-eight hours, effectively closing the British primary school operated by the Jerusalem

Girls' College; many teachers left, too. The government commandeered the college buildings; Jews evicted by British authorities from Arab areas of the city were allocated space in them. The school organized classes in Arab neighborhoods, at St. George's, and in the American Colony.[102]

The atmosphere in the city continued to deteriorate as the British created security zones surrounded by barbed wire. Moving from one zone to another now required passes; nightfall brought curfews as residents waited impatiently for daylight and freedom of movement within their zones. In April, the British informed the United Nations that it would ask the UN General Assembly, due to open in five months, to recommend a future government for Palestine. A United Nations Special Committee on Palestine (UNSCOP) was formed to address the issue. Eleven UNSCOP delegates visited Palestine and Europe in an attempt to fulfill their mission. Arabs hoped for recognition of their rights as the large majority of the population of Palestine. Jewish leaders pointed to the hundreds of thousands of refugees in European displaced persons camps and their need for the homeland promised in the Balfour Declaration. The delegates recognized that the basic conflict was a clash of two nationalisms. Sophie's last cartoon in 1937 had captured that conflict. Their final recommendation was published on September 8, 1947; it came in two parts. The majority recommended partition; the minority recommended a federated state of Jews and Arabs. The majority recommendation, with the proviso that Jerusalem was to be placed under an international trusteeship controlled by the UN, was scheduled for a vote by the General Assembly.

Three weeks after the recommendation was published, the British announced that they would leave Palestine in six months even if no settlement had been reached. On November 29, 1947, the vote took place: thirty-three delegates voted for partition, thirteen against, and ten abstained. Among those who voted against were Egypt, Syria, Lebanon, Iraq, and Iran. The United States and the Soviet Union voted in favor. The positive vote carried. Zion Square erupted in euphoric dancing as Jews celebrated what they saw as a victory. The Arab reaction was a mixture of incredulity and anger.[103] The dream of tolerance promulgated by the Jerusalem Girls' College and internalized by its graduates had become a nightmare.

Around 97 percent of the nearly 100,000 Jews living in Jerusalem lived in the New City, whereas roughly 48 percent, or 31,500, of the 65,000 Arabs lived there, with a preponderance of Christian Arabs living outside the city walls.[104] Following the announcement of the vote, Jerusalem's inhabitants entered a period of anarchy. In December, a procession of school boys and young men carrying Arab national flags went to the Commercial Center and torched about fifty shops, mostly Jewish-owned. In retaliation, Jews burned down the Rex, an Arab cinema. High Commissioner Alan Cunningham spoke to both Ben Gurion and Dr. Khalidi, Jewish and Arab leaders, in an attempt to quell the fighting. Bertha Spafford Vester observed in her diary, "He might as well appeal to the stones to act sensibly."[105]

4

Jordanian Jerusalem

1948–1967

> At times I would be possessed by unfathomable feelings and a vague excitement, especially when listening to music or singing. Feeling the urge to give expression to something I sensed but did not understand, I would run to get a pencil and paper that in no time would be covered with a jumble of interconnected words. . . . The practice of giving the best we have, knowing that our days are not spent in vain, gives us a sense of self-possession, peace and tranquility.
>
> —Fadwa Tuqan, *A Mountainous Journey*

Leaving West Jerusalem

Before 1948, the Palestinian Arab community of West Jerusalem numbered about twenty-eight thousand. It was one of the most prosperous in the Middle East, inhabiting spacious homes mainly in the southern neighborhoods of Talbieh, the Greek and German colonies, Katamon, and Baq`a', and in the eastern neighborhoods of Musrara and Abu Tor. Ninety-five thousand Jews lived mainly in the northern and western parts of the city, areas ringed by the Arab villages of Lifta, Sheikh Badr, Deir Yassin, Ein Karem, Malha, and Beit Safafa. As the New Year began, two bombings by the Irgun, a Zionist paramilitary organization, at the main portals to the Old City, the Damascus Gate and the Jaffa Gate, resulted in dozens of Palestinian deaths.[1] Bertha Spafford Vester, the stalwart leader of the American Colony relief efforts during World War I and World War II, wrote in her diary, "What a beginning to 1948! Civil war!"[2]

British authorities, in a futile effort to keep the warring sides apart, divided the New City into zones separated by barbed wire. Official passes were required to move from one area to another; the authorities regularly imposed curfews. Despite these measures, sporadic violence continued. Jewish, Muslim, and Christian families who lived in neighborhoods outside the Old City were unprepared for the ineffectiveness of the British in preventing attacks that followed the vote for partition.

On the stormy night of January 5, 1948, the Semiramis Hotel, which was situated on high ground in Katamon, and from which attacks had been launched against the Jewish neighborhoods of Rehavia and Kiryat Shmuel, was blown up by Jewish forces. Ghada Karmi, only eight years old at the time, remembered the events of that night in Katamon, where she lived with her brother and parents: "When the explosion came, it was almost like another clap of thunder. But it was so terrific that it blew out our windows, scattering glass everywhere. Immediately after, the whole sky was lit up with fire. My brother and I were terrified, and I can remember my mother dragging us from our beds onto the floor and pressing us against the wall. I did not understand that it was an explosion and kept asking if the glow in the sky was the sun rising . . . what remains vivid is the terror of my parents and the fear that began to grip me as I saw it."[3]

Years later Ghada recalled that her parents tried to shelter her from the grim reality of the situation, but that their furtive behavior filled her with fear. She reported that the streets of Katamon, recently teeming with life, became a ghostly place; food disappeared from the shops. The Karmi family remained in their home until they fled by car to Damascus on April 27, leaving all of their papers, documents, family photographs, and mementos, certain that they would return to their home within two to three weeks.[4] Years later, Ghada reflected on the enormous impact of the decision: "We were an ordinary family with ordinary lives and ordinary hopes. Left to ourselves, we would have remained a natural part of our society, married people like ourselves, raised children, traveled perhaps, but always knowing we had a home to return to. Eventually, we would have grown old with our families, died, and been buried in the same cemetery as our ancestors. Instead, we were displaced, uprooted, and sent into exile."[5]

The Sakakini family also lived in Katamon in 1948. They had previously lived in rented homes, but in 1937 they built a house in a neighborhood where they were surrounded by Christian Arab neighbors. On the same stormy night remembered by Ghada Karmi, Hala Sakakini, twenty-four years old, who had taken first aid lessons offered by the Catholic Club in anticipation of violence, wrote in her diary: "We had terrible weather last night—rain, lightning, thunder and a violent, howling wind. About a quarter past one we were awakened by an awful explosion that lighted the sky and shook the house. The explosion, we learned later, was in the Semiramis Hotel. I put my clothes on and, according to Dr. Freij's instructions, hurried to the Villa Maurice, just across from Hotel Semiramis, to help nurses with the wounded."[6]

Sixteen people died in Katamon that night. Frightened residents were concerned for their safety but reluctant to leave their homes. Following the explosion, the men of Katamon took out their guns and prepared to defend their families. The women, led by Hala's aunt, Melia Sakakini, called on the Iraqi consul, whose residence was in Katamon, to request that he send for soldiers from the Arab Legion (the army of Transjordan) to protect the Iraqi consulate and the surrounding neighborhood. Five soldiers soon arrived, to the relief of the women delegates. Nevertheless, as the violence continued, residents began to leave the area.

Hala Sakakini remembered: "All day long you could see people carrying their belongings and moving from their houses to safer ones in Katamon or to another quarter altogether. They reminded us of pictures we used to see of European refugees during the war. People were simply panic-stricken."[7] Hala, who had strong nationalistic feelings, noted that she and her sister, Dumia, scolded people scurrying to leave: "You ought to be ashamed to leave. This is just what the Jews want you to do; you leave and they occupy your houses and then one day you will find Katamon has become another Jewish quarter!" A few weeks later, on March 11, her diary revealed new compassion for those who fled: "Today, from early morning, we could see trucks piled with furniture passing by. Many more families from Katamon are moving away, and they are not to blame. Who likes to be buried alive under debris?!"[8] The Sakakini family, like the Karmi family, remained in Katamon for three difficult months following the bombing of the Semiramis. They left for Cairo on April 30.

The final battle for Katamon began that day and lasted for three days. One hundred fifty Arabs were killed. Widespread looting followed. An observer recorded: "For days you could see people walking by carrying looted goods. . . . Not only soldiers, civilians as well. They were looting like mad. They were even carrying dining tables. This was in broad daylight." Another saw "horse-drawn carts and pick-up trucks laded with pianos, refrigerators, radios, paintings, ornaments and furniture, some wrapped in Persian carpets."[9]

Violence in Musrara began in February. George Halaby's widow and children still lived in the spacious home surrounded by a large garden that had been their refuge since they returned at the end of World War I. Their neighbors, the families of Musa Alami, Tawfiq Canaan, and Ibrahim Tleel, shared the fear and insecurity produced by the violence in the city. On February 22, a bomb landed on residential buildings near the Halaby home. This event was the catalyst for Sophie to roll up the paintings she had brought back from Paris as well as the work she had finished since her return to Jerusalem. She packed canvases, brushes, and paints; she would not leave the city without her paintings. Her collection—including pencil, charcoal, and ink sketches as well as watercolor and oil paintings—is the only one by a professional painter of the Arab community in Jerusalem to survive.[10] Sophie also safeguarded family photograph albums that were brought from Kiev and documents pertaining to family history. She expected to return, but she was not taking any chances with her life's work and treasured family photos and documents.

At this moment, Sophie's resolute nature emerged from behind her quiet veneer. She was determined to move her paintings to a safe refuge in a city divided into cantons by barbed-wire barriers. It is possible that she packed them in Asia's car and was driven with them into the Old City. It is more likely that Asia secured help from British officials to move the paintings. It is also possible that Russian clergy aided her in bringing out paintings and in storing them until the hostilities were over.[11] Irrespective of who helped her, it was Sophie's clear understanding of the value of her work that prompted her to mobilize support for the rescue mission. Sophie's paintings comprise an important part of her story; their survival was of critical importance to her identity as an artist. Without them it would also have been impossible to understand her life and her legacy.

During March, Palestinian militias continued to encourage Arab families to remain in their homes. Knowing that her work was safely stored strengthened Sophie's resolve to remain in Musrara. Throughout this difficult time Asia continued to work for the British, not leaving her post until her employers left the city. Slowly, neighboring families in Musrara sought refuge in less violent areas. Finally, in April, Sophie brought her ailing mother, Olga, to the safety of the Old City, leaving Asia in Musrara.

Sophie and her mother joined the swelling tide of Arabs who left violent neighborhoods in the New City, seeking refuge in the Old City. Like the Karmis, who went to stay with family in Damascus, and the Sakakinis, who settled temporarily in Cairo, Sophie and her mother hoped to return to their Jerusalem home in a short time. The Old City, less than a mile from Musrara, was familiar to Sophie and her mother. The Halaby Pharmacy, opened in 1907 by a cousin, Anton Halaby, and located near the Damascus Gate, was the fourth to be established in the Old City.[12] In recognition of their family's long service to the Russian Orthodox Church, Olga and Sophie were given space in a convent adjacent to the Alexander Nevsky Church, called "al-Moscobiya" by residents of the Old City.[13] Entering their temporary home each day brought them into contact with ornate icons and paintings, and living in a church facility named for a thirteenth-century Russian warrior prince reinforced their strong ties to the Orthodox community. The convent was a relatively comfortable place to wait for an end to the fighting in Jerusalem.

Sophie and Olga were joined in the Old City by the Canaan family and the Tleel family, their neighbors in Musrara. Like Sophie, Tawfik Canaan was prudent in safeguarding his artistic collection. Dr. Canaan deposited his folklore collection of amulets and icons with an international organization in West Jerusalem. His biographer, Khaled Nashef, didn't identify the organization, which was possibly the YMCA, as Dr. Canaan served there for many years as chairman of the board. Like the Halaby family, Dr. Canaan, his wife, Margot Eilender, his sister, Badra, and his sister-in-law, Nora, remained stoically in their home following the bombing of Musrara in February. Margot and Badra were founding members of the Arab Women's Committee. They were determined to remain in their home for as long as possible. All four of the Canaan children were out of harm's way, as they were studying abroad. Their resolve crumbled when a direct hit on the Canaan house on May 9 destroyed the third floor. The family, each carrying a small suitcase, left swiftly and entered the Old City in accord with arrangements made previously. Under cover of darkness, they entered through a small door that led to the roof of a Catholic convent. Once inside the relative safety of the Old City, they walked to the offices of the Greek Orthodox Church, which owned many buildings. Canaan, who was Lutheran, and his family were given shelter in a small room.[14]

Leila, one of the Canaan children, described her parents' life in the Old City: "Mother and father would go daily up to the top of the Wall of Jerusalem to look at their home. They witnessed it being ransacked, together with priceless library and manuscripts. . . . They saw Mother's Biedermeyer furniture being loaded into trucks and then their home being set on fire."[15] Canaan began to operate a clinic in their living quarters, but soon joined Dr. Ibrahim Tleel in the Austrian Hospice. The Tawfiq Canaan collection is housed today at the Birzeit University Museum.

The Tleel family had several homes in Musrara. Dr. Ibrahim Tleel lived adjacent to a small park on a street with no name. John Tleel, his nephew, lived with his family in a building adjacent to the wall of the Old City, near Notre Dame. He described the fighting in 1948: "Jews and Arabs fought each other. Israeli soldiers fired from the Notre Dame rooftop, the Arab Legion from the Old City walls. Our house was part of the battlefield. We abandoned its spacious rooms, the new and old equipment for the dental clinic, and the two long wooden balconies, one looking toward Suleiman Road and Notre Dame, the other toward the wall. My childhood and teenage days are buried under the new road, which the Israelis have landscaped just outside the New Gate."[16]

John Tleel was in Beirut during the spring of 1948, preparing to sit for his first-year dental examinations at the AUB, when his family became refugees. John's father and older brother, Daoud, told him their stories when he returned to Jerusalem. They explained that they had walked fifty feet through the New Gate to begin life in rooms provided by the Greek Orthodox Church in the Old City. Dr. Ibrahim Tleel had already abandoned his home and was busy tending to the wounded in the Old City. John's house was still accessible when the first truce took effect in June 1948. John's father and brother, both dentists, were determined to return home to retrieve additional dental instruments. His father obtained a permit from Abdullah el-Tal, the Arab military governor. Israeli soldiers patrolling outside the walls of the Old City gave him five minutes to leave their refuge and return. An Israeli soldier and John's friend, Khalil Jancho, managed to carry a heavy dental chair into the Old City. The Tleels were able to install it in an improvised space within Saint Nicholas Convent. A few days later, Daoud procured a permit from the UN Office in Jerusalem and was thus able to retrieve some of his easily portable equipment and some dental instruments. Margarita Gavrielides, a Greek neighbor, went with him. She managed to secure her sewing machine, her only means of livelihood.[17]

Dr. Canaan and Sophie Halaby were not the only ones who had looked for safe storage space in the months before the British left. Daoud had tried to protect his dental equipment by moving it from the clinic in the Tleel house to what he thought was a safer place, the nearby French convent of the Reparatrice Sisters, near the New Gate. These sisters, who were cloistered nuns, had been Daoud's patients. They kept many valuable things safe for many people at that time. However, part of the convent caught fire in the fighting and was destroyed; the dental equipment was lost in the blaze.[18]

Jewish militias continued to attack Arabs in southern and eastern neighborhoods of Jerusalem. They also razed Arab villages on the periphery of the city. On April 9, Deir Yassin residents were the victims of a massive attack. Hala Sakakini described the outcome: "Ever since the massacre at Deir Yassin we have been thinking seriously of leaving Jerusalem. . . . I never thought Jews could be so cruel, so barbarous, so brutal. Pregnant women and children were tortured to death; young women were stripped naked, humiliated and driven through Jewish quarters to be spit upon by crowds. . . . One day, perhaps very soon, we will be forced to leave our house. I don't like to think of it."[19]

Hind al-Husseini, a young friend of Sophie's and Asia's, had led a student demonstration during the Arab Revolt while enrolled at the Jerusalem Girls' College. She became a trained social worker and, like Sophie, had found temporary refuge in the Old City during the spring of 1948. Following the destruction of Deir Yassin, she encountered children who had fled the village wandering around the Old City in a state of great despair. Many had been orphaned by the attack. Hind was committed to saving them, finding a room for them in the convent of the Soeurs de Sion. In a matter of weeks, she organized a kindergarten, a school, a vocational training center, and a small farm all in a large property built by her grandfather in Sheikh Jarrah, outside the Old City. She called the project *Dar al-Tifl al-Arabi*, The Home of the Arab Child. Hind became the headmistress of the school, incorporating lessons she learned in the Jerusalem Girls' College. She eventually started a women's college affiliated with al-Quds University, which was then in development. She traveled to raise funds abroad to ensure the continuity of her school.[20]

A few days after the attack on Deir Yassin, as the residents of Jerusalem mourned the dead, the *Palestine Post* sought to refocus the narrative with an announcement titled, "Declaration of Independence." This piece ignored the plight of Arab villagers, emphasizing instead the pressing needs of European Jews languishing in displaced persons camps and excoriating the British for their failure to fulfill the Mandate. The declaration presented readers with an unrealistic vision of the future: a Jewish state that offered peace and friendship to Arab citizens:

> On May 15, His Majesty's Government will surrender to the United Nations the trust it received from the League of Nations 27 years ago and which it has failed to fulfill. . . . As a result our refugees were refused entry in the hour of their direst need. They were interned, instead, and condemned to lead a life of danger, humiliation, and homelessness. . . . And now the Mandatory is proposing to destroy the very foundation of our existence and leave the country in utter chaos. To prevent this, we have resolved this day that the termination of the Mandate in Palestine shall in fact mark the end of all foreign domination in this country. With the termination of the Mandate, the Government of the Jewish State shall come into being. In this hour, we turn to the Arab citizens of the Jewish State and our Arab neighbours. We offer peace and friendship. We desire to build our State in common with Arabs as equal citizens.[21]

Not surprisingly, the Jewish attack on Deir Yassin had a greater impact than the words of the declaration.

On May 14, 1948, the British lowered their flag over Government House for the last time. Asia Halaby, loyal to the end, walked to the King David Hotel that morning to say goodbye to her British coworkers and friends. The previous afternoon, in her third-floor office in the hotel, she had signed a supplementary expenditure warrant authorizing the Agricultural Department to hire two additional guards in the forest of Jenin. When she returned home she found a note from her brother, Nicola, urging her to join the family in the safety of the Old City. She packed up a few belongings, including her portable typewriter and a copy of George Antonius's book, *The Arab Awakening*, and walked into the Old City.[22] Asia had acquired first aid experience during her service in the ATS. She joined Drs. Tleel and Canaan in the Austrian Hospice on the Via Dolorosa, which served as an emergency clinic to care for the wounded. She was easily identified in the Old City as the nurse who wore a pair of scissors on a black ribbon around her neck. She needed scissors to cut off the soiled bandages of patients and, as they were in short supply, she took to keeping a pair close by her. It is possible that she also offered her services to the Arab Legion at this time; family lore credits Asia with being a major in the organization. She wore the keffiyeh, the checked headscarf, of the legion and drove a military jeep for years.[23]

Dividing Jerusalem

Israel declared its independence hours after the last British officials sailed from the new port in Haifa. Fighting in Jerusalem, which had been sporadic for months, now became persistent. On May 16, the Arab Legion, under the command of Glubb Pasha, a former British officer, entered the Old City. The Haganah (precursor of the Israel Defense Force) continued to fire artillery from outside the city and periodically succeeded in bringing small numbers of soldiers into the city. Fierce fighting continued until May 27, when the remaining residents of the Jewish Quarter surrendered, and the Old City was ceded to Arab control. Arabs who resided in the Old City as well as refugees from other parts of Jerusalem and surrounding villages scavenged for food and water, which were in short supply. The dying and wounded were everywhere.

The UN announced a four-week truce on June 11. At this point Israeli forces held most of the New City, and the Arab Legion held the Old City as well as some eastern parts of the New City. During this period thousands of noncombatants left the city. In the Old City, out of a population of sixty thousand plus ten thousand refugees, only about five thousand to seven thousand remained. Among those who stayed were the clerics of the different monasteries, patriarchates, and other religious establishments, as well as consular and municipal employees.[24] Fighting resumed briefly on July 10. A second lull in the fighting, ordered by the UN Security Council, took effect on July 17. On August 2, the Israeli government declared West Jerusalem "territory occupied by Israel" and appointed a military governor. It enacted absentee property regulations to confiscate Arab homes, lands, and businesses.[25] During August and early September the city remained quiet, though there were sporadic outbursts of heavy firing at night. On November 30, 1948, a little more than six months after the British left, Transjordan and Israel agreed to "an absolute and sincere cease-fire" in Jerusalem.[26]

At the end of the fighting, no Arab residents remained in seven neighborhoods of west Jerusalem—Baq`a', Katamon, Talbieh, Musrara, Mamilla, and the German and Greek colonies that had been populated by Arabs before the war. Nearly all the Arab villages to the west of the city—Romema, Lifta, Malha, Ein Karem, and Deir Yassin—were empty; residents had been expelled or fled in fear. The Old City, in contrast, was entirely Arab. Several of the gates that had been important during the Mandate—the Jaffa Gate, Zion Gate, and New Gate—were now sealed. Herod's Gate gained prominence. Saint Stephen's Gate and Dung Gate became accessible to cars, which began to circulate in the Old City for the first time. Damascus Gate was accessible but was frequently closed when Israeli snipers attacked.[27]

Within the Old City, refugee families struggled to obtain food and water. Relief programs were organized. A soup kitchen located in the Greek Orthodox St. Nicolas Monastery provided food for four hundred children. Milk was also distributed to children who lived nearby. Each of the religious communities took care of members who had found refuge in the Old City. The Franciscan Fathers placed the Casa Nova Hospice at the disposal of the Catholic community. The Armenian Church assisted the Armenian community. The Coptic and Syriac monasteries opened their doors to refugees from their communities. The Lutheran Church distributed sacks of used clothing widely; most of it came from the United States. The International Red Cross and the United Nations joined the relief effort. In St. Nicholas, the Tleels set up a makeshift dental clinic without electricity. John Tleel was forced to use an old pedal-drilling machine when he returned from Beirut to join his father in the clinic.[28]

The Arab Legion remained in military control of the Old City and its eastern suburbs. Palestinian notables, meeting in Amman on October 1, 1948, asked King Abdullah of Transjordan, the Arab leader who had fought for their cause, to place Palestine under his protection. In November, Abdullah was ceremonially crowned king of Jerusalem by the Coptic bishop of the city. A few weeks later, at a conference of Arab notables from Palestine who were meeting in Jericho, Abdullah was declared king of Palestine. These men, now identifying exclusively as Palestinian, were distraught over the humiliating

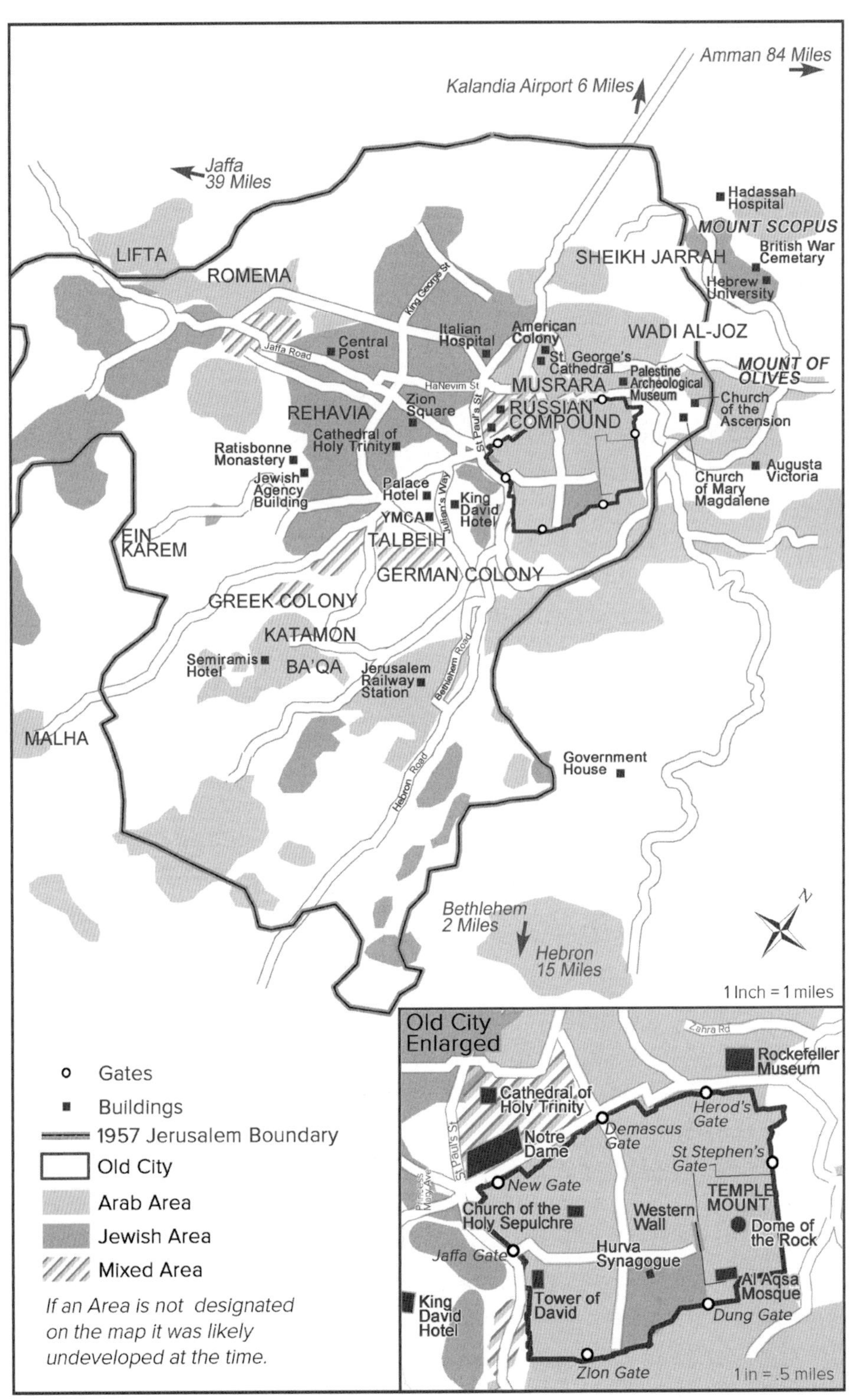

Map 1. Jerusalem during the British Mandate. Chelsea Gross, cartographer.

defeat of the Arabs on the battlefield. They began to call the war, which had destroyed Arab villages and urban neighborhoods and forced hundreds of thousands to become refugees, Nakba, meaning "catastrophe." They asked King Abdullah, their only proven ally in the Arab world, to aid them in their call for a unification of the two banks of the Jordan River.

In New York, the future of Jerusalem continued to be a cause of deep concern to the General Assembly of the UN. On December 11, 1948, the UN adopted Resolution 194, which reaffirmed the intent of the UN to establish an international regime for the city. A Conciliation Commission was appointed to present a detailed proposal for governing Jerusalem, one that would provide for maximum local autonomy for distinctive groups consistent with the special international status of the Jerusalem area. Resolution 194 called on Israel to permit Arab refugees who wished to return to their homes and live at peace with their neighbors to go home and called for compensation to be paid to those who chose not to return.[29] Israel, faced with absorbing thousands of destitute Jewish immigrants, did not reply to Resolution 194.

In like manner, King Abdullah ignored the UN resolutions and incorporated the West Bank of the Jordan River, which had been part of Palestine, into Transjordan, which had been independent since 1946. The new country was called "The Hashemite Kingdom of Jordan." King Abdullah appointed four Palestinian ministers to his government. Elections for the National Assembly in April 1950 guaranteed an equal number of Palestinian (West Bank) and formerly Transjordanian (East Bank) representatives.[30] On April 24, 1950, the National Assembly in Amman adopted a resolution confirming the unification of Palestine and Jordan into one state. The League of Arab States, unwilling to give up the idea of an independent Palestine, resolved that the territories occupied by the Jordanian Army in Palestine were to be held in trust for the people of Palestine.

Palestinian families like that of ten-year-old Hanan Ashrawi, who became a political activist and professor of English at Birzeit University, quietly protested the eradication of their national identity. Ashrawi remembered: "The word 'Palestine' was then taboo. I remember my father telling us that we were Palestinians, not Jordanians, but cautioning us against saying it out loud. It was safe to whisper the word at home and to listen to Sawt al-Arab (the Voice of the Arabs) radio station broadcasting from Gamal Abdel Nasser's Egypt, provided the volume was low and the windows were closed."[31]

Israeli leaders moved quickly to proclaim West Jerusalem, a term that came into existence with the Armistice Agreement of 1949,[32] Israel's capital. Government offices, which had been located in Tel Aviv, were moved to the new capital. In 1950, Israel enacted the Law of Return, granting every Jew in the world potential citizenship on arrival in Israel. Thousands began to arrive from displaced persons camps in Europe and soon from Arab countries where they had lived for generations, but where they no longer felt safe. Sophie knew very little about these developments, as there was no communication between East and West Jerusalem. The *Palestine Post*, which had been a source of information throughout the Mandate, had become the *Jerusalem Post* and was not for sale in East Jerusalem.

The division of Jerusalem greatly affected the Christian residents of the city. Nearly half of those now living in Jordanian Jerusalem, like Sophie and her family, had lived in the New City and had left homes and property behind. They had found refuge in the monasteries and church institutions of the Old City.[33] Many, like John Tleel, understood that there was, as yet, no going back to Musrara or Katamon. He tried to make the best of his new situation in the Old City. He was a young man in his twenties when Jerusalem was divided. He described his feelings about living in a completely Arab city: "We started gradually building a new Jerusalem, a Jerusalem completely ours. A Jerusalem that almost surpassed in beauty and style the one that was only a few paces away . . . the pious pilgrims who visited it lived a more biblical and holy Jerusalem then. It was a city for prayers, with little cosmopolitan outlook. Walking in the clean streets and climbing the steep, narrow alleys one could strongly feel the presence of holiness."[34]

Despite his hopeful rhetoric, Tleel lamented that East Jerusalem, including the Old City, was "a city at a dead end." Jordanian Jerusalem and the rest of the West Bank stagnated economically throughout the 1950s, leading to large-scale Christian emigration, reducing the Christian population from 29,350 in 1944 to 10,982 in 1964.[35] Tleel noted the sharp contrast between the beautiful sixteenth-century wall of the Old City and the ugly twentieth-century wall of barbed wire and concrete blocks, a result of the war of 1948.[36] Tleel was somewhat reassured by the proximity of the Kalandia Airport. This airport, built by the British, just north of East Jerusalem, was now part of Jordan. From there one could fly to Europe and to other Arab capitals. It was also possible to travel by car to all the Middle East and Europe.[37]

Sophie was able to remain in Jerusalem, but many other Palestinian artists were not. Jabra Ibrahim Jabra left for Baghdad, where he founded the Baghdad Group for Modern Art with Iraqi artist Jawad Salim. He wrote art criticism, translated art books from English into Arabic, and also published novels, short stories, and poems. Ismail Shammout, a teenager in 1948, dedicated his work to documenting the Nakba. He lived in a refugee camp in Gaza and later moved to Cairo, Rome, and Beirut. His work captured the life of Palestinians in exile longing for home. Salim Tamari noted that Shammout's work focused on the theme of "Paradise Lost" and on idyllic peasant landscapes.[38] Zulfa al-Sa'idi fled to Damascus, where she became a teacher in a refugee camp and stopped painting. Faten Nastas Mitwasi explained that exiled artists often painted from memories and from stories of the homeland; for them, the homeland was an idea.[39] Sophie was not part of this group; her homeland was all around her. Her art remained independent of the ideology and its attendant aesthetic that were created in the diaspora.

Sophie remained in her temporary home in the Old City during the first half of 1949 while a series of armistice agreements were signed individually between Israel and Egypt, Lebanon, Jordan, and Syria. Iraq did not sign an armistice, as it had no border with Israel. With the fighting ended and no prospect of returning to their home in Musrara, the Halaby sisters prepared to put down new roots. Their brother, Nicola, was a civil engineer who had worked on the Palestine Archaeological Museum in the 1930s. Perhaps it was then that he identified an excellent spot for a new home on Nur al-Din Street, on high land near the museum. Temporarily living in Beirut, Nicola planned the three-story stone house with a large garden and its own well. Nicola did not return to live in Jerusalem. He became a partner in a successful construction company founded by Lebanese entrepreneur Emile Bustani and spent several years in Kuwait supervising projects.[40]

The top story of the new house was designed as a studio for Sophie. From here she would be able to look out over the hills of her beloved city and paint. With the new house under construction and her paintings safely stored, Sophie decided to return to Paris for a few weeks of study. This time, she traveled with her sister, Asia. They could not sail from the ports of Jaffa or Haifa, both now in enemy territory. They may have taken advantage of a flight from the Kalandia Airport to Cairo, but it is more likely that the first part of their journey was completed by car, followed by a ship from Cairo or Alexandria to a port in Italy, and from there by train to Paris. While many refugees in the Old City had no passports, Sophie and Asia, who would later become Jordanian citizens, traveled with Palestinian passports that had been issued by the Mandatory government.[41]

Sophie and Asia registered at the Foyer International des Etudiantes on September 6, 1949, and lived together in room 316 for one week. The Foyer was across the street from the Luxembourg Gardens and near many of the city's famous landmarks. It is likely that Sophie took Asia on a tour of the city, perhaps showing her the studios where she had studied and introducing her to friends. Sophie remained alone at the Foyer for six weeks, while Asia may have continued on to London, where she could have visited former Jerusalem Girls' College teachers. It is reasonable to assume that both sisters wanted relief from the crowded conditions in the Old City. Sophie's stay in Paris was an opportunity for her to review the work in the galleries and museums that she hadn't seen since she left Paris in 1933. Like Mary Cassatt, Elizabeth Nourse, Paula Modersohn-Becker, and countless others who returned to Paris to continue their art studies, Sophie felt connected to the city because of its artistic culture. She went to galleries and museums in Paris to look at the work of favorite artists, still seeking to learn from them.

Sophie may have traveled through Italy on her way back to Jerusalem.[42] Not long after she returned to Jerusalem, she moved with Asia and their mother, Olga, into their new home. It was less grand than the Halaby home in Musrara, which had been located on Baldwin Street (now Elisha), named for the Crusader King Baldwin III of Jerusalem. The new house, however, was spacious and comfortable. Unlike their previous homes in Kiev and in West Jerusalem, they would never be forced to flee the house on Nur al-Din Street, named for a twelfth-century Turkic ruler of Aleppo who fought the Crusaders, including King Baldwin.

Life on Nur al-Din Street

Like John Tleel, Sophie was disappointed by the division of their city into East and West, with the more dynamic half of the city in the newly declared State of Israel. For Sophie, the division marked the end of her freedom to borrow books from the YMCA and to attend concerts and lectures in its beautiful auditorium. The fashionable shops on Ben Yehuda Street were no longer accessible. The art galleries where she could see the work of contemporary Jewish and British artists and read about them in articles in the *Palestine Post* were also no longer available.[43] Jerusalem had been the capital of Palestine during the Mandate. Its population had included a host of foreign diplomats and many British civil servants. These men and their educated wives added to the vibrancy of the city, which also included many tourists from all over the world. East Jerusalem, in contrast, was not a capital city; Amman remained the capital of Jordan. Some Palestinians left East Jerusalem to live and work in Amman; others went to work in Kuwait; still others left for Europe or the United States.

Anna Grace Vester, who grew up at the American Colony in East Jerusalem, described the changes Sophie experienced:

> Jerusalem in Jordan was very different from Jerusalem in Mandatory Palestine. Then, there had been a large British community and a distinct flavor of the British Raj, with tennis parties and picnics, dinner and dancing at the King David Hotel (now in West Jerusalem) with the numerous army and police officers. It was a city facing both east and west. Now, it faced east. Amman was the capital of Jordan, housing the government and the ministries and big businesses. The commercial side of Jerusalem had always developed to the west and, apart from two streets of modern shops, was virtually non-existent in East Jerusalem. There were serious water problems with the cutting in half of the water system, periodic times of crisis when water had to be brought in by tankers. As things got sorted out by degrees, East Jerusalem settled down into a quiet little town, but still a major tourist attraction, since it contained the whole of the Old City and its holy places and had easy access across the Jordan to the wonders of Petra and Damascus.[44]

Sophie and Asia settled into their new home, located near the Palestine Archaeological Museum, which would become a focus of their social lives. Olga moved into an apartment designed for her by Nicola within the new house. Sophie retrieved her paintings, canvas, paints, and brushes and installed them in her studio on the top floor. She spent most of her time at her easel, permitting very few guests to visit her private space. The lower level of the house, in contrast, teemed with women. It was used by Asia as a sewing workshop for destitute refugees, whom she taught to do traditional embroidery, enabling them to sell their work and provide themselves with an income so they could remain in the city. Not long after they moved into the new house, on December 31, 1952, Olga Halaby died. She was buried in the family plot of the Mary Magdalene churchyard on the Mount of Olives, next to her husband.[45]

Sophie and Asia slowly replaced the furniture and household necessities they had left behind in Musrara. They lived comfortably, surrounded by mother-of-pearl chests, a brass samovar, and Damascene vases. The floors were covered with Oriental rugs. A traditional Russian stove provided warmth in winter.[46]

The two sisters, so different in temperament, lived together in harmony for the rest of their lives in their well-appointed house. They celebrated holidays, prepared traditional foods, and spoke to each other in Russian. Two years after Olga's death, the Halaby children presented a silver icon of St. Vladimir, the patron saint of Kiev, to the Church of the Ascension in memory of their parents. Together they attended annual church services on St. Vladimir's Day, when their icon was venerated. Anya Berezina Derrick, then a young Russian refugee, observed approvingly that Sophie always visited her parents' graves on the appropriate days according to the Orthodox calendar.[47]

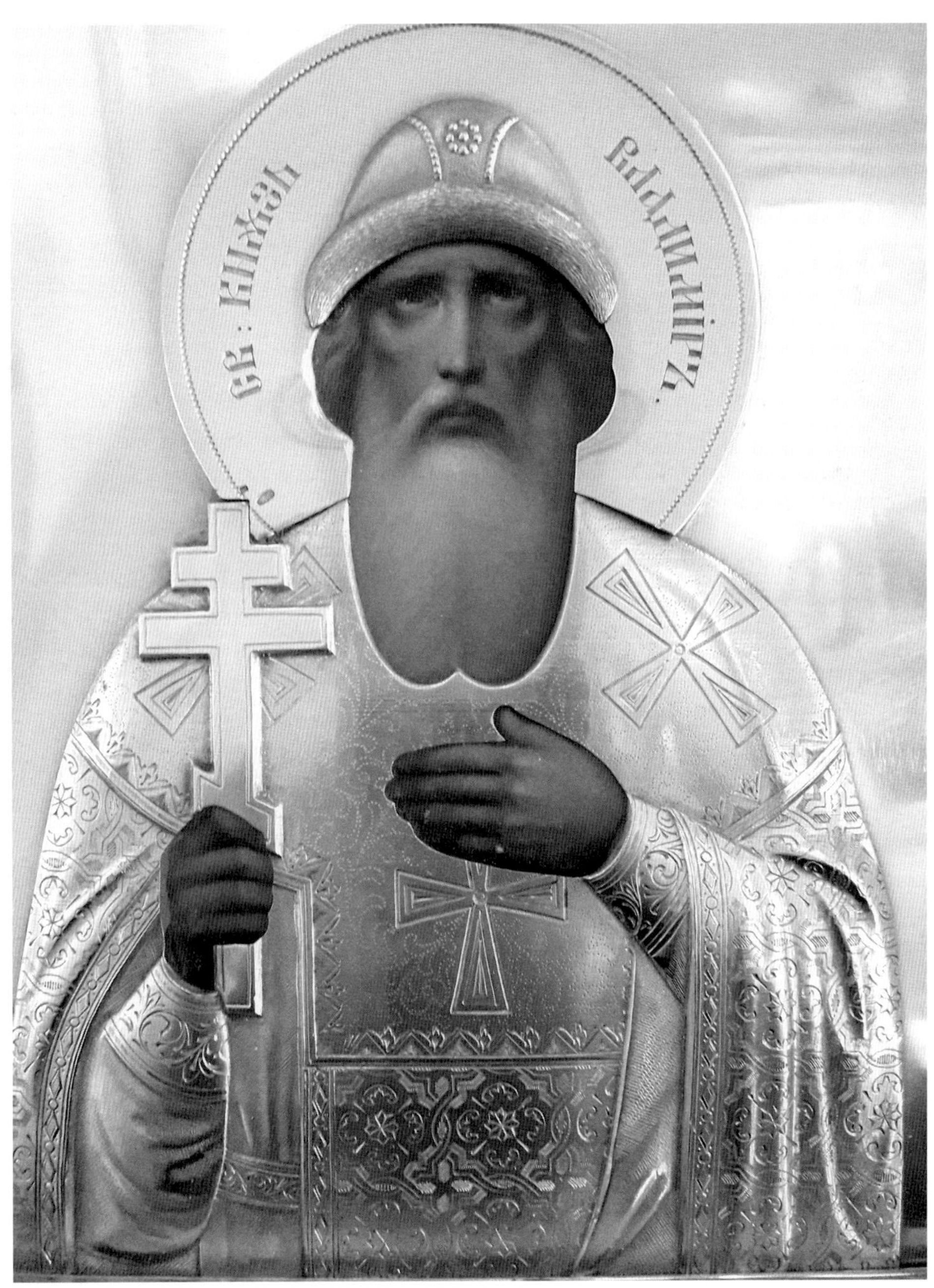

11. St. Vladimir icon. Russian ecclesiastical mission in Jerusalem, Russian Orthodox Church Outside of Russia.

Sophie's continuing connection to the church is remembered by Sisters Veronica and Tamara, both Arab orphans who lived and studied in the monastery of the Church of the Ascension. Sophie befriended the eighteen-year-old Tamara and eight-year-old Veronica; both ultimately became nuns. Beginning in 1957, they regularly visited the Halaby home, coming to celebrate Sophie's and Asia's name days. Veronica was accorded the rare privilege of being invited to Sophie's studio. She remembered looking at the paintings and listening to Sophie's stories about her childhood in Kiev. Sophie showed the youngster the family photograph album containing photos of herself as a little girl. Veronica and Tamara continued to visit Sophie and Asia for decades. Sophie also became especially close to Mother Superior Paraskeva, who arrived in Jerusalem in 1971. The mother superior was close in age to Sophie, having been born in Warsaw one year before Sophie's birth in Kiev. She died in Jerusalem two years before Sophie's death.

Samia Halaby offered a different view of her cousins' Christianity. She cited a neighbor, Randa Atalla, who lived nearby until 1967. Atalla, who was also related to the Halaby family, remembered that the sisters did not attend Sunday morning services and that Asia referred to those services as *kalam fadi*, or "empty words." While Asia's dismissive remarks about the religious service reflect her feisty personality, they don't capture the full picture of Sophie and Asia's relationship to the church. The two women were identified in Jerusalem as "the Russian ladies," and they remained culturally and socially affiliated with the Russian Orthodox Church and its community throughout their long lives. It was the church that gave them shelter in 1948 and possibly aided Sophie in protecting her paintings. It was the church that housed the burial plots of the Halaby family and of their closest relatives, the Wahbe family. In 1967, Asia brought bolts of expensive linen fabric purchased for the embroidery workshop to the church for safekeeping. It was the church that Sophie and Asia entrusted with their funds to create a home for the aged. Sophie also demonstrated her ties to the Russian Orthodox Church through her devotion to Mother Paraskeva by paying for her medical expenses at the end of her life.[48]

Sophie was never alone when she was at home, as Asia was always nearby. They met during the day to have meals or to take tea, often just the two of them, sometimes inviting friends and family. Neither sister was an accomplished cook. They frequently ordered food for their dinner from a nearby restaurant. Sometimes the Wahbe aunts would bring them food from Beit Jala. The sisters continued to use their childhood language, Russian, when they were alone. When friends came, they spoke English, the language they had studied in the Jerusalem Girls' College. Sophie developed an eccentric hobby more commonly found among Englishwomen than among Jerusalemites: she lavished affection on a pet cat, which was trained to eat at the table and was sometimes dressed up. She named it "Omdurman," after the site of a battle in the Sudan where British General George Kitchener defeated the revolt of the Mahdi in 1898.[49]

The sisters rented a storefront on neighboring Zahra Street from which they sold the embroidered tablecloths, napkins, sheets, and pillowcases made by the refugees that Asia taught. Rosemary Sayigh credited Sophie and Asia with "rescuing Palestinian peasants' designs in their Jerusalem workshop."[50] Sophie placed a new watercolor painting in the shop window each week. Kamal Boullata and his young artist friends, Sari Khoury and Vladimir Tamari, always stopped to look at her work, which left a deep impression on them. Boullata reflected, "Her watercolour landscapes in particular were an inspiration to each of us before we went to any art school."[51]

The 1950s were a time of transition for Arab Jerusalemites. Some of the men were appointed to government positions in Amman and tried to serve their people through political leadership. Educated and affluent women like Sophie and Asia tried to help their community, as they had been encouraged to do in the Jerusalem Girls' College. Rosemary Sayigh visited the Halaby sisters at this time. She described them as part of a group of women leaders, or *shakhsiya*, who came from "known" (property-owning) families.[52] They were concerned about those who experienced difficult times and lost their homes and land as a result of the division of the city. They were Palestinian nationalists, but they did not belong to political groups.

Asia's embroidery workshop grew. She taught hundreds of women to do traditional cross-stitch embroidery using high quality linen that she imported from Aden and silk thread from France. The resulting tablecloths, napkins, bookmarks, and samplers were sold worldwide through friends in the United States and the Middle East. Consular officials stationed in East Jerusalem were steady customers. Asia's shop, the Arab Refugee Handicrafts Centre, became a favorite place for tourists looking for gifts to bring home to Europe or the United States.[53] For a time, Asia went into partnership with Hanneh Majaj, a former classmate from the Jerusalem Girls' College who, like Asia, had completed a diploma in education. Hanneh's mother, Bahia Majaj, who had been active in the YWCA before 1948, was instrumental in reestablishing the organization on the Jordanian side of the city. Hanneh and Asia offered cross-stitch embroidery classes there to encourage refugee women to become self-reliant.[54]

Sophie also contributed to the activities of the YWCA. During the 1950s, she attended cultural and educational events there with her sister. When needed, Sophie and Asia offered the use of their mother's apartment, now vacant, to visiting leaders of the organization. Sophie sometimes exhibited her paintings at the YWCA. Doris Salah, the director, remembered that the very private Sophie showed her works, offering Palestinian women something beautiful in a time of despair.[55] Sporting a tweed jacket and skirt, wearing a big brooch on her lapel and rings on her fingers, Sophie presented a modern European style to the quiet city.[56] Her commitment to the women of Jerusalem is evident in the rare donation of a large watercolor, an arrangement of wild and cultivated flowers in a vase of glazed pottery, to the YWCA. The painting hung in a place of honor over the piano in the grand reception room for many years.[57] Rima, Doris's younger sister, remembered that Sophie was a short, fair-skinned Russian who wore conservative clothing and her hair in a bun. She also noticed that beneath the severe exterior there was a passionate spirit. Sophie had a sense of humor. She spoke English to the young Rima, encouraging her to continue her studies.[58]

In 1959, the elderly Miss Warburton visited Jerusalem for the last time. The photograph of the diminutive headmistress, wearing a black hat, standing in the center of her former pupils, provides a rare look at the continuing influence of the Jerusalem Girls' College on its graduates, so many of whom became leading figures in Palestine. To Warburton's right sits the white-haired Nabiha Nasir, founder of Birzeit High School (later, Birzeit University). Seated in the front row, at the far right is Olga Wahbe, teacher of generations of Palestinian teachers. Next to her is Sophie Halaby, wearing glasses. Standing behind Sophie, with her face in profile, is Asia Halaby. In the back row, near the center, wearing a white blouse, is Hind al-Husseini. These women gathered to pay tribute to their headmistress. She had believed in them and helped them find ways to live meaningful lives. The value of their education can be seen in the leadership roles they played in Jerusalem and elsewhere in Palestine. Their continuing use of English whenever they were together is another example of the influence of the education they received at the Jerusalem Girls' College.[59]

Sophie and Asia remained single throughout their long lives. If they ever had romantic relationships, they are not part of the historical record. It is likely that they would have agreed with the poet Fadwa Tuqan that marriage was unnecessary for women who had proved themselves and established a place in society. Tuqan scolded a friend who lamented that she had married a man with whom she had no rapport: "To begin with, you should never

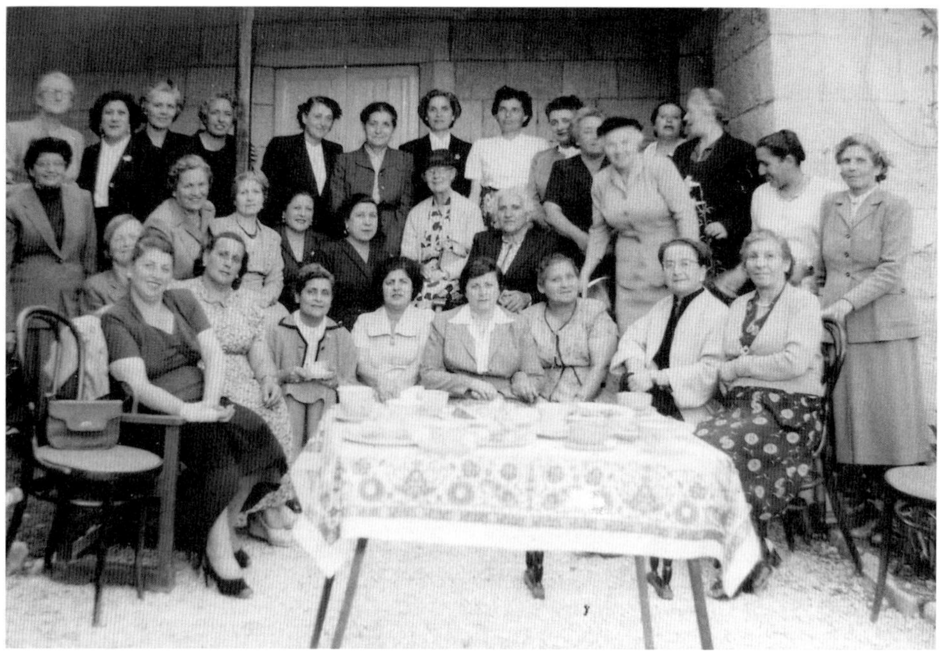

12. Mabel Warburton and alumnae of Jerusalem Girls' College, ca. 1959. Courtesy of Teddy and Nadia Theodorie.

have accepted such an incompatible husband." The friend explained that she feared being a spinster. Tuqan, who remained single, rejoined: "The spinster complex arises only for ordinary girls. What ordinary people say about being single does not apply to one with a strong personality who is socially and economically independent, freed from feelings of subordination, weakness and submission."[60]

Tuqan's views about marriage are reflected in the choices made by the many graduates of the Jerusalem Girls' College who remained single.[61] In this, they followed in the footsteps of their teachers at the JGC, most of whom were also single. Sophie and Asia followed this path, as did their cousins, the Wahbe sisters, three of whom did not marry. The Sakakini sisters also remained single. Like the Halaby sisters and the Wahbe sisters, they lived together throughout their lives. In this period of gradually changing gender roles, it's possible that these educated women found a shortage of educated men to marry.

Sophia and Asia had begun their working lives in Mandatory Jerusalem, where the authorities were Christian. Now, they were citizens of Jordan, where the authorities were Muslim. When Sophie and Asia worked for the British, Sunday was the weekly holiday for all workers. Under Jordanian rule, Friday was the day when work ceased. Christians were allowed to come to work at 10:00 a.m. on Sunday in deference to their holy day. Likewise, Christians were permitted to absent themselves from work on their religious holidays. Despite these accommodations, new laws were enacted restricting the activities of Christian charitable associations and their purchase of land.[62]

Sophie and Asia enjoyed their lives in Jordanian Jerusalem despite these new conditions. The sisters lived well in their comfortable home, supported by an inheritance of landed property in East Jerusalem, Bethlehem, and Amman that allowed them to maintain their upper-class status. Asia drove expensive British cars, usually a Vauxhall or an Aston. The sisters frequently ventured to nearby villages, where they would buy fresh fruit and vegetables. They also collected embroidered dresses, each representing a different village. George al-Ama, an important collector, thought that they had amassed one of the finest collections of embroidered dresses in Palestine. They also bought mother-of-pearl-inlaid furniture, ornate tableware, and cutlery. Their home became a model for Jerusalem-style gracious living.[63]

Many Palestinian Jerusalemites were comfortable under Jordanian rule. Betty Majaj, a nurse who came to Jerusalem from Lebanon in 1948 with her husband, Dr. Amin Majaj, noted that those days were the best days of her life: "There was stability and security. People could leave their cars unlocked, day or night, and their house doors too. If there were robberies, the culprits were usually quickly caught."[64]

Following their mother's death, Sophie and Asia were alone in Jerusalem. Nicola left in 1948 and never returned to live in the city. Though Sophie and Asia were independent women, they doubtless felt the loss of their brother. The culture of Jerusalem was deeply patriarchal. Nicola had assumed the role of head of the family after the death of George Halaby. Looking for opportunities for employment, he took up residence in Beirut. With their brother living in Beirut and later working in Kuwait, Sophie and Asia found other ways to get practical help and advice, hiring a bookkeeper to handle their business records, including the sale of Sophie's paintings and the receipts from Asia's embroidery business.[65] The sisters had also accepted advice from their cousin Hana Halaby in Amman about renting their property in his city. Hana and other family members aided Asia Halaby in selling the embroidery produced in her workshop.

In 1960, Nicola married the widow of their cousin, Bandali Halaby. This action led Sophie and Asia to permanently break with their brother. Beatrice Habesch, who inherited a printing company from her father, remembered an order she received from Sophie and Asia to print an official announcement declaring that the sisters would have no further communication with their brother following his marriage.[66] Nicola, in a letter to their Aunt Vera, stated: "Vera [his wife] and I have settled now in our flat in Beirut. I am very happy with her. She is a very good wife and we are happy together. Unfortunately, as you no doubt know, my sisters do not approve of my wife nor of my marriage and are doing their utmost to make us unhappy. They will not succeed. I am only sorry for them and pity them and their attitude to life and people. I do not know what to do with them and how to prevent them from making themselves unnecessarily miserable."[67]

Nicola's wife was pregnant at the time of the marriage and soon gave birth to a son, Rurik. Sophie and Asia may have believed that Rurik was Nicola's illegitimate son. Now middle-aged and fearful of unscrupulous men, the sisters were also fearful that Nicola would abandon them once he married, and thus preemptively severed contact with their brother.[68] Following the Israeli occupation, they worried about their land in Bethlehem, as it was undeveloped and hence was vulnerable to seizure by Israeli authorities. Ultimately, they lost that land to the mayor of Bethlehem, who promised to build an Orthodox home for the elderly but instead took the money for personal gain. Several years later, feeling more alone as Asia succumbed to dementia, Sophie hired Issa Hamed, a lawyer, to protect her property. This decision was costly, as he stole her remaining property and funds.[69] While it is not clear that Nicola's presence would have prevented these calamities, it is probable that Sophie felt his absence as a betrayal.

Sophie's Art

Sophie continued to work in her studio on the top floor of the house that she shared with Asia. She filled the room with various objects, which she drew and painted. Particularly, Sophie surrounded herself with flowers—in her garden, in her home, and in her paintings. She often left the studio to gather wild black irises, her favorite flower according to her friend Ada Kalbian,[70] along with red poppies and pink cyclamens, which grew on the hills outside Jerusalem. She also cultivated a flower garden that included roses, tulips, and dahlias. She brought them inside, arranged them, and painted them. Lydia Atalla, who was a florist and a friend, frequently brought Sophie additional fresh flowers.[71] Kamal Boullata explained: "She painted and repainted each arrangement, as if she were trying to furtively capture the scent of the season outside and in the process bring indoors her home landscape."[72]

Sophie's many depictions of flowers, in watercolor and oil, are different from the work of amateurs like Bertha Spafford Vester. The influence of French artists on her flowers is evident. One of Sophie's paintings of a vase of flowers sitting on a table next to a sculpture of a bust resembles one by Odilon Redon that she might have seen in Paris. The flowers of Jerusalem clearly represented something important to her. Perhaps the predictability of the seasonal blooming of the flowers, in contrast to the constant political change that marked her life, comforted Sophie, or it may have been that the sheer beauty of the brilliant colors in the sunlight that she captured on canvas created optimism and joy in the face of the bleak political reality. Whatever her motivation, her studio became her sanctuary. She surrounded herself with sketches and finished paintings that covered the walls and were propped on tabletops. Sophie's personal vision of Jerusalem imbued her studio. When she was certain that the painting was finished, she signed her name and sometimes added "Jerusalem."

Sophie began to paint flowers on cards in the mid-1930s and continued this practice for decades. The cards were a way for her to share the beauty of Jerusalem flowers with those who couldn't afford to buy her flower paintings. Asia often included a post card with each of the embroidery orders she delivered, perhaps seeking to establish a wider audience for her sister's work. In the 1950s and 1960s, the cards were sold as souvenirs to tourists and to Jerusalemites who used them as Christmas cards and to decorate their homes. Dr. John Tleel, who became Sophie's dentist, kept a collection of six cards in his home in the Old City until his death. The Kalbians, neighbors and friends in Jerusalem, brought a set of six cards with them to the United States when they emigrated. They framed the cards, displaying them in their new home, along with three of Sophie's paintings as well as several embroidered items from Asia's workshop. These items are poignant reminders of the city they left. Widad Kawar has a collection of Sophie's painted postcards in Amman.[73]

The wildflowers of Jerusalem and the surrounding villages had special meaning in Palestinian culture. Many Jerusalemites pressed flowers and included them as a remembrance of the Holy City in letters abroad. Hanan Ashrawi recalled that her parents showed her and her sisters how to pick wildflowers without damaging their roots, taught them which ones had medicinal properties, and recited stories from Palestinian folklore about wild tulips, violets, anemones, lilies, and shepherd's staff.[74]

Bertha Spafford Vester, who became a friend of the Halaby sisters, was one of many amateur artists who also painted wildflowers. Vester published a collection of thirty reproductions of her watercolors, *Flowers of the Holy Land*, in 1962. Her book contained a note by Lord Allenby, written decades earlier when he saw a collection of her watercolors: "I have had, more than once, the good fortune to see the Miracle of Spring in Palestine. . . . Those who have not yet seen that gorgeous display will be irresistibly lured to the hills and valleys where such wonders exist; and this book will enable them easily to identify each bloom."[75]

Allenby wasn't the only British visitor to enthuse about the flowers of Palestine. Hilda Ridler, who was employed in Jerusalem as an educational supervisor for many years and who was remembered by Melia Sakakini for her colonialist behavior, described the wild flowers of Palestine with great enthusiasm to a British audience in 1949:

> Never, except in the Swiss Alps, have I seen their equal. In Spring the whole country is like a vast rock garden, sheets of blue lupins and iris clothe the hillside; cyclamens and anemones and scarlet tulips spring up everywhere; tiny scented stocks, tall yellow daisies, hollyhocks, honeysuckle, rock roses, gladioli, and all kinds of orchids, make a glorious pattern of scent and colour . . . although coloured anemones of every hue are found throughout the country, only the scarlet type blossoms in or near Jerusalem. Tradition has it that this is in memory of the Crucifixion of Our Lord, the blood that poured from His side.[76]

American Consul General Evan Wilson wrote about spring flowers against the rocky background as a "sight never to be forgotten." His memoir mentioned white or pink cyclamen sprouting from every crevice. Scarlet anemones in great abundance appeared, followed by tulips, poppies, ranunculus, and countless varieties of "enchanting small orchids." Later, black iris and brilliant blue lupin emerged on the higher slopes around the city. As summer approached, golden daisies filled the fields, their color dotted by tiny phlox.[77]

Sophie also created landscapes of Jerusalem drawn from what she could see from her studio windows or from her rooftop, where she sometimes set up her easel. In these paintings, the artist's identification with the land is clear, according to Kamal Boullata. The Mount of Olives, visible from her studio, was a subject that she returned to repeatedly. Boullata compared her focus on the Mount with that of Cezanne's focus on Mont Sainte-Victoire. He explained:

> The first thing that strikes the viewer familiar with the site is how Halaby depicted it as if it were a virgin stretch of land denuded of its historic

> buildings. Though it is the Mount where two major Russian monuments were erected in the nineteenth century, the hilly ridge with its gentle horizon appears almost bare save for hints of scattered olive trees and some humble dwelling. Always painted from distant panoramic angles and from a number of approaches in variable seasons and under changing skies, the Mount is recognized in some of her paintings only by her suggestion of the mosque and belfry of the Ascension Church of the Russian Convent that crowns the summit of the rounded knoll in the ridge. The rest is merely intimated with stenographic brevity where the eye is left to complete the forms.[78]

Boullata continued his creative assessment of her landscapes by noting that her originality can be observed by studying the way she identified with the hilly ridge that was her primary subject. Halaby's identification with her Mount comes to light as the swelling bareness of the landscape becomes synonymous with the naked body. The undulating hills, washed with rose tints and earthy dots and shades, assume the nuances of skin, with its freckles and birthmarks, just as the brush strokes suggestion of distant trees or scattered bushes resemble the curls of body hair.[79]

Many of the landscapes that Halaby repeatedly painted were left unsigned, giving the impression, in Boullata's view, that "the paintings are unfinished, that she could not fully express her inner world." Whatever the reason, Sophie continued to paint, often taking her easel and watercolors outdoors to paint "en plein air" as she had learned to do in Paris. Sometimes she went up to the roof of her home and painted there. The scene of the Old City below could be viewed from that vantage point.

Sophie thought of herself as a professional artist, a position that was not as highly regarded in Jerusalem then as now.[80] She continued to use painting supplies imported from Paris—canvases, paints, and brushes were ordered and delivered to her studio. She sketched many versions of still-life arrangements, flowers, and landscapes before settling on a final version to be painted and repainted.

In the 1960s, Sophie's work was occasionally interrupted by visits of family members from nearby Amman and from the United States. In 1965, cousins, twin sisters from America, came to visit and asked Sophie to give them each a painting. Sophie explained that she was a professional artist and would have to charge them a nominal amount, five dollars for each painting. Nelly Barrett and Lily Porter bought the paintings and later inherited two additional paintings from their parents.[81] The following year, Samia Halaby, another American-based cousin and today a noted artist, arrived for a visit.

Sophie was not keen to show her studio to the younger artist and decades later refused Samia's offer of help to organize her work using acid free portfolios and slip-sheets.[82]

Dr. Hana Halaby, in charge of a military hospital near Ramallah, visited Jerusalem in 1967. He asked Sophie if he could buy one of her paintings, of which he was particularly fond. Sophie demurred, saying that she had promised it to a prospective buyer, but if it was not sold she promised to give it to Hana. He never received the painting.[83] Suheil Halaby, another cousin, visited and asked Sophie if he could see her paintings. At first, Sophie refused. Not one to be deterred, Suheil returned several times, each time bringing a box of chocolates, until finally Sophie agreed to show him her works.[84] Issa Halaby, a young cousin, attended boarding school in Jerusalem in the mid-1960s. He arrived in Sophie's home with his father, Raouf. All of the family in Amman helped Asia to sell embroidery that supported Palestinian refugees. Though Sophie was grateful for the support they provided to her sister's project, she apparently was especially fond of Raouf, as he was the only relative from Amman to whom she gave a painting.[85]

Clearly, Sophie enjoyed the solitude of her studio, as did Fadwa Tuqan, who described going into her safe refuge to be alone with her books, giving her a chance to read and meditate and producing a sense of security. Tuqan concluded: "I enjoyed my own company and could only find it by isolating myself."[86] Boullata wrote that he often wished he could see Sophie at work, but that he never visited her studio. He explained: "With her reserved nature, I was too shy to even attempt to approach her or to speak with her even after I saw her once from a distance standing for a little while before a set of my own watercolors that was displayed in a group exhibition at the Arab Orthodox Club in Jerusalem."[87]

Asia and Archaeology

In contrast to her sister's need for privacy when she worked, Asia enjoyed working with people. Following her service in the Arab Legion during the 1948 war, Asia was hired by the Jordanian government to supervise arrivals and departures at the Kalandia Imperial Airport (later Atarot Airport, now closed) in Jerusalem. Daniel Newberry, an American assigned as vice consul to Jerusalem, landed there in 1949 and was confronted by Asia, who examined Newberry's passport and determined that his duties were in West Jerusalem. She initiated the following exchange in English, as described by Newberry: "'Mr. Newberry, you can not land here!' I said, 'Where can I land? I don't have an assignment to Beirut. At least, I'm assigned as a vice consul in Jerusalem. It says so in my passport.' She repeated, 'You can't land here.' Finally, Major Halaby said, 'Okay, you can stay, but you're a prisoner of war!'"[88] She was, he noted, the only officer in the legion who spoke four languages.

Asia also worked as a guard at the Mandelbaum Gate, which was not a gate at all but rather a crossroads in the middle of no-man's-land adjoining the ruins of a house that had belonged to a wealthy Jewish merchant named Mandelbaum. Her forthright manner and confident approach to interacting with foreigners served her well during the years that she worked on the Jordanian side of this checkpoint, which was the unique passage between the two enemy jurisdictions of the city. There was no telephone, no mail service, and no commercial traffic of any kind between the two sides of the city. The signs at the crossing read: "Stop! Danger! Frontier Ahead!" in English, Hebrew, and Arabic. The checkpoints were about two hundred yards apart. Vehicles were not permitted to cross, except for consular cars that had two drivers, one for each side of the city, as unlimited crossing was a privilege reserved for consular officers and their families, members of the United Nations Truce Supervision Organization, and heads of ecclesiastical establishments.[89]

Kai Bird, an American, was a youngster living in East Jerusalem in the 1950s while his father was posted as a consular official there. Kai was driven through the Mandelbaum Gate each morning and each afternoon to attend the International School in West Jerusalem. He recalled the sounds in the neighborhood of the border: braying donkeys, crowing roosters, barking dogs, ringing church bells, and the Muslim call to prayer. These were accompanied by the sight of camels roaming as well as flocks of sheep and goats. Americans were told never to mention Israel when they were in East Jerusalem. Therefore, Kai told his friends that he went to school in "Dixieland."[90] Kai was not aware that the major who allowed him to pass through each day was Asia Halaby.

In addition to her duties at the Mandelbaum Gate and her embroidery workshop, Asia also developed a strong interest in archaeology during the decades following the division of the city. Though she remained an amateur archaeologist, Asia's work with two of the outstanding scholars of the period, Dame Kathleen Kenyon and Professor James Pritchard, led to assignments of increasing responsibility in the field. Both Asia and Sophie became regular visitors at the American School for Oriental Research and the Palestine Archaeological Museum. As was common in the 1950s and early 1960s, artifacts from excavations in which Asia participated were put on display in the Halaby home.[91]

Kathleen Kenyon became a mentor and friend. Like Sophie Halaby, Kenyon was born in 1906. Like Asia, she was outgoing and strong; she played hockey, lacrosse, and cricket, becoming Head Girl of St. Paul's School for Girls in London in 1924. At Somerville College, Oxford, she belonged to the tennis club and went ice-skating and riding. Like both Halaby sisters, she remained devout all her life, attending church regularly. From 1931 to 1935 she spent each spring on expedition in Samaria, thirty-five miles north of Jerusalem, near Sebastia. The expedition at Samaria was sponsored by the British School of Archaeology in Jerusalem, which had been established in 1919 to continue the work of the Palestine Exploration Fund, founded in 1865 "for the accurate and systematic investigation of the archeology, topography, geology and physical geography, natural history, manners and customs of the Holy Land." There, Kenyon was introduced to organizing excavation in Palestine despite difficulties introduced periodically by local labor and landowners. Despite her hard work, Kenyon enjoyed the social life of ending the day with cocktails, playing bridge after dinner, and listening to jazz records on a gramophone. Kenyon was one of a small group of single women who established independent careers as archaeologists before World War II.[92]

Like Asia, Kenyon volunteered to help the British war effort. She was trained for the Volunteer Aid Detachment, a Red Cross unit prepared to deal with national emergencies. Like Asia, Kenyon learned from her war experience; both women confidently handled a variety of tasks typically thought beyond the ability of women. Following the war, Kenyon became the director of the British School of Archaeology in Jerusalem, and by 1951, she was excavating in Jericho, thirty miles from Jerusalem, nine hundred feet below sea level. The dig lasted seven years, involved fifty-eight field supervisors, six surveyors, three draftsmen, three photographers, five conservators, five camp managers, and hundreds of laborers.[93]

Asia Halaby began her work in archaeology under the supervision of Kenyon, whose discoveries in Jericho focused on the first known examples of realistic human portraiture, seven skulls partially modeled from plaster, dating from 6000 BC. These skulls brought a great deal of attention to Kenyon, who was appointed a trustee of the Palestine Archaeological Museum and who continued to work in and around the Old City of Jerusalem until 1967. Asia and Sophie were regularly invited to events at the American Colony to greet Kenyon on her frequent visits to the city. In 1973, Kenyon was awarded the title Dame Commander of the Order of the British Empire for her services to archaeology.[94]

Asia also worked with Professor James B. Pritchard of the University of Pennsylvania, whose teacher was William Albright, a pioneer in American archaeology in the Holy Land for whom the American School for Oriental Research was later named. Like Kenyon, Pritchard was a devout Christian. He taught religious thought as well as archaeology and was well versed in the Bible. Beginning in 1957, there is evidence of Asia's work with Pritchard on the dig that uncovered the biblical town of Gibeon, north of Jerusalem. Records of the excavation note Asia Halaby as "cataloguer" in 1957 and 1958. Records of 1960 and 1962 show that she had reached a higher level of work, as she was listed as a "supervisor." Asia continued to work with Pritchard in 1964 and 1965 in excavating the cemetery at Tell Es-Sa'adiyeh. Pritchard was awarded a medal by King Hussein in 1964 as well as a gold medal from the Archaeological Institute of America.[95] Asia and Sophie were invited to events at the American Colony to greet Pritchard and his family, who stayed at the hotel on their frequent visits to East Jerusalem. The sisters frequently attended lectures and social events at the Albright Institute. Sophie donated a beautiful and rare still life of fruit to the institute; the painting remains on display there.

Political Developments

As noted above, following the division of Palestine in 1948, King Abdullah embarked on a plan to create a Jordanian national identity for all Jordanian citizens, including those of Palestinian origin, who had become the demographic majority of his kingdom.[96] The focal point of this effort was Jerusalem, specifically its holy sites. King Hussein, who succeeded to the throne in 1952, continued this policy. A series of postage stamps issued in 1952 illustrated the commitment to the unity of Jordan. The stamps identified the sections of the country as the East Bank and West Bank. Indeed, as of 1950, all official documents ceased to use the term "Palestine," replacing it with "West Bank." Some stamps carried images of the Dome of the Rock and of the Nabatean Treasury of Petra (in southern Jordan) side by side, again emphasizing the unity of the nation. King Hussein often visited Jerusalem to attend Friday prayers at al-Aqsa. Flouting the Armistice Agreement of 1949, he refused to allow passage for Jews to pray at the Western Wall, demonstrating that the Old City belonged to Jordan. He ignored the Vatican's demands to internationalize Jerusalem and similar requests by the Arab League.[97]

The Jordanian Nationality Law of 1954 granted Jordanian citizenship to "every person other than a Jew who was a holder of Palestinian citizenship before May 15, 1948, and who normally resided in the Kingdom of Jordan during the period December 20, 1949–February 16, 1954."[98] Sophie and Asia thus became Jordanian citizens. Some Palestinians urged the king to move the Jordanian capital from Amman to Jerusalem. This proposal was regularly debated in the press and on the radio. The fact that Israel had moved its capital from Tel Aviv to Jerusalem and that British and American ambassadors presented their credentials to the Israeli president in Jerusalem led to further concern among Palestinians. Yusuf Hanna, writing in *al-Difa*, charged that Israel had made Jerusalem their capital while Jordan "reduced Jerusalem from a position of preeminence to its current place that does not rise above the rank of village."[99] Cairo Radio, reflecting the policy of media-savvy Egyptian President Nasser, also took up the cry for the Old City to become the capital of Jordan. Referring to a plan to transfer the Jordanian Ministry of Foreign Affairs to Jerusalem, Nasser explained that this move would require Western ambassadors to present their credentials to Jordan in the Old City. In his view, this move would refute Israeli claims to Jerusalem as their capital.[100] Though Jordan never intended to move their Foreign Ministry, the claim continued to appear in the Arab press for years.

The Jordanian dinar became the only currency in the kingdom, replacing the Palestine pound. Jordan's king tried to consolidate his kingdom while simultaneously adjusting to the new politics of President Nasser of Egypt, who urged nonalignment with the West. Nasser's nationalization of the Suez Canal in 1956, followed by the attack on Egypt by Britain, France, and Israel, and the subsequent withdrawal of those armies due to international pressure, was seen as a victory for Nasser by the Arab world.

While President Nasser focused his talents on consolidating power among Arabs, King Hussein worked steadily to establish his control over Jerusalem. The Church of the Holy Sepulchre had suffered a major earthquake in 1927 and a second quake in 1937. The British had made some repairs to the building but were unable to correct the damage due to rivalry among the Christian sects controlling the church. King Hussein, seeing an opportunity to win support from the Christian world, was determined to make additional repairs. Repairs were started but not yet completed in June 1967 when Israel occupied the Old City. In 1954, the Jordanian government also promulgated the Law for the Restoration of the Aqsa Mosque and the Dome of the Rock, establishing Jordanian authority over the renovation. This was another move by the king to make Jerusalem a Jordanian city. In a tourism brochure published in 1960, Hussein articulated the sentiment that he had promulgated since the division of the city: "Jordan is a new name added to the frequently changing list of names by which the Holy Land is known today."[101]

Four years later, in early January 1964, Pope Paul VI made a historic visit to Jerusalem, providing King Hussein with an opportunity to demonstrate his support for the Christian world. The pope flew into Amman and proceeded from there to the Old City of Jerusalem, where two large photos of the pope and the king were displayed above the Damascus Gate. The pope held an important meeting with the ecumenical patriarch of the Orthodox Church, who had arrived in Jerusalem from Turkey for a meeting of the two highest religious officials of the two largest churches in the world. King Hussein hosted the meeting, which was an attempt to heal the schism between the Western and Eastern churches that dated back to 1054. The pope served a mass at the Church of the Holy Sepulchre and visited several Christian holy sites—Bethany, Bethlehem, Nazareth, and Capernaum. In the aftermath of the visit, the pope and the king appeared together on Jordanian stamps. However, while Christians applauded the pope's visit, it did nothing to resolve the underlying tension in Jerusalem. The Vatican continued to advocate a *corpus separatum* for Jerusalem.[102]

Simultaneously, the Arab League convened in Cairo. Under Nasser's leadership they discussed the creation of a liberation organization, something feared by the Jordanian monarchy. The Palestinian National Congress met in Jerusalem with King Hussein in attendance in May 1964. Hussein supported the appointment of Ahmad Shuqayri as chairman of the Palestine Liberation Organization (PLO), an organization committed to the liberation of Palestine through armed struggle. Shuqayri, aware of Hussein's concerns, pledged that the PLO would not interfere with the territory of any sovereign Arab state, but would restrict its efforts to liberating those parts of Palestine occupied by Israel.[103]

The creation of the PLO marked the end of the period begun in the 1950s, when the East and West Banks had been united and Palestinians had been granted Jordanian citizenship. During this time, an attempt was made to absorb Palestinians into Jordan legally, socially, and nationally. The PLO posed a challenge to this effort. By early 1967, King Hussein lost confidence in his ability to control the PLO and closed their offices in Jerusalem.

Palestinians followed these political developments with concern. Nevertheless, those like Sophie and Asia who had Jordanian citizenship were able to travel freely throughout the Arab world. Sophie and Asia had family whom they visited in Beirut, Amman, and Beit Jala.[104] They owned land in Bethlehem and Amman and traveled there to review their holdings. Their travels made them familiar with conditions for Palestinians in the wider Arab world. In addition, they were frequent guests at consular events in East Jerusalem and at the American Colony social evenings. They regularly attended archaeological lectures and events. Their contacts with an elite social class gave them access to pro-Western views that were at odds with the increasingly bellicose Arab unity rhetoric coming from Egypt.

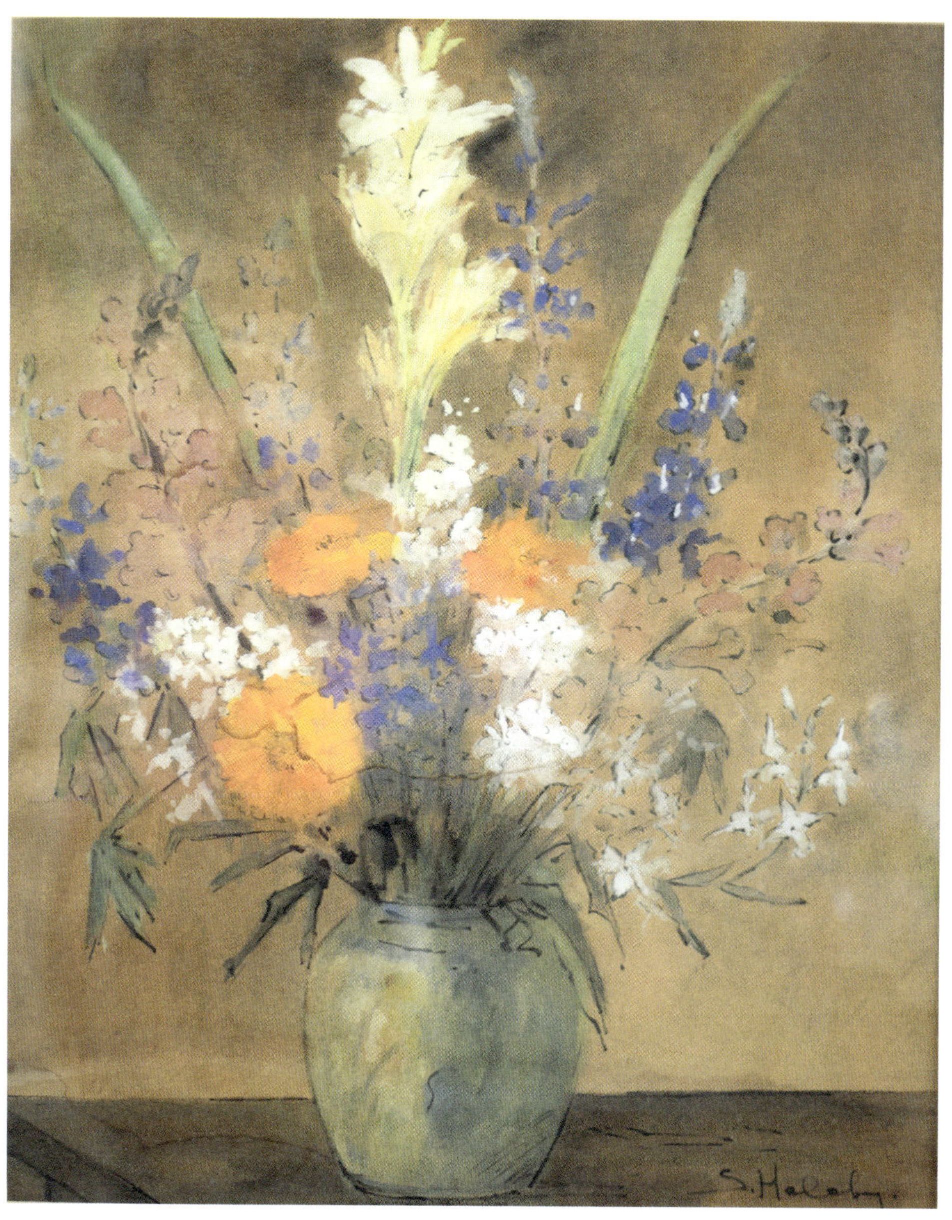

G1. Courtesy of YWCA, Jerusalem. Photograph by Aline Khoury.

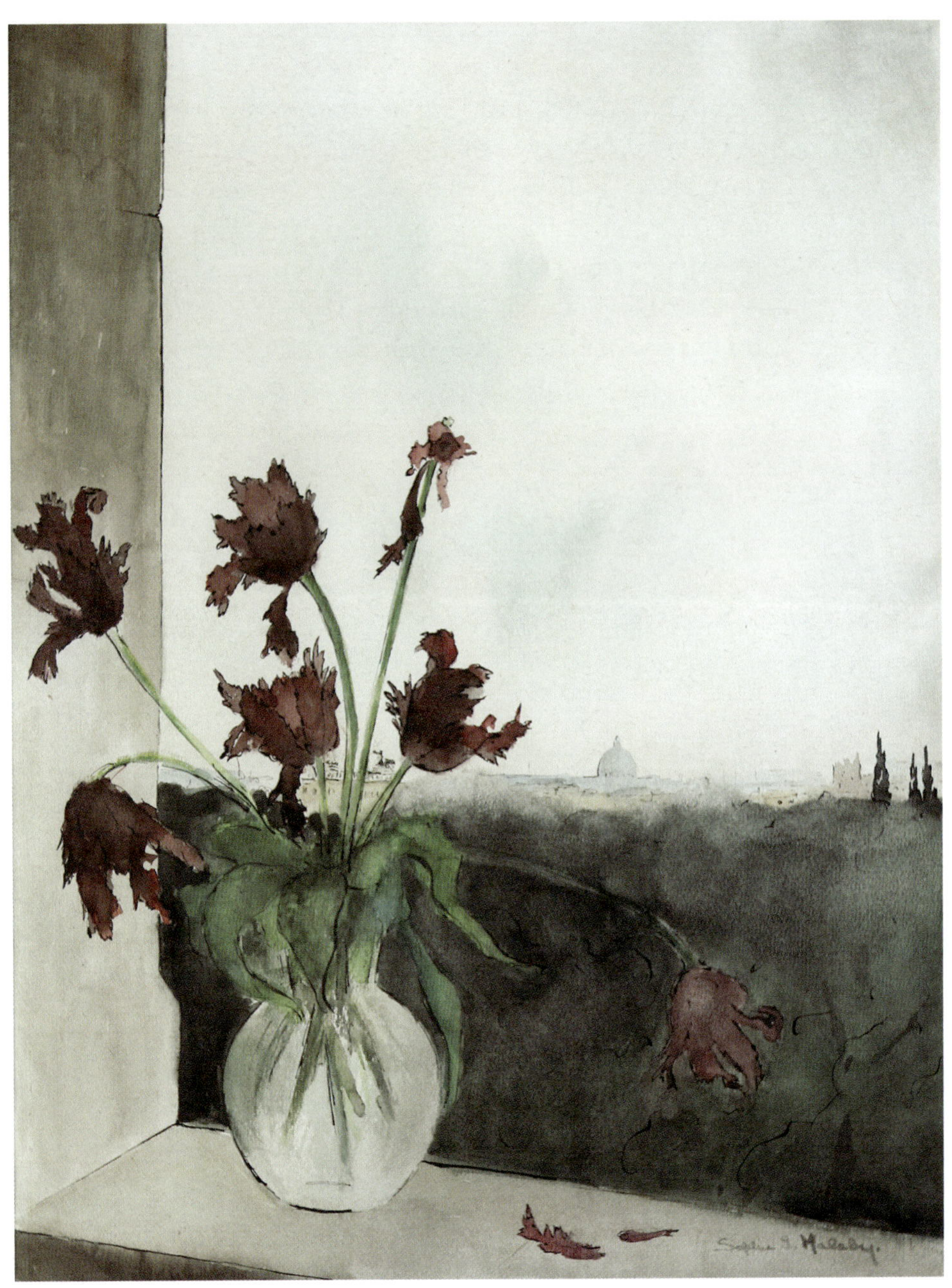

G2. George al-Ama Collection. Photograph by Aline Khoury.

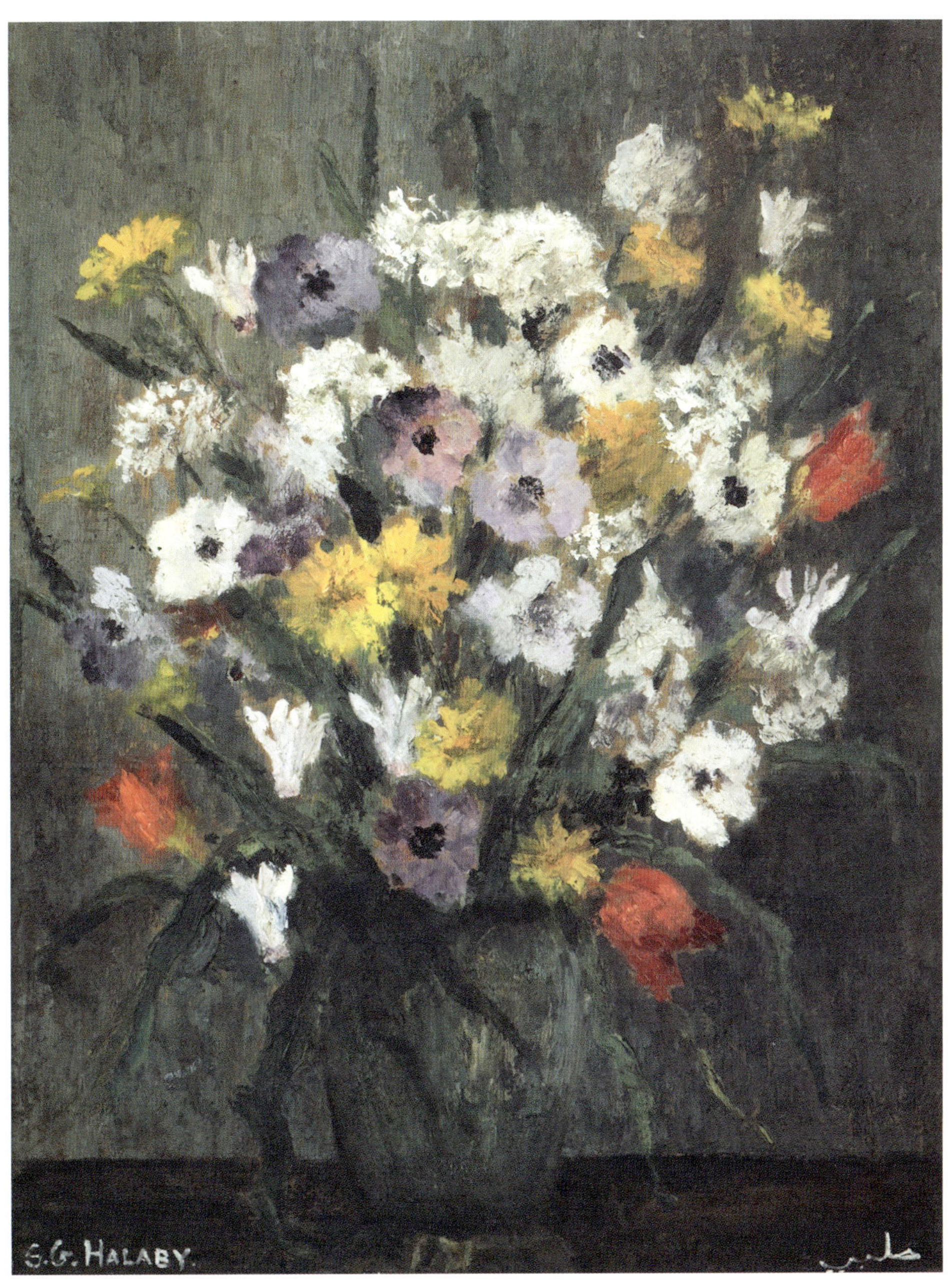

G3. Courtesy of Lily W. Porter and Nelly W. Barrett.

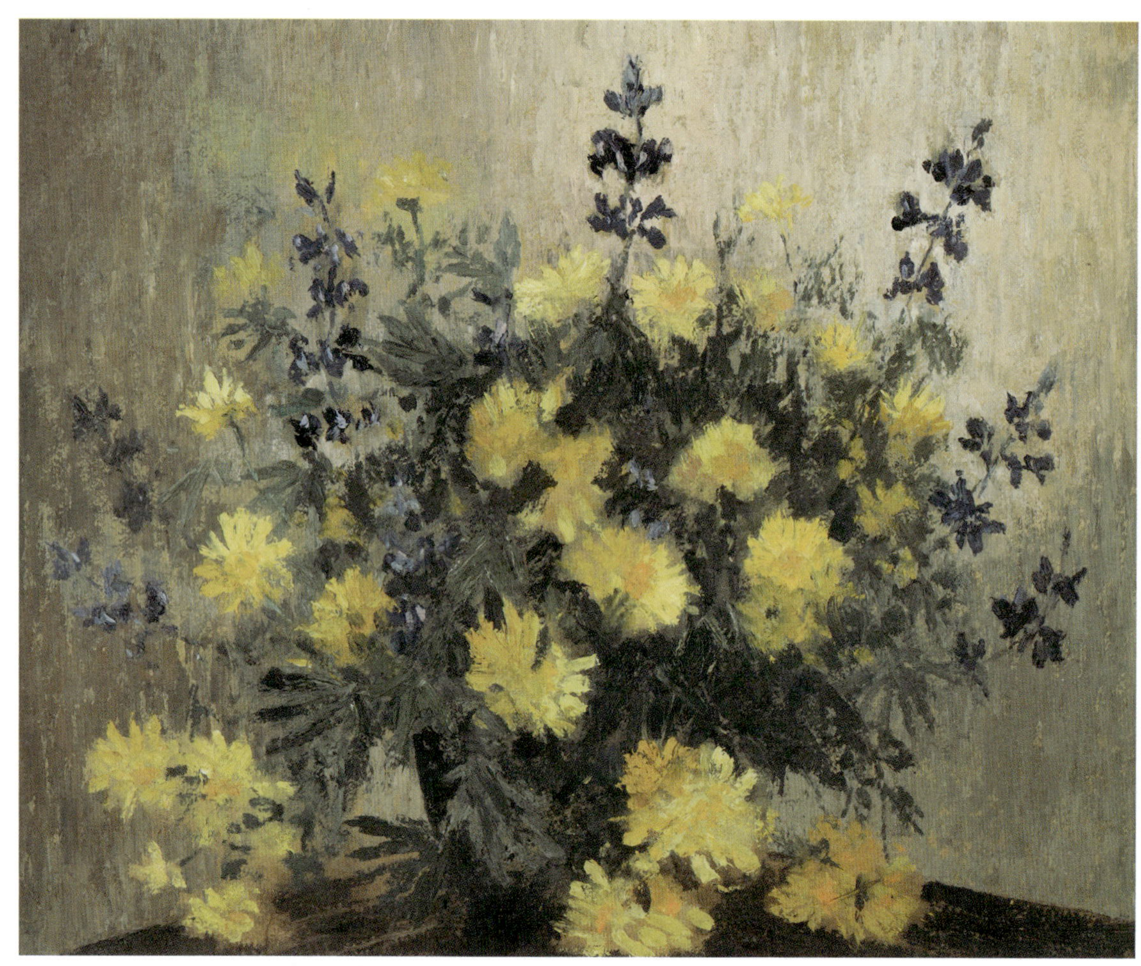

G4. Courtesy of Lily W. Porter and Nelly W. Barrett.

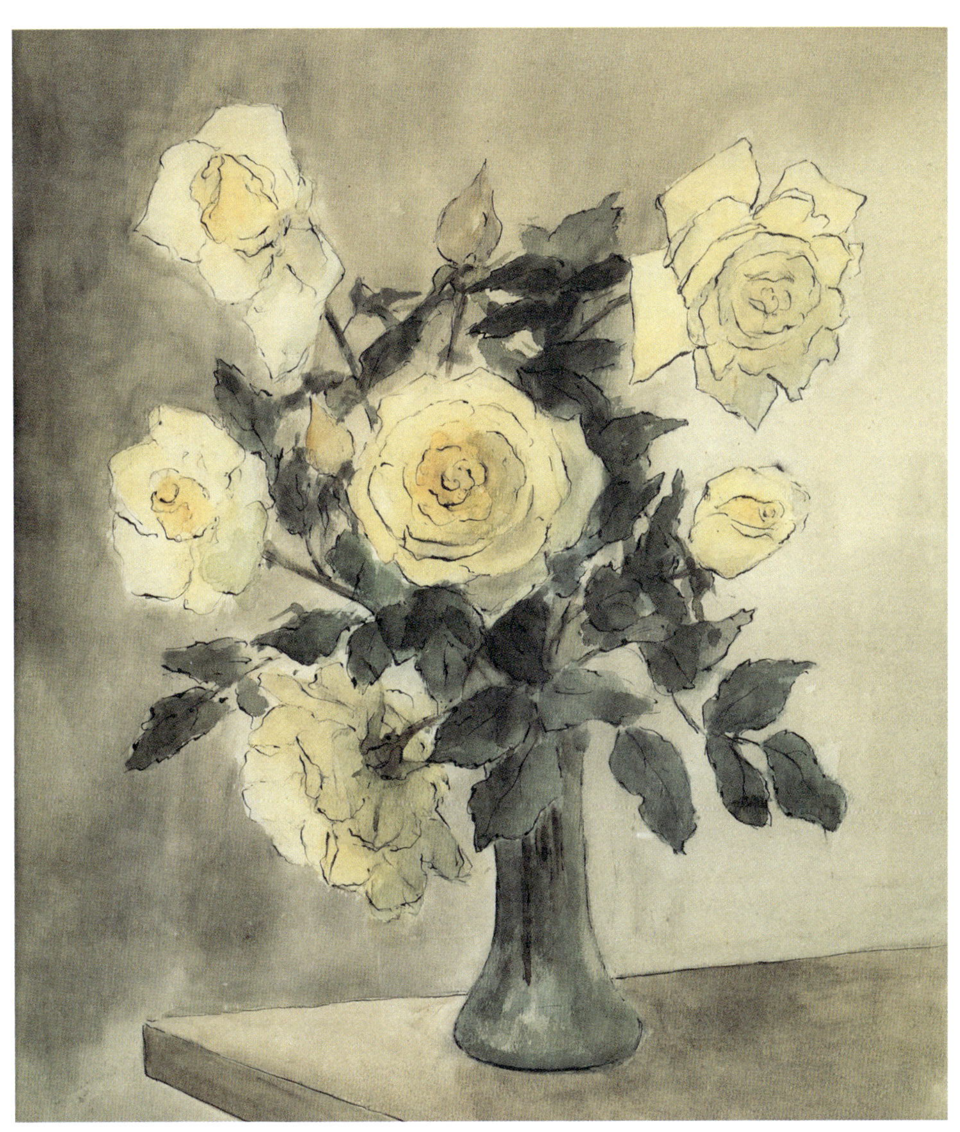

G5. Courtesy of Lily W. Porter and Nelly W. Barrett.

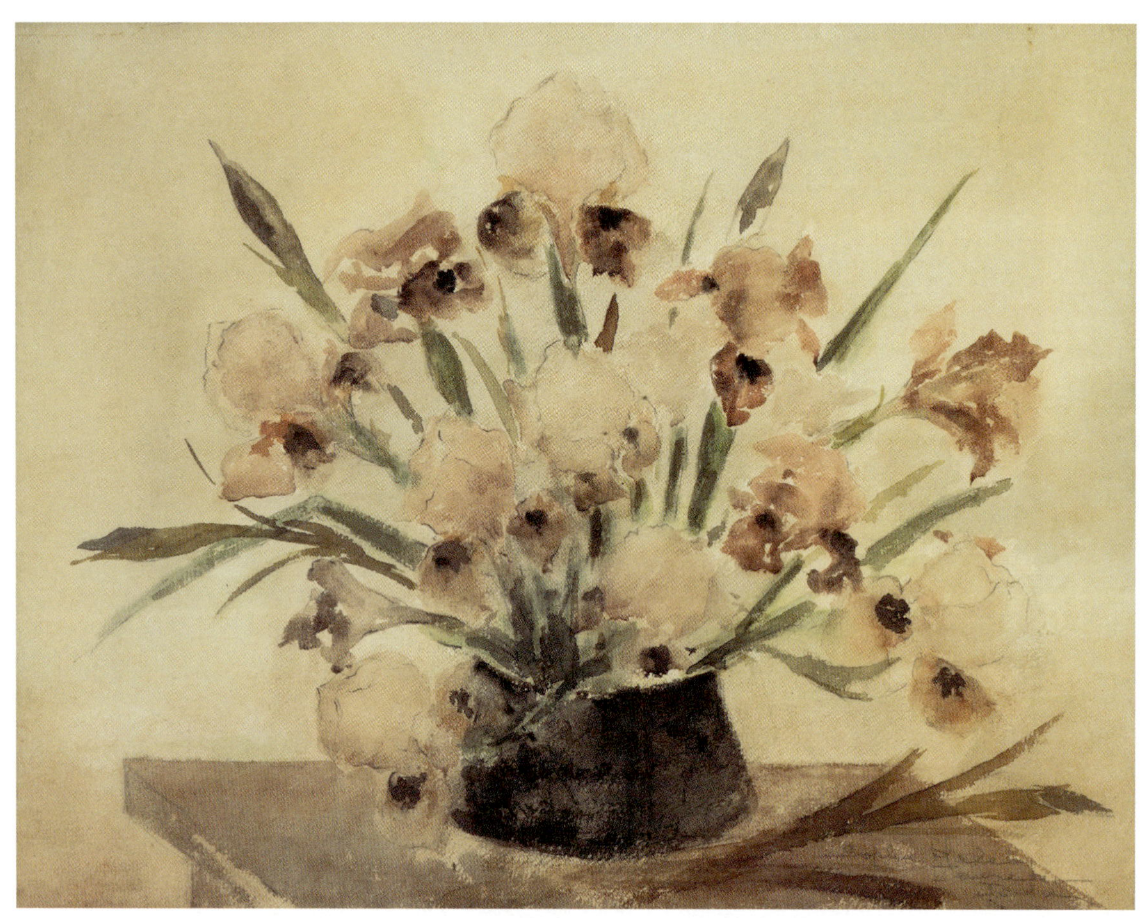

G6. From the collection of Vicken and Ada Kalbian.

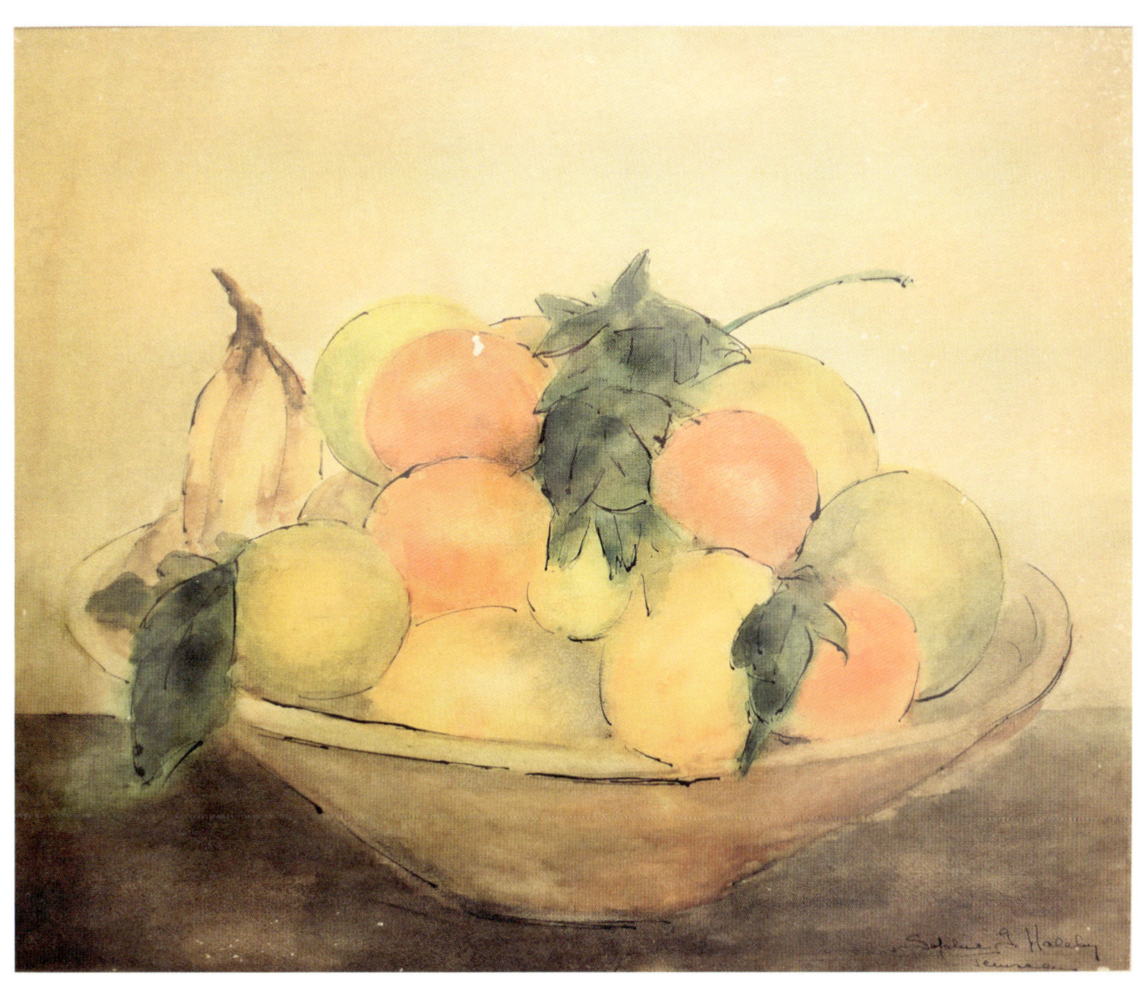

G7. Courtesy of the Albright Institute, Jerusalem. Photograph by Aline Khoury.

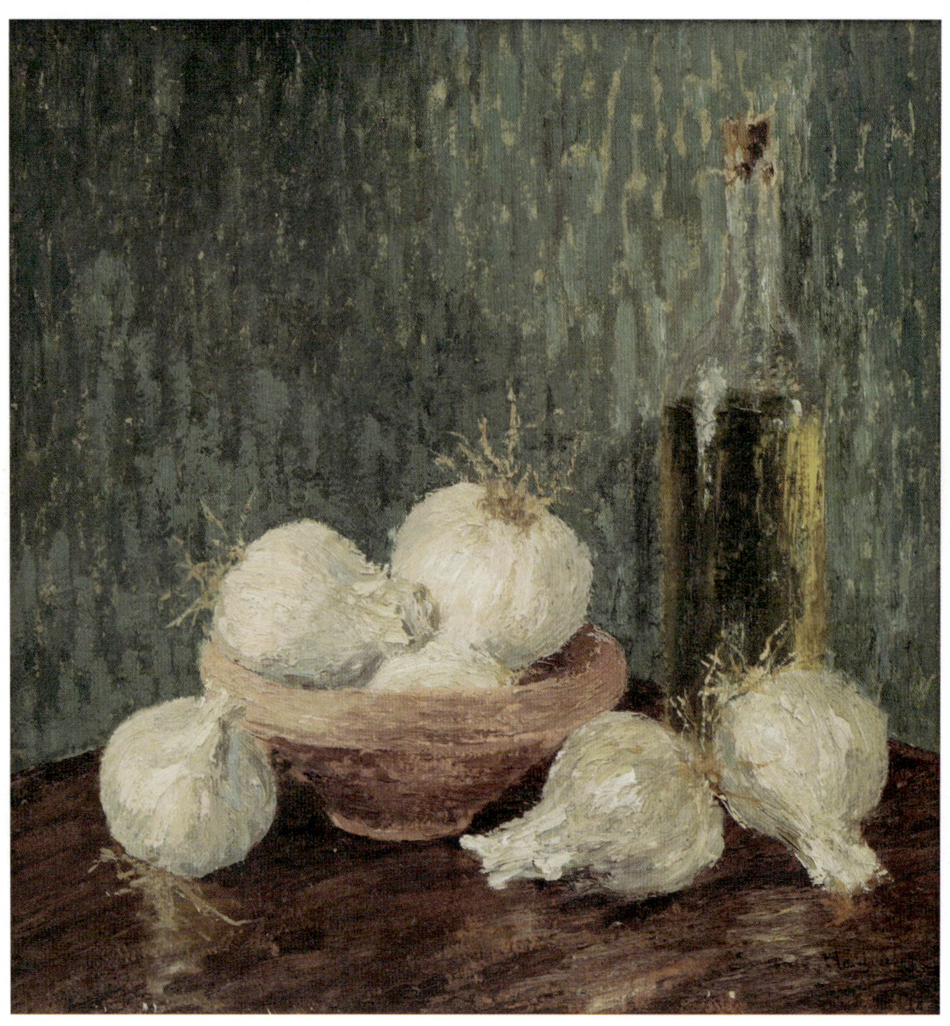

G8. Yvette and Mazen Qupty Collection.

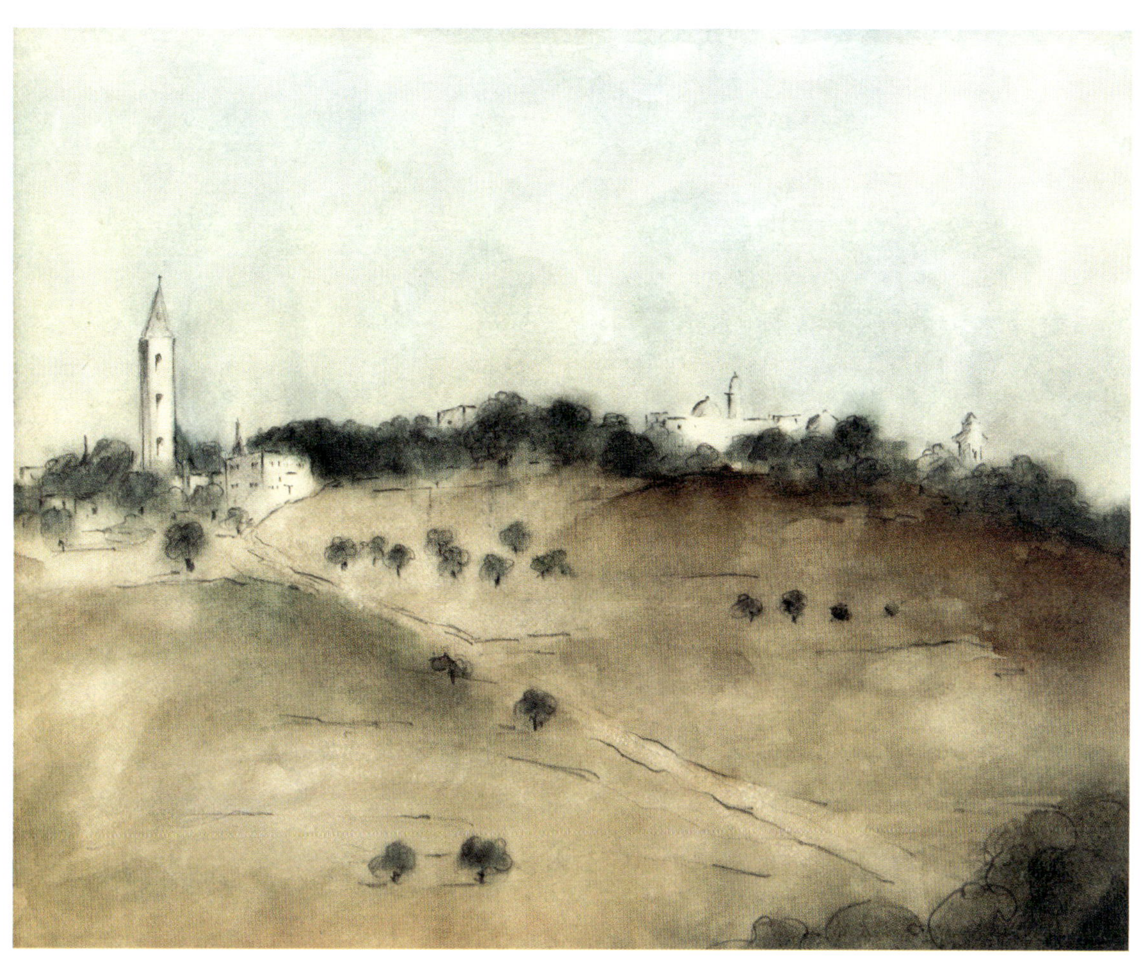

G9. Yvette and Mazen Qupty Collection.

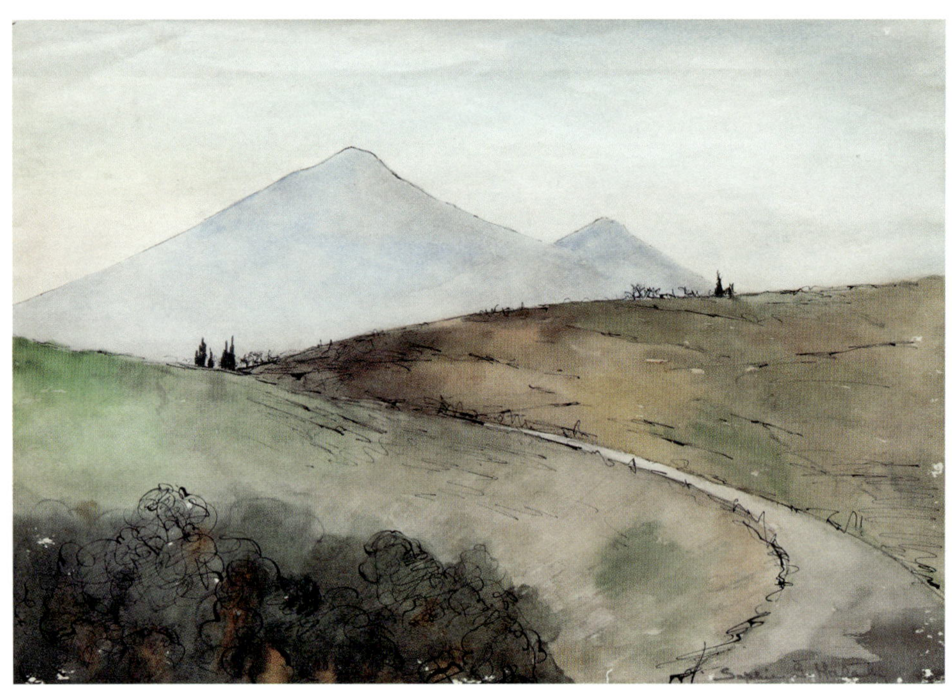

G10. Yvette and Mazen Qupty Collection.

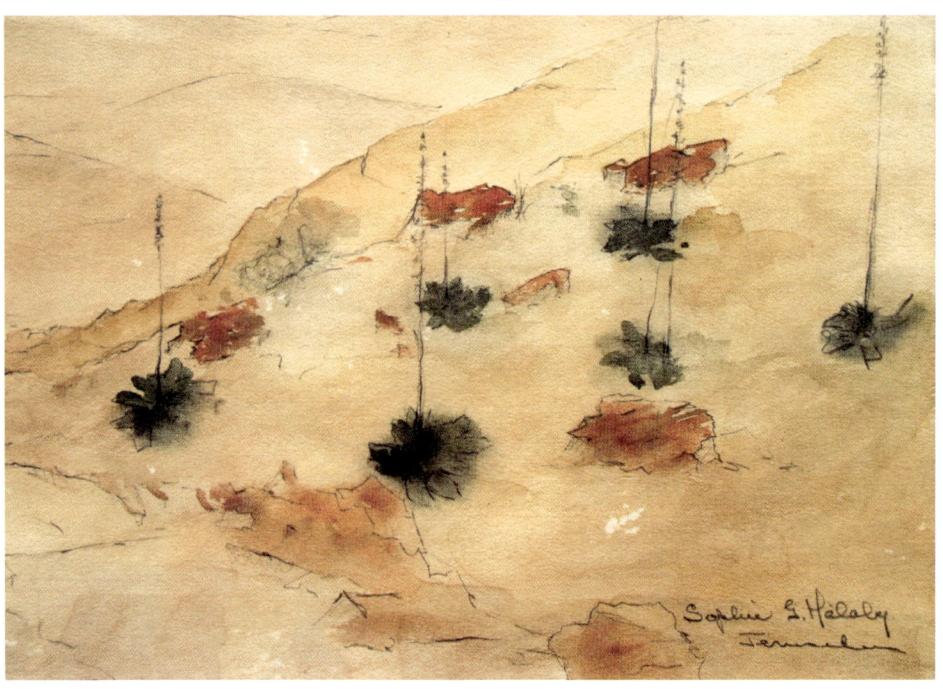

G11. Yvette and Mazen Qupty Collection.

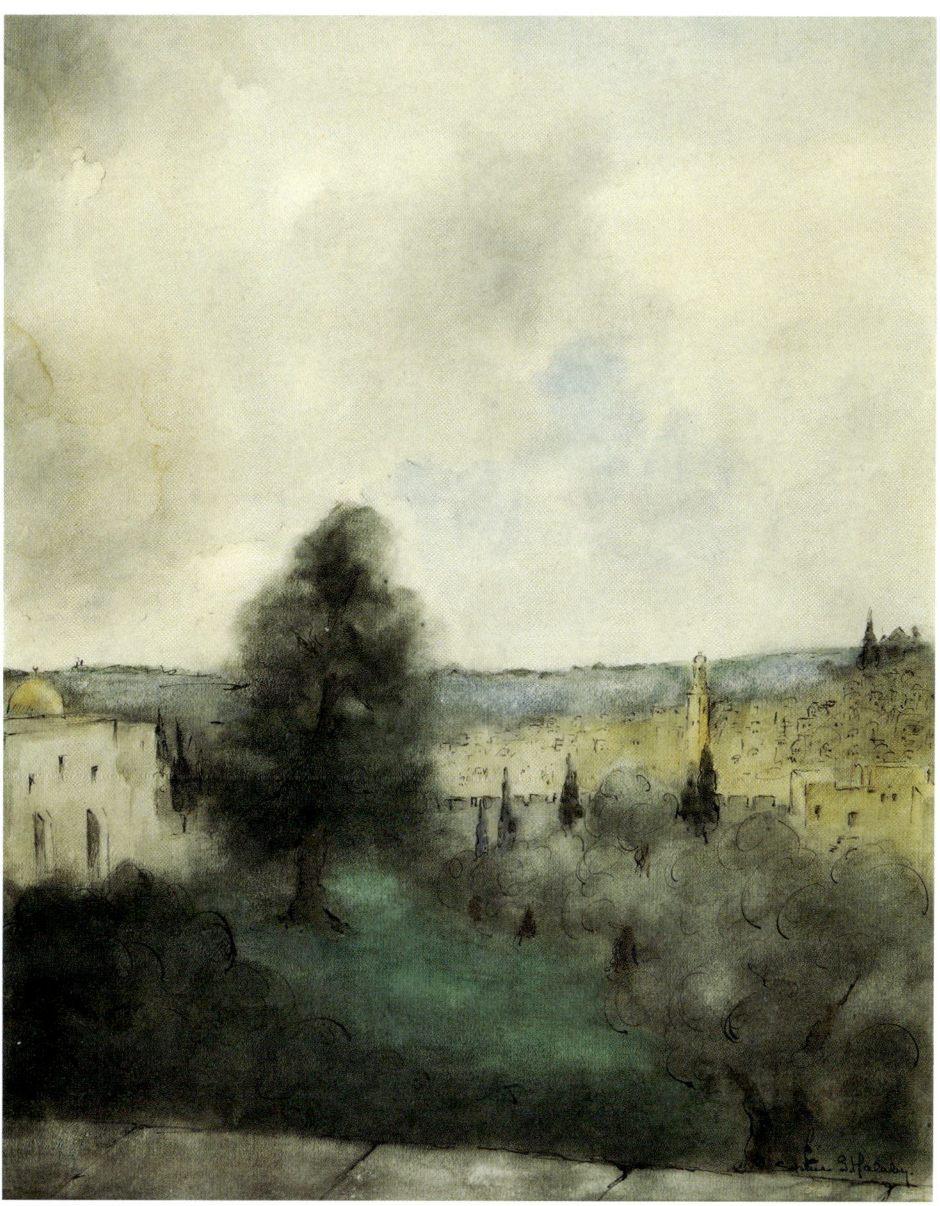

G12. From the collection of Vicken and Ada Kalbian.

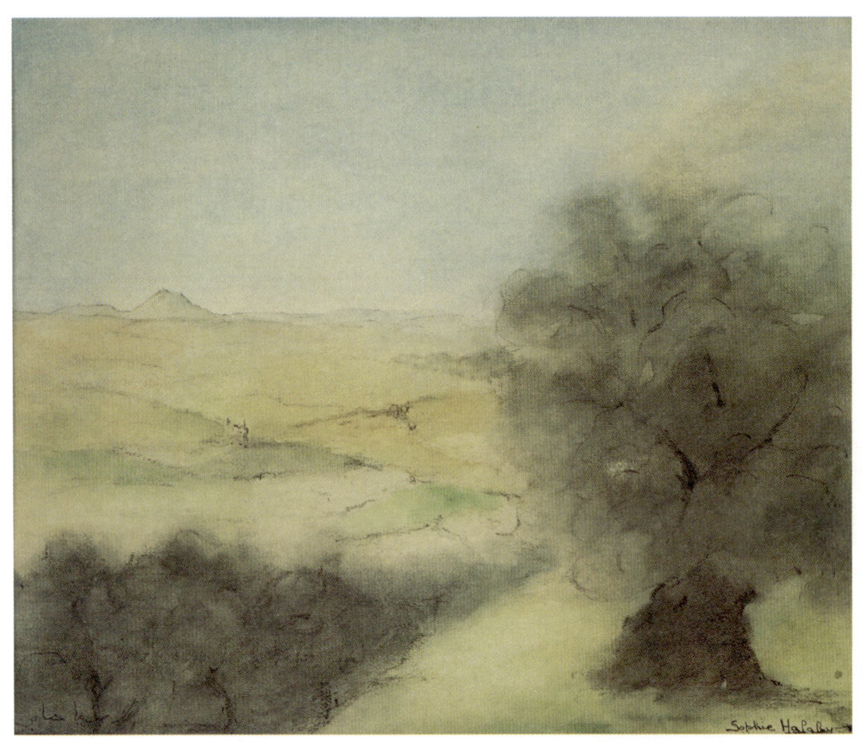

G13. Courtesy of Michael C. Hudson.

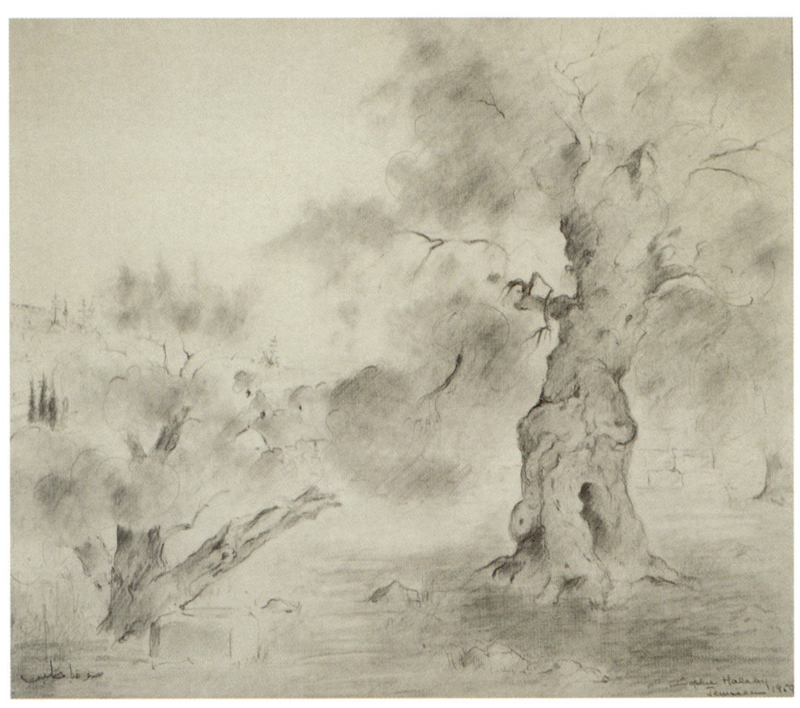

G14. Courtesy of Michael C. Hudson.

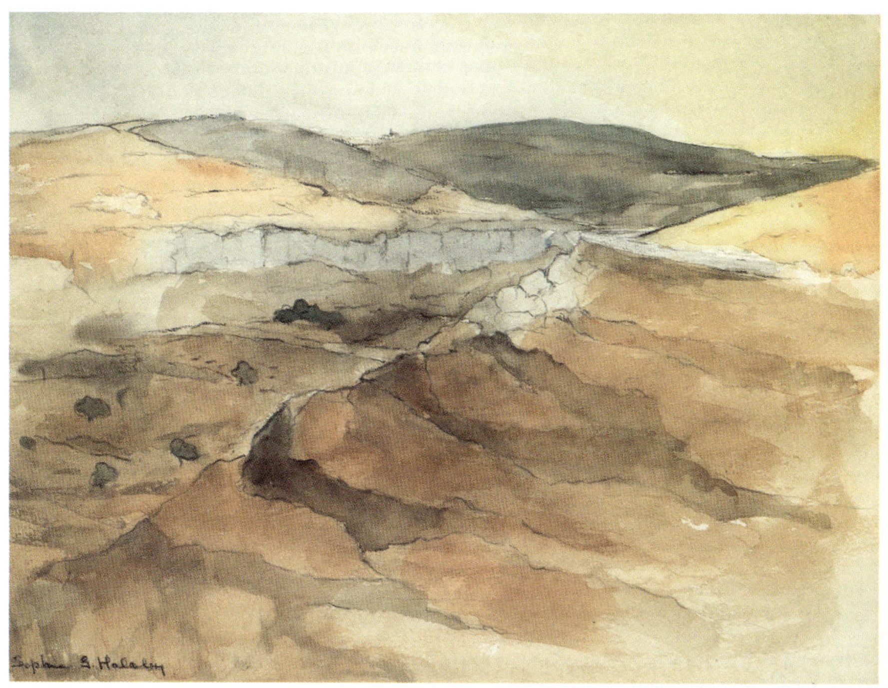

G15. Courtesy of Michael C. Hudson.

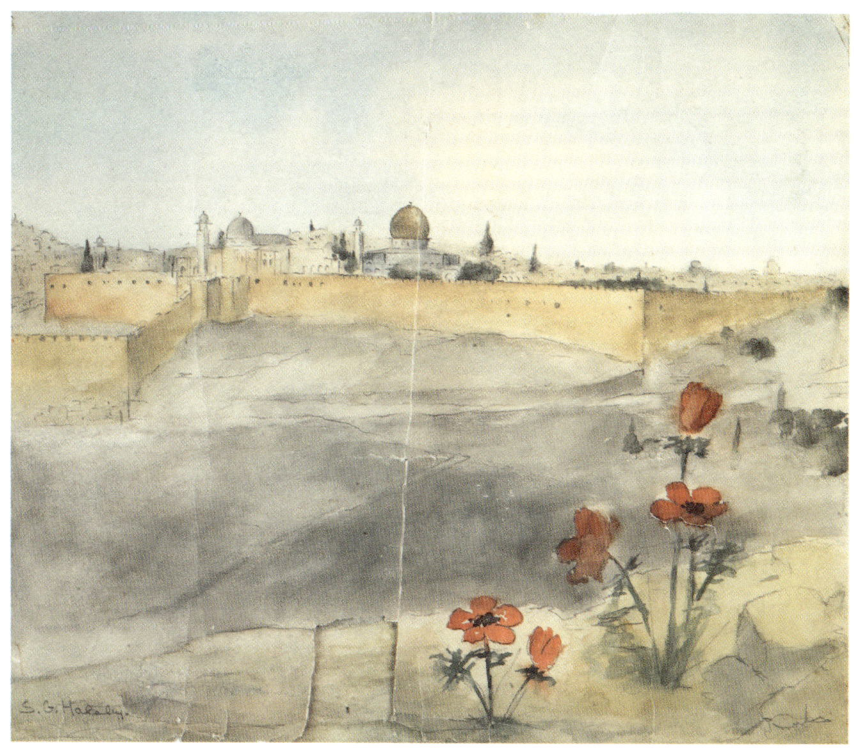

G16. Courtesy of Lily W. Porter and Nelly W. Barrett.

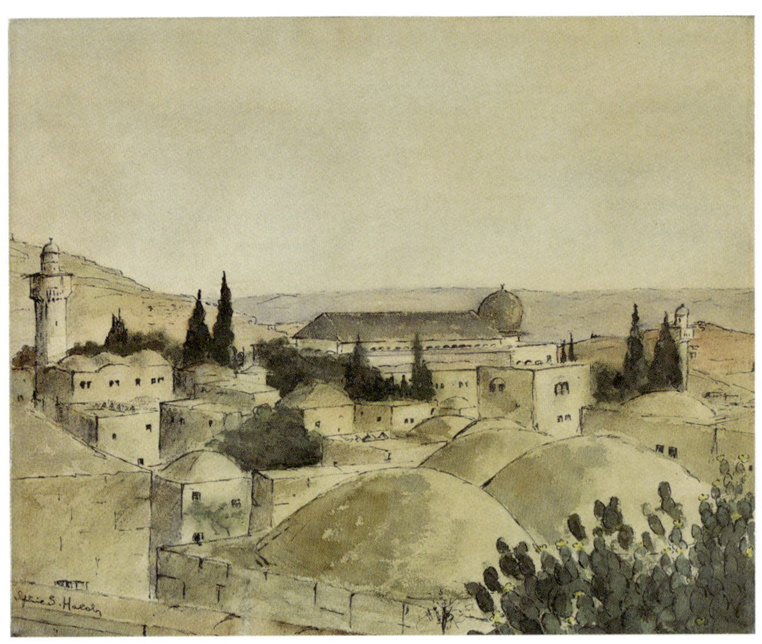

G17. Courtesy of Mary and Rafiq Husseini.

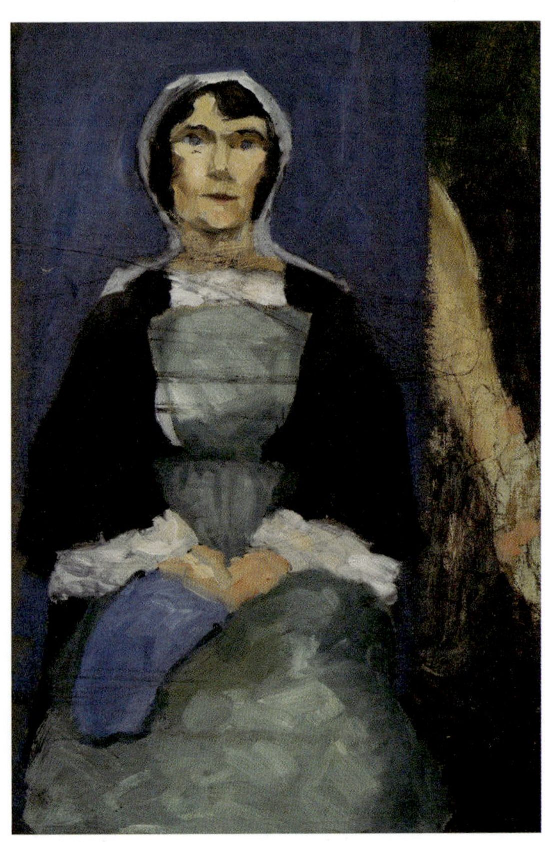

G18. Yvette and Mazen Qupty Collection.

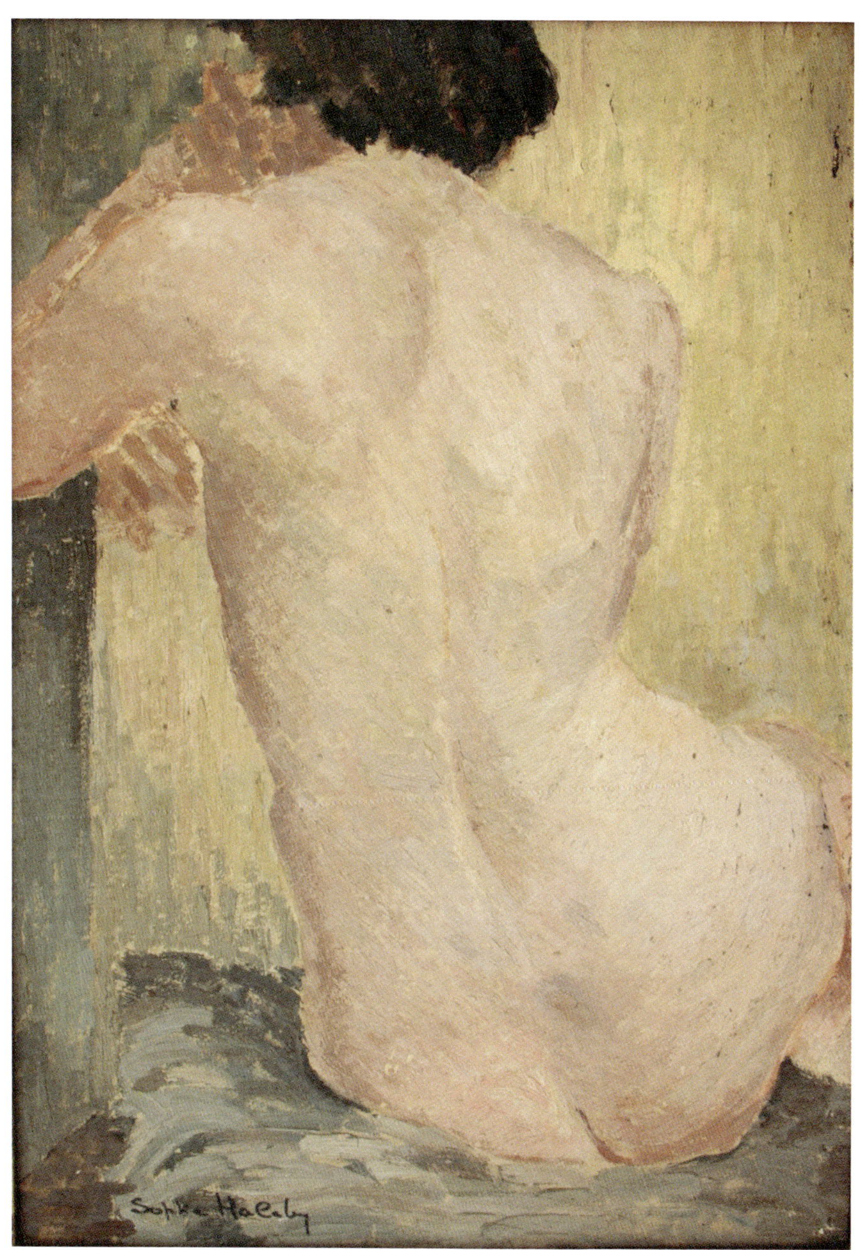

G19. Yvette and Mazen Qupty Collection.

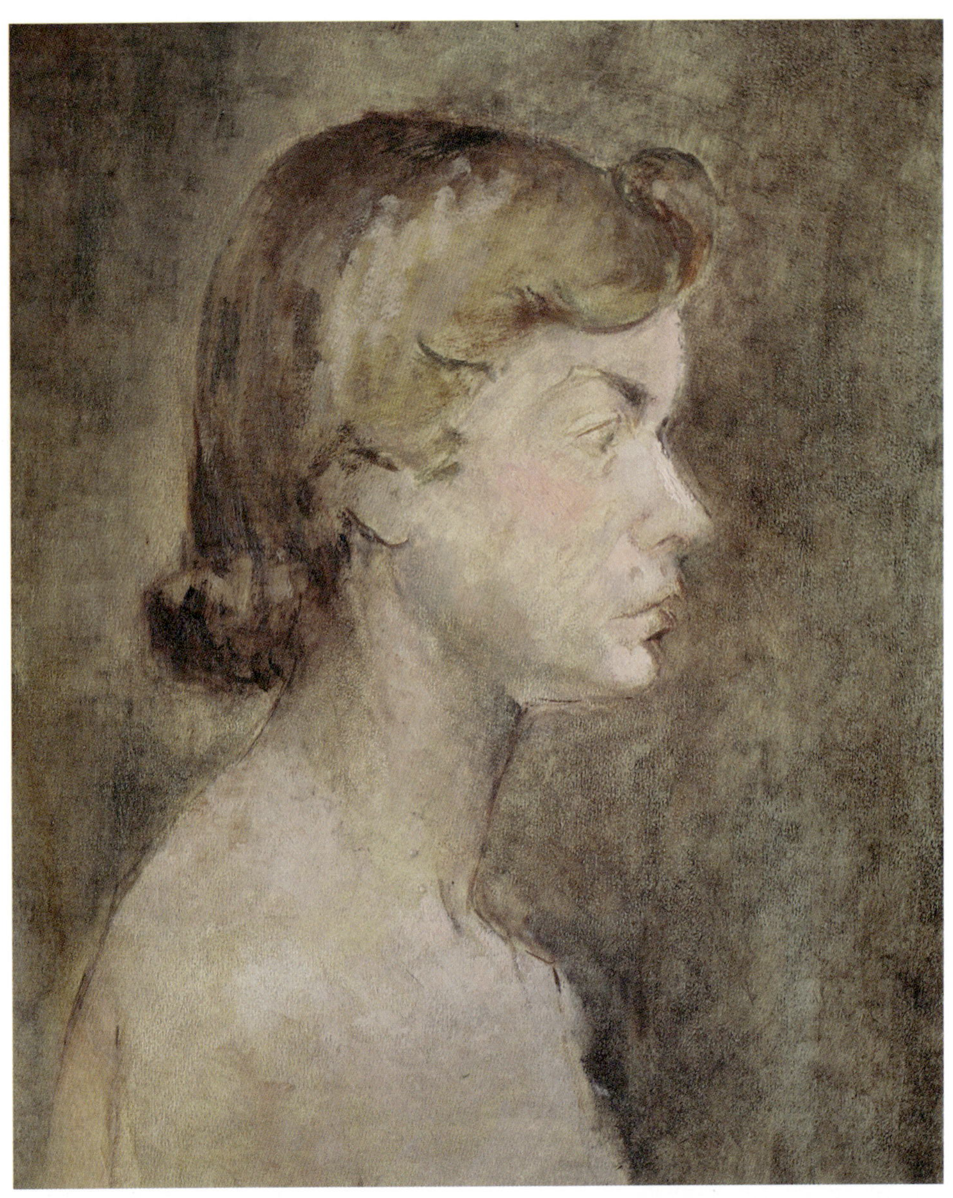

G20. George al-Ama Collection. Photograph by Aline Khoury.

5

Jerusalem Occupied

1967–1986

> In June 1967 another momentous change in the city and its borders occurred when the Israeli army occupied the west bank of Jordan and the eastern part of Jerusalem . . . the city was transformed almost beyond recognition. A long time resident or visitor would still be able to identify the Old City and the surrounding basin, the main religious and cultural features, and the overall topography of the city. But the enormous wide boulevards and shops, fast roads swirling through tunnels and across bridges, housing stretching star-shaped into the hills and valleys around the city, and the dominance of the motor vehicle are all disorienting . . . the main driver of these changes upon the city has been the determination of the Israeli government to consolidate the Israeli Jewish presence in the city and to constrain that of the Palestinians—in all fields—housing, population growth, economy, and cultural expression.
>
> —Michael Dumper, *Jerusalem Unbound*

The Six-Day War in Jerusalem

During the nearly two decades that Sophie and Asia Halaby lived in Jordanian Jerusalem, they were part of Palestinian Christian high society, regularly attending consular events and frequently invited to teas and other social occasions by Bertha Spafford Vester and later by her son Horatio and his wife, Valentine, at the American Colony, which became a hotel after the division of the city in 1948. They also attended fancy dress events at the Hospital of the Order of St. John, which cared for the blind. That building (today an arts center), which Sophie had drawn in one of her political cartoons in 1936, remained on the western side of the city, but a new building was erected to meet the needs of the children in East Jerusalem. Sophie and Asia were affluent landowners, well-spoken in English and French, connected to European and American archaeologists in the city, and affiliated with Christian Orthodox social welfare programs through Halaby relatives. They maintained the comfortable lifestyle they were accustomed to from their childhood as well as the purposeful existence they learned during their years at the Jerusalem Girls' College and developed during the ensuing years of struggle as Palestinians. While other members of the Christian elite were motivated to move to places where their children would have greater opportunities, Sophie and Asia, childless, remained in their home, near family and friends.

In the spring of 1967, there was no hint in Sophie and Asia's social circle of the change that was about to take place in Jordanian Jerusalem and in the villages and towns of the West Bank. Horatio Vester's diary recorded pleasant warm-weather activities that spring, including picnics and bird watching with the Armenian physician Vicken Kalbian and his wife, Ada, close friends of the Halaby sisters. The American Colony Hotel continued to serve Jordanian government representatives and members of old elite Palestinian families: Anwar Khatib, Hazem Khalidi, and Anwar Nusseibeh. Foreign visitors also continued to stay at the hotel. The American archaeologist James Pritchard and his family spent time at the American Colony in March 1967. Upon leaving for the United States, they were driven to the Kalandia Airport by their friend Asia Halaby. Nathan M. Pusey, president of Harvard, and his wife were guests at the hotel in March, too.[1]

These routine spring activities were interrupted in mid-May by threatening announcements broadcast on Radio Cairo. President Nasser, in a continuing bid for leadership of the Arab world, demanded that the UN withdraw its peacekeeping troops from the Sinai, where they had been stationed to protect access to the Suez Canal since 1956. Having achieved this goal, Nasser proceeded to inject a note of bellicosity into the languid Jerusalem days: "As of today there no longer exists an international emergency force to protect Israel. We shall exercise patience no more. We shall not complain anymore to the UN about Israel. The sole method we shall apply against Israel is total war, which will result in the extermination of Zionist existence."[2]

Nasser continued his verbal attack by threatening to close the Straits of Tiran, a ten-mile sea passage between the Sinai and the Arabian Peninsula, to all Israeli shipping and to all ships bound for the Israeli port of Eilat. The American consulate responded by instructing American tourists to leave Jerusalem in anticipation of Israeli retaliation. Horatio Vester, listening to ominous commentary on the BBC, was not convinced that anything dire was in the offing. In his diary, he observed that the BBC misunderstood issues in the Middle East frequently. He left the American Colony on a business trip after Nasser closed the Straits of Tiran to Israeli shipping on May 23, confident that there would be no Israeli retaliation. This time, however, Horatio misjudged the situation.[3]

John Melkon Rose, an Armenian Jerusalemite who had lived in the western part of the city, crossed into East Jerusalem in 1953, where he soon became the chief administrator of St. George's Close (later St. George's Cathedral Guest House). Melkon Rose also kept a diary in 1967. Early in the year, he reported border clashes between Israel and Syria and rumors of war between the two countries. Nevertheless, he noted that panicked buying of food and candles gave way to complacency as the weeks and months passed with no further escalation. He reported the removal of UN forces from the Sinai Peninsula, the occupation of Sharm el Sheikh by Egyptian troops, and the closing of the Straits of Tiran to Israeli shipping. He also noted that on May 30, King Hussein, pressured by Nasser, followed Syria and signed a defense pact with Egypt. Melkon Rose's diary account demonstrates how Jerusalemites, at first unconcerned by this new development, adjusted to the rapid changes that unfolded: "Monday, June 5th was business as usual in East Jerusalem. I was out shopping in the Old City when I was told that the Egyptian air force had been destroyed on the ground and that the war had started. Destruction of Syrian, Jordanian and Iraqi planes followed. By late morning there was an eerie silence in the streets, no traffic moved and we could hear occasional gunfire."[4]

Melkon Rose returned to St. George's Close, covered all the windows and doors with blankets and pillows, creating a shelter within the hallway, and prepared food for all the residents. On June 7, when word reached St. George's that Jordanian Jerusalem had surrendered to Israeli soldiers, he wrote: "Outside on Salah el Din Street stood a dreadful symbol of war. A small Red Crescent ambulance carrying four stretcher cases had been incinerated by napalm. . . . In the streets around and on the school playing field, lay many bodies of Arab fighters . . . more than a week passed before their removal."[5]

Horatio Vester was in Beirut during this invasion of Jerusalem, which became known as the Six-Day War. He was unable to return to the city until the war ended. By that time, Israel had declared that East and West Jerusalem were unified and that the newly integrated city was the capital. This assertion has remained contested for more than half a century.[6] Vester flew from Beirut to Cyprus and then directly to Ben Gurion airport in Tel Aviv, where he hired a taxi and was driven home on a road that he had not seen since 1948. The rhythm of life at the American Colony Hotel quickened after the war. Favored by foreign journalists like the American Dorothy Thompson, who was assigned to cover the changes to the city, life at the American Colony returned to the more cosmopolitan atmosphere it had known during the British Mandate. A few months after the war, James Pritchard returned, signaling the continued interest of foreign archaeologists in the layers of civilization that lay beneath the surface of the Holy Land.[7]

For years, Nasser and Palestinian leaders targeted Israel, the archenemy around whom they could rally support. Israel, the state that had been established in 1948 after bloody battles, had little reality to Palestinians who had sought refuge in East Jerusalem while it was under Jordanian rule. Since there was no communication at any level following the signing of the armistice agreement in 1949, Sophie and Asia had no way of knowing what went on behind the barbed wire that separated East and West Jerusalem.[8] Like many other Palestinians, Sophie and Asia had fond memories of the home they had left in Musrara and of Jerusalem during the British Mandate. They hoped to regain control of the property they had lost in the Nakba, land that was only a few miles away from their new home in East Jerusalem. They did not know that according to Israeli law, they had no right to that land.[9]

The sisters had long reminisced about their life in cosmopolitan Jerusalem, the life they remembered with fondness under the Mandate. East Jerusalem, in contrast, had remained a quiet town. The sisters, no longer young, were content in their home. They had their work, their church, their friends, and a position of status in society. Over the years, they had watched King Abdullah and later King Hussein try to integrate East Jerusalem into Jordan. They had also observed competing Palestinian groups try to create a governance structure for Palestine. Sophie and Asia were not involved in these political efforts. Asia remained loyal to the Jordanian monarchy, her employer, as she had been to the British Mandatory authorities. Sophie, who was not inclined to be politically involved, remained quietly supportive of Asia. Sophie's civic activities were limited to participation in traditional sewing circles that met at the American Colony to produce garments for the needy while the women, many of them friends since their school days, conversed in English about lectures they attended or films they watched. Asia participated in the sewing circles too, but her civic involvement was broader, focused on her embroidery workshop and the women it helped support. These activities were well within the sphere of social service efforts tolerated by Jordanian authorities.[10]

Anwar Nusseibeh, whose sisters often participated in the sewing circle, had served in Palestinian governing circles for decades. His participation in politics gave him a clearer vision of the immediate future than that of either Horatio Vester or Sophie Halaby. Nusseibeh recognized that Nasser's bombastic rhetoric provided Israel with the excuse they needed to attack. Concerned for the safety of his extended family, who lived near the border with West Jerusalem, Nusseibeh made plans to move them to shelter. As soon as he heard the first gunshots on June 5, 1967, he evacuated his entire family, moving them into the basement of a shuttered school down the street. The two adjacent Nusseibeh houses were left vacant. They became an open invitation to plunder by Israeli soldiers. Crystal, silver, tennis trophies, and gold medals, symbols of affluence and a westernized lifestyle, were scooped up while the family waited to emerge from hiding.[11]

Anwar's sons, Zaki and Sari, both studying in England, listened to Nasser's radio speech on May 23. They believed that the humiliating defeat of 1948 was about to be avenged. The brothers gathered with other young Arabs in the Egyptian Information Office in London. All of them assumed that war was inevitable. Led by Nasser, aided by Soviet support, Arab victory appeared certain to them. On June 5, rumors spread in London that the victorious Arab armies were marching into Tel Aviv. Sari and his friends wanted to join a victory march. They rushed to the Egyptian embassy and found it closed. From there they went to the Soviet embassy. Slavic guards threw them out. Within hours, the BBC reported a very different story. Israel had crossed the Jordanian border, and hundreds of thousands of Palestinians were fleeing to the East Bank.[12]

The telephone lines in Jerusalem were cut; the Nusseibeh sons could not reach their family in Jerusalem to get information. Israel, as their father Anwar had predicted, attacked and decimated the Egyptian and Syrian air forces and the Jordanian army.[13] This time, unlike the battles of 1948, inhabitants of the Old City did not rally to defend themselves. Israeli soldiers blasted a hole through the New Gate and flooded the Christian Quarter with soldiers who raced to the Western Wall, where they sang the Israel national anthem, "Hatikva," expressing the hopes of Jews in the diaspora to return to Jerusalem.

Zaki Nusseibeh, who had finished his studies at Cambridge, flew immediately to Amman; from there he paid smugglers to take him across the river to the West Bank. He hitchhiked to Jerusalem, realized that his family was not in danger, and rapidly decided that there was no future for him in Palestine. He continued his journey to Abu Dhabi, where he held several key government positions including minister of state. His brother, Sari, remained in England to complete his exams. Not wanting to return clandestinely to Jerusalem, Sari wrote an open letter to the *London Times* demanding that the Israeli government allow him to return home. Within days, the Israeli embassy in London stamped a visa into his Jordanian laissez-passer, and he boarded an El-Al flight to Tel Aviv. At the taxi stand outside the airport, Sari jostled with Israelis for a cab to Jerusalem. As he crossed the former no-man's-land that had divided East and West Jerusalem, he realized that the war had ended the division of his country. Defeat, he thought, had given him back his homeland. He had always felt that Palestine should include Jerusalem and Jaffa, not Amman. A youthful optimist, he saw no reason why he couldn't live in a democratic, secular state with the "aggressive" people who had cut in line for a taxi at the airport.[14]

Older Palestinians responded in different ways to the war. Sophie and Asia, now respectively sixty-one and fifty-eight years old, remained in their home on Nur al-Din Street, surrounded by their furniture, Damascene ewers and vases, samovars and other brass curios, embroidered silk cushions, Asia's antiquities, and Sophie's paintings. Their home, situated on high ground near the Palestine Archaeological Museum, which had recently been nationalized by King Hussein and was flying a Jordanian flag, was one of the first to be entered by Israeli soldiers on June 5, 1967.[15]

Moshe Amirav, an Israeli paratrooper officer, expected to be flown to the Sinai to jump, but instead received an order to go to Jerusalem. He and his men were disappointed with the command, having no idea that they were heading to the Old City. The soldiers approached East Jerusalem through no-man's-land near the museum, where they encountered snipers shooting from houses. They were ordered to enter each house to make certain that there were no enemy soldiers inside. They reached 12 Nur al-Din Street, Sophie's house, at 5:00 a.m., minutes after an officer had been severely wounded by a sniper at the previous stop.[16]

The soldiers were ordered not to enter any house until they were certain that all the inhabitants had emerged. Thus, they stood in front of the Halaby house and demanded that everyone come out, threatening to throw in a grenade if the residents did not follow orders. Amirav reported that several people emerged and were ordered to lie down on the street. The soldiers entered the house to make certain it was empty. Amirav and two others went upstairs to Sophie's studio to search for snipers. In the studio, surrounded by Sophie's paintings, Amirav was badly wounded by shrapnel from a shell that was fired into the house. Sophie's sanctuary was left in shambles. Soldiers searched the rest of the house, leaving havoc behind when they left.[17]

The solid stone house designed by their brother had been a safe haven for Sophie and Asia since they left the Old City. Being forced to evacuate their home at gunpoint and to lie on the ground while soldiers ransacked their belongings was a traumatic event for the sisters. The next few days presented more challenges. After Amirav was evacuated to the hospital with a serious head injury and the rest of the soldiers headed for the Old City, Sophie and Asia returned to their damaged home. According to Dr. Hana Halaby, a cousin living in Amman who stayed in close touch with Sophie and Asia, two

Jordanian legionnaires sought refuge a few hours later with the already shaken sisters. Despite their traumatic experience, the sisters rallied to the occasion, hiding the men in Asia's basement workroom and clandestinely burning their uniforms. They kept the men hidden until they came up with a plan for their escape. Eventually, dressed in women's robes, the legionnaires left the city.[18]

Another version of the story was told by Randa Atalla, also a cousin, to Samia Halaby, who recounted this version in her article about Sophie: "There was a clinic for the Jordanian army across the street from their [Sophie and Asia's] house. Approximately ten soldiers took refuge at their house. They kept them hidden for several days while they surreptitiously went out to neighbors begging for men's clothing. Then they made the soldiers change from uniform to civilian dress and snuck them out one at a time. After that they had to burn the uniforms slowly so that the smell would not attract suspicion from the Israeli soldiers."[19]

Both accounts of the event emphasize the heroic nature of Sophie and Asia. Barely recovered from their traumatic experience with Israeli soldiers, the sisters acted bravely to shelter the Jordanian soldiers and to help them escape. Their action was prized by the Halaby family, who focused on the story of the legionnaires rather than the story of the Israeli paratroopers. Lisa Taraki observed that as individuals perform acts of resistance they feel that they are part of something larger than themselves.[20] The story of the Halaby sisters helping the legionnaires suggests that Sophie and Asia felt like part of the resistance rather than like victims of the occupation.

Israeli soldiers returned a few days after the Jordanian soldiers left in order to review the scene of the shrapnel attack. Once again, Sophie and Asia were forced to give up their house to enemy soldiers, who sifted through the debris in Sophie's studio. The soldiers' report concluded that the shell that had wounded their commander was not fired by Jordanians, but rather was errant Israeli fire. For the soldiers, the incident at the Halaby home was a minor episode in the story of the capture of the Old City.[21] For Sophie and Asia, it was cause for great distress, no doubt reminding them of what they had lost when exiled from Jerusalem during World War I and again when they left their home in Musrara in 1948. Knowing that they had helped the legionnaires escape capture made the experience less painful.[22]

John Tleel, who had resided in the Old City since taking refuge there in 1948, listened to the news on June 5, 1967. In the morning, he heard a report from Radio Jerusalem broadcasting from Jordan announcing that the Jordanian Legion had overtaken the UN Headquarters and the surrounding area. Later that day, Tleel heard Kol Yisrael, the Israeli station, broadcasting that the Israeli army counterattacked and captured that strategic location. The following day, disruptions in the electrical supply led to intermittent radio broadcasts. A friend ran to tell Tleel about heavy fighting in the area near the Palestine Archaeological Museum. By noon, Tleel was again able to listen to Kol Yisrael. He heard Israeli instructions to Jordanian citizens in Jerusalem to remain indoors with their doors and windows closed. People were told to hoist white flags.

That night the fighting intensified. Battles were fought on Mount Scopus, the Mount of Olives, and all around the old Hadassah Hospital and Hebrew University, which were in no-man's-land. The nearby Augusta Victoria Hospital was ablaze. John Tleel worried about his uncle, Dr. Ibrahim Tleel, now the chief surgeon at Augusta Victoria, and about friends like Dr. Amin Majaj and Dr. Vicken Kalbian. On June 7, house-to-house fighting in the Old City intensified; the Christian Quarter surrendered to Israeli forces that afternoon.[23]

John Tleel had fond memories of West Jerusalem; he was eager to see the cafés where he had enjoyed eating ice cream and the grand cinemas where he had seen films such as *Gone with the Wind* and *Tarzan* featuring famous American movie stars. When the fighting stopped, he emerged from the Old City to assess the situation. He went first to Musrara, where his family had lived until 1948. He saw houses destroyed by war and the rubble left by the destruction. He recorded: "The first house on the left side corner of the main Musrara street that used to belong to the Russians was in ruins [this was the Halaby home]; on the right corner, the Swiss Pension Almazie was almost razed to the ground; next to it Dr. Tawfiq Canaan's house was damaged."[24]

Augusta Victoria, completed in 1910 following the visit of Kaiser Wilhelm to Jerusalem, was built as a Lutheran hospice for pilgrims. During World War II, the British had occupied the hospice and used it as a military hospital. In 1950, the Lutheran Worldwide Federation took over the building, renaming it the Augusta Victoria Hospital. It had 485 beds, making it the largest hospital in Jordan. On the first day of the Six-Day War, all the patients and staff of the hospital evacuated the main building and went into the basement shelter. Israeli planes bombed the hospital despite the presence of big UN and Red Cross flags.

Dr. Amin Majaj, the head of the department of pediatrics at Augusta Victoria, and his wife, Betty, a nurse, had returned hurriedly from a brief vacation in Vienna upon hearing news of the closing of the Straits of Tiran on the Viennese radio. Amin, like Anwar Nusseibeh, anticipated war and knew that he would be needed in Jerusalem. Once at home, Betty listened to the Israeli news station in French. The broadcaster advised mothers to make sure they were well equipped for emergency with chocolate, fruit salads, biscuits, and drinking water for their children. When the war began on June 5, Dr. Majaj drove quickly to the hospital. He remained there until the cease-fire. He watched as the new pediatrics department, which had taken him years to build, was completely destroyed. Dr. Majaj's lab, in an adjacent building, was damaged but not ruined.[25]

Betty and their four young children, a maid, and an elderly woman who wandered in from the street, remained in the Majaj family home, just outside the Old City walls near Herod's Gate. Surrounded by an iron railing, climbing roses, a row of cypress and lemon trees, and a jasmine vine, their stone house had three bedrooms. She listened as the sounds of war drew closer. A Jordanian antiaircraft gun positioned around the corner from the house fired repeatedly. Telephone lines were cut and the electric supply interrupted. On the second day of the war, Dr. Haydar, a family friend, arrived by car and offered to take Betty and the children to Lebanon. Betty decided to remain in Jerusalem. She moved all the children into her bedroom and placed mattresses and pillows against the windows. Not long after she finished, a loud blast shattered all the windows in the house. A balcony above the bedroom sustained a direct hit; rubble fell onto the front patio of the garden. Recognizing that the bedroom was no longer safe, Betty moved everyone into a narrow hallway, where they remained until the war ended.

When the firing stopped, neighbors called to Betty, urging her to come out to see the dead bodies of Jordanian soldiers. She struggled to keep the children inside. Dr. Majaj returned home shortly thereafter, devastated by the horrors he had witnessed. Amin Majaj fell into a deep depression that lasted six months. Unlike Zaki Nusseibeh, who went on to a successful business career in the Gulf, and Sari Nusseibeh, who became an educational and political leader in Jerusalem, Amin Majaj never resumed his career as an internationally recognized researcher and pediatrician. After the war, Betty and Amin found themselves isolated, on the other side of the border from Amin's mother, sister, brother, and numerous cousins, all of whom lived in Jordan. Routine communication with family and friends became difficult. Betty concluded, "We were totally isolated."[26]

Jerusalem: "Integrated"

As soon as the fighting stopped, the barriers and debris that had divided the city for nineteen years were torn down and carted away. The separation between the eastern and western sides of the city was nevertheless maintained. A green belt was planted around the Old City, framing its new, marginal role as a tourist destination and religious center to be visited rather than as an integral part of the city. The Israeli view of unified Jerusalem was that of a bustling metropolitan city in which Jewish and Arab residents lived separately, while they worked and shopped together in the western part of the city. Despite the announced unification of the city, the terms "East Jerusalem" and "West Jerusalem" remained in use. Israeli authorities had nearly two decades of experience in assimilating distinctive groups into the Israeli mosaic. In 1962, the Knesset had passed a law recognizing the Druze as an independent nationality; the Circassians in Kafr Kama and the Bedouin tribes in the Beersheba region had also been recognized as independent groups. Israeli authorities expected to continue to suppress the national attributes that Palestinian communities had in common and to absorb them as small groups within a predominantly Jewish society.[27]

In the immediate aftermath of the Six-Day War, the Jordanian, Palestinian, and Israeli dead were buried, and the separate water systems of East and West Jerusalem were connected. Telephone wires and electric lines were repaired. A sense of normalcy returned to the city after the bloody war. Two weeks after the fighting ended, tens of thousands of Israelis walked from the western into the eastern side of the city, while several dozen Palestinian Arabs walked west to see the homes and neighborhoods they had lost in 1948.

Hala Sakakini and her sister, Dumia, came quickly from Ramallah, part of the West Bank captured by Israel, to see the home they had left in Katamon in 1948. Like John Tleel, they were disappointed with what they found in West Jerusalem. Hala described walking from the Jaffa Gate with her sister and expecting to see the familiar sites of their youth. Instead, the shoeshine shop where the sisters had often climbed onto the high chairs to watch an Armenian polish shoes was in ruins; the delicatessen run by Abu Shafiq was no more, nor was the fruit shop run by Jawdat al-Amad, who also sold Palestinian newspapers. Hala and Dumia continued walking along Mamilla Road, which had been a busy shopping street. Hammoudi's beauty salon and barbershop, which had been a lively place with customers entering and exiting through a wide, colorful bead-hung doorway, was gone. Across the street, Piccadilly, the busy coffee house and meeting place favored by their father, Khalil Sakakini, was only a memory.[28]

They turned left on King David Street, known previously as Julian's Way. They found the YMCA and the King David Hotel exactly as they had remembered them. As they walked to Katamon, they passed the railway station and the gas station opposite, also familiar sites, but the houses looked shabbier than they remembered, and the gardens were neglected and full of litter. Nothing remained of Spinney's department store, Sayegh's pharmacy, Dajhani's greengrocery, or Kaloti's butcher shop. When they reached their house, they were happy to see that the building still stood, but all their plants had died: the fragrant honeysuckle over the garden gate was gone, the jasmine shrub that had leaned against the house was missing. The big dahlias of many colors in front of the house were gone too. The garden was dry and brown.

The Sakakini family home had been converted into a nursery school. As no one responded to their knock on the door, the sisters entered. The shock of seeing what had been their living room and dining room converted into a large play area for toddlers was too much for Hala, who wrote: "I would have liked for us to spend some more time all alone in the house in order to quietly relive the many memories that came rushing through my mind, but this could not be. We were afraid someone would come out of a room and start accusing us of trespassing (as happened to several of our friends who had gone to visit their houses)."[29]

Hala continued to describe the unhappy meeting with the current occupant of the house, an elderly European woman who had fled her home in Poland. Hala was unsympathetic to the woman's story, feeling that she was being blamed for the loss. The sisters walked through the whole house, noting that it was in good condition, but that everything was different. None of their neighbors—the Tleels, the Sliheets, or the Srujis—were about. The neighborhood was no longer the same. They left with a feeling of emptiness, disappointment, and frustration. Thirty years later, in 1997, Hala, not reconciled to her loss, wrote: "Jerusalem in its present state is not whole . . . give me back my home in Qatamon where I long to live, then only will Jerusalem be whole to me. Only when all children of Jerusalem live in it, when the property the Arabs own is restored to them . . . will Jerusalem be whole."[30]

In contrast to the sadness experienced in the summer of 1967 by many Arabs visiting West Jerusalem, Israelis—religious and secular alike—who passed freely into the Old City for the first time in nineteen years, were euphoric. Shop owners in the Old City, accustomed to selling to the Arab Jerusalem population, quickly refocused their products to appeal to Israeli tourists. They learned a little Hebrew and did a brisk business. Most Israelis came to shop; many came to pray at the Western Wall, which had been forbidden to them since 1948, while others came to the Old City in search of long lost friends. John Tleel reported visits from his father's friends and former patients; some of Tleel's Israeli college classmates from AUB came to say hello. But the old ties were frayed. He reported, "The enthusiasm was great, but the bonds, with the passing of time and the circumstances, never regained their old strength and died out."[31]

Some Arabs crossed into West Jerusalem to visit old friends, too. Anna Ticho, the seventy-one-year-old artist and widow of the famed ophthalmologist, was pleased with surprise visits from friends she hadn't seen in nearly two decades. Not all overtures of friendship, however, were received well. Professor Guggenheim of the Nutrition Department of Hadassah Hospital contacted Dr. Amin Majaj, whose research he had apparently been following for years. He asked for a meeting to discuss working together. Majaj, broken in spirit by the destruction of the pediatric department of Augusta Victoria that he had built, refused.[32]

While individual Israelis and Arabs adjusted to the new freedom of access, the Israeli government passed two laws that would have lasting effect on the city. On June 27, 1967, the Law of Protection of Holy Places was enacted, providing for access by all religious groups to places sacred to them.[33] The following day, the Law of Enlargement of the Area of Municipality of Jerusalem was passed, authorizing the integration of Jordanian Jerusalem into Jerusalem, Israel. On the twenty-ninth, the East Jerusalem municipality was officially dissolved. Mayor Ruhi al-Khatib, who had hoped to merge his city council into the West Jerusalem City Council, was rebuffed and later deported to Jordan. The councilors of the East Jerusalem municipality refused to join the Jerusalem City Council, leaving the population of East Jerusalem with no representation in city affairs.[34]

In conjunction with the expansion of Jerusalem, the Israel Ministry of the Interior held a census to verify who lived in East Jerusalem: 57,996 people were counted on June 27, 1967. They were entitled to Israeli identity cards establishing them as residents of the State of Israel, while those living in the towns and villages of the West Bank exclusive of Jerusalem received different cards, restricting their access to the city and their rights within Israel. The Israeli government's position that East Jerusalem was not annexed but rather "integrated" was significant, as under international law, if the city had been annexed its residents would have had to be given citizenship, whereas as residents, their rights could be revoked if deemed necessary.[35] The ministry registered ten thousand additional people in the next ten days. Six months later, less than half of those registered had received their blue identity cards due to a lengthy process to verify that the individual was actually a Jerusalem resident. In September, a second census counted 65,857, including 6,000 people who had not appeared on the first census. Clearly, people were migrating in and out of the city.[36]

Dispersion following the 1948 war resulted in distinct groups of Palestinians: those with Jordanian citizenship; those who lived in refugee camps in Syria, Lebanon, and Gaza; those who lived in Damascus, Beirut, Cairo, and the Gulf states; and those who had departed for countries in the West. Additionally, there was a population of Palestinians living within the Israeli border who were effectively cut off from the other groups in the Middle East. After the 1967 war, the first group—those with Jordanian citizenship—was subdivided into two categories: those with permanent residence rights in Jerusalem and those who lived in the West Bank outside of the city, who were no longer free to live in Jerusalem. All Palestinians, despite their segmentation, embraced a newly nationalist outlook after 1967. Lisa Taraki explained that they were united by a central tenet: the idea that the establishment of a Palestinian national authority could alone fulfill Palestinian nationalist aspirations.[37]

Though they shared a common goal, each of these groups faced different challenges. Palestinians living in the West Bank, now called the Occupied Territories, were confronted by Israeli officialdom for the first time since 1948. They were required to obtain building permits from Israeli authorities if they wished to renovate or add to their homes or shops; they also needed to provide Israeli authorities with documents if they wanted to work in Israel or to visit Jordan. Palestinian Jerusalemites were free to travel within Israel and were given the opportunity to become Israeli citizens. The vast majority, harboring hopes for national autonomy, did not apply.[38]

Like roughly seventy thousand other Palestinian residents of East Jerusalem, Sophie and Asia Halaby received their Jerusalem identity cards and remained Jordanian citizens. They were thus simultaneously residents of the State of Israel and enemies of the state under Israeli law because of their Jordanian citizenship. According to the Penal Amendment Law of 1957, which was not implemented, their property could have been confiscated by the state.[39] Israeli policy in the Occupied Territories included attacks on private homes and work sites. These attacks were often collective punishment for families of suspected "terrorists." The demolitions violated international convention and human rights law.[40]

By virtue of their new identity cards, Sophie and Asia were entitled to continue to reside in Jerusalem, and, like all Israeli citizens, they were now required to pay the *arnona*, a municipal tax. As residents of Jerusalem, they were entitled to vote in municipal elections. Few Palestinians chose to exercise the right to vote, not wanting to validate the unification of the city by voting for representatives.

Some regulations were not optional. For example, all Jerusalemites and residents of the West Bank were obligated to renew their car registrations and driving licenses. Jerusalemites were instructed to go to the barracks erected behind the King David Hotel for car inspection and the issuance of new license plates. John Tleel's car passed the test; he handed in his white Jordanian plates and received yellow Israeli ones. Asia Halaby was required to go through the identical procedure. West Bank residents went through a similar procedure and received different colored plates to identify their vehicles as belonging to Palestinians who had no right to live in Jerusalem.

Israeli laws, jurisdiction, and civil administration extended over a Jerusalem much larger than it had ever been in the past. Combining East and West Jerusalem, as well as adding several adjacent villages, ultimately resulted in a city of one hundred square kilometers. However, Bethlehem, Beit Jala, and Beit Sahour, towns that had been part of a shared cultural community with Jerusalem since Ottoman times, were now officially part of the West Bank. Sophie owned land in Bethlehem and had close family in Beit Jala. The new division made her anxious about her freedom to visit these towns. As a "permanent resident" of Jerusalem, Sophie knew that residency rights could be revoked by Israel.[41] This was not an empty threat. Between 1967 and 2008, over thirteen thousand Palestinians lost their right to reside in Jerusalem.[42]

Israeli law was the catalyst for many changes to daily living in East Jerusalem in subsequent decades. In June 1967, the population of Jerusalem included approximately two hundred thousand Jews and sixty-five thousand Arabs. Israeli leaders wanted that ratio to remain constant. In anticipation of Arab demographic pressure in the city, Israel began to build settlements on expropriated land to house Jewish residents.[43] During the Mandate years, Jewish immigration and land acquisition were catalysts for Arab nationalism. Decades later, under Israeli occupation, these issues again became central to the growing opposition to the unification of the city. As new neighborhoods were quickly built, Jerusalem became a noisy place; large construction cranes dotted the skyline. Tourist buses did a brisk business. Private cars, previously a luxury, became more affordable and soon choked the city's narrow streets.

Most Israelis celebrated the growth and reveled in the economic prosperity. Palestinians saw the new order through a decidedly different lens, referring to the city as occupied, not unified. Arab heads of state, meeting in Khartoum in late August, demanded that Israel pull back from all the land it seized as a result of the June war. These demands were ignored. On September 1, in response to the humiliating loss, especially to the loss of the Old City of Jerusalem and its holy places, the meeting participants declared that there would be "no peace, no recognition, and no negotiation" with Israel.

This declaration had immediate consequences in Jerusalem. Arab lawyers refused to argue cases in Israeli courts. Arab professional organizations opposed merging with parallel Israeli ones. Teachers and students went on strike. Merchants closed their shops. Nevertheless, lower-level employees of the municipality, who had formerly received their salaries from Jordan, continued to do their jobs and were now paid by Israel. Arab police officers were given new uniforms and reported to Israeli commanding officers. Wherever possible, however, resistance to implicit recognition of Israeli sovereignty over East Jerusalem continued.[44]

The Arabs of East Jerusalem, seeing themselves as part of the Palestinian nation, proved to be a more difficult group to integrate than the Druze, the Circassians, and the Bedouin. The aggressive actions of Israel in refashioning East Jerusalem drew more public attention than previous attempts at integration. Israeli law guaranteeing freedom of the press had an unintended consequence in Jerusalem. Unlike Beirut, Amman, Damascus, and Cairo, where press censorship was practiced, in Jerusalem, Palestinian resistance activities were featured in the press and other media. *Al-Quds*, a pro-Jordanian daily, began to appear in 1968. It was soon followed by the pro-PLO *al-Fajr* and *al-Sha'b*.[45] These papers reported daily incidents in which Palestinian Jerusalemites were subjected to humiliation by Israeli soldiers patrolling their neighborhoods and checking their identity papers. These events were also reported on the radio and were soon watched on TV. Resistance in the form of student strikes and the closing of shops were features of daily life. Reporting these events ensured their popularization.

Israeli building for residential and industrial use on land expropriated by the state in violation of international law was another topic that drew the interest of Palestinian journalists. Ultimately, nearly one third of the area of East Jerusalem was expropriated. The first area to be razed, and the most sensitive politically, was in the Old City. The Mugrahbi Quarter, abutting the Western Wall, was leveled, forcing the removal of hundreds of residents, days after the conquest. A wide plaza designed to accommodate Jewish religious and Israeli national needs replaced the homes that were destroyed. More Arabs were removed from the Old City to renovate an area that had been the Jewish Quarter until 1948. The removal of Arabs from the Old City stirred a lot of enmity, which was exacerbated as the plans to renovate the Jewish Quarter were realized and hundreds of Jews moved into the Old City.[46]

Building in what had been no-man's-land followed. The construction of the garden belt around the Old City and the new municipal center resulted in the expropriation of most of the Halaby property in Musrara. Sophie and Asia both wrote to friends about the noise and dirt produced by new construction. Their angry reactions to these changes were intensified by their personal losses. New residential areas, named Ramat Eshkol and French Hill, were erected between West Jerusalem and Mount Scopus. These projects were followed by four large suburban satellites: Neve Ya'akov, Ramot Alon, Gilo, and East Talpiot; each was in a strategic area controlling approaches to the city. Finally, another big housing project—Pisgat Ze'ev—was built on the northeast edge of the city. Many of these modern apartments added domes, arches, and courtyards, giving them a partly Middle Eastern look. These new enclaves, all illegal under international law, completed the continuous Jewish residential area from Neve Ya'akov to Mount Scopus, where the Hebrew University campus and Hadassah Hospital had been isolated since 1948. A new government center and an industrial park were built in nearby Atarot, near the airport.[47] This small airport, as well as Jordanian army facilities and police stations, were also expropriated for Israeli use. The airport, originally designed for British military use, had become a civilian airport under the Jordanians, allowing Palestinians and tourists to fly from Jerusalem to Arab capitals as well as to Europe. It was repurposed once more in 1967; Israelis bound for vacations in Eilat could now fly there from Jerusalem.

Post offices and schools in East Jerusalem continued to serve an all-Arab population. The curriculum of the schools was a contentious issue. Israel's effort to replace Jordanian texts with books used in Israeli Arab schools, and to replace the Jordanian matriculation examination with the Israeli matriculation exam, failed. Palestinians, seeing their future as part of the Arab world, wanted their children to study the Jordanian curriculum so that they could pursue higher education in Beirut or Cairo. Few saw Hebrew University as an option for their children.

The Israeli Ministry of Justice and the Jerusalem district court moved into former Jordanian government and municipal spaces within the Arab business district of East Jerusalem. The Histadrut (General Federation of Workers) opened offices and clinics in East Jerusalem to facilitate services for Arab members. Israeli banks opened, but few Arabs used them. Israeli-owned hotels did not open in East Jerusalem, despite demand. Similarly, East Jerusalem enterprises did not open branches in the West.[48]

John Melkon Rose, the Armenian who had grown up in West Jerusalem and had relocated to East Jerusalem in 1953, observed that life in the city

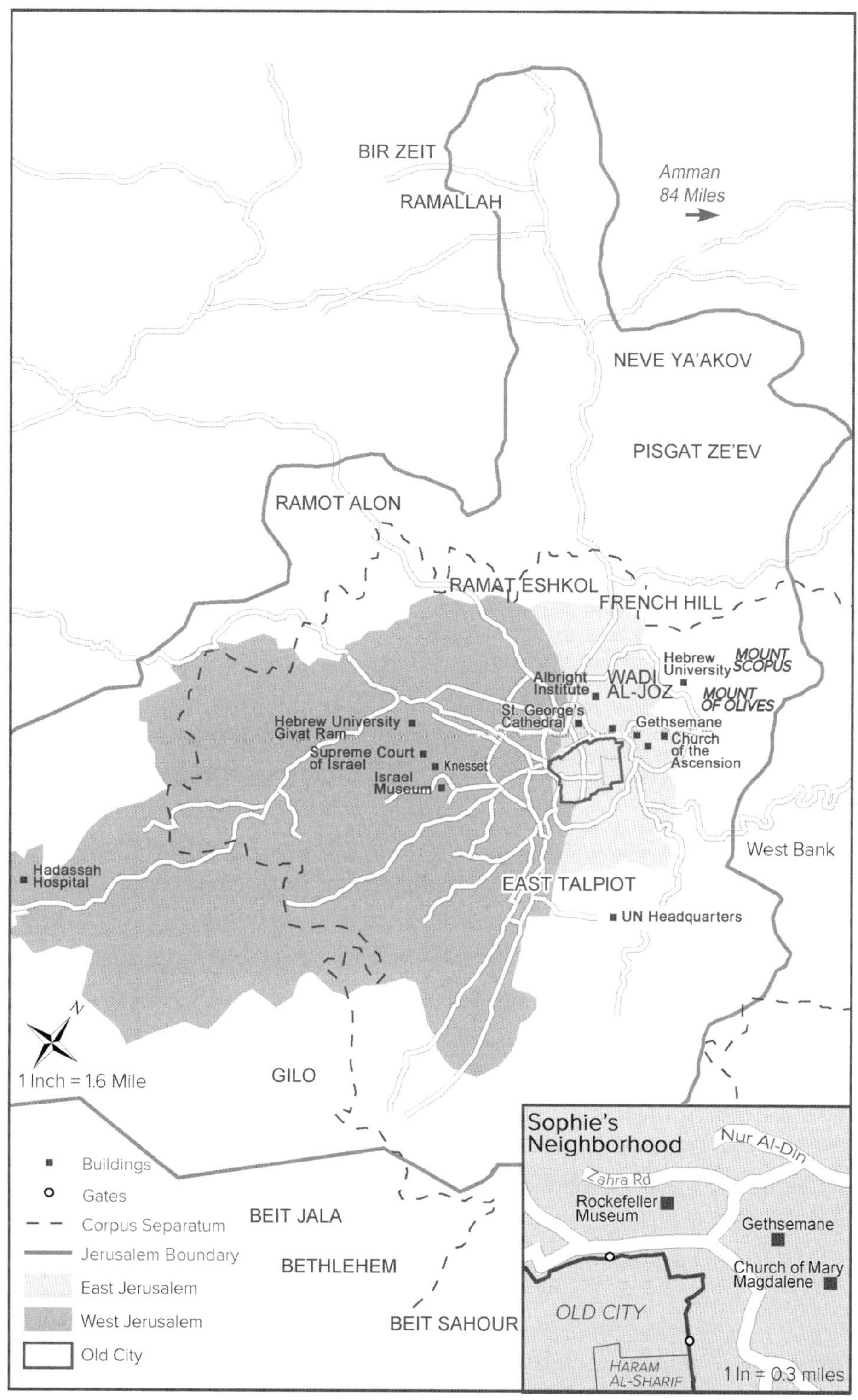

Map 2. Jerusalem after 1967. Chelsea Gross, cartographer.

changed rapidly after 1967. Employment opportunities, especially in the construction sector, grew rapidly, providing higher income for the many village Arabs who left farming for urban work. The Old City, which had been the focus of Jordanian Jerusalem life, was slowly modernized in the years following its annexation. Running water had existed in only 40 percent of the houses; many homes were not connected to the electric grid; sewage removal was not centralized. Each of these issues was addressed. Shops were also modernized. With these changes, the city lost a lot of its Arab character, as traditional trades vanished, making way for souvenir sellers who catered to tourists. New suburbs with high-rise buildings began to appear on the hills, in the view of Melkon Rose, "encircling the city with a noose of concrete."[49]

Asia's Protest

Sophie and Asia Halaby shared the experience of rapid change and profound dislocation described by John Melkon Rose. Like Hala Sakakini, John Tleel, and so many others, they recognized that there was no returning to the Jerusalem they had kept alive in their collective imagination until June 1967. Asia Halaby, who had worked first for the British Mandate and later for the Jordanian monarchy, did not work for the Israeli government. Though nearing the end of her sixth decade, Asia remained energetic and accustomed to being in charge. It was not surprising to find her name in Horatio Vester's diary entry on March 25, 1968, describing a protest activity: "The women of Jerusalem paraded in protest against a Jewish parade and were beaten by the police and jailed. Among them were Asia Halaby, Mrs. Khatib, and Mrs. Nusseibeh."[50]

On August 18, 1968, a group of ninety Arab women of East Jerusalem sent a telegram to the prime minister of Israel demanding protection for a group of young women, including one who was pregnant, who had been arrested and were being held in the same room as common criminals. These girls, the protestors claimed, were beaten by this rough element while police watched and did nothing to protect them from harm. The protestors alleged that the girls suffered cigarette burns while in prison; again, the guards did nothing. The signatories included many members of the Nusseibeh family, the Dajhani family, and Betty Majaj. Many of the signatures are unclear; it is likely that Asia Halaby's was one of them.[51]

A few days later, on August 23, Asia sent a postcard to her friends Ada and Vicken Kalbian, who had immigrated to Virginia. The picture on the reverse side of the card was that of a cyclamen. Below the image was a notation: Flowers of the Holy Land by Sophie Halaby:

> Dear Ada and Vicken,
> We miss you and appreciate news of you and are interested to learn always of your adjustments. It is not neglect that keeps us from writing! It is the inability to get used to the chaotic dirty smoky atmosphere surrounding us, even though occasionally we get some refreshing thoughts through visitors from abroad interested to eye witness the turmoil continuing at a very fast pace in the Helly Land. In the last 12 months I have covered some 22,000 kms in my faithful donkey, conveying visitors, acquainting them with the countryside and the atrocities perpetrated to the "Holy Land." It is time Christians would even awake to the reality. What great achievements the anti-Christian faction is reaching in changing the atmosphere. The physical appearance of Palestine by destruction of our slow moving into the 20th century Arab culture! No doubt the occupiers are mad maniacs. I wish I could write sweetly. Please forgive me. Love from both of us.
>
> Yours,
> Asia[52]

Asia had been busy taking foreign guests on tours of the West Bank and of the enlarged Jerusalem during the year following the Six-Day War. She had developed friendships with American and European archaeologists in the previous fifteen years. Many were eager to resume their work and required new licenses from Israeli authorities. Asia drove them to the various sites. She became aware of the growing politicization of archaeology, as Jewish nationalists saw the study as a way to prove Jewish residence in the Holy Land for millennia. Asia called out to Christians to awaken to the anti-Christian spirit she believed had taken over the Holy Land, which she bitterly called the "Helly Land."

It is possible that Asia was still smarting from an incident that had occurred several months earlier, when she accompanied Horatio Vester and James Pritchard to an excavation site at Tel Hatzor in Galilee. This site, originally excavated by the British archaeologist John Garstang in 1926, and later by the Israeli Yigael Yadin from 1955 to 1958, continued to yield rich archaeological discoveries. It is likely that Pritchard asked Horatio Vester to arrange the expedition and that Vester invited the intrepid Asia Halaby to accompany them. Vester described the beautiful day, the visit to the nearby museum, and a picnic lunch at Tel Hatzor. The pleasant afternoon with friends was ruined for Asia by an Israeli security guard stationed at the site, who asked Asia if she was an Israeli. She replied, "No, I am an Arab." He continued his banter, "You look just like one of us." She was incensed by this attempt at familiarity, according to Vester. When the guard took her arm to assist her in descending Tel Hatzor, she quickly withdrew it.[53] For Asia, this trip was not an opportunity for Israelis and Palestinians to exchange pleasantries.

Asia's fiery temperament and opposition to Israeli occupation of her city did not go unnoticed by the occupiers. On May 15, 1969, Vester reported that Asia Halaby was summoned to the Israeli police station in the Russian Compound and held there all day. The police tried to get her to sign a statement confirming that she had not taken part, was not currently taking part, and would not in the future take part in political protest activities. Asia was apparently willing to lie about the first two parts of the statement, agreeing to sign them, but she refused to sign a statement that she would not participate in the future. The next day, Vester reported that Asia came to a party at the American Colony and regaled the guests with a spirited account of her experiences.[54]

Asia Halaby appeared in Horatio Vester's diary again on February 1, 1970. This time he noted the ferocity of her attack on him for closing the Anna Spafford Baby Hospital, thereby, she charged, undoing sixty years of his mother's work. Vester, who had sought to redesign the small and now out-of-date hospital to focus on preventive medicine for mothers and babies, told Asia not to believe the gossip swirling about him. His words, he noted, had no effect on her. Asia had developed what he called "a protest personality." In fact, Vester successfully transformed the aged Anna Spafford Baby Hospital into the Spafford Children's Center, housing a modern outpatient clinic, a prenatal care program, and a well-baby clinic.

The following day, Asia met Horatio again. She asserted that she understood better than most the changes underway in Jerusalem. She proclaimed, "I am fully western and perhaps can understand to a minute degree how western minds work, as well as understanding the Arab point of view."[55] Asia believed that her dual identity aided her understanding of the political situation. Her declaration notwithstanding, Asia's participation in protests was less an expression of her dual identity and more the result of her commitment to action during times of political upheaval. Asia had taken decisive action when she volunteered for the ATS, when she tended the wounded in the Old City, and when she organized refugee women into an embroidery cooperative. After the occupation of East Jerusalem, she continued to protest efforts by Israel to assume control over the lives of Arabs.

One area over which she remained particularly vigilant was archaeology in the Old City. In 1972, Kathleen Kenyon wrote a blistering article in the *London Times* denouncing the "tunneling" in Jerusalem. She reported that she had just returned from Jerusalem, where she certainly discussed this issue with Asia, and could confirm that an Israeli team had tunneled under the Western Wall. The southern part of the wall was cleared of all buildings while a tunnel was opened under the northern part of the wall. Kenyon criticized the use of tunneling as an old practice no longer in use in modern archaeology because of the damage it had often caused. She noted that severe cracks had appeared in the excavation site of a hospice built for pilgrims in 1293. She acknowledged that Israel's Department of Antiquities had made efforts to repair the damage while members of the British School of Archaeology were documenting the plan of the building, but she warned that plans to resume tunneling were rumored: "It is also unbelievable that the exposure of ancient remains by tunneling should be undertaken in the 1970s. In the 1860s this was the way Jerusalem was explored; now, tunneling is a hundred years out of date, and is a disgrace in a country with many excellent practicing archaeologists. World opinion should give every possible help to strengthen the hands of the excellent Department in opposing this vandalism."[56]

Asia shared Kenyon's views about the irresponsible use of dated archaeological practices in the Old City. Unlike Kenyon, who returned to England, she could keep a vigilant eye on archaeological developments in the Old City.

Sophie's Protest

Sophie was aware of Kenyon's letter and of Asia's continued protest activity. However, she did not follow her sister into the streets. Though she shared her sister's anguish at the changes to Jerusalem, she remained at home, often in her studio, painting. At times, she would don a big straw hat to protect her fair skin against the sun and would set up her easel on the roof of the house. From this vantage point, she could see inside the walls of the Old City.[57] Unlike Asia, she remained silent as she bore witness to the constant changes in her city. Sophie continued to paint the hills surrounding Jerusalem as barren ridges. She removed from her canvas any expression of the new construction. This was her form of protest.

Though she remained withdrawn from the public arena, Sophie voiced her feelings in a private two-page handwritten letter to her close friend Ada Kalbian, dated three weeks after the postcard sent by Asia mentioned above. She began it formally with the date, September 17, 1968, creating a new place name, "Old City, Jerusalem, Palestine," a symbolic protest against the integration of East Jerusalem into the capital of Israel and evidence of her national allegiance. She began the letter:

> My dear Ada,
> Sincere apology for not having written to you on receipt of your first letter and for delaying answer to your second letter of 26.7.68. In normal circumstances this would have been inexcusable, but with the present situation in spite of yourself you begin to act in a peculiar way—to say the least!

Sophie was aware that the trauma resulting from the Six-Day War, specifically the invasion of her home by Israeli soldiers and the destruction of her studio by shrapnel, continued to affect her. She missed her friends Ada and Vicken Kalbian, for whom she had given a farewell party a few months earlier. She tried to remain the cosmopolitan woman they knew, but it was difficult. She continued her letter: "Certainly we were glad to learn your news and appreciate your thinking about us. If Haig [the Kalbian's oldest child] finds difficulty in merging into the new life it would not be a bad idea to keep up his interest in this part of the world through news, books and personal letters. The girls are much younger, most likely they will become Americans without much fuss but I hope they keep up their knowledge of other languages besides 'American.'"

Sophie's expression of concern for the Kalbians' children was a rare example of her interest in educating the next generation to maintain their Palestinian identity by emphasizing the importance of multilingualism and an appreciation for her city, the historic Jerusalem. Sophie wrote to Ada about the situation in her beloved homeland: "Probably you get some news from time to time about the general situation here, naturally no improvement and no hope of any settlement. We are in it—we still think it is a bad dream. The maddening, sickening happenings around us cannot—and should not be a reality. We were 'liberated' now everything is done to 'integrate' us and [to] facilitate their process 'laws' are being passed."[58]

The normally taciturn Sophie expressed her feelings candidly in this part of the letter. She likened the events of the recent past to living in a nightmare. Sophie's understanding of the events of the day was clearly in line with Asia's. Though she did not join Palestinian women who petitioned or marched, she was anguished by the changes. Sophie continued describing the "feverish activity to destroy as much as possible" of the Arab section of Jerusalem and its culture. She referred to bulldozers as "modern machinery of destruction" and noted that they were often employed day and night. Finally, she turned to Musrara, the area where the Halaby family had lived before 1948: "Musrara is melting away. Heaps of rubble are being thrown along the roads leading into town or filling valleys and natural depressions. The character of the landscape has already changed with the hilltops flattened and rows of prefabricated houses rising near the British War Cemetery on the 'requisitioned' land."[59]

Sophie was particularly distraught by the building boom that surrounded her. She did not know that a few years after she wrote this letter, a new circle with a traffic light would be installed by the municipality of Jerusalem between her home and the Rockefeller Museum.[60] The contractor for the project was Moshe Amirav, the Israeli officer who had led his troops into her house on June 5, 1967.

Sophie's letter ended with a brief personal note, "Asia and me are, thank God, keeping well and still retain some sense of humor." She continued with a professional update, explaining that the journalist Lowell Thomas, a great favorite of Bertha Spafford Vester, was staying at the American Colony. His photographer, Mr. Chase, also came to Jerusalem, bringing his wife. Mrs. Chase was a painter who asked Sophie to join her in an exhibit at the YWCA hall. Sophie reported: "The Exhibition was not much advertised but proved a great success among our friends. All my pictures (15) were sold and a number of orders placed!" Sophie concluded her letter with the observation that the political situation had become so boring that it was a relief to "plunge again into the serene world of art." She sent her love to Ada's family and added Asia's love, and asked to be remembered to all their common friends.[61]

Jerusalem: The Personal and the Political

Sophie and Asia were not alone in trying to understand the new reality for Palestinian Jerusalemites. Following the Six-Day War, Palestinians who left Jerusalem in 1948 continued to return to the city to see their homes and their old way of life. Some returned from other Arab countries, Europe, or the United States. Often, they were saddened by what they found. In 1972, Serene Husseini Shahid visited her old home in Musrara with her mother and sisters. At first, Serene was opposed to going, but her eighty-year-old mother insisted. Their house was near the Damascus Gate. Serene recorded her strong emotions:

> As the car drew up outside the front door, none of us could move. Each of us tried to hide our tears, and our deep, silent, grief. Looking up at our former home apparently unchanged, with the same balcony, the same old tree, the same bedroom windows looking up to the Virgin and Child in the Dominican compound against the blue sky, I felt the years of separation and they set me trembling. Across the street was the site of Dr. Tawfiq Canaan's house,

> razed to the ground now, and newly planted trees covering the distance to the Damascus Gate. . . . Now, Mother, the only one of us undaunted, got out of the car. Leaning on her cane, she walked up the three steps leading to the main door, and, with her stick knocked on the door three times. The door opened and a middle-aged Jewish woman appeared. From the car, we heard Mother say politely but firmly "May I have your permission to see the inside of my house?"
>
> "Your house?" the woman gasped. "But we bought it!" Mother said: "I did not sell it." The woman spoke with an Iraqi accent. Realizing what this sudden confrontation meant, she cursed the Israeli authorities who sold her the house: "Damn them. We had our own house in Iraq. We didn't have to come and face a situation like this."[62]

Serene explained that she learned from her mother to have courage to face the "new reality." Later, she set out alone or with her sisters to explore the city that she had loved so much and from which she had been separated so long. She noted, "At every turn we were confronted by the Israeli military occupation, and at every turn we were confronted by our memories. . . . We also felt that we had no time to waste, that we had to soak up the precious memories and store them."

While middle-class Palestinians who had obtained foreign passports visited Jerusalem, those living in nearby refugee camps had little access to the city. Increasingly, their lives were disrupted by violence; this time from a new enemy. In September 1970, following continuing conflict with the PLO in Amman, King Hussein expelled Arafat and his followers. This event was known as Black September by the Palestinians because of the thousands of casualties suffered when King Hussein ordered his troops to attack Palestinian refugee camps, ostensibly to kill members of the Palestinian Resistance Movement, a group loosely affiliated with the PLO.[63] The Palestinian leadership began years of nomadic existence, first in Damascus, later in Beirut, and finally in Tunis.

Mistrust of the PLO in the West reached new heights after the 1972 murders of Israeli Olympic athletes in Munich. The following year, the 1973 Arab-Israeli War (Yom Kippur War) caught Israel off guard. However, initial Arab victories in the Sinai and in the Golan Heights were repulsed. Following the defeat of Arab forces, the Arab League, responding to the continuing condemnation of the PLO by Western powers, met in Algiers and designated the PLO the "sole legitimate representative of the Palestinian people."[64] King Hussein, who had hoped to keep the loyalty of his Palestinian citizens, saw this as a direct challenge. In response, he suspended the Jordanian Parliament, whose seats were held in equal number by Palestinian and East Bank citizens.[65]

A new generation of Palestinian leadership began to develop among students and faculty at Birzeit University in the West Bank. Israel responded with frequent military incursions on campus. The West Bank was officially governed by Israeli military law. Military Order 854, issued in 1980, granted near absolute power to Israeli authorities over faculty appointments, student admission, and curriculum. Every book taught required the stamp of the military governor. The order also required all foreign nationals teaching at Birzeit to sign a loyalty oath that they would not be involved with any "hostile" organization, specifically the PLO.[66] Tom Ricks, an American who taught at Birzeit, socialized with archaeologists and their friends in Jerusalem. Sophie and Asia were part of his circle. Ricks refused to sign the oath.[67]

In the years that followed, the visual arts experienced a sharp growth in Palestine. Young artists from the West Bank, Jerusalem, and Gaza, as well as those who lived within the 1948 boundaries of Israel, met to discuss the political situation, to rediscover their traditions, to plan art activities, and to resist the occupation. Many were arrested, but they continued to meet and eventually established the League of Palestine Artists under the direction of Sliman Mansour. These artists became part of the national movement to represent Palestinian identity and culture. For them, the aesthetic value of their work was secondary. The league held exhibits in Jerusalem and Ramallah. The members tried to express the essence of Palestinian identity in their paintings and ceramics. Sophie Halaby didn't join them. She attended their exhibits, but she continued to paint the subjects she had always painted using the techniques she had learned in Paris, even as her style evolved.[68]

In 1978, the Women's Work Committee was founded, representing progressive women from different academic, vocational, and professional backgrounds. These women tried to develop a strategy addressing both national liberation and social emancipation. This effort split into subgroups based on different political agendas. In 1980, the original committee tried again to bring women together under a new name, the Palestinian Union of Women's Work Committees. The new effort at an umbrella organization did not survive differences stemming from loyalties to trade unions, student groups, and voluntary associations.[69]

The Halaby sisters did not participate in the above committees. They continued their work—Sophie in her studio and Asia in her workshop. They remained close to their young cousin, Hana Halaby, who lived in Amman. On

June 12, 1979, Asia sent him a postcard with a painting by Sophie titled *Thorns and Thistles of the Holy Land.* She wrote:

> My dearest Hana,
> Your last request for a tablecloth set left me with a big question mark as to size, color, scheme, etc. So please let me know. But, now thanks to our mutual kind friend this has been cleared—your interest in one set has grown into the advanced figure of 50 JDs [Jordanian dinars].
>
> There are not enough expressions of appreciation and gratitude to be conveyed to you in any written form. Your attitude to be of service to the "less privileged" staying put in our homeland is more than marvelous!
>
> May the almighty bless you and yours in your heartfelt humanitarian acts, starting so early in your life, and may He always help you to succeed in every enterprise.
>
> With love for you and yours.
>
> Yours lovingly and eagerly
> to meet you all.
> AGH[70]

Eight months later, in February 1980, Asia wrote to him again thanking him for his past assistance with her project and excitedly anticipating his trip to Jerusalem.

> My dear Hana,
> Tons of appreciations: included in your interest and kindness the good news that you have decided and we shall be seeing you soon! Naturally staying with us. Thank you for the 42 JD for the past, for the 100 JD advanced for the new lot herewith (with the exception of forty oblong sachets which are not immediately available but which will be following with the first opportunity). My helpers are delighted and thank you very much for your help, and are also looking forward to meeting you. This is a very hurried note—greetings to your mother and brothers and hoping that you are doing well at your studies, and that in your case your interest in sales is not detracting from your studies! Wish well to your Granny and Uncles and all the family.
>
> Yours,
> AGH

Asia's postscript to the letter revealed that the Halaby home had acquired a telephone, with the number 282680. In her note, Asia identified the neighboring archaeological museum, where she spent a lot of time, as the Rockefeller Museum, the name given to the Palestine Archaeological Museum following the Israeli occupation. This museum, formerly administered by an international committee and briefly taken over by the Jordanian government, became part of the Israel Museum founded before the Six-Day War by Teddy Kollek.

Sophie added a few words of caution about the process of traveling to Jerusalem at the bottom of her sister's letter:

> Dear Hana
> We are glad to know that you leave to visit us soon. We intend to get your permit valid from March 20th to April 20th, and send it to you (hopefully) sometime after March 15th with the first opportunity c/o Sari or Yacub with the request to contact your uncle.
> *Important-indispensable* to get an absolutely *new passport in Amman and leave your old one at home.* The less you carry with you the better—just a weekend bag! Salams.
>
> Sincerely Aunt Sophie[71]

Betty Majaj described the difficulties of visiting family in Amman that was implied in Sophie's letter: "The trip to Amman that used to be a short drive was now a humiliating all day ordeal. Toiletries, printed or handwritten materials, cameras, film and photos were forbidden. It was dehumanizing, humiliating, and terrifying. We were stripped naked and then had a metal detector passed over our bodies. This went on for many years."[72]

Sophie and Asia remained close to the Wahbe family, who lived in nearby Beit Jala. Their friendship with Olga and her sisters went back to their childhood at the Jerusalem Girls' College. In the late 1970s, Leila Hudson, the American daughter of Vera Wahbe Hudson, visited Sophie and Asia in Jerusalem. Leila remembered that Asia wore pants, unusual dress for an Arab woman. Raouf Halaby, another young cousin, born in Jerusalem, visited from Arkansas. He described the exquisite interior of their home—its mother-of-pearl-inlay furniture, richly embroidered cushions, rugs, Roman-era marble busts, coin collections, octagonal coffee tables, and prayer beads. Helen Khader, another young relative, lived nearby. She was urged by her parents to visit Sophie and Asia with her young children. Helen reported that Asia knew how to play with children, while Sophie was always eager to return to her studio.[73]

While the Jerusalem they knew and loved continued to change, Sophie and Asia were comforted by the familiar music and ceremonies of the Russian Orthodox Church. In May of 1982, they joined the Russian Orthodox community in Jerusalem for a splendid service held at the Church of Mary Magdalene for the canonization of the Russian Grand Duchess Elizabeth. After losing her husband to an assassin's bomb, the duchess had opened a convent in Moscow to serve the poor. She was murdered by Bolsheviks in July of 1918. Her remains and those of Sister Varvara Yakovleva, her close companion, were brought to Jerusalem and buried in the crypt of the church. At the time of her canonization, her remains and those of Sister Varvara were brought up from the crypt and placed in the main body of the church.[74]

While the church continued to remain a source of support for Sophie and Asia, they were aware that some Arab leaders supported the Soviet government, which denounced their church, the Russian Orthodox Church Outside of Russia, and had long claimed church property. In the 1970s, Sophie and Asia sought a broader community to help them understand the complicated twists and turns of Middle Eastern politics. They began to hold regular salon meetings of journalists in their home. The Halaby sisters were part of the "old" women's movement, defined by Eileen Kuttab as those known for their charitable work in urban areas and for limiting their ranks to upper-class women. Their salon meetings were an expression of their transition to the "new" women's movement, which Kuttab designates as those dedicated, among other objectives, to educating women so that they could participate in public life. Guests came to listen to journalists and to question those who had access to political news. Nora Kort, who attended these "at-homes," remembered Sophie and Asia as gracious hosts and as being very circumspect. It is likely that Asia was losing her zeal for protest as she approached old age. Nora described the sisters: "They were elegant, regal women who listened to the thoughts of others and kept their own thoughts private." Sophie and Asia, she said, commented to each other only in Russian, out of a desire for privacy.[75]

In the 1980s, public opinion among Palestinians began to change. Many no longer demanded an end to the State of Israel as they had since 1948; instead, they spoke of regaining the land seized by Israel in 1967. The idea of two states for two peoples represented a new phase in Palestinian thinking about the future, but not all factions agreed. In June 1982, an attempt on the life of the Israeli ambassador to Great Britain was the casus belli for Israeli incursion into Lebanon, which resulted in four hundred thousand Lebanese and Palestinian people uprooted from their homes and from refugee camps in southern Lebanon. The massacre of Palestinian refugees at the Sabra and Shatila camps was the source of growing support for two new militant groups: Hezbollah and Hamas.[76]

Simultaneously in Jerusalem, a new center of political action with a very different approach emerged. Orient House, the family home of Faisal Husseini, who had been exiled in 1969 and returned in the late 1970s, became the center for peace discussions. Faisal, son of the revered military leader Abdel Qader al-Husseini, slain at Castel in 1948, was well educated and multilingual. He soon became the person most sought after by Western visitors. Faisal Husseini started an Arab Studies Society in the early 1980s and invited Jewish intellectuals like Yeshayahu Leibowitz to participate in discussion. Raymonda Tawil (Yasser Arafat's future mother-in-law), a journalist and friend of Ruth Dayan, participated. The editors of the pro-PLO newspaper *al-Fajr*, Hanna Siniora and Ziad Abu Zayyad, also attended meetings of the society.[77]

Sophie and Asia Halaby were not part of the guest list at Orient House. As they aged, their social world contracted. Young Palestinians referred to them as the "two old Russian ladies." Some celebrated the sisters' patriotic practice of boycotting Israeli-made products. Others remembered Asia's participation in protests and her arrest by Israeli authorities. Rumors circulated that the sisters refused to pay taxes and that their well had been sabotaged by Israeli soldiers.[78] Nonetheless, the sisters felt increasingly isolated. Their community, the Christians of Jerusalem, continued to leave the city in search of higher education and jobs.

As their city changed, the sisters continued to work: Sophie painted in her studio and corresponded with family and friends, often writing on postcards on which she had painted flowers. Asia provided linen fabric and thread to poor women, teaching them to embroider and marketing their work through a network of friends and family abroad. During their final years, the sisters, who had been recognized as modern women in their youth, struggled to understand the ideas articulated by new leaders.

6

Sophie's Legacy

1986–2016

> Visual production in its diverse forms is a critical constituent of our individual and collective memory and thus a contributor to the incessant formation of our cultural identity.
>
> —Rawan Sharaf, *Otherwise Occupied: Biennale Art*

Tallat (Outlook): Women's Art in Palestine

After 1967, young Palestinian artists from the West Bank, Jerusalem, and Gaza, as well as those who lived within the 1948 boundaries of Israel, met to discuss the political situation, rediscover their traditions, plan art activities, and resist the occupation. Many were arrested, but they continued to meet, eventually establishing the League of Palestinian Artists or Rabita. During the 1970s and 1980s, they focused on the relationship of politics to art. The art of the Rabita artists was communal, not individualistic. Its purpose was Palestinian liberation.[1]

Vera Tamari and Sliman Mansour, leading young artists, described the popularity of exhibitions in Gaza and the West Bank in the 1970s. They noted that poster reproductions of paintings were prized possessions in the poorest and most remote villages. Full of questions and eager to converse, people attended group exhibitions that featured themes of resistance to occupation. Artists painted subjects and used symbols directly meaningful to the Palestinian masses: the Dome of the Rock; the land and landscape of Palestinian villages; symbols of Canaanite and Philistine tribes; cactus, olive, and orange trees; and Palestinian village dress.[2]

Sophie was aware of the work of younger Palestinian artists, and she regularly attended exhibits of the league to see their paintings, but she did not join them.[3] She continued to spend hours alone in her studio, surrounded by her lifetime of work. She found meaning in her paintings of flowers and in the landscapes that removed man-made structures and allowed her to create the city as she wished it to be. She accompanied Asia to lectures at the Rockefeller Museum and at the Albright Institute, eager to learn about new evidence of previous life in the Holy Land. The sisters continued to participate in sewing circles at the American Colony Hotel, making clothing and blankets for poor families.

In 1986, a group of young Palestinian women artists under the leadership of Vera Tamari, a ceramicist, and Faten Toubasi, a painter, organized an exhibit at the Hakawati Theatre in East Jerusalem, then under the direction of human rights scholar Fateh Azzam. The exhibit that they created thirty years ago and its star, Sophie Halaby, are today barely remembered in Jerusalem. The event was, however, an important milestone for Sophie and for Palestinian women artists.

Tallat: Women's Art in Palestine included works by ten women, including three paintings by Sophie Halaby. This was the only time that Sophie participated in a group exhibition in Jerusalem outside the familiar environs of the YWCA. Though her works were selected to hang in the Salon des Tuileries in 1932 and again in 1933 when she was an art student in Paris, Sophie did not build a career based on exhibitions following her return to Palestine. She did not join the League of Palestinian Artists after 1967 or any of the other groups of young artists with a nationalist focus who exhibited at the Arab Orthodox Club of East Jerusalem. Kamal Boullata explained: "Halaby was a fiercely independent woman who could not respond to what might be expected of her as an artist in a time of political and national turmoil."[4] Thus, her decision to participate in the 1986 exhibit was not taken casually.

Faten Toubasi remembered accompanying Vera Tamari to Nur al-Din Street to meet Sophie and to request some of her paintings for the exhibit. The other artists who had agreed to participate belonged to a younger generation of women who had grown up after the Nakba. Some of them had heard of Sophie; they may even have glimpsed her work in Asia's embroidery shop window. Vera Tamari knew about the reclusive artist since her older sister, Tania Tamari Nasir, was a friend of Sophie's. At first, Toubasi recounted, Sophie was reluctant to agree to their request to participate in the exhibit. Nevertheless, the octogenarian graciously served them coffee and cakes and ultimately selected two landscapes to include in the exhibit. A third painting, the portrait of an elderly man sketched in charcoal on paper, made while Sophie was a student, was added to the exhibit later.[5]

Vera Tamari curated the exhibit, draping the walls of the theater with white cloth, arranging the paintings symmetrically, placing clay works on wooden stands. She used lighting to enhance the features of each work.[6] Regrettably, a catalog describing the paintings was not produced. The only documentation about the exhibit is a review that appeared in *al Fajr* on November 28, 1986; thus, there is no way of knowing which of Sophie's many landscape paintings were shown. The portrait, from Sophie's student days in Paris, dated 1930, is described in the review, written by Behar Ashhab. The model was a bearded, longhaired old man wearing only shorts. He was drawn in charcoal using lines and hatchings. His right hand, dangling between his thighs, was misshapen and redrawn separately on the side with great clarity. Samia Halaby, in a recent review of Sophie's work, noted that the artist may have redrawn the hand after receiving criticism from an instructor. It's also possible that her teacher redrew the hand. She concluded that her cousin's student drawings were of high quality.[7] It is possible that Sophie decided to include this drawing to demonstrate the work she did as a student in Paris, since in Jerusalem she was still known by many as the first Arab woman to study in the French capital. Nevertheless, the portrait of the nearly nude old man is an odd addition to an exhibit featuring Palestinian nationalist symbols. It is possible that Sophie was demonstrating the characteristics of women art students identified by Lita Whitesel: independence, impulsivity, freedom from inhibitions, and tendencies to deal with ideas in ways that were more sensory and aesthetic than verbal or logical.[8]

Ashhab, a leading art critic, used the platform of the review to comment more broadly on the restrictions placed on women's lives in Palestinian society, an issue that had gained attention through the work of several women's committees.[9] He contrasted women's limited social roles with the strength of their artistic contributions in the exhibit:

> Palestinian women may have a long way to go in achieving parity with Palestinian men in this male dominated society. But they seem already to have surpassed men in the world of artistic expression, technique, and evidently of art exhibition. The artists say they were not out to prove anything, but the 10 Palestinian women artists in the "Outlook: Women's Art in Palestine" exhibition November 15–21 at the Nuzha/el-Hakawati centre did not have to. Their art, judged by theme, brushwork or composition, must be considered among the most presentable in any local art exhibited in the occupied territories in more than two years.[10]

Ashhab added that many of the women artists held prestigious degrees: Vera Tamari had an MA in Islamic Art from Oxford. Suad Amiry and Suad Nassar both had MA degrees in city planning. Orayb Najjar was a PhD candidate in journalism at Indiana University. Faten Toubasi had an MA in oil painting from Leningrad. Samira Badran had a BA in art and education from Cairo. Sophie Halaby had studied in Paris. Kathy Soufan had studied in Sofia, Bulgaria. Teriz Azzam studied in Haifa. Mary McKone was an American teaching at the Ramallah Friends School who had studied in the United States. Of the ten women who exhibited, only two, Vera Tamari and Faten Toubasi, were well known to local exhibition followers, since they belonged to the League of Palestine Artists, which sponsored most art exhibitions in the occupied territories.

Ashhab noticed that the works were remarkably free of simplistic political statements, which, he observed, had dominated the local art scene in recent years. Ashhab, writing for *al-Fajr*, a PLO-supported newspaper, continued with some political observations. He noted that in many ways politics and art were inseparable under military occupation, and he concluded that the ten artists presented sophisticated sociopolitical messages that, whether intended or inadvertent, were all impressive. For example, Orayb Najjar's and Suad Amiry's various color and black-and-white photographs portrayed the beautiful Palestinian countryside. They showed unaltered rock formations, multicolored house fronts, gravel roads, and whitewashed interiors. Ashhab wrote: "The pictures said 'yes' to the Palestinian way of life." He commented that the watercolors of Halaby and Toubasi gave the same message, using soft colors and simple combinations.[11]

The elder stateswoman of the group, Sophie Halaby, was pictured in a photograph that accompanied the review. Surrounded by Vera Tamari, Faten Toubasi, Suad Nassar, Teriz Azzam, Mary McKone, and Suad Amiry, Sophie held a bouquet of flowers presented to her by the young artists. Ashhab singled her out for an interview. He asked her if she continued to paint. She said that she had stopped painting more than two decades before the exhibit, thus her last works would have been completed before the occupation of East Jerusalem.[12] However, her response to Ashhab was either intentionally misleading or simply mistaken. In her letter to Ada Kalbian, cited above, Sophie reported seeking solace from the turbulence of the occupation in painting. It is interesting that the works she selected to exhibit in 1986 were painted before many of the other participants were born: Sophie reported that her landscapes were from the 1950s, while the portrait was from her student days.[13]

Ashhab pursued his line of questioning, asking her why she had stopped painting. Sophie teasingly explained, "I don't want to get in trouble with the occupation," perhaps referring to a law forbidding artists to use green, black, red, and white, the colors of the Palestinian flag, in paintings. Her humorous response deflected the harsh reality she had experienced since the

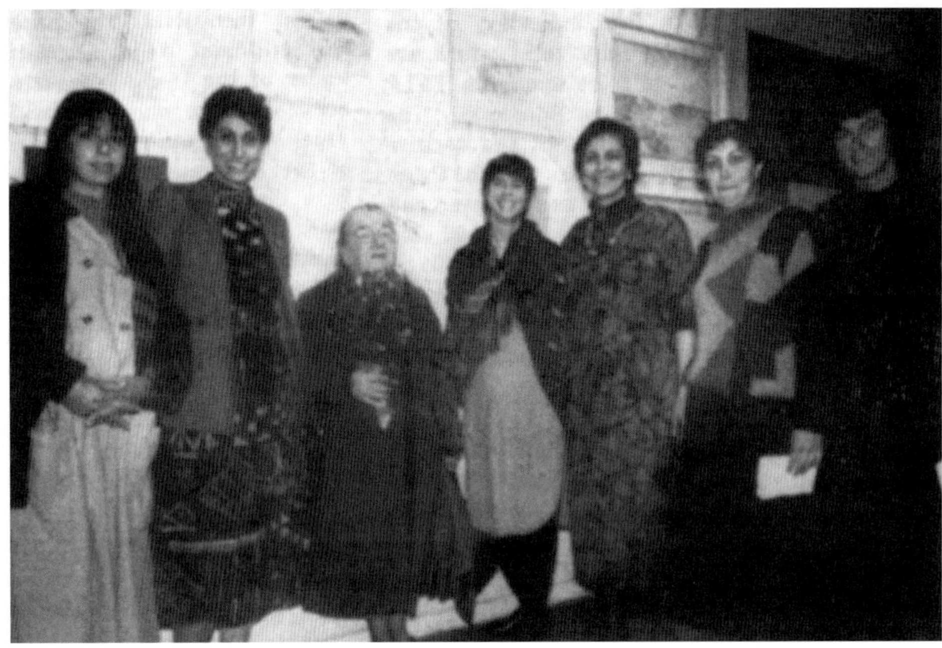

13. Sophie Halaby and young artists, 1986. *Left to right*: Suad Nassar, Suad Amiry, Sophie Halaby, Teriz Azzam, Vera Tamari, Faten Toubasi, Mary McKone. Private collection.

occupation. She didn't make reference to the fact that her studio had been badly damaged by a shell during the fighting that led to Israel's capture of the Old City in 1967. She didn't refer to the repeated arrests of her sister, Asia, for participating in resistance efforts. She didn't mention the routine harassment experienced by Jerusalemites who wished to travel to Beirut or Amman, where she had family and friends. In sum, she refused to discuss politics. To defuse the tension surrounding political questions, she added, "anyway, everything looks foggy to me now," no doubt referring to her failing vision. (A photo of Sophie taken in 1959 showed her wearing glasses; in old age, perhaps her vision was impaired.) When asked about her age, she replied: "I stopped counting after fifty."[14]

At the time of the exhibit, Sophie was nearing the beginning of the final decade of her life. Her younger sister, Asia, would soon begin to show signs of dementia, putting a strain on the enduring companionship the sisters had shared throughout their lives. Not long after the exhibit, Asia stopped driving with Sophie to the nearby villages where they purchased fresh fruit and vegetables, sometimes lingering so that Sophie could paint wildflowers. They no longer went on walking tours together led by the archaeological associations to which they belonged. Sophie was no longer able to share her thoughts with Asia as she had throughout their lives. Sophie cared for her sister for many years; they continued to entertain friends and family, but increasingly, Asia, the outspoken sister, was silent, looking to Sophie to answer questions for her.[15]

Perhaps Sophie overcame her reticence and agreed to have her work displayed at the Hakawati Theatre with young artists because Vera Tamari was the younger sister of her friend Tania Tamari Nasir.[16] Certainly, she also realized that there would not be many more opportunities to share her art with the public. Asia's declining health led to the closing of the embroidery shop that the sisters had maintained on Zahra Street, where Sophie had displayed one painting per week in a window frequented by young artists. In a culture that continued to privilege men and in which women were not supposed to have independent lives, the exhibit challenged conventional wisdom. Following a lifetime of work as an artist, perhaps Sophie was ready to claim a place in the growing group of Palestinian artists. Sophie knew that the exhibit at the Hakawati Theatre would provide the Jerusalem public with a rare chance to see her work. Today, Jerusalemites have vague memories of this exhibit, but no longer remember anything about the works shown or the people who attended.

The exhibit's curator, Vera Tamari, born in 1945, was nearly four decades younger than Sophie. By the time she was ready for college, the American University of Beirut had a fine arts department, something that had not existed in Sophie's day.[17] Vera graduated from AUB in 1966. Despite this new educational opportunity, professional careers for Palestinian women in the mid-1960s and 1970s were even narrower than the opportunities experienced by Sophie when she graduated from the Jerusalem Girls' College in 1924. At that time, Arab families were pleased when their daughters chose to work in British government offices, or to work for British companies. In the mid-1960s, there were no similar opportunities for girls. They could still train to be teachers. Few chose to study nursing or medicine, as the taboo against touching men remained strong. Some became social workers. Others went on to higher education. Forty years after Sophie had set an example for Arab girls who wanted to study art professionally, Vera lamented that there were only two possibilities open to her that would neither offend society nor cast aspersion on her family: she could become a housewife, painting in a small corner at home as her mother had, or she could become an art teacher. Despite Sophie's path-breaking example and despite the political upheaval caused by the occupation and the resultant interest in art as a medium to develop nationalism, there was still no social acceptance for Arab women as professional artists.

In the early 1970s, Vera followed Sophie's lead and traveled to Europe for further education, going to Florence to study ceramics. A decade later, having gained a reputation as a ceramicist and as a teacher, Vera returned to Europe, hungry for more education. This time, she studied for a master's degree at Oxford. Despite her talent and education, Vera felt that her opportunities were limited.

Vera was frequently asked if her art was political. She explained that she consciously tried to express herself through the colors of Palestine, village and landscape scenes, and traditional motifs. She used designs adapted from traditional embroidery. Nevertheless, she said: "My art probably doesn't stir violent emotions in people. It won't start a revolution, but it makes them happy inside because they are related to it."[18] Vladimir, Vera's brother, also chafed at the narrow opportunities opened to him as an artist in Palestine. Like his friend Kamal Boullata, he traveled until he found a more congenial space to engage his talents. Vladimir Tamari lived most of his life in Japan; Kamal Boullata lives in southern France. Vera Tamari, like Sophie Halaby, remained close to her Jerusalem birthplace. She lives and works in Ramallah.

Halaby Landed Property

On August 5, 1986, Asia Halaby took the American archaeologist Nancy Lapp and her daughter Sharry on a tour of what had been Halaby family property in Musrara. Asia had already taken many foreign visitors to see the changes that followed the unification of Jerusalem in 1967; this trip was probably her last. Mrs. Lapp and her archaeologist husband, the late Paul Lapp, were friends of the Halaby sisters. Paul Lapp had been the director of the American School of Oriental Research in East Jerusalem for six years, beginning in 1960. Paul, who died young in a swimming accident, had an illustrious career as an archaeologist of the Holy Land. Asia Halaby accompanied the Lapp family to several dig sites during the 1960s. In 1986, Mrs. Lapp returned to Jerusalem following a long absence to visit her daughter, who had settled in Ramallah. Asia offered to show the women her old neighborhood. Much of that land had remained untouched during the years the city was divided, as it lay in no-man's-land. Following the Israeli conquest of East Jerusalem, however, developers had leveled the Halaby homes in order to build a park around the Old City and to build a new office complex for the Jerusalem municipality. Much of an orchard had been destroyed to make room for high-rise apartment buildings to accommodate new immigrants, primarily Moroccan Jews. A playground was built on a corner lot to provide a place for children to play. Lilac trees were uprooted to create space for yet another apartment building. Mrs. Lapp took ten photos to document the areas formerly owned by the Halaby family. The last photo is of Asia picking wild flowers in the one open area remaining of the former Halaby estate.[19] Many family and friends remembered that Sophie Halaby railed against Teddy Kollek, mayor of Jerusalem, for stealing her land; it was the Musrara property she had in mind.[20]

Both Sophie and Asia harbored anguished feelings about the loss of their property, similar to the feelings expressed by others who returned to Jerusalem to look at homes lost in 1948. They felt especially aggrieved since their houses and gardens were not destroyed until 1967. For nineteen years the sisters had continued to hope that they might still regain possession of their property. However, following the victory of Israel in the Six-Day War, their land was expropriated by the state under the terms of the Absentee Property Act, which had been enacted in 1950. This Israeli law authorized the Custodian of Absentee Property to sell the property of Arab refugees. Thus, in continued defiance of UN resolutions, Arab property was confiscated by the State of Israel. In some cases, Jews moved into formerly Arab homes, and in other cases the houses were demolished to make way for new building projects.[21]

Sophie and Asia owned property in Bethlehem in addition to their home in East Jerusalem. They were keen to avoid losing it to expropriation by the state. Diana Safieh was a trusted family friend, the daughter and niece of old friends of the Halaby family. When she learned that Sophie and Asia planned to make a gift of their land in Bethlehem to a church to establish a home for the elderly, she urged them to work with the Catholic Church, which had agreed to build the home and to provide a small house for Sophie and Asia where they could be cared for in their advanced years. After a lot of discussion with Diana, who was Catholic, Sophie and Asia decided to donate their land to the Orthodox Church in Bethlehem through Mayor Freij. Sadly, Freij did not do as promised; he took the land for himself. The old age home was not built. Sophie also railed against the perfidious Freij for years.[22]

At about the same time, Hana Halaby, a cousin who lived in Amman, warned Sophie and Asia that the man who was renting the house they owned in Amman was trying to take legal possession, in effect stealing it from them. Hana Halaby was able to help prevent the theft of this property, which remained in their estate, by intervening on their behalf.[23] The land that had been the source of their wealth for decades was threatened by new laws and unscrupulous dealings.

John Tleel, who knew the sisters for thirty years, said that they were fearful that their land in East Jerusalem might be expropriated. They asked him to help them donate their land and their home to the Orthodox Church in Jerusalem to create a *waqf* (charitable foundation). He made some inquiries for them, but his offer of help was ultimately turned down as Sophie came under the influence of Issa Hamed, a lawyer recommended by Nora Kort. Sophie and Asia had gone to school with members of the Kort family. When Nora recommended Hamed, they were confident of his trustworthiness.

Hamed, however, was also eager to realize personal benefits from his association with the Halaby sisters. Nora Kort soon recognized her error in recommending him and tried to convince Sophie to fire him, but it was too late. In her last decade of life, Sophie struggled to care for her sister, who needed increasing levels of attention. No family members offered to live with her or to assist her at home. Hamed, who lived nearby, moved in with his wife and child. His wife cooked for all of them. Hamed provided companionship for Sophie in the last years of her life. Family and friends, including the nuns on the Mount of Olives, resented him, as he restricted their access to Sophie.[24]

Intifada in Jerusalem

Until the mid-1980s, East Jerusalem remained the major urban center for the West Bank, serving as a locus for banking and credit, an employment hub, and an educational and cultural magnet. The city contained the major specialized and general hospitals, the major shopping centers, educational and research centers, religious sites, and religious service organizations for both Muslims and Christians of all denominations. However, as a result of Israel's policies, East Jerusalem gradually lost its role as the center of the West Bank. It lost its service and market status to Ramallah, Nablus, and Hebron. Its economy became dependent on West Jerusalem as a supplier of cheap labor and as a minor market for Israeli commodities. East Jerusalem continues to evoke considerable passion as a center for Christian and Muslim worship and as a contested future capital for Palestine.[25]

Ali Qleibo, an artist and anthropologist, returned to live in the Old City in December 1987, following an absence of thirteen years in Europe, the United States, and Japan. He returned to teach at Bethlehem University as the intifada began. The intifada was the name given collectively to the acts of civil disobedience—refusal to pay taxes, merchant strikes, noncompliance with military orders, and demonstrations—that were a new expression of the Palestinian protest against Israeli occupation that began in December 1987 and lasted until 1993. Political graffiti appeared under cover of night, denouncing the occupation.[26] University students, women, and children participated, challenging the traditional patriarchal leadership of Palestinian society. The intifada reoriented Palestinian identity toward the conditions of occupation.[27]

Qleibo used his poetic skills to capture the changes brought on by occupation. He recorded what he saw in *Before the Mountains Disappear*, published in 1992. The book begins with a poem that explains his title:

> Before the mountains disappear
> I returned to what is left to us of Palestine,
> I live within the walls of Jerusalem and I long for its alleys, its covered
> passageways, its domes and
> I look forward to them every morning and every evening.
> I drive through our countryside and feel nostalgic for our fields and valleys
> as I look at them.
> I breathe our mountain air and yearn for it at the same moment.
> I fear that before this century is over the mountains of the West Bank and the
> Gaza Strip will have turned into residential barracks for Jewish settlers.
> This fear is no longer a transient nightmare that disturbs our sleep.
> The truth is clear and bitter:
> In the near future, each Arab city and each Arab village will be surrounded
> by a thick belt of settlements and we will be strangers in our own land.
> Sooner or later, short of a miracle, the mountain tops will disappear from
> the horizon, will become extinct and will retreat to become hostage in a few
> nature reserves.[28]

Sophie spent decades expressing similar feelings in her paintings of Jerusalem. Like Qleibo, she felt that her city was changing and in the process becoming alien. Her landscapes were images of Jerusalem as she remembered it in her childhood, before the noise of construction filled the air and dust polluted the atmosphere. Like Qleibo, Sophie had studied abroad. Like him, she returned home, where her paintings exhibited "that deep mysterious sense of contentment produced by the feeling of belonging."[29] Sophie rarely painted buildings; when she did they were limited to those elements of the Old City of Jerusalem that she viewed from her studio windows or her rooftop.

Qleibo reported on the international coverage of the intifada and on the measures taken by Israel to quell the rebellion. He noted that Joan Baez gave a concert in the National Palace Hotel and Richard Dreyfuss came to express his support. The American Colony Hotel and the National Palace Hotel were crowded with international press, television and radio reporters. In the streets, masked youths wearing kaffiyehs attacked a municipal van, a symbol of the occupation. Failing to overturn the van, they used stones to break all the windows. Finally, they pushed a burning tire under the van hoping for an explosion of the gas tank. Nothing happened. Israeli soldiers firing tear gas appeared and the youngsters disappeared. Reporters ran between the two groups, eager to film the event, sniffing onion slices to counteract the tear gas.[30]

Many Palestinian Jerusalemites shared the excitement described by Qleibo when learning of Palestinian resistance: "The euphoria accompanying confrontations with the Israeli soldier is contagious. The excitement moves from the street and through the windows to us, the crowds of spectators inside our houses. We respond with sporadic thundering burst of applause. Commonplace clichés are reiterated by the throngs of men and women watching from windows and balconies. 'May God's support be with you.'"[31]

Jerusalemites told and retold stories of defiance and repression. One story described an event that took place on Sunday, January 10, 1988, when a group of women marched to protest the occupation, starting at the Damascus Gate and heading toward Herod's Gate. The marchers were quiet. No stones were thrown. Nevertheless, halfway between the gates, near the Pilgrims Palace Hotel, simultaneously from two directions, horsemen, jeeps, and vans filled with armed Israeli soldiers descended on them. The soldiers came from the east, from the direction of the Halaby home on Nur al-Din Street, and from the west, from Musrara. The women were trapped; soldiers attacked them with clubs and carried them into the vans. As one tried to free herself, her dress was torn, exposing her flesh. A taxi driver parked near Herod's Gate rushed over to one of the soldiers shouting, "For shame, you cannot treat a young lady this way!" He was told to mind his own business.[32]

At the end of July 1988, nearly forty years after annexing the West Bank and East Jerusalem, Jordan renounced claims to the area and recognized the PLO as the sole legitimate representative of the Palestinian people. On November 15, 1988, the Palestinian Parliament in exile, the Palestinian National Council, met in Algiers and declared statehood. It also adopted a resolution that accepted the two-state solution. Many Palestinians were unprepared for these changes in policy; they felt deceived by their leadership. A few years later, the PLO sided with Iraq against the United States in the Gulf War of 1991; the outcome of the war left the PLO leadership in a weakened position.[33]

The United States sought to create a peaceful solution to the years of Israeli occupation through the peace process developed at the Madrid Peace Conference, in which the Palestinians had no direct representation. Simultaneously secret talks held in Oslo led to the Declaration of Principles signed by Yasser Arafat and Yitzchak Rabin on the White House lawn in 1993. This Oslo agreement created the Palestinian Authority, which had administrative jurisdiction over civilian affairs in the West Bank and Gaza. The response to the agreement in Jerusalem was at first euphoric. Palestinians, anticipating that East Jerusalem would become the capital of Palestine, distributed flowers to Israeli soldiers and placed olive branches in the barrels of their guns. Their reactions changed when they understood that discussions about Jerusalem would await "final status talks," with no indication of when they would begin. There were other developments. Arafat returned to Jericho and Gaza. In 1994, Jordan and Israel signed a peace treaty, the first between Israel and an Arab country since the Egyptian treaty of 1979.[34]

Declining Years

Political events continued to draw those interested in peace to Jerusalem. Many stayed at the American Colony Hotel, where Sophie and Asia had spent sociable afternoons in previous years. Sophie now had trouble keeping up with changes in Jerusalem. Her life became more circumscribed, more inward looking. After many years of caring for Asia, the companion she had relied on for decades, Sophie moved her to a nursing home run by a Halaby cousin in nearby Emmaus. Not long thereafter, Sophie's dear friend, Mother Superior Paraskeva, died following a long illness. Sophie paid for her medical expenses. Suffering from heart disease, Sophie was now alone except for Hamed. Friends who visited her were often turned away by Hamed, who hovered nearby and limited access to Sophie. At the end of her life, Sophie spent several months in the cardiac ward of St. Joseph's Hospital in East Jerusalem, where Dr. Ahmed cared for her.[35]

During her last months, Sophie amended her will, naming Hamed as her sole heir. The deceitful lawyer also had her sign over all the property deeds to him, perhaps forging her signature. Sophie died on May 22, 1997; she was buried on the Mount of Olives, which she had painted so many times, next to her parents in the graveyard of the Church of Mary Magdalene. Few attended her funeral. Nine months later, on February 12, 1998, her sister, Asia, died and was buried next to Sophie. Though the sisters left property valued at millions of dollars to Issa Hamed, proper headstones have not been erected on their graves.

Hamed remained alone in the Halaby house on Nur al-Din. His wife left him, taking their child. His lifestyle became profligate. He bought fancy sports cars with the ill-gotten inheritance and drove them around the city. Hamed died a few years after the Halaby sisters. His corpse was discovered in the house. Efforts to restore ownership of the house to the Halaby family are still underway.[36]

Hamed had no appreciation for Sophie's art. Taher Nusseibeh, the former neighborhood delivery boy, claimed to have come into possession of Sophie's paintings by finding them in the garbage. Nusseibeh contacted Mazen Qupty, an early collector of Palestinian artists, and offered him the opportunity to buy Sophie's paintings. Qupty, recognizing the importance of her work, bought seventy-five paintings—oils and watercolors—for five thousand dollars. George al-Ama, another collector, was also offered an opportunity to acquire paintings and bought a similar number, mostly watercolors. Had it not been for Taher Nusseibeh and these two collectors, Sophie Halaby's work would have been forgotten.[37]

Sophie's Legacy

In 2000, fourteen years after the *Tallat* exhibit at Hakawati, a second exhibit devoted to Palestinian women artists was organized. The organizer was Tal Ben Zvi, an Israeli graduate student who was writing an MA thesis in art history titled, "Between Nation and Gender: The Representation of the Female Body in Palestinian Art" at Tel Aviv University. Funded by the European Commission, this exhibit, *Self-Portrait: Palestinian Woman's Art*, was designed to open at the al-Wasiti Art Center in Jerusalem, which was under the direction of Sliman Mansour, and to travel to the Ami Steinitz Gallery in Tel Aviv and then to the International Center in Bethlehem. Regrettably, the exhibit was postponed indefinitely because of the Al-Aqsa Intifada. Fortunately, funding for a catalog remained intact. Ben Zvi edited a catalog that was to have accompanied the exhibit. Published in 2001, the catalog reviewed the nine artists scheduled to exhibit and included images of their works. In addition to her own essay, Ben Zvi solicited articles from Tina Sherwell and Kamal Boullata. Their work allowed scholars to study the planned exhibit, which was to have been a conversation among women artists, part of a larger discussion on identity, culture, and Palestinian art.

None of the nine women artists whose work was to have been included in the 2000 exhibit had participated in the previous exhibit in 1986, yet they clearly stood on the shoulders of earlier Palestinian women, including Sophie Halaby. Ben Zvi wrote: "*Self-Portrait* represents each artist's commitment to move from the personal sphere into the public sphere in terms of her modes of representation and the ways her work will be experienced, viewed, and criticized. The outing of the personal and the subjective is a conscious choice. It is a political act an authorial position, an assertion of self-definition."[38]

Kamal Boullata contributed the essay "Pioneering Women in Palestinian Art." Boullata, who remembered Sophie's art from the window display on Zahra Street, was now a well-known artist who had begun to write about Palestinian art history. He observed that in earlier times, Arab women wrote poetry to express their inner feelings, while more recently they expressed themselves using the visual arts as well. He felt that each of the young artists participating in this project had captured images from their own worlds to escape the prison—the occupation or the exile—in which she had been conceived. Boullata chose to write about three women whose works may have inspired those participating in the exhibit: Zulfa al-Sa'di, whose paintings were exhibited at the first National Arab Fair in Jerusalem; Juliana Seraphim, whose family fled Jaffa and moved to Beirut in 1948; and Mona Hatoum, born in Beirut, the daughter of refugees from Haifa. The portraits that al-Sa'di hung in the halls of the Supreme Muslim Council in Jerusalem, he explained, ignored inherited conventions associated with image-making as much as Seraphim's erotic imagery defied the inhibitions prevalent in her cultural milieu. Hatoum, Boullata continued, chose a visual language that broke with the pictorial tradition of Lebanon, where she resided. Their work reflected themselves, their political memory, and their reality.[39] Boullata's decision to exclude Sophie Halaby from this group of pioneers is understandable; living abroad, he didn't have access to her paintings. A few years later, Boullata returned to Jerusalem, where he interviewed Russian nuns on the Mount of Olives to learn about Sophie's life. At that time, he was also able to study Qupty's collection. He was therefore able to include a study of her work in his important book, *Palestinian Art.*

Tina Sherwell's essay "Imaging Palestine as the Motherland" pointed out the difference between Palestinian artists who lived within their historic homeland, like Sophie, and those who lived in exile: "Palestinians on the inside experience a particular form of displacement . . . because they do not live in what they imagine and desire Palestine to be . . . while those living in exile hold a more static memory of Palestine normally centered around the moment of their departure."[40]

Sherwell, who grew up in England, observed that the Zionist project of searching for and claiming exclusively Jewish roots in Palestine, such as the archaeological work that concerned Asia Halaby, had the effect of denying the Arab historical presence there. It was not surprising to Sherwell that representations of the landscape would dominate the artistic expression of Palestinians and Israelis alike, each seeking to find validation for their historic claims. She noted that as Palestinian art gained popularity with the Palestinian public from the mid-1970s to the mid-1980s, Israeli authorities began to confiscate paintings and to close exhibitions containing political messages. (Sophie Halaby's cryptic response to Ashhab's questions in 1986 alluded to these measures.) Exhibits required permission from the Israeli military government; artists and exhibits were banned from foreign travel, and the colors of the Palestinian flag were not permitted in paintings.[41]

Ben Zvi contributed a review essay for the catalog which identified each of the artists whose works were to have been included in the exhibit: Iman Abu Hamid, a native of Acre, dealt with the concept of home; Faten Fawzy Nastas addressed domestic space, conveying a sense of claustrophobia; Manar Zu'abi used black silk stockings to delimit space, to mark boundaries; Ahlam Shibli sketched a game of hopscotch in which participants were forbidden to cross the lines; Suheir Isma'il Farraj's film told the story of a Palestinian woman about to give birth, emphasizing the value of sons; Jumana Emil Abboud created collages of symbolic figures—the Virgin Mary, a Pharaonic-Egyptian woman, and the Egyptian actress Nabila Ebeid; Hanan Abu Hussein created a carpet of paraffin breasts; Manal Murqus's ceramic work dealt with ignorance, repression, and lack of awareness among women with regard to their bodies, especially their genitals; Aida Nasrallah displayed four paintings representing four female types: the poet, the dejected one, the naïve one, and "Fatima," who died in an honor killing, falsely suspected.[42]

Had the European Commission not funded the catalog, none of these essays documenting the participation of Palestinian women in the visual arts would have been written and published. Ben Zvi noted ruefully that there were still no art academies under the auspices of the Palestinian Authority; nor were there any Arabic-language art schools in Israel. Thus, young Palestinians still went abroad to study art.[43] Sophie Halaby, who had pioneered study abroad so many decades earlier and whose work was featured in the 1986 exhibit, was not included in the planned exhibit in 2000, nor was she mentioned in any of the catalog essays, though her early work depicting portraits of women, dressed and nude, were harbingers of the work discussed in the catalog. After Sophie's death, her work disappeared for several years and her reputation faded.

Sliman Mansour, an established artist and the founder and director of the al-Wasiti Art Center, had arrived in Jerusalem from a neighboring village in 1965 to study art. Though he had heard of Sophie Halaby, he was too shy to request permission to visit her studio. Thus, he did not see her work during her lifetime. Shortly after her death, he made an effort to acquire some of her pieces. Mansour went to Sophie's home on Nur al-Din Street to ask about using some of her paintings for a planned exhibit to be called *Pioneer Palestinian Artists*. Hamed turned him away, telling him that he had burned everything.[44] Mansour subsequently learned that Taher Nusseibeh had some sketches and paintings. As the plans for the exhibit matured, Sliman went to see Nusseibeh, who loaned him several works for an exhibit that took place in 2003. It was in Nusseibeh's storage area that Sliman first saw Sophie's work, which had not been shown to the public since 1986.[45]

The exhibit organized by Mansour opened at the al-Wasiti Art Center in Jerusalem and traveled to the al-Hallaj Gallery in Ramallah. Regrettably, no reviews of this exhibit have been found, so it is impossible to know how it was received. Fortunately, the Swiss Agency for Development Cooperation funded the publication of a catalog of the exhibit. The catalog, written by Tina Sherwell, was difficult to find. There may be copies in private collections, but there is only one copy available to scholars; it is located in a library in Geneva. *Forgotten Scene: Pioneer Artists from Palestine* includes a discussion of six Jerusalem artists: Sophie Halaby, Nihal Bishara, Daoud Zalatimo, Jabra Ibrahim Jabra, Mubarak Sa'ad, and Zulfa Sa'di. Sherwell explained that "pioneer Palestinian artists" are those who worked in the visual arts before the founding of the State of Israel and the subsequent dispersal of the Palestinian people. She noted that there is little written about these artists because of the fragmentation of Palestinian society after 1948 and the loss of documentation. She concluded: "from the outset, one must acknowledge that Palestinian art history is a discourse that is founded on fragmented narratives."[46] Rather than attempting to create a timeline for all Palestinian art, Sherwell organized the catalog by genre: landscape paintings, Palestinian landscapes, portraiture and figurative paintings, and historical portraits.

Fourteen of Sophie's works were included in the catalog. There is no indication of their provenance, but it is likely that they all came from Taher Nusseibeh's collection. Nine are landscapes in watercolor on paper, and one, lush and verdant, is in oil on canvas. All but one of these ten landscapes feature Jerusalem and its vicinity. Three are portraits: two pencil on paper, one charcoal on paper, as well as one watercolor flower painting. It is unclear where these works are today.

By the time Sherwell wrote about Sophie's art, the artist was no longer alive to read of the recognition she received. It is likely that she would have agreed with Sherwell's opening statement: "The landscape surrounding Jerusalem was one of her favourite subjects and sources of inspiration. In her works Jerusalem's hills are portrayed in different moods, nearly always vacant of human presence, as it was rather the hues and contours of the land that Halaby continually studied."[47] Sherwell went on to contrast Halaby's art with that of the European tradition of depicting the Holy Land: "Halaby does not choose to portray grand panoramas . . . rather her paintings express a more intimate relationship to the land. At times one can discern the silhouette of the Dome of the Rock and other buildings in her paintings. However landmarks are never glorified in her images, rather they are registered via a few simple brush-strokes. Similarly, in a number of her watercolours, the landscape dissolves away from the horizon line into strokes of colour."[48] Sherwell concluded her review of Halaby's landscapes by noting the lack of religious buildings in her work. Her landscapes are, in Sherwell's view, a "tender study of the qualities of the hilly terrain surrounding the city."[49]

Sherwell's appreciation of Sophie Halaby's work was not limited to her landscapes. She included two pencil sketches by Sophie in the catalog. The first, the portrait of a nude seated woman, dated 1932, was used by Sherwell to illustrate her belief that the genres of painting pursued by Palestinian artists in this period mirrored the education they received in Western academies. The second, the face of a woman, dated 1930, was based on a model also found in sketches in George al-Ama's collection. These sketches were made during Sophie's student years in Paris. The third portrait, also from the 1930s, is charcoal on paper and is an image of a woman working in a kitchen. Sherwell noted that this is one of the few images in existence by Palestinian artists of the domestic interior. She states: "this sketch . . . recalls the work of French women impressionists who executed many studies of the middle and upper class home environment." The drawing shows a burly woman busily preparing food. Sophie included a view from the kitchen window that appears to be Paris.[50]

Seven years after the unsuccessful effort of Ben Zvi to exhibit Palestinian women's work at al-Wasiti, Reem Fadda, a Palestinian art historian and curator, organized an exhibit at the new Palestinian art center, al-Hoash, in East Jerusalem. The exhibit was titled *Palestinian Women Artists*. In the catalog, Fadda devoted considerable attention to landscape painting, noting that especially after the Nakba, Palestinian women artists used this genre as a way to claim their rightful place in the land. She singled out several artists, including Sophie, for their landscapes: "The vast Palestinian landscape has been portrayed beautifully in the watercolors and oil paintings of artists such as Nihal Bishara, Sophie Halaby, Faten Toubasi, and Afaf Arafat. Its hillsides, beaches, mountains, and flora are recurring subject matter in the still life work of women artists from the beginning of the twentieth century, and they persist in the artwork of today."[51]

Fadda quoted Sherwell, who posited landscape painting as a form of self-definition: "Landscapes came to dominate Palestinian art, as they were conceived as the locus of Palestinian identity."[52] She also noted Boullata's observation, "the closer artists live to the home culture, the more figurative their art, and the farther away they settle the more their art evolves into abstraction."[53] In addition to her wide reading about Palestinian art, Fadda had access to the Qupty collection of Halaby works. She was particularly impressed by the landscapes and also by still-life paintings she saw: "The Qupty collection of Sophie Halaby's works shows multiple depictions of olive groves and traditional Palestinian rugged landscapes, a divergence from the lavish and green impressionistic paintings she would have been exposed to early in the century. This reveals her ability to internalize—and localize—the language of art. Even in her still life work, Halaby reproduced elements of Palestinian nature and tradition: garlic and a bottle of olive oil, pomegranates and oranges."[54]

Fadda included four images of Sophie's work in her catalog of the exhibit; all are from the Qupty collection. Three are watercolors on paper that capture Sophie's interest in wild flowers and in the landscape of Jerusalem: pink cyclamens, the Garden Gate from Gethsemane, and the Mount of Olives with the Church of Ascension tower in background. The final image, of a nude woman, is vibrantly painted in oil on canvas.

Two years after the exhibit, Kamal Boullata's comprehensive history of Palestinian art was published in English. He devoted several pages to Sophie Halaby's life and work. Boullata, who had been inspired by Sophie's work when he was a boy, continued to value it after he became an accomplished artist and art historian. Boullata's extensive comments on Sophie's nudes, her flowers, and her landscapes are described in chapters 2 and 4. He included eight of Sophie's paintings in his book, all from the Qupty collection. They were untitled and undated. The first is a watercolor; Boullata called the painting *Basilica of the Resurrection*, a location more commonly known as the Church of the Holy Sepulchre. He grouped five of the paintings, calling the series *The Mount of Olives*. In one of them, the artist added pencil to the watercolor; in another she added black ink. Two paintings are female nudes seen from the back: one is a watercolor; the other is tempera on paper.[55]

In 2014, Esmail Neshif published *On Palestinian Abstraction*, a study of Zohdy Qadry, a Palestinian who studied art in St. Petersburg. Neshif's introduction to Qadry's work devotes substantial attention to Sophie Halaby, positing that her works, like his, used elements of the visual culture of both Russia and Palestine to create unique images. Neshif described her watercolor technique in detail: "she divides the watercolor into various shades, and then uses a pencil or a pen to define the different forms and the relationship between them, which, in turn, build up the painting." He continued to explain that she used two main colors in most of her works: the color of the human body, and a sandy, soil-earthy color. She also used different shades of green as an interface color that links the bottom to the top of the painting. Neshif noted: "In the watercolor paintings, the equal distribution of light is predominant, recalling the Jerusalem climate, with the use of color spectrums going from the public-light and the private-dark for shading, in order to illustrate the curves, angles, and sides."[56]

Neshif continued his review of Sophie's works, explaining how she employed a vertical axis with a right angle to create the sections of her canvas. In the background of her paintings she added a wild scene—uninhabited nature in her landscapes and random arrangement in her still-life paintings of flowers. He also noted her use of watercolor spots that brought her "fixed shape to a state of fluidity." Her paintings, however, were not completely fluid, as the lines of her flowers, mountains, and ribs were clear.[57]

Neshif summarized the basic contradiction within Palestinian society of Sophie's era as the relationship between the human body and the land on the one hand and the colonial regime which sought to cut that tie on the other. He credits Sophie Halaby for contributing to Palestinian art history work that "transferred the basic material contradictions within Palestinian society at the time, and re-positioned it in an artistic context."[58] He elaborated: "One may argue that Sophie Halaby's record has formed the prototype of the Palestinian modernist abstract plastic arts, in the sense that it established the basic mechanisms of transference, the positioning, and the generation of the Palestinian material in the colonial context."[59]

In 2015, the *Jerusalem Quarterly* devoted its summer issue to a critical study of visual culture. Samia Halaby contributed an essay about her cousin. She titled it "Sophie Halaby, Palestinian Artist of the Twentieth Century." Like Sherwell, Fadda, Boullata, and Neshif, Samia Halaby was attracted to Sophie's landscapes, finding in them "a precious record of the beauty of the land and of the love affair Palestinians have with it."[60] Samia described the technical skills that enabled Sophie to create her beautiful landscapes: "Based on an academic foundation, Sophie Halaby developed a substantial formal capability, creating illusions of space. Her painter's eye is never lost in details, she perceives the general visual attributes of the view before her and fearlessly represents it. . . . She made hundreds of line drawings in pencil. They were formally economical, using a minimum number of lines to indicate the hills and to articulate various foci scattered in the landscape, such as houses, rocks or trees."[61]

Samia studied several of Sophie's landscapes in detail. Most of them are undated and untitled. One, however, was given a title by the artist, *The Garden Gate from the Gethsemane Garden*. This very special vantage point, a few feet below the graveyard where Sophie's parents were interred, had a view of the sealed double gate into the Old City. This gate, also known as the Golden Gate, has religious meaning for Jews, Christians, and Muslims. Sophie's painting features an ancient, large olive tree dominating the foreground on the left and another one, smaller, on the right. In the distance were rows of olive trees. Under her signature, Sophie wrote, "Jerusalem, Palestine," the same important signifier of location she had claimed in the address to her letter to Ada Kalbian in 1968.

Samia Halaby's description of the painting concludes that it was clearly painted on site, with attention paid to the accuracy of the general principles of the scene and disregarding unessential detail. Sophie used dark lines that seem to lie on the surface of the painting to outline the main shapes. Samia noted, "This is a sophisticated way of playing the surface of the painting against the illusion of depth. The lines of the surface stress the picture plane through which we see the space of the scene executed in broad swashes of color."[62]

Samia included seven images of Sophie's works in her article, all from the Qupty collection: One is the old man, charcoal on paper, featured in the exhibit at the Hakawati Theatre in 1986. The second is a watercolor still life of fruit. The third is a watercolor landscape, also included by Boullata. The fourth is *The Garden Gate from Gethsemane Garden* described above. The fifth is a watercolor of the Church of the Holy Sepulchre, included by Boullata. The sixth is a watercolor, perhaps from a balcony overlooking the Mediterranean. The seventh is oil on paper, an untitled still life of tulips.[63]

Despite the important contributions of Kamal Boullata, Tina Sherwell, Reem Fadda, Esmail Neshif, and Samia Halaby, the full impact of Sophie Halaby's legacy as an artist remains to be addressed. In the two decades since her demise, a major retrospective of her works has not been held. Such an exhibit, with a catalog covering the full range of her works, would establish Sophie Halaby's enduring importance in the history of Palestinian art. It would stimulate discussion on the role of art and of this artist in particular in reflecting and explaining her era. One indication of the fragile condition of Sophie Halaby's legacy is her absence from a recent book, *The Origins of Palestinian Art*, by Bashir Makhoul and Gordon Hon, published by Liverpool University Press in 2013. In reply to my letter about this omission, Professor Hon apologized for the error and affirmed that Palestinian art historian Rawan Sharaf was writing an Arabic translation of the book that would include information about Sophie Halaby.[64]

Sharaf explained that visual production is a critical constituent of individual and collective memory, and thus contributes to the formation of cultural identity. For this reason, knowing Sophie's landscapes and her flowers is important to understanding the cultural identity of the Palestinian people. Sharaf, like Boullata, recognized that Sophie was incapable of changing her artistic sensibilities to meet the directives of Palestinian nationalists who sought to mold visual expression to form a more militant identity for the Palestinian people after 1967. Sharaf astutely noted that Sophie's identity—that of Palestinian, Russian Orthodox, and artist—forecasted the fragmented identity of Palestinians in the diaspora today.[65]

The Palestine Museum, opened in 2016 in Birzeit, has not yet established a permanent collection. When it does, hopefully a collection of Sophie's paintings will be included. This biography of Sophie Halaby is designed to encourage others to continue the process of expanding the boundaries of Palestinian history to document and to interpret the lives and work of Palestinian women. Women like Sophie and her sister Asia, who responded to challenging times with creativity and compassion for others, should be studied for their contributions to the history of the last century.

As this book goes to press, dozens of Sophie's sketches remain in Taher Nusseibeh's studio. The big book in which she recorded her work, mentioned by Diana Safieh and others, may lurk there as well. Sophie left a clue about this book by including it in one of her paintings: a big book with the title, *Hist(ory) of Drawings*, on the spine.[66] This important source disappeared after the artist's death along with all of her personal papers. Fortunately, most of Sophie's paintings are preserved in two collections, that of Yvette and Mazen Qupty and that of George al-Ama, but others are scattered around the globe like diaspora Palestinians. An effort to document all of her work through digitization would create an important resource for future scholars of Palestinian art. We can only hope that a permanent exhibit of Sophie Halaby's works will be established in the house on Nur al-Din Street, with an exhibit of Palestinian embroidery installed downstairs, so that the world of the Halaby sisters may be memorialized for future generations.

Afterword

I first learned of Sophie Halaby by reading an interview with Mazen Qupty in the *Jerusalem Post* in August 2008.[1] I was motivated to contact Qupty because of his passionate declaration: "It's important for everyone, including Israelis, to see that Palestinians have a cultural life and cultural history and are not just shooting and throwing stones and blowing themselves up." Like Jean Said Makdisi, Mazen Qupty expressed dissatisfaction with the picture of Palestinian life being presented to the public. I was moved by his statement and wanted to know more about Palestinian art and culture. My long interest in women's history, combined with my research on Jerusalem, gave rise to thoughts about a new project featuring the life and work of Sophie Halaby. A visit to the home of Mazen and Yvette Qupty in Beit Hanina, East Jerusalem, began the process. I looked with great appreciation at their collection of Sophie's paintings, some displayed in their home and others captured on slides. The variety and beauty of the works moved me. I decided to learn more about the artist and her work.

The years after my introduction to Sophie Halaby's paintings in Beit Hanina were replete with repeated episodes of violence in the Middle East, including three wars between Israel and Gaza.[2] I used this politically sensitive time to search through the material that I had gathered for my first book about Jerusalem, looking for any mention of Sophie. My search led me back to the Middle East Center Archives (MECA) at St. Anthony's College, Oxford, and a collection of papers from the Jerusalem Girls' College. I suspected that Sophie might have attended that important school. A thorough search led me to discover Sophie's name in several issues of the college magazine. I learned when she took the Oxford and Cambridge matriculation examinations and in what fields, and I discovered when she went to France to study painting.

In Oxford, I also found files about Mabel Warburton, the determined founder of the Jerusalem Girls' College. Warburton encouraged her students to develop their skills to lead a meaningful life; she further urged them to contribute to their people through civic involvement, usually in the form of social service. In the archives, I learned about the school Sophie had attended, the courses she had taken, and her graduation date, but what did it all mean to her? Traditional historical research had provided only limited information. For more information I would need to interview people who knew Sophie.

My second meeting with Mazen Qupty took place in November 2013. I asked him to give me the name of anyone who might remember Sophie, who had died in 1997. He suggested Beatrice Habesch, a friend who had been attentive to Sophie in her last years. Qupty called Habesch and set up an appointment for me to meet her at the Ambassador Hotel in Jerusalem. Habesch began by telling me about Sophie's mother, Olga, referring to her as a White Russian and observing that she spoke little Arabic. The family, she remembered, conversed in Russian. She also remembered Sophie's father, George, whom she called "an intellectual"; she often saw him sitting at his desk writing. She also shared memories of Asia, Sophie's sister, who had studied with the British archaeologist Kathleen Kenyon.

My meeting with Habesch was the first of many extraordinary teas and coffees with Palestinians who had stories to tell and who trusted me to share them with a wider audience. Her warm response was not replicated by everyone I approached. Some were clearly uncomfortable with the idea of being interviewed by an American academic. They were suspicious of my motives. Others suffered from the multiple traumas of dispersal from their homeland and decades of failed political efforts to return. One elderly family member refused to talk about Sophie because she found the history of Palestine too painful to recall. My book could not have been written without the generosity of spirit and thoughtful responses from Habesch and the many others described below. Interviews conducted in hotels, restaurants, offices, and homes often lasted several hours. They were often continued via email, telephone, and second visits over a period of several years.

Habesch, a sprightly octogenarian at the time of our meeting, not only shared her recollections of Sophie, she also took me on an impromptu walking tour of East Jerusalem. She showed me Sophie's house on Nur al-Din Street; the nearby restaurant, previously called Aya, where Sophie often called to order dinner to be delivered; and the shop with a big window where Sophie's paintings were on regular display.

As was to happen time and again during my early search for information about Sophie Halaby, each informant left me with more questions than I had when I started the interview. Habesch, who had inherited her father's printing business, mentioned that Sophie and Asia asked her to print an announcement declaring that they had severed all ties with their brother, Nicola. She didn't know why. It took me two years to learn one reason from Dr. Hana Halaby in Amman. He explained that Sophie and Asia considered Nicola's marriage to Vera, the widow of their late cousin Dandali, scandalous. This circuitous method of piecing together information from different informants was to prove a constant in the coming years.

Each informant led me to others who might have answers to my growing list of questions. Habesch urged me to interview Doris Salah, the former director of the YWCA in East Jerusalem, where Sophie sometimes lectured about art. I located Doris in New York City, where she lived with her sister, Rima, who worked for the UN. Doris explained that Sophie showed her work to the women of Jerusalem at the YWCA, giving them hope at times when cultural life in the city was bleak. Rima remembered that Sophie wore her hair in a bun and that she had a sense of humor and was passionate about art. Three years later, interviewing Archie Wallis, a British archaeologist who knew Sophie and Asia in the 1970s, I was told that she was "a grand eccentric."[3] I wondered if Rima and Archie were describing the same behavior using different words.

It became clear that I would have to find many informants to learn Sophie's story. Ultimately, I would interview dozens of friends and family, some living in Jerusalem, the majority scattered in New York, Baltimore, Washington DC, London, Paris, Amman, and Bethlehem. Oral testimony served in place of the diary that I craved but never found. It also replaced many of the official documents—birth certificate and travel documents—that have been lost. Some of the people I contacted showed me paintings and postcards created by Sophie. Others shared letters saved for decades written by Sophie and Asia.

Mazen Qupty also suggested that I get in touch with Kamal Boullata, a Palestinian artist and art historian living in southern France, who knew Sophie when he was a youngster in Jerusalem. I purchased Boullata's *Palestinian Art* and read with great interest his insightful description of Halaby's life and works. I wanted to ask him many questions. Communication was a challenge. Letters written to his publisher were not answered. Finally, through Awad Halabi (no relation to the Halaby family), a former student of Issa Boullata, Kamal's brother, I obtained the correct email address. Kamal's response was thoughtful. He described Sophie as "a loner and a very introverted kind of private person." He added that after the annexation of Jerusalem in 1967, Sophie must have been "crushed and indignant." She probably became more withdrawn at this point.[4] Boullata encouraged me to pursue the project. He wrote several times suggesting people I might interview.

Qupty also suggested that I write to Tina Sherwell, an art historian who lived in the Shu'fat refugee camp in Jerusalem. Sherwell, who grew up in England, never met Sophie, but she knew about the collection of Sophie's work owned by George al-Ama and sent me his email address. Sherwell also sent me images of paintings in Qupty's collection on file at al-Hoash. Having images of Sophie's work close at hand inspired further research.

Slowly, I discovered several additional Palestinian art historians. Reem Fadda, an art historian and curator associated with the Guggenheim Museum, grew up, like Sherwell, in the diaspora. We met in New York City; she was enthusiastic about my research and offered a few suggestions. I found Faten Toubasi's name in a review article about an exhibit that took place in East Jerusalem in 1986. An internet search revealed that she was now teaching and working in Canada. Toubasi generously answered repeated email questions about her meeting with Sophie in relation to the exhibit. Rawan Sharaf, a Palestinian art historian studying in Birmingham, was suggested as a potential source by a British colleague. She wrote enthusiastically when I told her that I was working on a biography of Sophie Halaby. We met in London, where she provided useful information and offered additional suggestions for research.

Issam Nassar, a specialist in the history of photography of Palestine, teaches at Illinois State University. We have never met, but after repeated emails he thoughtfully introduced me to Raouf Halaby and Samer Wahbe, both distant relatives of Sophie who live in the United States. I contacted them electronically at first; later we spoke on the phone. Eventually, I met Raouf when he visited New York. Both men appreciated my effort to bring Sophie Halaby onto the historical stage and were happy to share information. Raouf, who was born in Jerusalem, is an artist who explained that he had photographic visual memory. He had visited Sophie and Asia several times at their home on Nur al-Din Street and remembered its lavish interior. Their home, he believed, was typical of the homes of elite Palestinians. Samer Wahbe shared a family tree. He also suggested that I get in touch with Mona Halaby, who had written an article about the Soeurs de Sion School in Jerusalem. I knew this article, as I had referenced it in my previous research, and contacted Mona to ask for her help. She responded by sending me a marvelous photograph of Sophie and Asia with many other graduates of the Jerusalem Girls' College surrounding their retired headmistress, Mabel Warburton. The photo, taken shortly before Warburton's death in 1961, was evidence of the continuing connections between the graduates and the headmistress they revered.

Salim Tamari is a professor of sociology at Birzeit University and the director of the Institute for Palestine Studies. He also edits *Jerusalem Quarterly.*

Tamari was encouraging about my research on Sophie Halaby. He sent me email addresses of others whom he thought would have information, including Suad Amiry, his wife and an artist who participated with Sophie and Faten Toubasi in an exhibit in 1986.

At a particularly difficult stage of the project, I met with noted historian Rashid Khalidi in his office at Columbia University. I was discouraged about finding people to interview and documents to consult. Khalidi listened patiently to my hopes of launching an exhibit of Sophie's works in the United States and wisely advised me to concentrate on a biography, noting that once the biography was completed it might be possible to launch an exhibit.

In Jerusalem I met Helen Khader, a Halaby family member identified by Raouf Halaby. Khader invited me to her home in East Jerusalem during a particularly painful moment leading up to the Gaza War of 2014. I sat at her kitchen table while she prepared traditional Palestinian food for a gathering that night. She stopped chopping vegetables to show me several items of embroidery made in Asia's workshop, treasured embroidered linen tablecloths and napkins, which she used on special occasions. She also took time to tell me all she could remember from her visits with her rambunctious young children to the Halaby home. She remembered that Asia had "a heart of gold," while Sophie was stern, having no patience for the children.

As I got up to leave, Khader offered to walk me over to the entrance of al-Hoash, the art gallery mentioned by Qupty in the 2008 interview that was showing some of Sophie's works. I had looked for the gallery a few days earlier, but couldn't find it. This time, Khader escorted me to the back entrance and introduced me to a member of the staff, who guided me to the main exhibit room, where I saw two of Sophie's paintings, both portraits of women. The first was an oil painting of a severe-looking woman dressed in green that I had seen previously at Mazen's house. The other was the chiseled profile of a woman in gold, a watercolor, part of George al-Ama's collection. I later learned that both of these works were painted during Sophie's student years in Paris.

Before we parted, Khader suggested that I walk over to the YWCA to see a large flower painting, one of Sophie's watercolors that she remembered hanging in a place of honor over the piano. When I went there a few days later, the painting was not in sight. I was told that it had been misplaced during a recent renovation. Though I was happy to learn of its longtime public presence in the city, its absence was disappointing. Was it a sign that Sophie's legacy was being forgotten in Jerusalem? Four years later, I went back to the Y; the wonderful flower painting remembered by Helen Khader had been found.

Happily, there were other indications of Sophie's life in the city. In the newly opened American Colony Archives I found lists of invitations to events hosted by Bertha Spafford Vester, including the names of Sophie and Asia Halaby. Inspired by reading the guest lists, I later read Bertha's diaries, beginning in 1926 and ending in 1968, housed at the Library of Congress. In Jerusalem, I read the diaries of Horatio Vester, Bertha's son, which begin in 1968. Both sets of diaries mention Sophie and her sister, Asia, as members of the elite society of Jerusalem who attended teas and other social functions at the American Colony.

Arriving at the archives one morning before the opening, I perused the holdings in the American Colony bookstore. I told the manager about my project and asked if he could recommend a book. Without hesitation, he showed me John Tleel's *I Am Jerusalem*, an extraordinary memoir by an elderly resident of the Old City. I purchased the book and asked the manager to try to acquire contact information for Tleel. Within twenty-four hours he provided the email address.

My interview with the eighty-eight-year-old Dr. John Tleel took place two weeks later, giving me time to devour every page of his memoir. I learned about Tleel's family of doctors and dentists, who had lived in Musrara near the Halaby family, about Tleel's education at the American University of Beirut, about the family's move to the Old City in 1948, and about Tleel joining his father and brother in the practice of dentistry. I appreciated the effort involved in documenting the tumultuous events of Tleel's long life and the emotions accompanying them.

Tleel lived across from the offices of the Greek Patriarchate in the Old City in a large and elegantly furnished house. We met in a sunlit room that had dozens of photos of Tleel with world leaders who have visited Jerusalem. We spoke about Sophie and Asia Halaby, both of whom had been his patients for thirty years, from the late 1960s through the end of their lives. The interview went on for more than ninety minutes as Tleel continued to remember people and events that he thought would be of interest to my research. At one point in the conversation, he remembered that he had a collection of Sophie's postcards. These cards were hand painted with floral images similar to those in the paintings I had seen in the Qupty collection. Tleel opened a huge drawer in an ancient bureau and located them. At the time, I didn't know anything about Sophie's postcards. I was thrilled to discover them and deeply appreciative when he gave me one to further my endeavor.

Reviewing my notes back in New York City, I remembered a book by Kai Bird, *Crossing the Mandelbaum Gate*, about his childhood in Jerusalem, where his father, Gene Bird, had served in the American consulate. Through a friend, I was able to find Bird's email address. I wrote to ask if his father was still alive and if he might remember two Russian-Palestinian ladies—Sophie and Asia Halaby—who lived in East Jerusalem when he was posted there. Happily, Bird responded quickly. His father did not remember much about them, but he had suggested that I get in touch with Vicken and Ada Kalbian, friends who knew the Halaby sisters well and had continued to correspond with them after departing from Jerusalem in 1968. I wrote to them immediately. This suggestion turned out to be one of the most valuable in the years of research that ensued.

Vicken Kalbian answered my first email on October 16, 2014: "We are Jerusalemites and lived in Jerusalem till 1968. My wife, Ada, and I knew the Halaby girls very well. We were frequent guests at their home in East Jerusalem next to the Rockefeller Museum. Actually they had a tea party for our family just before we immigrated to the US in 1968. We own three watercolor paintings of Sophie. In the States we also helped the sisters by selling embroideries by Palestinian refugee girls that Asia designed. I saw them last in 1981 on a visit to Jerusalem."[5] Kalbian wrote that he and his wife would be happy to be interviewed and suggested that we meet in Washington, DC.

The interview took place a week later in their son's law offices. The Kalbians brought photocopies of letters from Sophie and Asia, as well as copies of paintings, postcards, and embroidery. Their descriptions of life in Jerusalem were rich in detail and feeling. Vicken, an Armenian, described his childhood in Jerusalem living at 4 Balfour Street, just behind the YMCA, attending St. George's College, where his best friend was Lucian Meysels, the son of a Viennese Jewish immigrant who was an art critic for the *Palestine Post*. From 1948 to 1950, Vicken and some of his family sought refuge in Beirut. His father, a physician who cared for the Halaby family, was in East Jerusalem and urged his son to join him, as there was a need for more physicians in the city. Vicken arrived in East Jerusalem in 1950 to become the chief resident of the Augusta Victoria Hospital on Mount Scopus. Vicken and Ada, a Roman Catholic who grew up in the German Colony, married in 1954.

My interview with the Kalbians yielded a lot of information about Sophie and Asia; some of it added confusion to the unfolding story. For example, Vicken thought that the Halaby family lived in Katamon before moving to East Jerusalem. Ada was certain they had lived in Musrara. Raouf Halaby told me they had lived in Upper Baq`a'. Beatrice Habesch, like Vicken, remembered a home in Katamon. The *Directory of Arab Trade, Industries, Crafts, and Professions in Palestine*, printed in 1937, listed Sophie living in Musrara.[6] Testimony from Asia Halaby in an interview with Nancy Lapp in 1986 confirmed that the Halabys lived in Musrara until 1948. It is possible that they lived in Katamon at one point and later moved to Musrara. More likely, another Halaby relative lived in Katamon.

There are also conflicting accounts about where the family went when they left Musrara in 1948. Vicken believed that the family fled to the Old City, a story described in *O Jerusalem*,[7] a book based on research by Diana Safieh, a family friend of the Halabys. Others believed that they lived with the Russian nuns on the Mount of Olives. Here, it is likely that both stories are true. It is clear that the sisters and their mother fled first to the Old City, and it is possible that they later moved to the Mount of Olives and finally to East Jerusalem.

The interview with the Kalbians also resulted in suggestions for further reading: the memoir of Wilson Evans, a former US consul in Jerusalem, was very useful, as was the memoir of John Melkon Rose, an Armenian who remained in West Jerusalem after 1948. Vicken also suggested that I contact Professor Michael Hudson, the widower of Vera, a cousin of Sophie and Asia. This suggestion led to a lively meeting in Washington, DC, with Michael's daughter, Leila Hudson, an anthropologist at the University of Arizona. She shared her impressions of a visit with Sophie and Asia as well as family photos, letters, and copies of paintings owned by her father.

Later, I corresponded with Lily Porter, another family member, and ultimately met her and her twin sister, Nelly Barrett, in Baltimore. They also shared family photos and letters to document the story I was writing. They had visited Sophie and Asia in 1965 and each purchased a painting for five dollars. They had inherited two additional paintings from their parents. Looking at all four paintings in Lily's living room in Baltimore was deeply moving. Three were vibrant watercolors of flowers and one was an unusual painting, sadly damaged, of the Old City of Jerusalem with red flowers in the foreground and the golden dome shining in the distance. Lily Porter urged me to contact Mother Catherine at the Church of Mary Magdalene in Jerusalem. She thought that Mother Catherine might have additional information.

Subsequent correspondence with the Kalbians and a second meeting in March 2016 produced additional names for research and some help in deciphering names and events in the diaries of Bertha Spafford Vester. The Kalbians were particularly helpful in understanding the Christian communities of Jerusalem. For example, Vicken asserted that Catholic girls in Jerusalem attended Schmidt's Girls' School or Soeurs de Sion, as the Latin patriarch, the head of the Catholic Church in Jerusalem, forbade their attendance at the Jerusalem Girls' College, which received support from the Anglican Church.

Similarly, Vicken reported that the Latin patriarch threatened any Catholic who entered the YMCA with excommunication.

Among the many people recommended by Vicken and Ada Kalbian as potentially useful sources about Sophie and Asia Halaby was the aforementioned Diana Safieh, whom I met at the Notre Dame Hotel in Jerusalem. Safieh remembered the Halaby home in Musrara; she had also visited the family in the Old City and later in East Jerusalem. She knew about Sophie's failed attempt to establish a home for the elderly in Bethlehem under the auspices of the Greek Orthodox Church. A letter from Sophie to Hana Halaby, a cousin in Amman, indicated that she also had difficulty with a tenant who tried to challenge her ownership of property in that city. Sophie's sense of loss resulting from the theft of Halaby land in Bethlehem and the threats to ownership in Amman were compounded by the previous loss of homes and land in Musrara, a short walk from the Halaby house in East Jerusalem.

My group of sources expanded to include Khaled Khatib, the director of the Palestine Heritage Museum and the nephew of the last mayor of East Jerusalem, whom I met while on a tour of the museum. I was particularly interested in the Hind al-Husseini room in his museum. Hind had attended the Jerusalem Girls' College and knew Sophie Halaby. Learning my interest in Sophie, Khatib offered to introduce me to Taher Nusseibeh, who had recently contacted him in an effort to sell him some of Sophie's sketches. Khatib set up a meeting for us to view the work.

Our meeting took place on a very hot day summer day. The iron shutters of all the shops were closed that day, as a strike had been declared in response to the occupation. Nusseibeh's studio was accessed through a dark alleyway and up a flight of rickety steps. Without Khatib, I would have been hesitant to proceed with the visit. As soon as we entered the studio, I saw Sophie's work. Her sketches lined the walls. Some were signed; her style was clearly recognizable. I was thrilled. I thought I knew all of her works, having seen originals and slides of paintings owned by Mazen Qupty and later the slides of works owned by George al-Ama. Some of the sketches were clearly preparatory to the later oils or watercolors; others were totally new to me. Taher Nusseibeh had agreed to be interviewed, but once we were in his studio he was only moderately interested in telling me about Sophie and more interested in selling the works. He assumed that I was a collector and repeatedly boasted that he had offers for them "from the Gulf" for millions. Ultimately, he focused on my questions and began to tell me the story of how he came to own the sketches.

He began with his childhood, explaining that he had lived near the Halaby sisters and had often ridden over to their house on his bicycle, hoping to be offered an ice cream, which happened when Sophie was not working. When she was working, she would quickly send him off with a commission to deliver something to the American Colony or pick something up from the post office. I had already learned from Beatrice Habesch and others that Sophie's last years were full of strife. She had hired Issa Hamed as her legal advisor. Hamed gradually took over the management of all her finances and ultimately robbed her heirs of her home and other properties. Hamed was not interested in her artwork and, according to Nusseibeh, threw all the sketches into the garbage, from whence Nusseibeh retrieved them. My interview with Rawan Sharaf two years later revealed a more complete story. Apparently, Nusseibeh bought all of Sophie's work from Hamed and soon sold seventy-five paintings to Qupty, later selling about an equal number of paintings and some sketches to al-Ama. The remainder of the sketches and dozens of blank canvasses ordered from Paris remained with Nusseibeh.[8]

I had learned from others that Sophie kept a large notebook in which she recorded information about her paintings. I asked Nusseibeh if he had the notebook; at first, he seemed confused about the question. Then he said he had it somewhere else, not in the studio, and that he would sell it to me. Later, Sliman Mansour, the celebrated artist, told me that he had gone to Sophie's house after her death to ask Hamed for this book, knowing that it would be important to be able to date her work. He was told that it had been burned. There was one final lead. Nusseibeh remembered a woman who had worked for Sophie and Asia for decades; she was a clerical assistant who helped Asia with the embroidery business and Sophie with her art sales. The woman was no longer alive, but Khatib knew her brother. He called and asked the brother to search among her possessions to see if there were any papers that might shed light on Sophie's art sales. Nothing was ever found.

In Jerusalem, I followed one more lead for information about Sophie. I knew that Asia worked on several archaeological digs. It occurred to me that both sisters might have frequented gatherings sponsored by the Albright Institute. I called to find out if the institute maintained a register of guests and was encouraged to visit. A few days later, my visit to the institute produced some useful information. Nadia Bandak, the finance manager, remembered Sophie and Asia. They had been friends of her parents and grandparents, often stopping to buy fresh eggs, fruit, and vegetables at her grandparents' farm. Bandak remembered that one of Sophie's still-life paintings of a bowl of fruit had hung in the institute. At first, she couldn't find it, but a subsequent visit confirmed that it had been found and was being reframed. The last time I visited, Bandak and I walked across the street to retrieve the painting from the framer and accompanied it home.

Later, an interview in London with Archie Wallis, an archaeologist who had worked with the British School for Archaeology in Jerusalem, yielded colorful details of British social events in the 1970s that included Sophie and Asia. He described them as belonging to the English social set of the city. Sophie smiled a lot and had sparkling blue eyes. Her laugh was deep. She wore a tweed jacket and skirt, a big brooch, and rings on her fingers. Asia worked with the American archaeologist James Pritchard and the British archaeologist Kathleen Kenyon. She was their unofficial dragoman, working out difficulties between laborers and landowners at the sites being investigated.

Sophie and Asia attended lectures by visiting archaeologists at the Albright Institute and at the Palestine Archaeological Museum. They also participated in walks led by Father Fitzgerald and Father Murphy O'Connor of the École biblique. Given the lax attitudes of the times toward artifacts found at the sites, it is not surprising that Raouf Halaby remarked on the "Roman-era" sculpture that he remembered in the Halaby home. All the antiquities disappeared after the death of the sisters.

Elias Khoury, the lawyer hired by the Halaby family after Sophie's and Asia's deaths, also consented to an interview. Khoury had worked for Sophie Halaby in the early 1990s as she sought to defend the property rights of Halaby relatives living in Amman to land on the Mount of Olives. He gave me copies of several letters written by Sophie and Asia, some of which were written on Sophie's postcards. From him I learned a bit more about the financial and legal difficulties experienced by Sophie at the end of her life, problems alluded to by several informants. Khoury explained in greater detail how Sophie had been tricked by Hamed, whom she had hired at the recommendation of Nora Kurt, an old friend, to assist with financial matters. Sophie, who came to rely on the much younger man, ultimately made him her sole heir. In addition to her will, she signed over all of the properties jointly owned by both sisters to Hamed. Thus, the property she worked hard to protect during her life was lost to a swindler. Her failure to ensure the future of her paintings is particularly hard to understand and surely is a sign of her great distress at the end of her life.

Still searching for more information, I learned about Alexander Zanemonets, a Russian deacon, who had recently published a book about the history of the Russian Orthodox Church in Jerusalem. I contacted Deacon Zanemonets with many questions about the church and asked for his help to break through the barriers I had encountered when I tried, unsuccessfully, to interview one of the nuns who remembered Sophie. He scheduled a meeting for me with Abbess Elizabeth at the Mary Magdalene Convent and went with me to facilitate the discussion. Abbess Elizabeth remembered Sophie and Asia but could shed little light on them as she had spent many years in Australia. Neither Mother Seraphim, who had spoken to Kamal Boullata years earlier, nor Mother Catherine, who had spoken with Lily Porter, was available. On a subsequent trip to Jerusalem, Deacon Zanemonets provided an introduction to Sister Marina at the Mount of Olives Convent. She introduced me to Sister Veronica and Sister Tamara, who knew Sophie and Asia over a period of forty years. Their interviews proved very valuable.

Dominique Trimbur, a scholar who studied French influence in Palestine, thought that it would be possible to find an address for Sophie during the years she spent in Paris. A visit to the diplomatic archives on the outskirts of Paris was fruitless, but a trip to the Frick library in New York City solved the mystery. There, in a compendium of lists of artists who exhibited at the Salon des Tuileries, I found Sophie's name and her address in 1932 and 1933: 93 Boulevard St. Michel.[9]

A few months later, I continued my investigation in Paris, where I found, to my amazement and joy, the Foyer International des Etudiantes. I reasoned that if Sophie had lived here, there could be a record of her arrival and departure. I asked to meet with the director of the Foyer and returned the next day to interview MaryAnn Piwowarczyk. I learned that the Foyer in Sophie's day accepted students from all over the world. I walked through the library and saw books in English, French, and Russian. I imagined Sophie sitting in the grand room reading those books. The director informed me that the archives of the Foyer were in the process of being inventoried and that I would have to wait about six months to learn if Sophie's name appeared in any register. She took me on a tour of the building before I returned to New York to await the outcome of the research. Six months later, I received a note from Maria Czerniak, the librarian of the Foyer, confirming Sophie's presence there.

A second conversation with Sliman Mansour in June 2016 led to the discovery of the *Palestine and Transjordan Weekly*, published during the Arab Revolt of 1936–39. Perusal of issues held in the New York Public Library yielded a surprising find, eight political cartoons signed S.G.H. I knew these were Sophie Halaby's initials and I was 95 percent certain that they were her cartoons. An email query to Kamal Boullata produced a definitive confirmation: the cartoons were certainly Sophie's work. He pointed to the characteristic way she sketched the backgrounds, a little mosque or some humble dwellings among the hills that recalled the top of the Mount of Olives, scenes she repeatedly depicted in her watercolors and oils. These political cartoons represent a moment in the artist's usually private life when she became directly involved with the vigorous political discussion in Palestine. The cartoons added another dimension to the picture I had been forming of her long life.

In January 2018, though I had finished the research and completed a draft of the manuscript, I made one more trip to London and Amman to meet additional members of the Halaby family and friends. This final group of interviews deepened my understanding of the talented artist and of her life in Jerusalem during the last century. I learned of the continuing relations Sophie and Asia had with Halaby cousins in Amman, who were actively involved in selling embroidery to help support Palestinian refugees. Sophie and Asia were welcome guests in Amman. Nevertheless, Sophie did not share her paintings with her family. I discovered only one painting belonging to the family in Amman and none in London.

In addition to the significant contributions to this project made by each of those interviewed, my research was facilitated by numerous archivists and librarians on three continents. Among them, three provided sustained and extraordinary support: Debbie Usher at the Middle East Center Archives, Oxford; Barbara Bair at the American Colony in Jerusalem Papers, Library of Congress, Washington, DC; and Rachel Lev at the American Colony Archives, Jerusalem. Barbara Porter of the American Council on Oriental Research in Amman, Eleanor Yadin at the New York Public Library, and Claibourne Williams at the Hunter College Library provided support at critical stages of the project. Two art historians in Jerusalem, Emily Bilsky and Aline Khoury, guided me in selecting Sophie's paintings for this book. The editing process was supported by the skillful work of Jessica DeCoux.

I began this project with the intent of bringing Sophie Halaby's life and works onto the stage of history. During the years of research and writing, I met many friends and family of the artist who deeply enriched my understanding of her life. This book could not have been written without their patient replies to my questions. The book represents the fulfillment of one stage of the project. Additional research is needed to digitize all of her paintings and to make them available to art historians and other scholars. The next step would be an exhibit of her works, ideally accompanied by a conference to discuss her place in Palestinian art history. This project will be complete when Palestinian schools include Sophie Halaby in their curriculum and when her paintings are included in the collections of major museums.

Notes

Bibliography

Index

Notes

Introduction

1. Ellen Fleischmann, "Crossing the Boundaries of History: Exploring Oral History in Researching Palestinian Women in the Mandate Period," *Women's History Review* 5, no. 3 (1996): 351–52.

2. Elias Sanbar, "Out of Place, Out of Time," *Mediterranean Historical Review* 16, 87 [87–94], cited in Ahmad Sa'di and Lila Abu-Lughod, eds., *NAKBA: Palestine, 1948, and the Claims of Memory* (New York: Columbia Univ. Press, 2007), 4.

3. Rosemary Sayigh, "Women's Nakba Stories," in Sa'di and Abu-Lughod, *NAKBA*, 136.

4. Shahid, Serene Husseini, *Jerusalem Memories*, ed. Jean Said Makdisi (Beirut: Naufal, 1999), iv.

5. Mary Joury, interview by the author, January 2018. Dr. John Tleel, the dentist who cared for Sophie and Asia Halaby for thirty years, added that artists were not valued in the Jerusalem society of Sophie's youth as they are today. John Tleel, interview by the author, June 2014.

6. Suad Amiry, "An Obsession," in *Seeking Palestine: New Palestinian Writing on Exile and Home*, ed. Penny Johnson and Raja Shehadeh (Northampton, MA: Olive Branch Press, 2013), 74–77.

7. Samia Halaby, "Sophie Halaby, Palestinian Artist of the Twentieth Century," *Jerusalem Quarterly* 61 (Winter 2015): 84–100.

1. Forming Sophie's Identity

1. Michelle Campos, *Ottoman Brothers: Muslims, Christians, and Jews in Early Twentieth-Century Palestine* (Stanford, CA: Stanford Univ. Press, 2011), 63.

2. Information about Olga Akimovna provided by Alexander Zanemonets from a genealogical book about the Khudobasheva family. Alexander Zanemonets, interview by the author, May 2016 and December 2016. The Imperial Orthodox Society of Palestine took over the management of many elementary schools of the Orthodox Patriarchate of Antioch at the end of the nineteenth century. Interview with Beatrice Habesch provided information about the place of the marriage. Beatrice Habesch, interview by the author, November 2013.

3. Vypuskniki Kievskoi Dukhovnoi Akademii (Graduates of the Kiev Theological Academy) 1823–69, 1885–1915, http.//www.petergen.com/bovkalo/duhov/kievda.html.

4. Elias Khoury, interview by the author, Jerusalem, July 2014.

5. Abbess Elizabeth, Mother Superior, Convent of St. Mary Magdalene, Jerusalem, to Elias Khoury, May 26, 2000. Copy in author's possession.

6. Kamal Boullata, in his important book *Palestinian Art*, asserted that Sophie was born in Kiev in 1906. Boullata searched through Halaby birth records in the Christian Arab Orthodox birth registry in 2003 and did not find her name. He also consulted with Mother Serafina of the Church of Mary Magdalene, who confirmed Halaby family lore that Sophie was born in Kiev. Sisters Veronica and Tamara of the Russian Convent, friends of Sophie's, share this belief. Recently, however, Samia Halaby, a distant relative of Sophie's, obtained a copy of Sophie's death certificate from the Jerusalem municipality that noted Sophie's birthplace as Jerusalem. Elias Khoury, a lawyer hired by the Halaby family, explained that this is not definitive as clerks routinely completed unknown birthplaces with the local city. Sisters Veronica and Tamara, interview with author, June 2016. See also Kamal Boullata, *Palestinian Art: From 1850 to the Present* (London: Saqi, 2009), 170, and email to author, October 2016. Samia Halaby, "Sophie Halaby," 61, 85.

7. Three family trees: descendants of Costandi Halaby, undated, commissioned by the Halaby family. Copies in the author's possession.

8. Hana Halaby, interview by the author, January 2018.

9. Derek Hopwood, *Russian Presence in Syria and Palestine, 1843–1914* (Oxford: Oxford Univ. Press, 1969), 92.

10. Father Kapustin had the strong support of Alexander II and Alexander III, both of whom sought to expand Russian influence in the Ottoman Empire following Russia's defeat in the Crimean War. The Russian Orthodox Church became independent of the Eastern Orthodox Church in 1453 with the fall of Constantinople. Hopwood, *Russian Presence*, 2, 93.

11. Hopwood, 72.

12. Hopwood, 115.

13. Sister Marina, Convent of Mount of Olives, interview by the author, June 2016.

14. Alexander Zanemonets provided this information in translation from a booklet in Russian, *The First Pilgrim Journey of Students of the Kiev Theological Academy to the Holy Land in Summer 1911* (Kiev: Kiev Academy, 1914), n.p. Republished in 2005 as *By the Holy Places from Kiev to Jerusalem*.

15. Salim Tamari, *Year of the Locust: A Soldier's Diary and the Erasure of Palestine's Ottoman Past* (Berkeley: Univ. of California Press, 2011), 91–94.

16. Edward Said, "Reflections on Exile," in *Reflections on Exile and Other Essays* (Cambridge, MA: Harvard Univ. Press, 2000), 186.

17. Sisters Veronica and Tamara, interview. The Sisters reported that the Halaby family fled the Russian Revolution, returned to Jerusalem, and never returned to Kiev.

18. Sisters Veronica and Tamara, interview.

19. See Michael Ignatieff, *The Russian Album* (New York: Viking, 1987), 92, for a report about a similar family in Kiev.

20. See chapter 6. These included papers with ornate seals of the Russian Empire appointing her father as dragoman. Sophie described these papers to Elias Khoury near the end of her life. Elias Khoury, interview by the author, July 2014.

21. Evgeny Dobrenko, introduction to *The White Guard* by Mikhail Bulgakov (New Haven, CT: Yale Univ. Press, 2008), xxv. In 1917, Kiev was more than 50 percent Russian, 20 percent Jewish, 16 percent Ukrainian, and 10 percent Polish.

22. Hopwood, *Russian Presence*, 137–38.

23. Abigail Jacobson, "A City Living through Crisis: Jerusalem during World War I," *British Journal of Middle Eastern Studies* 36, no. 1 (April 2009): 84.

24. Bertha Spafford Vester, *Our Jerusalem* (Jerusalem: Ariel, 1950; facsimile edition, 1988), 264. See also Jacobson, "City Living through Crisis," 84–85.

25. Donna Robinson Divine, "Palestine in World War I," in *The Middle East and North Africa: Essays in Honor of J. C. Hurewitz*, ed. Reeva S. Simon (New York: Columbia Univ. Press, 1990), 76–77, 81.

26. Sakakini diary, quoted in translation in Divine, "Palestine in World War I," 71.

27. Vester, *Our Jerusalem*, 280.

28. Laura Robson, *Colonialism and Christianity in Mandate Palestine* (Austin: Univ. of Texas Press, 2011), 1–2, 6.

29. See Tamari, *Year of the Locust*, 54–56 for testimony about the cruelty of Jemal Pasha.

30. Bernard Wasserstein, *Divided Jerusalem* (New Haven, CT: Yale Univ. Press, 2008), 80.

31. Susan P. Emery, "Mabel Warburton," notes prepared for St. Anthony's College archive, 121–23, MECA.

32. Talitha Kumi, meaning "Rise, walk," comes from the Gospel of Mark and refers to the resurrection of a girl by Jesus. The building was torn down, but its iconic entranceway remains on Jaffa Road.

33. "Girls' High School in Jerusalem," *Bible Lands*, January 1921, 98.

34. Diana Safieh, interview by the author, February 2015.

35. Sakakini, diary, quoted in translation in Divine, "Palestine in World War I," 71.

36. A letter marked "SECRET" from Alan Cunningham, high commissioner for Palestine, to G. H. Hall, His Majesty's principal secretary of state for the colonies, January 31, 1946, revealed ongoing quarrels within the Russian Orthodox Church. CO/733/248/22, National Archives of Great Britain.

37. Sophie attested to the fact that there were papers, today missing, in her possession that granted him the title dragoman. Khoury, interview.

38. Habesch, interview. In 1964, the State of Israel, grateful to the Soviet Union for its vote for partition at the United Nations in November 1947, recognized their claim to the Russian Compound and purchased the land from them.

39. Salim Tamari, *Mountain against the Sea: Essays on Palestinian Society and Culture* (Berkeley: Univ. of California Press, 2009), 81.

40. Tamari, 182.

41. Felicity Ashbee, *Child in Jerusalem* (Syracuse: Syracuse Univ. Press, 2013), 51–52.

42. Menachem Klein, *Lives in Common: Arabs and Jews in Jerusalem, Jaffa, and Hebron*, trans. Haim Watzman (Oxford: Oxford Univ. Press, 2014), 80, 7. Nathan Krystall, "The Fall of the New City," in *Jerusalem 1948: The Arab Neighbourhoods and Their Fate in the War*, 2nd ed., ed. Salim Tamari (Jerusalem: Institute of Jerusalem Studies, 2002), 93.

43. Wasif Jawhariyyeh. *The Storyteller of Jerusalem: The Life and Times of Wasif Jawhariyyeh, 1904–1948*, ed. Salim Tamari and Issam Nassar, trans. Nada Elzeer (Northampton, MA: Olive Branch Press, 2014), 216.

44. Anna Ticho, notes for a speech to be delivered in New York City, n.d., Ticho House Archives, The Israel Museum, Jerusalem. Ticho was exiled to Damascus during World War I.

45. Shahid, *Jerusalem Memories*, 14–15.

46. Nicola Halaby to Vera Wahbe, December 21, 1961, copy provided by Leila Hudson in the author's possession. Letters from Sophie and Asia to Ada and Vicken Kalbian were written in English, in 1968.

47. Ron Fuchs and Gilbert Herbert, "A Colonial Portrait of Jerusalem," in *Hybrid Urbanism*, ed. Nezar AlSayyad (Westport, CT: Praeger, 2001), 87.

48. Fuchs and Herbert, 88.

49. Fuchs and Herbert, 91. The original clock was damaged during its removal. Storrs tasked Holliday, who had replaced Ashbee, to construct a new tower. It stood near Allenby Square (today Zahal Square), near the since-demolished central post office.

50. Fuchs and Herbert, "Colonial Portrait," 98–100.

51. Anna Ticho, notes for a talk, 1912, Ticho House Archives. See also David Reifler, *Days of Ticho: Empire, Mandate, Medicine and Art in the Holy Land* (Springfield, NJ: Gefen Books, 2015), 81.

52. Susan P. Emery to mother, September 21, 1919, MECA. See also Anya Berezina Derrick, *Recollections of Jerusalem* (Jordanville, NY: Holy Trinity, 2014), 69.

53. Geoffrey Grigson and Charles Harvard Gibbs-Smith, eds., *People, Places, and Things* (London: Grosvenor Press, 1954), quoted in Evan Wilson, *Jerusalem Key to Peace* (Washington, DC: Middle East Institute, 1970), 158.

54. For discussion of increasing Arab resentment of Turkish rule see Moshe Ma'oz, *Ottoman Reform in Syria and Palestine, 1840–1861: The Impact of the Tanzimat on Politics and Society* (Oxford: Clarendon Press, 1968), 241–48.

55. Inger Marie Okkenhaug, "To Give the Boys Energy, Manliness, and Self-Command in Temper: Anglican Male Ideal and St. George's School in Jerusalem, c. 1900–40," in *Gender, Religion, and Change in the Middle East: Two Hundred Years of History*, ed. Inger Marie Okkenhaug and Ingvild Flaskerud (Oxford: Berg, 2005), 48.

56. *Bible Lands*, 1905, 96. Cited in Okkenhaug, "Give the Boys Energy," 53.

57. Mabel Warburton, "Opening Day Remarks," November 10, 1922, Jerusalem Girls' High School, MECA.

58. Emery, obituary for Mabel Warburton, MECA.

59. Emery, obituary.

60. Emery to mother, October 26, 1919, MECA.

61. Olga Wahbe, "Reminiscence," from the personal collection of Leila Hudson. Leila Hudson, interview by the author, November 2014. *Kalila wa-Dimna* is a folk tale that originated in Persia and remained popular in the Muslim world. Georgie Zeidan was a popular Lebanese historical novelist.

62. Wahbe; Hudson, interview.

63. Wahbe; Hudson, interview.

64. Reports of alumnae gatherings appear in annual publications of the *Jerusalem Girls' College Old Girls' Guild* beginning in 1924. In 1929, the publication would be retitled the *Jerusalem Girls' College Magazine*.

65. Emery to mother, April 27, 1923, MECA.

66. Emery, obituary for Mabel Warburton, MECA.

67. The school was renamed The Jerusalem Girls' College in 1922.

68. Emery to mother, October 26, 1919, MECA.

69. "The Jerusalem Girls' College," *Palestine Weekly*, November 10, 1922, 710.

70. Yigal Zalmona, "The Tower of David Days: The Birth of Controversy in Israel Art in the Twenties," in *The Tower of David Days: First Cultural Strife in Israel Art*, curated by Yigal Zalmona (Jerusalem: Tower of David Museum, 1991), 74.

71. Widad Kawar, interview by the author, January 2018.

72. *Old Girls' Guild Third Annual Report*, 1925–26, MECA.

73. "News Jerusalem," *Palestine Weekly*, November 3, 1922, box 41, file 3, MECA.

74. "News Jerusalem."

75. Mabel Warburton, "Looking Back and Looking Forward," *JGC Magazine*, June 1931, 7–9, MECA.

76. Warburton, 7–9.

77. Fortunée Sitton, a Jerusalem Girls' College graduate, brought her report card to Khartoum and later to London. Her son, David Dweik, brought it with him to Jerusalem after her death. David Dweik, interview by the author, June 2014.

78. *Old Girls' Guild First Annual Report*, 1923–24, 2, MECA.

79. *Old Girls' Guild Second Annual Report*, 1924–25, 5, MECA.

80. Izzat Tannous, *The Palestinians: A Detailed Documented Eyewitness History of Palestine under British Mandate* (New York: IGT, 1988), 15.

81. Nancy Stockdale, *Colonial Encounters among English and Palestinian Women, 1800–1948* (Gainesville: Univ. Press of Florida, 2007), 183–84.

82. Stewart Perowne to father, May 26, 1926, MECA, quoted in A. J. Sherman, *Mandate Days: British Lives in Palestine, 1918–1948* (Baltimore: Johns Hopkins Univ. Press, 2001), 72.

83. Stockdale, *Colonial Encounters*, 185–86.

84. Tannous, *The Palestinians*, 15.

85. Rashid Khalidi, *Palestinian Identity: The Construction of Modern National Consciousness* (New York: Columbia Univ. Press, 1997), 146.

86. Khalidi, 149.

2. Becoming a Modern Woman

1. Mabel Warburton, "Women's Education in Palestine," 1924, Jerusalem Girls' High School, MECA.

2. *Old Girls' Guild Annual Report 1924–25*, 5. The foundation stones of the first university in Jerusalem, Hebrew University, were laid in 1918. The classes that opened in 1925 were graduate courses in chemistry and were taught in Hebrew.

3. Pinhas Ofer, "A Scheme for the Establishment of a British University in Jerusalem in the Late 1920s," *Middle Eastern Studies* 22, no. 2 (April 1986): 274–75.

4. Olga Wahbe, Reminiscence, personal collection of Leila Hudson.

5. Derrick, *Recollections of Jerusalem*, 31.

6. Boullata, *Palestinian Art*, 167. Samia Halaby, "Sophie Halaby," 96–97.

7. Hana Halaby, phone interview by the author, July 2014.

8. *Old Girls' Guild Third Annual Report*, 1925–26, 17, MECA.

9. Robson, *Colonialism and Christianity*, 6.

10. Tom Ricks, phone interview by the author, December 2015.

11. Beatrice Habesch, interview by the author, November 2013.

12. Samia Halaby, "Sophie Halaby," 87. Widad Kawar remembered that Sophie had very high standards for her dress. Kawar, interview.

13. Widad Kawar, "The Silk Threads of Jerusalem: Attire and Handicrafts during the British Mandate," in *Jerusalem Interrupted: Modernity and Colonial Transformation, 1917–Present*, ed. Lena Jayyusi (Northampton, MA: Olive Branch Press, 2015), 178.

14. Helen Bentwich to Lady Caroline Franklin, July 10, 1925, Helen Bentwich Collection, Women's Library, London.

15. Tawfiq Canaan, "Unwritten Laws Affecting the Arab Women of Palestine," *Journal of the Palestine Oriental Society* 11, nos. 3–4 (1931): 190.

16. Bertha Vester diary, 1927, American Colony in Jerusalem Papers, Manuscript Division, Library of Congress, Washington, DC.

17. Fannie Fern Andrews, *The Holy Land under Mandate* (Boston: Houghton Mifflin, 1931), 89.

18. Emery to mother, December 9, 1924, MECA.

19. Andrews, *Holy Land*, 89.

20. Emery to mother, December 9, 1924, MECA.

21. For other examples of discrimination when working for the British government see Laura Schor, *The Best School in Jerusalem: Annie Landau's School for Girls, 1900–1960* (Waltham, MA: Brandeis Univ. Press, 2013), 156–57.

22. Rochelle Davis, "Growing Up in Palestinian Jerusalem before 1948: Childhood Memories of Communal Life, Education, and Political Awareness," in Jayyusi, *Jerusalem Interrupted*, 203.

23. Sandy Sufian, "Healing Jerusalem: Colonial Medicine and Arab Health from World War I to 1948," in Jayyusi, *Jerusalem Interrupted*, 121.

24. Bernard Wasserstein, "'Clipping the Claws of the Colonisers': Arab Officials in the Government of Palestine, 1917–48," *Middle Eastern Studies* 13, no. 2 (May 1977): 171.

25. Wasserstein, 189.

26. Nicola worked on the General Post Office (today, Central Post Office), the Palestine Archaeological Museum (today the Rockefeller Museum), and on Government House (today housing the United Nations Special Coordinator for the Middle East Peace Process). Khoury, interview, July 2014.

27. *JGC Magazine*, 1928, 21.

28. *JGC Magazine*, 1929, 44–46.

29. See chapters 3 and 4.

30. Ruth Woodsmall, Survey on Status of Middle Eastern Women, Ruth Woodsmall Papers, Sophia Smith Collection, Smith College. The religious affiliation of the students was indicated by Woodsmall on their response sheets.

31. Woodsmall, Survey.

32. Woodsmall, Survey.

33. Woodsmall, Survey. For a discussion of the conflict between modern values and nationalism among World War I soldiers, see Tamari, *Year of the Locust*, 85.

34. Kawar, interview.

35. *JGC Magazine*, 1933, 47.

36. Ofer, "Scheme for Establishment," 274–77.

37. Archie Wallis, interview by the author, April 2016.

38. Bezalel Academy closed in 1929 and reopened in 1935. See Ankori, *Palestinian Art*, 41.

39. Reem Fadda, ed., *Palestinian Women Artists* (Jerusalem: Palestinian Art Court—al-Hoash, 2007), 52.

40. Vicken Kalbian is certain that they knew of each other's work. Vicken and Ada Kalbian, interview by the author, November 2014.

41. Samia Halaby, "The Pictorial Arts of Jerusalem, 1900–1948," in Jayyusi, *Jerusalem Interrupted*, 23–28.

42. Ganit Ankori, *Palestinian Art* (London: Reaktion Books, 2006), 29–32.

43. Jacques d'Aumale, *Voix de l'Orient: Souvenirs d'un diplomate* (Montreal: Editions Variétés, 1945), 265–76.

44. Documents relating to applications, Service des œuvres françaises à l'étranger, box 47; serie O, XXVIII, dossier 2, Palestine 1930–32, Centre des Archives diplomatiques, La Courneuve, France.

45. Documents relating to applications.

46. Sitton's certificates are in the author's possession.

47. Samia Halaby, "Sophie Halaby," 84, 98–99.

48. Habesch, interview.

49. Paula Birnbaum, *Women Artists in Interwar France: Framing Femininities* (Surrey, UK: Ashgate, 2011), 2.

50. Bertha Vester diary, April 30, 1929, American Colony in Jerusalem Papers, Manuscript Division, Library of Congress, Washington, DC.

51. Hillel Cohen, *Year Zero of the Arab-Israeli Conflict: 1929* (Waltham, MA: Brandeis Univ. Press, 2015), xvii–xviii.

52. David Reifler, *Days of Ticho: Empire, Mandate, Medicine and Art in the Holy Land* (Jerusalem: Gefen, 2015), 262–63, 284–88.

53. "The Protest of the Arab Advocates," Beyt-Ul-Makdes Press, n.d., clippings file, American Colony Archives, Jerusalem.

54. Ellen Fleischmann, "Jerusalem Arab Women's Politicization during British Mandate," in Jayyusi, *Jerusalem Interrupted*, 156.

55. Anbara Salam Khalidi, *Memoirs of an Early Arab Feminist* (London: Pluto Press, 2013), 134. Another leader was Melia Sakakini. See Davis, "Growing Up in Palestinian Jerusalem," 203.

56. Khalidi, *Memoirs*, 134. See also Bertha Vester diary, October 26, 1929, American Colony in Jerusalem Papers, Manuscript Division, Library of Congress, Washington, DC.

57. Jenifer Glynn, ed., *Tidings from Zion: Helen Bentwich's Letters from Jerusalem, 1919–1931* (London: Tauris, 2000), 191.

58. Hana Halaby, interview, July 2014.

59. Mutaz Qafisheh, "The International Law Foundations of Palestinian Nationality," *Graduate Institute of International Studies* 7 (2008): 149.

60. Catherine Fehrer, "Women at the Académie Julian in Paris," *Burlington Magazine* 136, no. 1100 (November 1994): 753. See discussion of this portrait, chapter 5.

61. Edward Lucie-Smith, *Impressionist Women* (New York: Artsbras, 1989), 141.

62. Boullata, *Palestinian Art*, 170.

63. Poster, Ticho House Archive. The exhibit took place November 14–27, 1930.

64. Livre 5, feuillet 3, position 28. Archives, Foyer International des Etudiantes, Paris.

65. Paula Birnbaum, "Modern Madonnas and Working Mothers," in *Essays on Women's Artistic and Cultural Contributions 1919–1939*, ed. Paula Birnbaum and Anna Novakov (Lewiston, NY: Edwin Mellen Press, 2009), 84.

66. Birnbaum, 142–44. See also Pierre Paraf, "Foyer International des Etudiantes," *L'Illustration*, May 10, 1930, 64–67.

67. Carolyn Patch, *Grace Whitney Hoff: An Abundant Life* (Cambridge, MA: Riverside Press, 1933), 155.

68. Habesch, interview.

69. Patch, *Grace Whitney Hoff*, 141.

70. Tamar Garb, "Men of Genius, Women of Taste," in *Overcoming All Obstacles: The Women of the Académie Julian*, ed. Gabriel Weisberg and Jane Becker (New York: Dahesh Museum of Art, 1999), 131.

71. Patch, *Grace Whitney Hoff*, 153, 159.

72. Walker's Galleries, "An Exhibition of Paintings and Drawings of Essex, France, and Elsewhere by Annette Tritton" (London: Women's Printing Society, January 31–February 13, 1934), in the author's possession.

73. Mary Alice Heekin Burke, *Elizabeth Nourse, 1859–1938: A Salon Career* (Washington, DC: Smithsonian Institution Press, 1983), 15.

74. Nicolas Ross, *Sainte-Alexandre-Nevski: Centre spiritual de l'emigration russe, 1918–1939* (Paris: Editions des Syrtes, 2011), 573–91.

75. Gill Perry, *Women Artists and the Parisian Avant-Garde: Modernism and Feminine Art, 1900 to the late 1920s* (Manchester, UK: Manchester Univ. Press, 1995), 19.

76. Pauline Paul, "Letters from Old Friends," *JGC Magazine*, 1933, 43.

77. Habesch, interview.

78. "A La Galerie Zak," *L'art vivant*, February 1932, 118.

79. "A La Galerie Zak," 118.

80. "A La Galerie Pigalle," *L'art vivant*, March 1932, 161.

81. "A Travers Le Salon des Tuileries," *Les Beaux-Arts*, June 25, 1932, 10; "Les Salons du Printemps: La Peinture du Neo-Parnasse," *La revue de l'art*, June–December 1932, 72.

82. "Courrier: Académies et Ateliers," *La Semaine à Paris*, January 13–20, 1933, 14. Searching through all Sophie's portraits of women, I have been able to find none that bears her signature using a middle initial.

83. "Les Expositions: Le Salon des Tuileries," *La revue de l'art*, June–December 1933, 317.

84. Boullata, *Palestinian Art*, 167.

85. Birnbaum, *Women Artists*, 44.

86. Jane Kaillor, *Paula Modersohn-Becker: Germany's Pioneer Modernist* (New York: Galerie St. Etienne, 1983), [pages unnumbered].

87. Kaillor, [pages unnumbered].

88. Samia Halaby, "Sophie Halaby," 84–85.

89. Kaillor, *Paula Modersohn-Becker*), [pages unnumbered].

90. Yigal Zalmona, *The Art of Abel Pann: From Montparnasse to the Land of the Bible* (Jerusalem: Israel Museum, 2003), 8. In 1912, Boris Schatz convinced Pann to go to Jerusalem to teach at the Bezalel Academy. He remained in the city for the rest of his life.

91. *JGC Magazine*, 1933, 43.

92. "Jerusalem Girls' College," *Bible Lands*, April 1930–October 1934, 97.

93. *JGC Magazine*, 1931, 7.

94. *JGC Magazine*, 1931, 7.

3. The Art and Politics of Jerusalem

1. Helen Bentwich, "The Newest Jerusalem," typescript, 1, Helen Bentwich File, Central Zionist Archives, Jerusalem.

2. Bentwich, 1.

3. Raouf Halaby, interview by the author, April 2014. Helen Bentwich, "The Newest Jerusalem," 2.

4. Eunice Holliday, *Letters from Jerusalem during the Palestine Mandate* (London: Radcliffe Press, 1997), 124.

5. Bentwich, "The Newest Jerusalem," 2.

6. Klein, *Lives in Common*, 82. See also, Moshe Hananel, ed., *Ha-Yerushalmim: Masa' be-Sefer ha-Telefon ha-Mandatori* (The Jerusalemites, A Mandatory Telephone Directory) (Tel Aviv: Erets va-Teva, 2007), 270.

7. Bentwich, "The Newest Jerusalem," 3–4.

8. Bentwich, 3–4.

9. Bentwich, 3–4.

10. Patch, *Grace Whitney Hoff*, 61.

11. Bertha Vester diary, September 16, 1933, American Colony in Jerusalem Papers, Manuscript Division, Library of Congress, Washington, DC.

12. See chapter 2.

13. Bentwich, "The Newest Jerusalem," 3–4.

14. Taher Nusseibeh, interview by the author, June 2014.

15. Interview by the author with Beatrice Habesch and others.

16. Nadim Bawalsa, "Sakakini Defrocked," *Jerusalem Quarterly* 42 (2010): 16.

17. Tamari, *Year of the Locust*, 85.

18. Walid Khalidi, *Before Their Diaspora: A Photographic History of the Palestinians 1876–1948* (Washington, DC: Institute for Palestine Studies, 2010), 104.

19. Diary entry March 26, 1915, cited in Bawalsa, "Sakakini Defrocked," 6.

20. Jawhariyyeh, *Storyteller of Jerusalem*, 218.

21. Bawalsa, "Sakakini Defrocked," 11.

22. Fadwa Tuqan, *A Mountainous Journey: An Autobiography*, ed. Salma Khadra Jayyusi, trans. Olive Kenny, poetry trans. Naomi Shihab Nye, (St. Paul, MN: Graywolf Press, 1990), 26.

23. Holliday, *Letters from Jerusalem*, 141–42.

24. Bertha Vester diary, 1933, American Colony in Jerusalem Papers, Manuscript Division, Library of Congress, Washington, DC.

25. Bertha Vester diary, 1933.

26. Michael Romann and Alex Weingrod, *Living Together Separately: Arabs and Jews in Contemporary Jerusalem* (Princeton, NJ: Princeton Univ. Press, 1991), 9.

27. Walid Khalidi, *Before Their Diaspora*, 109. See also Norman Bentwich and Helen C. Bentwich, *Mandate Memories, 1918–1948* (New York: Schocken Books, 1965), 153–54.

28. John H. Melkon Rose, *Armenians of Jerusalem: Memories of Life in Palestine* (London: Radcliffe Press, 1993), 150.

29. Raouf Halaby, interview, and Nora Kort, interview by the author, June 21, 2014. Nadia Bandak, interview by the author, February 2015.

30. Melkon Rose, *Armenians of Jerusalem*, 151. For another interpretation of why the Arab university plan failed see, d'Aumale, *Voix de l'Orient*, 201.

31. Boullata, *Palestinian Art*, 69.

32. Faten Nastas Mitwasi, *Reflections on Palestinian Art: Art of Resistance or Aesthetics* (Beit Jala, Palestine: Diyar, 2015), 19.

33. Samia Halaby, "Pictorial Arts of Jerusalem," 47. Al-Sa'di fled Jerusalem in 1948 and spent the rest of her life in Damascus teaching art in Palestinian refugee camps. Her paintings are privately held.

34. Bertha Vester diary, 1934, American Colony in Jerusalem Papers, Manuscript Division, Library of Congress, Washington, DC.

35. Hala Sakakini, *Jerusalem and I: A Personal Record*, 2nd ed. (Amman, Jordan: Economic Press, 2000), 49.

36. Salim Tamari, "City of Riffraff: Crowds, Public Space, and New Urban Sensibilities in War-Time Jerusalem, 1917–1921," in *Comparing Cities: The Middle East and South Asia*, ed. Kamra Asdar Ali and Martina Rieker (Oxford: Oxford Univ. Press, 2009), 24.

37. Tamari, 24.

38. One exception was the Evelina de Rothschild School, which had a dual-language program, English and Hebrew, for Jewish girls. See Schor, *Best School*, 82–86.

39. Stockdale, *Colonial Encounters*, 191.

40. *JGC Magazine*, 1935, 35.

41. *JGC Magazine*, 1933, 59.

42. Matiel E. T. Mogannam, *The Arab Woman and the Palestinian Problem* (London: Herbert Joseph, 1937), 59–69.

43. Jerusalem Girls' College, box 43, file 3, Jerusalem and East Mission (J&EM), MECA.

44. Mabel Warburton, "A Survey of Education in the Middle East: Yesterday and Today," April 1935, box 37, J&EM, MECA.

45. *JGC Magazine*, July 1934, 13.

46. Bertha Vester diary, August 20, 1935, American Colony in Jerusalem Papers, Manuscript Division, Library of Congress, Washington, DC.

47. Rashid Khalidi, *Palestinian Identity*, 189–90.

48. Raouf Halaby, interview.

49. Dorothy Norman to family, May 19, 1936, MECA, quoted in Sherman, *Mandate Days*, 97.

50. Warburton to Edward Bickersteth, June 14, 1936, box 46, J&EM, MECA.

51. Eileen Kuttab, "Palestinian Women in the 'Intifada': Fighting on Two Fronts," *Arab Studies Quarterly* 15, no. 2 (Spring 1993): 71.

52. Sultaneh Halaby, "The Jews and Palestine," *Palestine and Transjordan: A Weekly Review of Political, Economic, Legal, and Social Affairs in Palestine, Transjordan and Other Parts of the Arab World*, June 27, 1936.

53. Ellen Fleischmann, *The Nation and its "New" Women: The Palestinian Women's Movement 1920–1948* (Berkeley: Univ. of California Press, 2003), 128. See also Noah Haiduc-Dale,

Arab Christians in British Mandate Palestine: Communalism and Nationalism, 1917–1948 (Edinburgh: Edinburgh Univ. Press, 2015).

54. *Palestine and Transjordan: A Weekly Review of Political, Economic, Legal and Social Affairs in Palestine, Transjordan and Other Parts of the Arab World*, August 29, 1936.

55. *Palestine and Transjordan*, September 19, 1936, October 10, 1936.

56. *Palestine and Transjordan*, October 17, 1936.

57. *Palestine and Transjordan*, November 7, 1936, November 14, 1936.

58. *Palestine and Transjordan*, November 21, 1936.

59. Bertha Vester diary, January 3, 1937, American Colony in Jerusalem Papers, Manuscript Division, Library of Congress, Washington, DC.

60. "The Folk Museum of Jerusalem," *Palestine and Transjordan*, January 16, 1937.

61. *Palestine and Transjordan*, March 6, 1937. The author thanks an anonymous reviewer for this interpretation of the cartoon.

62. Miss Landau was the headmistress of the Evelina de Rothschild School for Girls in Jerusalem. See *Palestine Post*, May 12, 1937.

63. Wasserstein, *Divided Jerusalem*, 110–15.

64. *Directory of Arab Trade, Industries, Crafts, and Professions in Palestine and Trans-Jordan, 1937–1938* (Jerusalem: Commercial Press, 1937), 194, 208.

65. Emery to mother, September 25, 1938, MECA, quoted in Inger Marie Okkenhaug, *The Quality of Heroic Living, of High Endeavour and Adventure: Anglican Mission, Women and Education in Palestine* (Leiden: Brill, 2002), 181. Ellen Fleischmann interview with Alexandra Aboud: "Muslims forced the Christians to wear black veils on their heads when they went out. The veils were to look like the ones the Muslims wore. They didn't want Christians to look like Jews when they went out. This act was both religious and national." Fleischmann, *The Nation*, 274n116.

66. Ted Swedenburg, *Memories of Revolt: The 1936–1939 Rebellion and the Palestinian National Past* (Fayetteville: Univ. of Arkansas Press, 2003), 32–34.

67. Bertha Vester diary, September 3, 1938, American Colony in Jerusalem Papers, Manuscript Division, Library of Congress, Washington, DC.

68. Winifred Coate, "Jerusalem Girls' College Reunion," *Bible Lands*, July 1937, 875.

69. Mabel Warburton, "Partitioning Jerusalem," box 42, J&EM, MECA.

70. Warburton, "Partitioning Jerusalem."

71. Norman Bentwich, inaugural address, quoted in Warburton, "Partitioning Jerusalem."

72. "The Arab Ladies Denounce Jewish Attacks on Arabs," *Palestine and Transjordan*, July 16, 1938.

73. Winifred Coate to J. G. Matthew, October 24, 1938, box 43, file 1, MECA.

74. "Alumnae News," *JGC Magazine*, 1938, 48.

75. Walid Khalidi, *Before Their Diaspora*, 194–95; Bentwich and Bentwich, *Mandate Memories*, 163.

76. Rashid Khalidi, *Palestinian Identity*, 190.

77. Tom Segev, *One Palestine Complete: Jews and Arabs under the Mandate*, (New York: Metropolitan Books, 2000), 450.

78. J. M. Cowper, *The Auxiliary Territorial Service* (London: War Office, 1949), 41, 77–78.

79. Hana Halaby, interview by the author, July 2014. Asia received a pension for her service during the war from the British government for the rest of her life. Adli and Naji Halaby, interview by the author, January 2018.

80. Vicken and Ada Kalbian, interview by the author, November 2014.

81. Odd Karsten Tveit, *Anna's House: The American Colony in Jerusalem* (Nicosia, Cyprus: Rimal, 2000), 373.

82. Sherene Seikaly, *Men of Capital: Scarcity and Economy in Mandate Palestine* (Stanford, CA: Stanford Univ. Press, 2016), 54.

83. Andrea Stanton, *This Is Jerusalem Calling* (Austin: Univ. of Texas Press, 2013), 140–43.

84. Sherman, *Mandate Days*, 160.

85. Hana Halaby, interview by the author, January 2018.

86. Cowper, *Auxiliary Territorial Service*, 104.

87. Okkenhaug, *Quality*, 176.

88. Martin Gilbert, *Jerusalem in the Twentieth Century* (New York: Wiley, 1996), 165.

89. Wasserstein, *Divided Jerusalem*, 119–20.

90. Gilbert, *Jerusalem in the Twentieth Century*, 167.

91. Danny Rubenstein, Jerusalem historian, in note to the author, including translation of information cited in Bahjat Abū Gharbīyah, *Fī khiḍam al-niḍāl al-'Arabī al-Filasṭīnī: mudhakkirāt al-munāḍil Bahjat Abū Gharbīyah, 1916–1949* (In the Ocean of Palestinian Arab Struggle: The Memoirs of the Fighter Bahjat Abu Gharbiyah, 1916–1949) (Beirut: Mu'assasat al-Dirāsāt al-Filasṭīnīyah, 1993).

92. Gilbert, *Jerusalem in the Twentieth Century*, 169–70.

93. Rochelle Davis, "The Growth of the Western Communities," in Tamari, *Jerusalem 1948*, 47–48.

94. Safrai Gallery on King David Street claims to have been in existence since 1935, but there is no documentation of a permanent art gallery space before 1948.

95. Th. F. M., "Jerusalem Art Notes: Fifteen Artists," *Palestine Post*, February 10, 1946.

96. "A la Galerie Zak," 118.

97. Hananel, *Ha-Yerushalmim*, 168–69.

98. "Jerusalem Art Notes," *Palestine Post*, June 4, 1942, April 28, 1944, November 2, 1945, February 10, 1946, May 24, 1946, July 1, 1946, September 12, 1946, April 10, 1947.

99. Leila Hudson, interview by the author, November 2014.

100. Leila Hudson believes that this was a galvanizing moment for the Wahbe and Halaby families, who lost hope for the future in the face of this family tragedy.

101. Melkon Rose, *Armenians of Jerusalem*, 166.

102. A year later, the college buildings were taken over by the Evelina de Rothschild School, which was fleeing from Musrara. See Schor, *Best School*, 218–20.

103. Wasserstein, *Divided Jerusalem*, 131.

104. Nicholas E. Roberts, "Dividing Jerusalem: British Urban Planning in the Holy City," *Journal of Palestine Studies* 42, no. 4 (Summer 2013): 22.

105. Bertha Vester diary, December 2, 1947, American Colony in Jerusalem Papers, Manuscript Division, Library of Congress, Washington, DC.

4. Jordanian Jerusalem

1. Krystall, "Fall of the New City," 85, 88.

2. Bertha Vester diary, January 1, 1948, American Colony in Jerusalem Papers, Manuscript Division, Library of Congress, Washington, DC.

3. Ghada Karmi, "The 1948 Exodus: A Family Story," *Journal of Palestine Studies* 23, no. 2 (Winter 1994): 34–35.

4. Karmi, 35.

5. Karmi, 40.

6. Hala Sakakini, *Jerusalem and I*, 110.

7. Sakakini, 111.

8. Sakakini, 113, 115.

9. Krystall, "Fall of the New City," 102.

10. Boullata, *Palestinian Art*, 167

11. Boullata, 167n12.

12. Hana Halaby, interview, January 2018. Though it changed ownership at the turn of this century, the shop maintains the old sign, continuing the visual connection to the Halaby presence in the Old City.

13. Sahar Hamouda, *Once Upon a Time in Jerusalem* (Reading, UK: Garnet, 2010), 39. Nikolai Woronstov, chairman of IOPS, email correspondence with the author, December 2015. Elderly Jerusalemites testified that Sophie and her family were housed in the Coptic Orthodox monastery, close to the Alexander Nevsky Church.

14. Khaled Nashef, *Ya Kafi, Ya Shfi, the Tawfik Canaan Collection of Palestinian Amulets* (Birzeit: Birzeit Univ. Publications, 1998), 14.

15. Khaled Nashef, "Tawfik Canaan: His Life and Works," *Jerusalem Quarterly File* 16 (November 2002): 24.

16. John Tleel, *I Am Jerusalem* (Jerusalem: J. N. Tleel, 2007), 32.

17. Tleel, 33.

18. Tleel, 34.

19. Sakakini, *Jerusalem and I*, 118. See also, Henry Cattan, *Jerusalem* (London: Saqi Books, 2000), 44, for a description of the massacre at Deir Yassin by Jacques de Reynier, chief delegate of the International Red Cross.

20. Anbara Salam Khalidi, *Memoirs*, 143. Today, the Dar al-Tifl Foundation supports a girls' school, a museum, a cultural center, and the Hind al-Husseini College for Women.

21. "Declaration of Independence," *Palestine Post*, April 13, 1948, 1.

22. Larry Collins and Dominique Lapierre, *O Jerusalem* (New York: Simon & Schuster, 1972), 11–12.

23. Collins and Lapierre, 414.

24. Krystall, "Fall of the New City," 110.

25. Krystall, 113. These regulations were later codified as the Absentee Property Law of 1950.

26. Wasserstein, *Divided Jerusalem*, 163.

27. Tleel, *I Am Jerusalem*, 45.

28. Tleel, 54–56, 74.

29. Cattan, *Jerusalem*, 62.

30. Kimberly Katz, *Jordanian Jerusalem: Holy Places and National Spaces* (Gainesville: Univ. Press of Florida, 2005), 52–53.

31. Hanan Ashrawi, *This Side of Peace* (New York: Simon & Schuster, 1995), 23.

32. Salim Tamari, "The Phantom City," in *Across the Wall: Narratives of Israeli-Palestinian History*, ed. Ilan Pappe and Jamil Hilal (London: Tauris, 2010), 87.

33. Daphne Tsimhoni, "Christians in Jerusalem: A Minority at Risk," *Journal of Human Rights* 4 (2005): 391.

34. Tleel, *I Am Jerusalem*, 104.

35. Tleel, 392.

36. See also Romann and Weingrod, *Living Together Separately*, 12. The border was composed of damaged or destroyed buildings, stretches of rubble that had become no-man's-land, minefields, and long strings of barbed wire. At various points high concrete walls were put up to protect residents from sniper fire. The only passage between the two cities was the Mandelbaum Gate.

37. Tleel, *I Am Jerusalem*, 106.

38. Salim Tamari, *Mountain against the Sea: Essays on Palestinian Society and Culture* (Berkeley: Univ. of California Press, 2009), 58.

39. Mitwasi, *Reflections on Palestinian Art*, 21–23.

40. Adli and Naji Halaby, interview.

41. Foyer International des Etudiantes, livre 19, feuillet 41, positions 1009 and 1010. These files record Sophie Halaby's passport #167652, delivered in Jerusalem on October 23, 1943, and Anastasia Halaby's passport #127358, delivered in Jerusalem on November 28, 1939.

42. Sophie may have studied in Italy. See Samia Halaby, "Palestinian Artist," 61.

43. Thomas Meysels, the father of Vicken Kalbian's classmate, Lucian, wrote a column, "Jerusalem Art Notes," that appeared frequently from 1942 through 1947.

44. Bertha Spafford Vester, epilogue to *Our Jerusalem*, 1.

45. Kort, interview, and Safieh, interview. Helen Khader, interview by the author, June 30, 2014.

46. Raouf Halaby, interview.

47. Sister Marina, interview. Anya Berezina Derrick, telephone interview by author, July 2016.

48. Samia Halaby, "Sophie Halaby," 95. Sisters Veronica and Tamara, interview.

49. Habesch, interview; Hudson, interview; Raouf Halaby, interview. Issa Halaby, interview by the author, January 2018.

50. Rosemary Sayigh, "Encounters with Palestinian Women under Occupation," *Journal of Palestine Studies* 10, no. 4 (Summer 1981): 10. Widad Kawar concurred with this assessment. Kawar, interview.

51. Boullata, *Palestinian Art*, 172n8.

52. Sayigh, "Encounters," 10.

53. Asia Halaby to Hana Halaby, February 23, 1980, in the author's possession; Vicken Kalbian, email correspondence with the author, October 16, 2014.

54. Betty Dagher Majaj, *A War without Chocolate: One Woman's Journey through Two Nations, Three Wars, and Four Children* (n.p., 2015), 139.

55. Doris Salah, interview by the author, December 3, 2013.

56. Wallis, interview.

57. Khader, interview. The painting was removed during a recent renovation and awaits a decision on its placement.

58. Rima Salah, interview by the author, December 3, 2013.

59. The identification of women in the photograph was aided by Mona Halaby.

60. Tuqan, *Mountainous Journey*, 178.

61. See also Inger Marie Okkenhaug, "She Loves Books and Ideas," *Islam and Christian-Muslim Relations* 13, no. 4 (2002): 463.

62. Daphne Tsimhoni, *Christian Communities in Jerusalem and the West Bank since 1948* (Westport, CT: Praeger, 1993), 2–6.

63. Bandak, interview. George al-Ama, interview by the author, December 2015. Kort, interview. Adli Halaby believed that some of the land was given to Sophie and Asia by their brother, Nicola. Adli Halaby, interview.

64. Majaj, *War without Chocolate*, 160.

65. Khaled Khatib, interview by the author, June 2014.

66. Habesch, interview.

67. Nicola Halaby to Vera Wahbe, December 21, 1961, copy in the author's possession.

68. Khoury, interview, July 2014.

69. Khoury, interview.

70. Ada Kalbian, interview with author, March 2016.

71. Kawar, interview.

72. Boullata, *Palestinian Art*, 167.

73. Vicken and Ada Kalbian, interview, November 2014. Tleel, interview; Kawar, interview.

74. Ashrawi, *This Side of Peace*, 226.

75. Bertha Spafford Vester, *Flowers of the Holy Land* (Kansas City, MO: Hallmark Cards, 1962), 8.

76. Hilda Ridler, "The Palestine I Knew, 1918–48," Hilda Ridler Papers, MECA.

77. Wilson, *Jerusalem*, 12.

78. Boullata, *Palestinian Art*, 172.

79. Boullata, 172.

80. Tleel, interview.

81. Lily Porter and Nelly Barrett, interview by author, March 2016.

82. Samia Halaby, "Sophie Halaby," 90, 99.

83. Hana Halaby, interview.

84. Suheil Halaby, telephone interview by author, January 2018.

85. Issa Halaby, interview.

86. Tuqan, *Mountainous Journey*, 84.

87. Boullata, email correspondence with the author, October 15, 2016.

88. Daniel Oliver Newberry, interview, December 1, 1997, *Foreign Affairs Oral History Project*, The Association for Diplomatic Studies and Training, http://www.adst.org/Readers/Israel.pdf.

89. Wilson, *Jerusalem*, 3–4.

90. Kai Bird, *Crossing Mandelbaum Gate: Coming of Age between the Arabs and Israelis, 1956–1978* (New York: Scribner, 2014), 15, 19.

91. Raouf Halaby, interview.

92. Miriam C. Davis, *Dame Kathleen Kenyon: Digging Up the Holy Land* (Walnut Creek, CA: Left Coast Press, 2008), 58–59.

93. Davis, 104–7.

94. Davis, 222.

95. In 1957, Asia Halaby was listed as a "cataloguer" for Pritchard's expedition. This position assumed experience on previous expeditions. Gibeon Expedition, 1956–64, University

Museum, University of Pennsylvania. James B. Pritchard, *The Cemetery at Tell Es-Sa'idiyeh, Jordan* (Philadelphia: University Museum, 1980), 66. See also obituary of James B. Pritchard, *New York Times*, January 19, 1997.

96. See also Laurie Brand, "The Politics of Passports," in *The Middle East and North Africa: Essays in Honor of C.J. Hurewitz*, ed. Reeva Simon (New York: Columbia Univ. Press, 1990), 28. Brand states: "Transjordan's population prior to the partition of Palestine is estimated at 340,000, divided between nomads and semi-nomads of the desert (160,000) on the one hand, and primarily rural town inhabitants (180,000) on the other. Transjordan's annexation of the West Bank increased the kingdom's population by 900,000 people: the native population of the West Bank (400,000–450,000) and some 450,000 refugees who came from what became the State of Israel."

97. Katz, *Jordanian Jerusalem*, 55–66.

98. Brand, "Politics of Passports," 28.

99. Katz, *Jordanian Jerusalem*, 85.

100. Katz, 85

101. Katz, 135.

102. Katz, 124.

103. Katz, 138.

104. Hana Halaby, interview, and Leila Hudson, interview.

5. Jerusalem Occupied

1. Horatio Vester, diary, March 14, 1967, American Colony Archives, Jerusalem.

2. Sari Nusseibeh, *Once Upon a Country* (New York: Farrar, Strauss, Giroux, 2007), 87.

3. Horatio Vester, diary, May 26, 1967, American Colony Archives, Jerusalem.

4. Melkon Rose, *Armenians of Jerusalem*, 260.

5. Melkon Rose, 265. Moshe Amirav also reported use of napalm. Moshe Amirav, *Jerusalem Syndrome: The Palestinian-Israeli Battle for the Holy City* (Brighton, UK: Sussex Academic Press, 2009), 13.

6. The United States broke with the rest of the world in 2018 when it moved its embassy to Jerusalem. See the *New York Times*, May 12, 14, and 15.

7. Horatio Vester, diary, 1968, American Colony Archives, Jerusalem.

8. Melkon Rose, *Armenians of Jerusalem*, 272.

9. Sami Hadawi, *Palestinian Rights and Losses in 1948* (London: Saqi Books, 1988), 85. Safieh, interview.

10. Sayigh, "Encounters with Palestinian Women," 10.

11. Nusseibeh, *Once Upon a Country*, 94.

12. Nusseibeh, 93.

13. During the Six-Day War, Israel conquered the Sinai Peninsula and Gaza from Egypt; the Golan Heights from Syria; East Jerusalem (including the Old City) and the West Bank from Jordan.

14. Nusseibeh, *Once Upon a Country*, 98.

15. "Jordan Antiquities Department Takes Over Palestine Museum," *Jerusalem Star*, September 2, 1966. See also Horatio Vester, diary, September 3, 1966, American Colony Archives, Jerusalem.

16. Moshe Amirav, interview by the author, December 2015. See also Amirav, *Jerusalem Syndrome*, 13.

17. Amirav, interview.

18. Hana Halaby, interview, July 2014.

19. Samia Halaby, "Sophie Halaby," 88.

20. Lisa Taraki, ed., *Living Palestine: Family Survival, Resistance, and Mobility under Occupation* (Syracuse: Syracuse Univ. Press, 2006), xxi.

21. Amirav, interview.

22. For a general discussion of the role of storytelling at this historical moment, see Rosemary Sayigh, "Palestinian Camp Women as Tellers of History," *Journal of Palestine Studies* 27, no. 2 (Winter 1998): 42–58.

23. Tleel, *I Am Jerusalem*, 156, 159.

24. Tleel, 201–3.

25. Majaj, *War without Chocolate*, 171.

26. Majaj, 170.

27. Ibrahim Dakkak, "Jerusalem's via Dolorosa," *Journal of Palestine Studies* 11, no. 1 (Autumn 1981):138, 143.

28. Sakakini, *Jerusalem and I*, xii.

29. Sakakini, xv.

30. Hala Sakakini, *The Years in Ramallah* (Jerusalem: Commercial Press, 1997), 28, quoted in Klein, *Lives in Common*, 202.

31. Tleel, *I Am Jerusalem*, 183.

32. Majaj, *War without Chocolate*, 169.

33. Ahmad Jamil Azem, "The Israeli Redefinition of Jerusalem," in Jayyusi, *Jerusalem Interrupted*, 328.

34. Elie Rekhess, "The Palestinian Political Leadership in East Jerusalem after 1967," in *Jerusalem: Idea and Reality*, ed. Tamar Mayer and Suleiman Ali Mourad (London: Routledge, 2008), 268–69; Azem, "Israeli Redefinition of Jerusalem," 328–29.

35. Terry Rempell, "The Significance of Israel's Partial Annexation of East Jerusalem," *Middle East Journal* 51, no. 4 (Autumn 1997): 525.

36. Meron Benvenisti, *Jerusalem* (Jerusalem: Isratypset, 1976), 163–65.

37. Lisa Taraki, "The Development of Political Consciousness among Palestinians in the Occupied Territories, 1967–1987," in *Intifada: Palestine at the Crossroads*, ed. Jamal R. Nassar and Roger Heacock (New York: Praeger, 1990), 53.

38. Rashid Khalidi, *Palestinian Identity*, 193–97.

39. Rempel, "Israel's Partial Annexation," 527.

40. Lamis Abu Nahleh, "Six Families: Survival and Mobility in Times of Crisis," in *Living Palestine*, ed. Lisa Taraki (Syracuse: Syracuse Univ. Press, 2006), 105–6.

41. Abu Nahleh, 71.

42. Michael Dumper, *Jerusalem Unbound: Geography, History, and the Future of the Holy City* (New York: Columbia Univ. Press, 2014), 91.

43. Romann and Weingrod, *Living Together Separately*, 18–20. See also Mehran Kamrava, *The Modern Middle East: A Political History since the First World War* (Berkeley: Univ. of California Press, 2011), 234–35.

44. Romann and Weingrod, 21.

45. Rekhess, "Palestinian Political Leadership," 271.

46. Thomas Phillip Abowd, *Colonial Jerusalem: The Spatial Construction of Identity and Difference in a City of Myth, 1948–2012* (Syracuse: Syracuse Univ. Press, 2014), 128.

47. Romann and Weingrod, *Living Together Separately*, 33.

48. Romann and Weingrod, 40

49. Melkon Rose, *Armenians of Jerusalem*, 271. See also Benvenisti, *Jerusalem*, cited in Klein, *Lives in Common*, 217.

50. Horatio Vester, diary, March 25, 1968, American Colony Archives, Jerusalem.

51. Telegram, August 18, 1968, file 6423/8, letter *gimel*, Israel State Archives.

52. Asia Halaby to Ada and Vicken Kalbian, August 23, 1968, copy in the author's possession.

53. Horatio Vester, diary, February 4, 1968, American Colony Archives, Jerusalem.

54. Horatio Vester, diary, May 16, 1969.

55. Horatio Vester, diary, February 2, 1970.

56. Kathleen Kenyon, "Tunneling in Jerusalem," *London Times*, August 17, 1972.

57. Vicken Kalbian, email correspondence with the author, October 26, 2016.

58. Sophie Halaby to Ada Kalbian, September 17, 1968, copy in the author's possession.

59. Sophie Halaby to Ada Kalbian, September 17, 1968.

60. Amirav, interview.

61. Sophie Halaby to Ada Kalbian, September 17, 1968.

62. Shahid, *Jerusalem Memories*, 195–200.

63. Samih K. Farsoun, *Palestine and the Palestinians* (Boulder, CO: Westview Press, 1997), 157.

64. Nusseibeh, *Once Upon a Country*, 136.

65. Laurie Brand, "Palestinians and Jordanians: A Crisis of Identity," *Journal of Palestine Studies* 24, no. 4 (Summer 1995): 53.

66. Foreign nationals included Palestinians who had lived abroad. Nusseibeh, *Once Upon a Country*, 189.

67. Ricks, interview.

68. Boullata, *Palestinian Art*, 172. Samia Halaby, *Liberation Art of Palestine* (London: HTTB, 2001), 5. Mitwasi, *Reflections on Palestinian Art*, 25.

69. Eileen Kuttab, "Palestinian Women," 74.

70. Asia Halaby to Hana Halaby, June 12, 1979, copy in the author's possession.

71. Asia Halaby to Hana Halaby, June 12, 1979.

72. Majaj, 170–71.

73. Khader, interview; Hudson, interview; Raouf Halaby, interview.

74. Melkon Rose, *Armenians in Jerusalem*, 240.

75. Kort, interview. See also Kuttab, "Palestinian Women," 74–75.

76. See Lisa Taraki, "Development of Political Consciousness," 67–68.

77. Nusseibeh, *Once Upon a Country*, 219.

78. Bandak, interview.

6. Sophie's Legacy

1. Mitwasi, *Reflections on Palestinian Art*, 25–26.

2. Samia Halaby, *Liberation Art*, 5.

3. Boullata, *Palestinian Art*, 172.

4. Boullata, 167, 172. See also, Fadwa Tuqan's refusal to write nationalist poetry in Tuqan, *Mountainous Journey*, 107–8.

5. Faten Toubasi, email correspondence with the author, January 7, 2016.

6. Behar Ashhab, "Women's Art in Palestine," *Al-Fajr*, November 28, 1986, 11.

7. Samia Halaby, "Sophie Halaby," 89.

8. Lita S. Whitesel, "Personalities of Women Art Students," *Studies in Art Education* 20, no. 1 (1978): 56.

9. The Women's Work Committee, inaugurated in 1978, addressed national liberation and social emancipation. In 1980 it regrouped as the Palestinian Union of Women's Work Committee, in 1981 as the Union of Palestinian Women's Committees, and in 1982 as the Women's Committee for Social Work. Eileen Kuttab, "Palestinian Women," 73–74.

10. Ashhab, "Women's Art in Palestine," 11.

11. Ashhab, 11.

12. Ashhab, 11.

13. Sophie Halaby to Ada Kalbian, September 17, 1968.

14. Sophie Halaby to Ada Kalbian.

15. Habesch, interview.

16. Samia Halaby, "Sophie Halaby," 90–91.

17. The department opened in 1954.

18. Orayb Aref Najjer, *Portraits of Palestinian Women* (Salt Lake City: Univ. of Utah Press, 1992), 211–12.

19. Najjer, 211–12. For discussion of Musrara, see Paola Caridi, "Musrara, the Center of the World," *Jerusalem Quarterly* 62 (Spring 2015): 29 48.

20. Nancy Lapp, telephone interview by the author, December 2015.

21. Hadawi, *Palestinian Rights*, 85. See also, Cattan, *Jerusalem*, 63.

22. Safieh, interview.

23. Hana Halaby, interview, July 2014.

24. Sisters Tamara and Veronica, interview.

25. Salim Tamari, "Jerusalem: Subordination and Governance in a Sacred Geography," in *Capital Cities: Ethnographies of Urban Governance in the Middle East*, ed. Seteney Shami (Toronto: Centre for Urban and Community Studies, Univ. of Toronto, 2001), 191–92.

26. Frances Hasso, *Resistance, Repression, and Gender Politics in Occupied Palestine and Jordan* (Syracuse: Syracuse Univ. Press, 2005), 119.

27. Kamrava, *Modern Middle East*, 227–28.

28. Ali Qleibo, *Before the Mountains Disappear: An Ethnographic Chronicle of the Modern Palestinians* (Cairo: Kloreus, 1992), x.

29. Qleibo, xiii.

30. Qleibo, 58–59.

31. Qleibo, 57.

32. Qleibo, 64.

33. Rashid Khalidi, *The Iron Cage: The Story of the Palestinian Struggle for Statehood* (Boston: Beacon Press, 2006), 146.

34. Ashrawi, *This Side of Peace*, 147–57. See also Taraki, *Living Palestine*, xxviii, and Khalidi, *Iron Cage*, 151.

35. Email from Dr. Deeb, director of St. Joseph's Hospital, February 2014.

36. Khoury, interview, July 2014.

37. Lauren Gelfond Feldinger, "Putting East Jerusalem (Back) on the Cultural Map," *Jerusalem Post*, August 1, 2008, 22–23. George al-Ama and Mazen Qupty, interview by the author, Jerusalem, July 2014.

38. Tal Ben Zvi, ed., *Self-Portrait: Palestinian Woman's Art* (Tel Aviv: Andalus, 2001), 158.

39. Kamal Boullata, "Pioneering Women in Palestinian Art," in Ben Zvi, *Self-Portrait*, 170–78.

40. Tina Sherwell, "Imaging Palestine as the Motherland," in Ben Zvi, *Self-Portrait*, 166.

41. Sherwell, 165.

42. Ben Zvi, *Self-Portrait*, 146–58.

43. The International Academy of Art, Palestine, in Ramallah, was founded in 2006.

44. Sliman Mansour, telephone interview by the author, June 2014.

45. Sliman Mansour, interview by the author, Jerusalem, July 2016.

46. Tina Sherwell, *Forgotten Scene: Pioneer Artists from Palestine* (Jerusalem: Al-Wasiti Art Center, 2003), 3.

47. Sherwell, 11.

48. Sherwell, 11.

49. Sherwell, 12.

50. Sherwell, 17.

51. Fadda, *Palestinian Women Artists*, 59.

52. Sherwell, "Imaging Palestine," 164, quoted in Fadda, *Palestinian Women Artists*, 59.

53. Kamal Boullata, "Artists Re-Member Palestine in Beirut," *Journal of Palestine Studies* 32, no. 4 (Summer 2003), cited in Fadda, *Palestinian Women Artists*, 59.

54. Boullata, 60.

55. Boullata, *Palestinian Art*, 40, 168–71.

56. Esmail Nashif, *On Palestinian Abstraction: Zohdy Qadry and the Geometrical Melody of Late Modernism* (Haifa, Israel: Dar Raya, 2014), 40–42.

57. Nashif, 43.

58. Nashif, 43

59. Nashif, 44.

60. Samia Halaby, "Sophie Halaby," 93.

61. Samia Halaby, 91–93.

62. Samia Halaby, 93.

63. Samia Halaby, 89, 92, 94–95.

64. Gordon Hon, email correspondence with the author, April 5, 2016.

65. Sharaf, interview.

66. In the collection of Mazen and Yvette Qupty.

Afterword

1. Feldinger, "Putting East Jerusalem (Back)."

2. The three Gaza wars were Operation Cast Lead 2008–9, Operation Pillar of Defense 2012, and Operation Protective Edge 2014.

3. Wallis, interview.

4. Kamal Boullata, email correspondence with the author, October 14, 2016.

5. Vicken Kalbian, email correspondence with the author, October 16, 2014.

6. *Directory of Arab Trade, Industries, Crafts, and Professions in Palestine and Trans-Jordan, 1937–38* (Jerusalem: Commercial Press, 1937), 194.

7. Collins and Lapierre, *O Jerusalem*, 11–12.

8. Rawan Sharaf, interview by the author, London, April 2016. This information was later confirmed for the author by Mazen Qupty.

9. Pierre Sanchez, ed., *Dictionnaire du salon des Tuileries: répertoire des exposants et listes des oeuvres présentées, 1923–1962*, vol. 2 (Dijon: L'Echelle de Jacob, 2007), 364.

Bibliography

Archival Sources

American Colony Archives, Jerusalem.
American Colony in Jerusalem Papers, Manuscript Division, Library of Congress, Washington, DC.
Elinor Moore Collection, Hartley Library, Univ. of Southampton, UK.
Foyer International des Etudiantes, Archives, Paris.
Frick Art Reference Library, The Frick Collection, New York City.
Gibeon Expedition, 1956–64, University Museum, Univ. of Pennsylvania.
Helen Bentwich Collection, Central Zionist Archives, Jerusalem.
Helen Bentwich Collection, Women's Library, London.
Jerusalem Girls' College Collections, Middle East Centre Archives, Saint Anthony's College, Oxford University (MECA).
Katy Antonius Papers, Israel State Archives, Jerusalem.
National Archives of Great Britain, Kew, UK.
Ruth Woodsmall Papers, Sophia Smith Collection, Smith College, Northampton, MA.
Service des œuvres françaises à l'étranger, Centre des Archives diplomatiques, La Courneuve, France.
Ticho House Archive, The Israel Museum, Jerusalem.

Interviews

Al-Ama, George. Bethlehem, December 2015.
Al-Ama, George, and Mazen Qupty. Jerusalem, July 2014.
Amirav, Moshe. Tel Aviv, December 2015.
Bandak, Nadia. Jerusalem, February 2015.
Boullata, Kamal. By email, October 2016 and December 2016.
Dajani, Mahira. Jerusalem, December 2015.
Derrick, Anya Berezina. By telephone, July 2016.
Dweik, David. Jerusalem, June 2014.
Elizabeth (Abbess), Mother Superior, Convent of St. Mary Magdalene, Jerusalem, December 2015.
Habesch, Beatrice. Jerusalem, November 2013.
Halaby, Adli and Naji. London, January 2018.

Halaby, Hana. By telephone, July 2014; Amman, January 2018.
Halaby, Issa. Amman, January 2018.
Halaby, Raouf. New York City, April 2014.
Halaby, Suheil. By telephone, January 2018.
Hudson, Leila. Washington, DC, November 6, 2014.
Joury, Mary. Amman, January 2018.
Kalbian, Vicken, and Ada Kalbian. Washington, DC, November 2014 and March 2016.
Kara'a, Nadia George. Jerusalem, June 2014.
Kawar, Widad. Amman, January 2018.
Khader, Helen. Jerusalem, June 30, 2014.
Khatib, Khaled. Jerusalem, June 2014.
Khouri, Jamia Nasir. By telephone, June 2014.
Khoury, Elias. Jerusalem, July 2014 and July 2016.
Kort, Nora. Jerusalem, June 21, 2014.
Lapp, Nancy. By telephone, December 2015.
Mansour, Sliman. By telephone, June 2014; Jerusalem, July 2016.
Marina (Sister). Convent of Mount of Olives, Jerusalem, June 2016.
Nusseibeh, Taher. Jerusalem, June 2014.
Porter, Lily. By telephone, December 2014.
Porter, Lily, and Nelly Barrett. Baltimore, March 2016.
Qupty, Mazen. Jerusalem, August 2008 and November 2013.
Ricks, Tom. By telephone, December 2015.
Rubenstein, Danny. Jerusalem, December 2015.
Safieh, Diana. Jerusalem, February 2015.
Salah, Doris. New York City, December 3, 2013.
Salah, Rima. New York City, December 3, 2013.
Sharaf, Rawan. London, April 2016.
Theodorie, Nadia, and Teddy Theodorie. By telephone, June 2014.
Tleel, John. Jerusalem, June 2014.
Toubasi, Faten. By email, March 2016.
Veronica (Sister) and Tamara (Sister). Russian Convent, Mount of Olives, Jerusalem, June 2016.
Wahbe, Samer. By telephone, March 2014.
Wallis, Archie. London, April 2016.
Woronstov, Nikolai, chairman of Imperial Orthodox Society of Palestine. By email, December 2015.
Zanemonets, Alexander. Jerusalem, May 2016 and December 2016.

Correspondence

Abbess Elizabeth, Mother Superior, Convent of St. Mary Magdalene, Jerusalem. To Elias Khoury, May 26, 2000. Copy in the author's possession.

Bentwich, Helen. To Lady Caroline Franklin, July 10, 1925, Helen Bentwich Collection, Women's Library, London.

Emery, Susan P. To mother, September 21, 1919, MECA.

Emery, Susan P. To mother, October 26, 1919, MECA.

Emery, Susan P. To mother, April 27, 1923, MECA.

Emery, Susan P. To mother, December 9, 1924, MECA.

Emery, Susan P. To mother, September 25, 1938, MECA.

Halaby, Asia. To Ada and Vicken Kalbian, August 23, 1968. Copy in author's possession.

Halaby, Asia. To Hana Halaby, June 12, 1979, and February 23, 1980. Copy in author's possession.

Halaby, Nicola. To Vera Wahbe, December 21, 1961. Copy in author's possession.

Halaby, Sophie. To Ada Kalbian, September 17, 1968. Copy in author's possession.

Warburton, Mabel. To Edward Bickersteth, June 14, 1936, MECA.

Periodicals

"A La Galerie Pigalle." *L'art vivant*, March 1932.

"The Arab Ladies Denounce Jewish Attacks on Arabs." *Palestine and Transjordan: A Weekly Review of Political, Economic, Legal, and Social Affairs in Palestine, Transjordan and Other Parts of the Arab World*, July 16, 1938.

Ashhab, Behar. "Women's Art in Palestine." *Al-Fajr*, November 28, 1986.

"A Travers le Salon des Tuileries." *L'Art et les artistes*, June 25, 1932.

"A Travers les Galeries." *La semaine* à *Paris*, January 13–20, 1933.

Beyt-Ul-Makdes Press, n.d., American Colony Archives, Jerusalem.

Bible Lands: Quarterly Paper of the Jerusalem and the East Mission, 1921, 1925–39.

"Courrier: Academies et Ateliers." *La semaine* à *Paris*, January 13–20, 1933.

"Declaration of Independence." *Palestine Post*, April 13, 1948.

"Les Expositions: Le Salon des Tuileries." *La revue de l'art*, June–December 1933.

Feldinger, Lauren Gelfond. "Putting East Jerusalem (Back) on the Cultural Map." *Jerusalem Post*, August 1, 2008.

"The Folk Museum of Jerusalem." *Palestine and Transjordan: A Weekly Review of Political, Economic, Legal, and Social Affairs in Palestine, Transjordan and Other Parts of the Arab World*, January 16, 1937.

"Girls' High School in Jerusalem." *Bible Lands: Quarterly Paper of the Jerusalem and the East Mission*, January 1921, 98.

Halaby, Sultaneh. "The Jews and Palestine." *Palestine and Transjordan: A Weekly Review of Political, Economic, Legal, and Social Affairs in Palestine, Transjordan and Other Parts of the Arab World*, June 27, 1936.

Jerusalem Girls' College Magazine, 1929, 1931, 1933–35, 1938.

Jerusalem Girls' College Old Girls' Guild, 1924–29.

"The Jerusalem Girls' College." *Palestine Weekly*, November 10, 1922, 710.

"Jordan Antiquities Department Takes Over Palestine Museum." *Jerusalem Star*, September 2, 1966.

Kenyon, Kathleen. "Tunneling in Jerusalem." *London Times*, August 17, 1972.

M., Th. F. [Meysels, Thomas]. "Jerusalem Art Notes." *Palestine Post*, June 4, 1942–April 10, 1947.

M., Th. F. [Meysels, Thomas]. "Jerusalem Art Notes: Fifteen Artists." *Palestine Post*, February 10, 1946.

Mikdadi, Salwa Nashashibi. "Badrans: A Century of Tradition and Innovation." *This Week in Palestine*, October 2007, 114.

Old Girls' Guild Annual Report, 1924–25, 1925–26, 1929–30 (published later as *Jerusalem Girls' College Magazine*—see above).

Palestine and Transjordan Weekly: A Weekly Review of Political, Economic, Legal, and Social Affairs in Palestine, Transjordan and Other Parts of the Arab World, 1936–38.

Paraf, Pierre. "Foyer International des Etudiantes." *L'Illustration*, May 10, 1930, 64–67.

Pritchard, James B. Obituary. *New York Times*, January 19, 1997.

"Le Salon des femmes artistes modernes a la Galerie Pigalle. *L'art vivant*, March 1932.

"Les Salons du Printemps: La Peinture du Neo-Parnasse." *La revue de l'art*, June–December 1932.

Books and Articles

Abowd, Thomas Philip. *Colonial Jerusalem: The Spatial Construction of Identity and Difference in a City of Myth, 1948–2012*. Syracuse: Syracuse Univ. Press, 2014.

Abu El-Haj, Nadia. *Facts on the Ground: Archaeological Practice and Territorial Self-Fashioning in Israeli Society*. Chicago: Univ. of Chicago Press, 2001.

Abulhawa, Susan. "Memories of an Un-Palestinian Story, in a Can of Tuna." In Johnson and Shehadeh, *Seeking Palestine*, 4–16.

Abu Nahleh, Lamis. "Six Families: Survival and Mobility in Times of Crisis." In *Living Palestine: Family Survival, Resistance, and Mobility under Occupation*, edited by Lisa Taraki, 103–84. Syracuse: Syracuse Univ. Press, 2006.

Aburish, Said K. *Children of Bethany: The Story of a Palestinian Family*. London: Bloomsbury Press, 1988.

Albina, Iris. "Souvenir from Gethsemane: Portrait of the Albina Brothers." *Institute for Palestine Studies* 60 (2014): 59–69.

Amirav, Moshe. *Jerusalem Syndrome: The Palestinian-Israeli Battle for the Holy City*. Brighton, UK: Sussex Academic Press, 2009.

Amiry, Suad. *Golda Slept Here*. Doha, Qatar: Bloomsbury Qatar Foundation, 2014.

———. "An Obsession." In Johnson and Shehadeh, *Seeking Palestine*, 74–85.

Amit, Gish. "Ownerless Objects? The Story of the Books the Palestinians Left Behind." *Jerusalem Quarterly* 33 (2008): 7–20.

Andrews, Fannie Fern. *The Holy Land under Mandate*. Boston: Houghton Mifflin, 1931.

Ankori, Gannit. "The Other Jerusalem: Images of the Holy City in Contemporary Palestinian Painting." *Jewish Art* 14 (1988): 74–92.

———. *Palestinian Art.* London: Reaktion Books, 2006.

Antonius, George. *The Arab Awakening: The Story of the Arab National Movement.* Beirut: Librairie du Liban, 1969.

Ashbee, Felicity. *Child in Jerusalem.* Syracuse: Syracuse Univ. Press, 2013.

Ashrawi, Hanan. *This Side of Peace.* New York: Simon & Schuster, 1995.

Ayalon, Ami. *Reading Palestine: Printing and Literacy, 1900–1948.* Austin: Univ. of Texas Press, 2004.

Azem, Ahmad Jamil. "Israeli Redefinition of Jerusalem." In Jayyusi, *Jerusalem Interrupted*, 311–58.

Ballobar, Conde de. *Jerusalem in World War I: The Palestine Diary of a European Diplomat.* London: Tauris, 2015.

Bawalsa, Nadim. "Sakakini Defrocked." *Jerusalem Quarterly* 42 (2010): 5–25.

Bentwich, Norman, and Helen C. Bentwich. *Mandate Memories, 1918–1948.* New York: Schocken, 1965.

Benvenisti, Meron. *Jerusalem.* Jerusalem: Isratypset, 1976.

Ben Zvi, Tal, ed. *Self-Portrait: Palestinian Women's Art.* Tel Aviv: Andalus, 2001. Exhibition catalog.

———. "Self-Portrait: Palestinian Women's Art." In Ben Zvi, *Self-Portrait*, 146–58.

Bird, Kai. *Crossing Mandelbaum Gate: Coming of Age between the Arabs and Israelis, 1956–1978.* New York: Scribner, 2014.

Birnbaum, Paula. "Modern Madonnas and Working Mothers." In *Essays on Women's Artistic and Cultural Contributions 1919–1939*, edited by Paula Birnbaum and Anna Novakov, 83–95. Lewiston, NY: Edwin Mellen, 2009.

———. *Women Artists in Interwar France: Framing Femininities.* Burlington, VT: Ashgate, 2011.

Blythe, Estelle. *When We Lived in Jerusalem.* London: John Murray, 1927.

Boullata, Kamal. "Artists Re-Member Palestine in Beirut." *Journal of Palestine Studies* 32, no. 4 (Summer 2003): 22–38.

———. "Art under the Siege." *Journal of Palestine Studies* 33, no. 4 (Summer 2004): 70–84.

———. *Palestinian Art: From 1850 to the Present.* London: Saqi, 2009.

———. "Palestinian Expression inside a Cultural Ghetto." *Middle East Research and Information Project* 159, no. 19 (July/August 1989): 24–28.

———. "Pioneering Women in Palestinian Art." In Ben Zvi, *Self-Portrait*, 170–78.

———. "To Measure Jerusalem: Explorations of the Square." *Journal of Palestine Studies* 28, no. 3 (Spring 1999): 83–91.

Brand, Laurie. "Palestinians and Jordanians: A Crisis of Identity." *Journal of Palestine Studies* 24, no. 4 (Summer 1995): 46–61.

———. "The Politics of Passports." In Simon, *The Middle East and North Africa*, 26–42.

Burke, Mary Alice Heekin. *Elizabeth Nourse, 1859–1938: A Salon Career.* Washington, DC: Smithsonian Institution Press, 1983.

Campos, Michelle U. *Ottoman Brothers: Muslims, Christians, and Jews in Early Twentieth-Century Palestine.* Stanford, CA: Stanford Univ. Press, 2011.

Canaan, Tawfiq. "Unwritten Laws Affecting the Arab Women of Palestine." *Journal of the Palestine Oriental Society* 11, nos. 3–4 (1931): 172–203.

Caridi, Paola. "Musrara, the Center of the World." *Jerusalem Quarterly* 62 (Spring 2015): 29–48.

Cattan, Henry. "The Status of Jerusalem under International Law and United Nations Resolutions." *Journal of Palestine Studies* 10, no. 3 (Spring 1981): 3–15.

———. *Jerusalem.* London: Saqi, 2000.

Chesin, Amir S., Bill Hutman, and Avi Melamed, eds. *Separate and Unequal: The Inside Story of Israeli Rule in East Jerusalem.* Cambridge, MA: Harvard Univ. Press, 1999.

Chisholm, Edwin. *The Jolly Book for Girls.* London: T. C. and E. C. Jack, n.d.

Clawson, Mary. *Letters from Jerusalem.* New York: Abelard-Schuman, 1957.

Cohen, Hillel. *Year Zero of the Arab-Israeli Conflict: 1929.* Waltham, MA: Brandeis Univ. Press 2015.

Collings, Rania Al Qass, Rifat Odeh Kassis, and Mitri Raheb, eds. *Palestinian Christians in the West Bank: Facts, Figures and Trends.* 2nd ed. Bethlehem: Diyar, 2012.

Collins, Larry, and Dominique Lapierre. *O Jerusalem.* New York: Simon & Schuster, 1972.

Cowper, J. M. *The Auxiliary Territorial Service.* London: War Office, 1949.

Dakkak, Ibrahim. "Jerusalem's via Dolorosa." *Journal of Palestine Studies* 11, no. 1 (Autumn 1981): 136–49.

d'Aumale, Jacques. *Voix de l'Orient: Souvenirs d'un diplomate.* Montreal: Editions Variétés, 1945.

Davidson, Henry Pomeroy. *The American Red Cross in the Great War.* New York: Macmillan, 1919.

Davis, Miriam C. *Dame Kathleen Kenyon: Digging Up the Holy Land.* Walnut Creek, CA: Left Coast Press, 2008.

Davis, Rochelle. "Growing Up in Palestinian Jerusalem before 1948: Childhood Memories of Communal Life, Education, and Political Awareness." In Jayyusi, *Jerusalem Interrupted*, 187–210.

———. "The Growth of the Western Communities." In Tamari, *Jerusalem 1948*, 10–29.

———. "Ottoman Jerusalem." In Tamari, *Jerusalem 1948*, 30–67.

Derrick, Anya Berezina. *Recollections of Jerusalem.* Jordanville, NY: Holy Trinity, 2014.

Directory of Arab Trade, Industries, Crafts, and Professions in Palestine and Trans-Jordan, 1937–1938. Jerusalem: Commercial Press, 1937.

Divine, Donna Robinson. "Palestine in World War I." In Simon, *The Middle East and North Africa*, 71–94.

Dobrenko, Evgeny. “Introduction.” In *The White Guard*, by Mikhail Bulgakov, xv–xlii. New Haven, CT: Yale Univ. Press, 2008.

Dumper, Michael. *Jerusalem Unbound: Geography, History, and the Future of the Holy City*. New York: Columbia Univ. Press, 2014.

———. *The Politics of Jerusalem since 1967*. New York: Columbia Univ. Press, 1997.

Einstein, Albert. “1925: The Mission of Our University.” *Scopus: The Magazine of the Hebrew University of Jerusalem*, April 1925. Reprint, 2015–16.

El Saadawi, Nawal. “The Political Challenges Facing Arab Women at the End of the Twentieth Century.” In *Women of the Arab World: The Coming Challenge*, edited by the Arab Women’s Solidarity Association, 7–26. London: Zed Books, 1988.

“An Exhibition of Paintings and Drawings of Essex, France, and Elsewhere by Annette Tritton.” London: Women’s Printing Society. A price list, published in conjunction with the exhibition of the same name, shown at Walker’s Galleries, London, UK, January 31–February 13, 1934.

Fadda, Reem, ed. *Palestinian Women Artists*. Jerusalem: Palestinian Art Court-al Hoash, 2007.

Farsoun, Samih K. *Palestine and the Palestinians*. Boulder, CO: Westview Press, 1997.

Fehrer, Catherine. “A Search for the Academie Julian.” *DRAWING: The International Review Published by the Drawing Society* 4, no. 2 (1982): 25–28.

———. “Women at the Academie Julian in Paris.” *Burlington Magazine* 136, no. 1100 (November 1994): 752–57.

Fleischmann, Ellen. “Crossing the Boundaries of History: Exploring Oral History in Researching Palestinian Women in the Mandate Period.” *Women’s History Review* 5, no. 3 (1996): 351–71.

———. “Jerusalem Arab Women’s Politicization during British Mandate.” In Jayyusi, *Jerusalem Interrupted*, 153–68.

———. *The Nation and its “New” Women: The Palestinian Women’s Movement 1920–1948*. Berkeley: Univ. of California Press, 2003.

———. “Selective Memory, Gender and Nationalism: Palestinian Women Leaders of the Mandate Period.” *History Workshop Journal* 47 (Spring 1999): 141–58.

———. “Young Women in the City: Mandate Memories.” *Jerusalem Quarterly* 27, no. 1 (Fall 1998): 31–39.

Fuchs, Ron, and Gilbert Herbert. “A Colonial Portrait of Jerusalem.” In *Hybrid Urbanism: On the Identity Discourse and the Built Environment*, edited by Nezar Al-Sayyad, 83–110. Westport, CT: Praeger, 2001.

Furlonge, Sir Geoffrey. *Palestine Is My Country: The Story of Musa Alami*. New York: Praeger, 1969.

Garb, Tamar. “Men of Genius, Women of Taste.” In *Overcoming All Obstacles: The Women of the Academie Julian*, edited by Gabriel Weisberg and Jane Becker, 115–33. New York: Dahesh Museum, 1999.

Gharbīyah, Bahjat Abū. *Fī khiḍam al-niḍāl al-ʿArabī al-Filasṭīnī: mudhakkirāt al-munāḍil Bahjat Abū Gharbīyah, 1916–1949* (The Ocean of Palestinian Arab

Struggle: The Memoirs of the Fighter Bahjat Abu Gharbiyah, 1916–1949). Beirut: Mu'assasat al-Dirāsāt al-Filasṭīnīyah, 1993.

Ghosheh, Subhi S. *Jerusalem: Arab Social Life, Traditions, and Everyday Pleasures in the 20th Century*. Northampton, MA: Olive Branch Press, 2013.

Gilbert, Martin. *Jerusalem in the Twentieth Century*. New York: Wiley, 1996.

Glock, Albert E. "Tradition and Change in Two Archaeologies." *American Antiquity* 50, no. 2 (April 1985): 464–77.

Glynn, Jenifer, ed. *Tidings from Zion: Helen Bentwich's Letters from Jerusalem, 1919–1931*. London: Tauris, 2000.

Graham, Stephen. *With the Russian Pilgrims to Jerusalem*. London: Macmillan, 1913.

Graham-Brown, Sarah. *Palestinians and Their Society 1880–1946: A Photographic Essay*. London: Quartet Books, 1980.

Gribetz, Jonathan Marc. *Defining Neighbors: Religion, Race and the Early Zionist-Arab Encounter*. Princeton, NJ: Princeton Univ. Press, 2014.

Grisgon, Geoffrey, and Charles Harvard Gibbs-Smith, eds. *People, Places, and Things*. London: Grosvenor Press, 1954.

Habash, Dahlia, and Terry Rempel. "Assessing Palestinian Property in the City." In Tamari, *Jerusalem 1948*, 167–99.

Hadawi, Sami. *Palestinian Rights and Losses in 1948*. London: Saqi Books, 1988.

Haiduc-Dale, Noah. *Arab Christians in British Mandate Palestine: Communalism and Nationalism, 1917–1948*. Edinburgh: Edinburgh Univ. Press, 2015.

Halaby, Mona Hajjar. "School Days in Mandate Jerusalem at Dames de Sion." *Jerusalem Quarterly* 31 (Summer 2007): 40–71.

Halaby, Samia. *Liberation Art of Palestine*. London: HTTB, 2001.

———. "The Pictorial Arts of Jerusalem, 1900–1948." In Jayyusi, *Jerusalem Interrupted*, 23–28.

———. "Sophie Halaby, Palestinian Artist of the Twentieth Century." *Jerusalem Quarterly* 61 (Winter 2015): 84–100.

Hamm, Michael E. *Kiev: A Portrait, 1800–1917*. Princeton, NJ: Princeton Univ. Press, 1993.

Hamouda, Sahar. *Once Upon a Time in Jerusalem*. Reading, UK: Garnet, 2010.

Hananel, Moshe, ed. *Ha-Yerushalmim: masa' be-sefer ha-telefon ha-mandatori* (The Jerusalemites, A Mandatory Telephone Directory). Tel Aviv: Erets va-teva, 2007.

Hasso, Frances S. "Modernity and Gender in Arab Accounts of the 1948 and 1967 Defeats." *International Journal of Middle East Studies* 32, no. 4 (November 2000): 491–510.

———. *Resistance, Repression, and Gender Politics in Occupied Palestine and Jordan*. Syracuse: Syracuse Univ. Press, 2005.

Hintlian, George. "An Attempt to Reconstruct the Pre-1948 Arab Commercial Center of Jerusalem." In *Between the Archival Forest and the Anecdotal Trees: A Multidisciplinary Approach to Palestinian Social History*, Birzeit University Ninth International Conference, November 21–22, 2004.

Hoffman, Adina. *House of Windows: Portraits from a Jerusalem Neighborhood.* New York: Broadway Books, 2000.

———. *Till We Have Built Jerusalem: Architects of a New City.* New York: Farrar, Straus and Giroux, 2016.

Holliday, Eunice. *Letters from Jerusalem during the Palestine Mandate.* London: Radcliffe Press, 1997.

Hopwood, Derek. "Russia and the Arab Orthodox Community in Palestine, 1882–1917." *Sobornost* 16, no. 2 (1994): 24–31.

———. *Russian Presence in Syria and Palestine, 1843–1914.* Oxford: Oxford Univ. Press, 1969.

Hurewitz, J. C. *The Struggle for Palestine.* New York: Greenwood Press, 1968.

Ignatieff, Michael. *The Russian Album.* New York: Viking, 1987.

Jacobson, Abigail. "A City Living through Crisis: Jerusalem during WWI." *British Journal of Middle Eastern Studies* 36, no. 1 (April 2009): 73–92.

———. *From Empire to Empire: Jerusalem between Ottoman and British Rule.* Syracuse: Syracuse Univ. Press, 2011.

Jacobson, Abigail, and Moshe Naor. *Oriental Neighbors: Middle Eastern Jews and Arabs in Mandatory Palestine.* Waltham, MA: Brandeis Univ. Press, 2016.

Jad, Islah. "From Salons to the Popular Committees: Palestinian Women, 1919–1989." In Nassar and Heacock, *Intifada*, 125–42.

Jawhariyyeh, Wasif. *The Storyteller of Jerusalem: The Life and Times of Wasif Jawhariyyeh, 1904–1948*, edited by Salim Tamari and Issam Nassar. Translated by Nada Elzeer. Northampton, MA: Olive Branch Press, 2014.

Jayyusi, Lena, ed. *Jerusalem Interrupted: Modernity and Colonial Transformation, 1917–Present.* Northampton, MA: Olive Branch Press, 2015.

Johnson, Penny, and Raja Shehadeh, eds. *Seeking Palestine: New Palestinian Writing on Exile and Home.* Northampton, MA: Olive Branch Press, 2013.

Jones, Christina. *The Untempered Wind: Forty Years in Palestine.* London: Longman, 1975.

Kaillor, Jane. *Paula Modersohn-Becker: Germany's Pioneer Modernist.* New York: Galerie St. Etienne, 1983. Published in conjunction with the exhibition of the same name, shown at the Galerie St. Etienne, New York City, November 15, 1983–January 7, 1984.

Kamrava, Mehran. *The Modern Middle East: A Political History since the First World War.* Berkeley: Univ. of California Press, 2011.

Karmi, Ghada. *Jerusalem Today: What Future for the Peace Process.* Reading, UK: Ithaca Press, 1996.

———. "The 1948 Exodus: A Family Story." *Journal of Palestine Studies* 23, no. 2 (Winter 1994): 31–40.

———. *Return: A Palestinian Memoir.* London: Verso, 2015.

Kartveit, Bard Helge. *Dilemmas of Attachment: Identity and Belonging among Palestinian Christians.* Leiden: Brill, 2014.

Katz, Kimberly. *Jordanian Jerusalem: Holy Places and National Spaces.* Gainesville: Univ. Press of Florida, 2005.

Kawar, Widad. "The Silk Threads of Jerusalem: Attire and Handicrafts during the British Mandate." In Jayyusi, *Jerusalem Interrupted,* 169–86.

Kawar, Widad Kamel, and Tania Tamari Nasir. *Palestinian Embroidery.* Beirut: Syco, 2003.

Kenyon, Kathleen. *Jerusalem: Excavating 3,000 Years of History.* New York: McGraw-Hill, 1967.

Khalidi, Anbara Salam. *Memoirs of an Early Arab Feminist.* London: Pluto Press, 2013.

Khalidi, Rashid. *The Iron Cage: The Story of the Palestinian Struggle for Statehood.* Boston: Beacon Press, 2006.

———. *Palestinian Identity: The Construction of Modern National Consciousness.* New York: Columbia Univ. Press, 1997.

Khalidi, Walid. *Before Their Diaspora: A Photographic History of the Palestinians 1876–1948.* Washington, DC: Institute for Palestine Studies, 2010.

Khoury, Samia Nasir. *Reflections from Palestine: A Journey of Hope.* Cyprus: Rimal, 2016.

Klein, Menachem. *Lives in Common: Arabs and Jews in Jerusalem, Jaffa, and Hebron,* translated by Haim Watzman. Oxford: Oxford Univ. Press, 2014.

Krystall, Nathan. "The Fall of the New City." In Tamari, *Jerusalem 1948,* 81–141.

Kuttab, Eileen. "Palestinian Women in the 'Intifada': Fighting on Two Fronts." *Arab Studies Quarterly* 15, no. 2 (Spring 1993): 69–85.

Lapp, Paul W., and W. F. Albright. "Tawfiq Canaan in Memorium." *Bulletin of the American Schools of Oriental Research* 174 (April 1964): 1–3.

Lazar, Hadara. *Out of Palestine: The Making of Modern Israel.* New York: Atlas, 2011.

Lloyd, Fran, ed. *Contemporary Arab Women's Art: Dialogues of the Present.* London: Women's Art Library, 1999.

Lucie-Smith, Edward. *Impressionist Women.* New York: Artsbras, 1989.

Mack, Merav, Angelos Dalachanis, and Vincent Lemire. "Matrimony and Baptism: Changing Landscapes in Greek (Rum) Orthodox Jerusalem (1900–1940)." *British Journal of Middle Eastern Studies* 45, no. 3 (May 2018): 443–63.

Madsen, Ann M. *Making Their Own Peace: Twelve Women of Jerusalem.* New York: Lantern Books, 2003.

Majaj, Betty Dagher. *A War without Chocolate: One Woman's Journey through Two Nations, Three Wars, and Four Children.* n.p.: 2015.

Makdisi, Jean Said. "Becoming Palestinian." In Johnson and Shehadeh, *Seeking Palestine,* 160–77.

———. *Teta, Mother and Me: An Arab Woman's Memoir.* London: Saqi, 2005.

Makhoul, Bashir, and Gordon Hon. *The Origins of Palestinian Art.* Liverpool, UK: Liverpool Univ. Press, 2013.

Mansour, Atallah. *Still Waiting for the Dawn*. Self-published, CreateSpace, 2013.

Ma'oz, Moshe. *Ottoman Reform in Syria and Palestine, 1840–1861: The Impact of the Tanzimat on Politics and Society*. Oxford: Clarendon Press, 1968.

Massad, Joseph. "Permission to Paint: Palestinian Art and the Colonial Encounter." *Art Journal*, Fall 2007.

Mathews, Nancy Mowll, ed. *Cassatt and Her Circle, Selected Letters*. New York: Abbeville Press, 1984.

Mayer, Tamer, and Suleiman Mourad. *Jerusalem: Idea and Reality*. London: Routledge, 2008.

Mazza, Roberto. *Jerusalem from the Ottomans to the British*. London: Tauris, 2009.

Meisler, Stanley. "Elements of Empowerment." In Lloyd, *Contemporary Arab Women's Art*, 70–110.

———. *Shocking Paris: Soutine, Chagall and the Outsiders of Montparnasse*. New York: Palgrave MacMillan, 2015.

Melkon Rose, John H. *Armenians of Jerusalem: Memories of Life in Palestine*. London: Radcliffe Press, 1993.

Mitwasi, Faten Nastas. *Reflections on Palestinian Art: Art of Resistance or Aesthetics*. Beit Jala, Palestine: Diyar, 2015.

———. *Sliman Mansour*. Petersburg, Germany: Michael Imhof Verlag, 2008.

Mogannam, Matiel E. T. *The Arab Woman and the Palestinian Problem*. London: Herbert Joseph, 1937.

Mrowat, Ahmad. "Karimeh Abbud: Early Women Photographer (1896–1955)." *Jerusalem Quarterly* 31 (Summer 2007): 72–78.

Najjer, Orayb Aref. *Portraits of Palestinian Women*. Salt Lake City: Univ. of Utah Press, 1992.

Nardi, Noah. *Education in Palestine, 1920–1945*. Washington, DC: Zionist Organization of America, 1945.

Nashashibi, Mikdadi Salwa, ed. *Forces of Change: Artists*. Washington, DC: National Museum of Women in the Arts, 1994.

Nashashibi, Nasser Eddin. *Jerusalem's Other Voice: Ragheb Nashashibi and Moderation in Palestinian Politics, 1920–1948*. Exeter, UK: Ithaca Press, 1990.

Nashef, Khaled. "Tawfik Canaan: His Life and Works." *Jerusalem Quarterly* 16 (November 2002): 12–26.

———. *Ya kafi, Ya shfi, The Tawfik Canaan Collection of Palestinian Amulets*. Birzeit: Birzeit Univ. Publications, 1998.

Nashif, Esmail. *On Palestinian Abstraction: Zohdy Qadry and the Geometrical Melody of Late Modernism*. Haifa, Israel: Dar Raya, 2014.

Nasir, Tania Tamari. "My Silk Road." *This Week in Palestine*, May 2007.

Nassar, Issam. "Early Local Photography in Palestine: The Legacy of Karimeh Abbud." *Jerusalem Quarterly* 46 (Summer 2011): 23–31.

———. "Photographing Jerusalem at War." In Tamari, *Jerusalem 1948*, 142–66.

Nassar, Jamal R., and Roger Heacock, eds. *Intifada: Palestine at the Crossroads*. New York: Praeger, 1990.

Newberry, Daniel. Interview. December 1, 1997. Foreign Affairs Oral History Project. The Association for Diplomatic Studies and Training. http://www.adst.org/Readers/Israel.pdf.

Nusseibeh, Sari. "Negotiating the City: A Perspective of a Jerusalemite." In *Jerusalem: Idea and Reality*, edited by Tamar Mayer and Suleiman Ali Mourad, 198–204. London: Routledge, 2008.

———. *Once Upon a Country*. New York: Farrar, Straus and Giroux, 2007.

Ofer, Pinhas. "A Scheme for the Establishment of a British University in Jerusalem in the Late 1920s." *Middle Eastern Studies* 22, no. 2 (April 1986): 274–85.

Okkenhaug, Inger Marie. *The Quality of Heroic Living, of High Endeavour and Adventure: Anglican Mission, Women and Education in Palestine*. Leiden: Brill, 2002.

———. "She Loves Books and Ideas." *Islam and Christian-Muslim Relations* 13, no. 4 (2002): 461–79.

———. "To Give the Boys Energy, Manliness, and Self-Command in Temper: Anglican Male Ideal and St. George's School in Jerusalem, c. 1900–40." In Okkenhaug and Flaskerud, *Gender, Religion, and Change in the Middle East*, 47–62.

———. "Women in Christian Mission: Protestant Encounters from the 19th and 20th Century." *Journal of Gender Research in Norway*, special edition (2004): 1–21.

Okkenhaug, Inger Marie, and Ingvild Flaskerud. *Gender, Religion and Change in the Middle East: Two Hundred Years of History*. Oxford: Berg, 2005.

Palumbo, Michael. *The Palestinian Catastrophe: The Expulsion of a People from Their Homeland*. London: Faber & Faber, 1987.

Patch, Carolyn. *Grace Whitney Hoff: An Abundant Life*. Cambridge, MA: Private printing at the Riverside Press, ca. 1933.

Perry, Gill. *Women Artists and the Parisian Avant-Garde: Modernism and Feminine Art, 1900 to the late 1920s*. Manchester, UK: Manchester Univ. Press, 1995.

Piroyansky, Danna. "From Island to Archipelago: The Sakakini House in Qatamon and Its Shifting Ownership throughout the Twentieth Century." *Middle Eastern Studies* 48, no. 6 (November 2012): 855–77.

Porath, Yehuda. *The Palestinian Arab National Movement, 1929–1939*. London: Frank Cass, 1977.

Pritchard, James B. *The Cemetery at Tell Es-Sa'idiyeh, Jordan*. Philadelphia: University Museum, 1980.

Pullan, Wendy, and Lefkos Kyriacou. "The Work of Charles Ashbee: Ideological Urban Visions with Everyday City Spaces." *Jerusalem Quarterly* 39 (Autumn 2009): 51–61.

Qafisheh, Mutaz. "The International Law Foundations of Palestinian Nationality." *Graduate Institute of International Studies* 7 (2008): 149.

Qleibo, Ali. *Before the Mountains Disappear: An Ethnographic Chronicle of the Modern Palestinians*. Cairo: Kloreus, 1992.

Radycki, J. Diane. "The Life of Lady Art Students: Changing Art Education at the Turn of the Century." *Art Journal* 42, no. 1 (1982): 9–13.

Reifler, David. *Days of Ticho: Empire, Mandate, Medicine and Art in the Holy Land*. Jerusalem: Gefen Books, 2015.

Rekhess, Elie. "The Palestinian Political Leadership in East Jerusalem after 1967." In *Jerusalem: Idea and Reality*, edited by Tamar Mayer and Suleiman Ali Mourad, 266–82. London: Routledge, 2008.

Rempel, Terry. "The Significance of Israel's Partial Annexation of East Jerusalem." *Middle East Journal* 51, no. 4 (Autumn 1997): 520–34.

Roberts, Nicholas E. "Dividing Jerusalem: British Urban Planning in the Holy City." *Journal of Palestine Studies* 42, no. 4 (Summer 2013): 7–26.

Robson, Laura. *Colonialism and Christianity in Mandate Palestine*. Austin: Univ. of Texas Press, 2011.

Rogers, Sarah A., and Eline van der Vlist, eds. *Arab Art Histories: The Khalid Shoman Collection*. Amman: Khalid Shoman Foundation, 2013.

Romann, Michael, and Alex Weingrod. *Living Together Separately: Arabs and Jews in Contemporary Jerusalem*. Princeton, NJ: Princeton Univ. Press, 1991.

Ronald Storrs. *The Memoirs of Sir Ronald Storrs*. New York: Putnam, 1937.

Ross, Nicolas. *Sainte-Alexandre-Nevski: Centre spiritual de l'emigration russe, 1918–1939*. Paris: Editions des Syrtes, 2011.

Sabbagh, Karl. *Palestine: History of a Lost Nation*. New York: Grove Press, 2006.

Sa'di, Ahmad, and Lila Abu-Lughod, eds. *NAKBA: Palestine, 1948, and the Claims of Memory*. New York: Columbia Univ. Press, 2007.

Said, Edward. "Reflections on Exile." In *Reflections on Exile and Other Essays*, 173–86. Cambridge, MA: Harvard Univ. Press, 2000.

Sakakini, Hala. *Jerusalem and I: A Personal Record*. 2nd ed. Amman, Jordan: Economic Press, 2000.

———. *The Years in Ramallah*. Jerusalem: Commercial Press, 1997.

Sanbar, Elias. "Out of Place, Out of Time," *Mediterranean Historical Review* 16, no. 1 (June 2001): 87–94.

Sanchez, Pierre, ed. *Dictionnaire du salon des Tuileries:* Répertoire des exposants et listes des oeuvres présentées, 1923–1962. 2 vols. Dijon: L'Echelle de Jacob, 2007.

Sayigh, Rosemary. "Encounters with Palestinian Women under Occupation." *Journal of Palestine Studies* 10, no. 4 (Summer 1981): 3–26.

———. "Palestinian Camp Women as Tellers of History." *Journal of Palestine Studies* 27, no. 2 (Winter 1998): 42–58.

———. *Palestinian Women: Triple Burden, Single Struggle*. London: Zed Books, 1989.

———. "Women's Nakba Stories." In Sa'di and Abu-Lughod, *NAKBA*, 135–60.

Schor, Laura. *The Best School in Jerusalem: Annie Landau's School for Girls, 1900–1960*. Waltham, MA: Brandeis Univ. Press, 2013.

Segev, Tom. *One Palestine Complete: Jews and Arabs under the Mandate*. New York: Metropolitan Books, 2000.

Seikaly, Sherene. *Men of Capital: Scarcity and Economy in Mandate Palestine*. Stanford, CA: Stanford Univ. Press, 2016.

Shahid, Serene Husseini. *Jerusalem Memories*. Edited by Jean Said Makdisi. Beirut: Naufal, 1999.

Sharaf, Rawan. *Otherwise Occupied: Biennale Art, 2013*. Jerusalem: Al-Hoash, 2013.

Sherman, A. J. *Mandate Days: British Lives in Palestine, 1918–1948*. Baltimore, MD: Johns Hopkins Univ. Press, 2001.

Sherwell, Tina. *Forgotten Scene: Pioneer Artists from Palestine*. Jerusalem: Al-Wasiti Art Center, 2003.

———. "Imaging Palestine as the Motherland." In Ben Zvi, *Self-Portrait*, 160–66.

Shomali, Qustandi. "Palestinian Christians: Politics, Press, and Religious Identity 1900–1948." In *The Christian Heritage in the Holy Land*, edited by Anthony O'Mahony, 225–36. London: Scorpion Cavendish, 1995.

Simon, Reeva S., ed. *The Middle East and North Africa: Essays in Honor of J. C. Hurewitz*. New York: Columbia Univ. Press, 1990.

Stanton, Andrea L. *This Is Jerusalem Calling*. Austin: Univ. of Texas Press, 2013.

Stockdale, Nancy. *Colonial Encounters among English and Palestinian Women, 1800–1948*. Gainesville: Univ. Press of Florida, 2007.

Sufian, Sandy. "Anatomy of the 1936–1939 Revolt: Images of the Body in Political Cartoons of Mandatory Palestine." *Journal of Palestine Studies* 37, no. 2 (Winter 2008): 23–42.

———. "Healing Jerusalem: Colonial Medicine and Arab Health from World War I to 1948." In Jayyusi, *Jerusalem Interrupted*, 115–38.

Swedenburg, Ted. *Memories of Revolt: The 1936–1939 Rebellion and the Palestinian National Past*. Fayetteville: Univ. of Arkansas Press, 2003.

Tamari, Salim. "The City and its Rural Hinterland." In Tamari, *Jerusalem 1948*, 68–83.

———. "City of Riffraff: Crowds, Public Space, and New Urban Sensibilities in War-Time Jerusalem, 1917–1921." In *Comparing Cities: The Middle East and South Asia*, edited by Kamra Asdar Ali and Martina Rieker, 23–48. Oxford: Oxford Univ. Press, 2009.

———. "Jerusalem: Subordination and Governance in a Sacred Geography." In *Capital Cities: Ethnographies of Urban Governance in the Middle East*, edited by Seteney Shami, 170–90. Toronto: Centre for Urban and Community Studies, Univ. of Toronto, 2001.

———. *Mountain against the Sea: Essays on Palestinian Society and Culture*. Berkeley: Univ. of California Press, 2009.

———. "The Phantom City." In *Across the Wall: Narrative of Israeli-Palestine History*, edited by Ilan Pappe and Jamil Hilal, 87–105. London: Tauris, 2010.

———. "The Revolt of the Petite Bourgeoisie: Urban Merchants and the Palestinian Uprising." In Nassar and Heacock, *Intifada*, 159–74.

———. *Year of the Locust: A Soldier's Diary and the Erasure of Palestine's Ottoman Past.* Berkeley: Univ. of California Press, 2011.

Tamari, Salim, ed. *Jerusalem 1948: The Arab Neighborhoods and Their Fate in the War.* 2nd rev. ed. Bethlehem: Institute for Jerusalem Studies, 2002.

———. *A Young Palestinian's Diary: 1941–1945. The Life of Sami 'Amr.* Translated by Kimberly Katz. Austin: Univ. of Texas Press, 2009.

Tannous, Izzat. *The Palestinians: A Detailed Documented Eyewitness History of Palestine under British Mandate.* New York: IGT, 1988.

Taraki, Lisa. "The Development of Political Consciousness among Palestinians in the Occupied Territories, 1967–1987." In Nassar and Heacock, *Intifada*, 53–72.

Taraki, Lisa, ed. *Living Palestine: Family Survival, Resistance, and Mobility under Occupation.* Syracuse: Syracuse Univ. Press, 2006.

Tleel, John. *I Am Jerusalem.* 2nd ed. Jerusalem: J. N. Tleel, 2007.

Tritton, Annette. *An Exhibition of Paintings and Drawings of Essex, France, and Elsewhere.* London: Walker's Galleries, 1934.

Tsimhoni, Daphne. "The Arab Christians and the Palestinian Arab National Movement during the Formative Stage." In *The Palestinians and the Middle East Conflict*, edited by Gabriel Ben-Dor, 73–98. Ramat Gan: Turtledove, 1978.

———. *Christian Communities in Jerusalem and the West Bank since 1948.* Westport, CT: Praeger, 1993.

———. "Christians in Jerusalem: A Minority at Risk." *Journal of Human Rights* 4 (2005): 391–417.

Tuqan, Fadwa. *A Mountainous Journey: An Autobiography.* Edited by Salma Khadra Jayyusi. Translated by Olive Kenny. Poetry translated by Naomi Shihab Nye. St. Paul, MN: Graywolf Press, 1990.

Tveit, Odd Karsten. *Anna's House: The American Colony in Jerusalem.* Nicosia, Cyprus: Rimal, 2000.

Usher, Graham. "Palestinian Women, the *Intifada* and the State of Independence: An Interview with Rita Giacaman." *Race and Class* 34, no. 3 (1992): 31–43.

Vester, Bertha Spafford. *Flowers of the Holy Land.* Kansas City, MO: Hallmark Cards, 1962.

———. *Our Jerusalem.* Jerusalem: Ariel, 1950. Facsimile edition 1988.

Vypuskniki Kievskoi Dukhovnoi Akademii, 1823–69, 1885–1915. http.//www.petergen.com/bovkalo/duhov/kievda.html.

Walker's Galleries. "An Exhibition of Paintings and Drawings of Essex, France, and Elsewhere by Annette Tritton." London: Women's Printing Society, January 31–February 13, 1934.

Warnock, Kitty. *Land before Honour.* Houndmills, UK: Macmillan Education, 1990.

Wasserstein, Bernard. "'Clipping the Claws of the Colonisers': Arab Officials in the Government of Palestine, 1917–48." *Middle Eastern Studies* 13, no. 2 (May 1977): 171–94.

———. *Divided Jerusalem*. New Haven, CT: Yale Univ. Press, 2008.

———. "Patterns of Communal Conflict in Palestine." In *Essential Papers on Zionism*, edited by Jehuda Reinharz and Anita Shapira, 671–88. New York: NYU Press, 1996.

Whitesel, Lita S. "Personalities of Women Art Students." *Studies in Art Education* 20, no. 1 (1978): 56–63.

Wilson, Evan. *Jerusalem: Key to Peace*. Washington, DC: Middle East Institute, 1970.

Zalmona, Yigal. *The Art of Abel Pann: From Montparnasse to the Land of the Bible*. Jerusalem: Israel Museum, 2003.

———. "The Tower of David Days: The Birth of Controversy in Israel Art in the Twenties." In *The Tower of David Days: First Cultural Strife in Israel Art*, edited by Yigal Zalmona, 66–74. Jerusalem: Tower of David Museum, 1991.

Zanemonets, Alexander. *The First Pilgrim Journey of Students of the Kiev Theological Academy to the Holy Land in Summer 1911* (Kiev: Kiev Academy, 1914), [unnumbered]. Republished in 2005 as *By the Holy Places from Kiev to Jerusalem*.

Index

Page numbers appearing in italics refer to illustrative material.

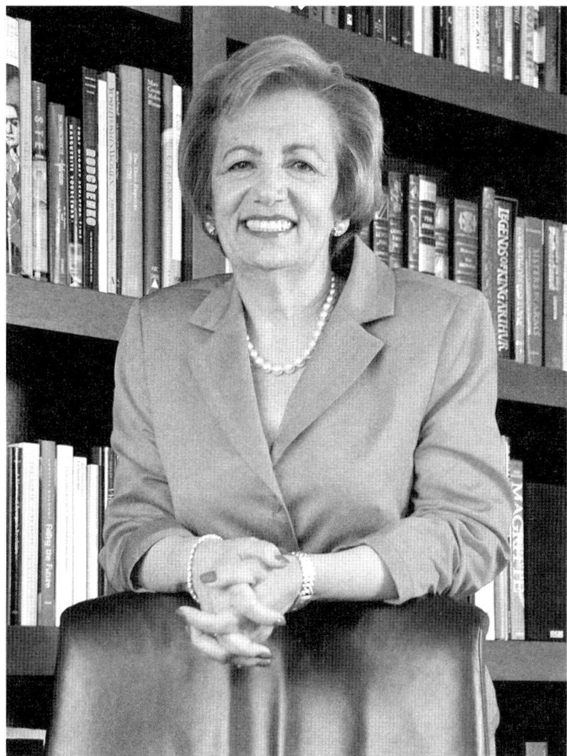

Photograph by Andre Beckles

Laura S. Schor is professor of history at Hunter College and the CUNY Graduate Center. She is the author of several books on women's history, including *The Odyssey of Flora Tristan*, a biography of the nineteenth-century French feminist-socialist; *Les Jolies femmes de Paris*, an exhibit catalog of the cartoons of Edmund de Beaumont, political satirist who depicted women's struggle for political rights in 1848; *The Life and Legacy of the Baroness Betty de Rothschild*; and *The Best School in Jerusalem: Annie Landau's School for Girls, 1900–1960.* Her research on twentieth-century Jerusalem brought little-known artist Sophie Halaby to her attention.